SCOUNDRELS
IN LAW

ALSO BY CAIT MURPHY

Crazy '08: How a Cast of Cranks, Rogues, Boneheads,
and Magnates Created the Greatest Year in Baseball History

Smithsonian Books

HARPER

An Imprint of HarperCollins*Publishers*
www.harpercollins.com

SCOUNDRELS IN LAW

THE TRIALS OF HOWE & HUMMEL,

LAWYERS TO THE GANGSTERS, COPS, STARLETS, AND RAKES WHO MADE THE GILDED AGE

Cait Murphy

HarperCollins books may be purchased for educational, business, or sales promotional use. For information, please write: Special Markets Department, HarperCollins Publishers, 10 East 53rd Street, New York, NY 10022.

FIRST EDITION

Designed by Cassandra J. Pappas

Library of Congress Cataloging-in-Publication Data
Murphy, Cait.
  Scoundrels in law : the trials of Howe & Hummel, lawyers to the gangsters, cops, starlets, and rakes who made the Gilded Age / Cait Murphy.
    p. cm.
  ISBN 978-0-06-171428-3
  Includes bibliographical references.
  1. Howe, William F., 1828–1902. 2. Hummel, Abraham H., 1849–1926. 3. Lawyers—New York (State)—New York—Biography. 4. Trials—United States. I. Title.
  KF355.N4M87 2010
  340.092'2—dc22
  [B]   2009049639

10 11 12 13 14   OV/RRD   10 9 8 7 6 5 4 3 2 1

My siblings have long been my personal defense team.
Though they have higher ethical standards than Howe & Hummel,
I nevertheless dedicate this book to them.

Mairead Walsh Murphy Nash
Brendan Woods Murphy
Robert Finn Murphy
Joan Byrne Murphy Sleeper
Katherine Siobhan Murphy Grogan
Mary Cullene Murphy
John Cullen Murphy

ACKNOWLEDGMENTS

The unacknowledged heroes of nonfiction are librarians. So let me acknowledge the staff of the New York Public Library, the New York Society Library, and the New-York Historical Society. Ellen Belcher of the John Jay College of Criminal Justice and Leonora Gidlund of the Municipal Archives of the City of New York were particularly helpful.

My agent, Rafe Sagalyn, always had my back, and my editor, Elisabeth Dyssegaard, was so easy to work with that I might just do this again. A number of people were kind enough to read this before publication; I did not take all their advice, but I appreciated it. So thanks, Sameena Ahmad, Cullen Murphy, Finn Murphy, and Margaret O'Connor. Gretchen Worth again provided an inspiring place to work at her Bangkok home, and Sam-ang took wonderful care of me. I also enjoyed the companionship of Sii-da, Zack, and especially Mack.

Finally, thanks to everyone who told me that of course I would finish. That sentiment was always less reassuring, and more irritating, than it was meant to be. But it was a good thought.

CONTENTS

PREFACE

DECEMBER 20, 1905

After deliberating for 130 minutes, the jury filed back into the court-room. The trial had lasted only a couple of days, but it had really taken more than four years to reach this moment, as a run-of-the-mill divorce turned into an epic of debauchery, mendacity, and not a little humor. At the heart of it all was lawyer Abraham Hummel. Bald, wiry, gorgeously mustached, and not even five feet tall,[1] Hummel was a friend to chorus girls and gangsters, to anarchists and high society. Except, that is, when he was their enemy. He wasn't choosy.

Hummel did have his principles. Not many, it has to be said. Indeed, they can be counted on one hand: He believed in being paid in cash, up front; he believed in winning; he believed discretion was the better part of affluence; and he believed that the calculated effrontery that had served him so well for so long would never fail. But now, as the clock ticked past 3:00 and the clerk asked for the verdict, that last principle was looking shaky. So it proved. "Guilty," called the jury foreman, of one count of conspiracy to pervert the course of justice.

The judge announced the sentence—a year in jail and a $500 fine. And then Hummel made the long walk: out of the court, up the stairs and over the Bridge of Sighs,[2] that awful link between the freedom of the court, where Hummel had had so many glorious moments, and into the Tombs, the New York City jail.[3]

He was ordered into cell 122, on the second tier.[4] One likes to think that the cops chose the cell with intent, for this was a room with a particular view. If Hummel stretched up on his tiptoes to peek out the window, he could see the exact site of his dingy old office.

As he settled into his uncomfortable surroundings, so different from his townhouse on the leafy precincts of the Upper East Side, Hummel might have thought back to 1863. That was when he first crossed the threshold of 89 Centre Street to ask for a job as an office boy at the premises of William Howe, a lawyer with oodles of brio but a decidedly small-time practice. Six years later, Hummel, age 20, was a full partner. Howe and Hummel became a glorious partnership and New York's most famous lawyers. They made a fortune, and a reputation, that glittered in their own time to such an extent that there was a common toast in the bars of New York. "Here's how," one drinker would suggest. The expected response: "Here's Hummel."[5]

When Howe died in 1902, he was eulogized as the "dean of the criminal bar."[6] Hummel soldiered on, honoring his mentor by continuing under the old name. Of course, that made business sense, too. At this point, Howe & Hummel was a brand. "There was not a criminal within a thousand miles who had not heard of Howe & Hummel," wrote District Attorney Francis Wellman, a frequent opponent.[7] Open 24 hours a day during their peak years, Howe & Hummel was the first phone call for villains of all varieties; cops or court clerks were paid to tip the partners off to likely cases.[8]

An hour after going into the Tombs as a prisoner, Hummel was in the corridor chatting with reporters, who had always liked the little fellow for his gift of pith. He assured them that he was "innocent as a newborn babe"—something that hadn't been true at least since the Civil War. Four hours later, he was out on bail. But seven months after that, he was disbarred, and in 1907 he took what was known as the "ferry of despair" to the jail on Blackwell's Island, his mustache shorn, to serve his sentence. When he got out in 1908, he set sail for England. Howe & Hummel was finished.

. . .

But it was a great ride while it lasted.

From 1869 to 1902, the two had a wonderful time of it, displaying a puckish humor (cable address: LENIENT)[9] and a legal flair that made them the favored advocates for scoundrels of all kinds. Like any memorable partnership, there were enough differences between the two to make each of them stand out individually. Howe was fat; Hummel was tiny. Howe was Catholic; Hummel was Jewish. Howe was married three times;[10] Hummel was a bachelor. Howe was known for his oratory; Hummel excelled at subtler arts. They shared a love of the racetrack and a cheerful disregard for ethical niceties.

Hummel was the more diffident of the two. Much of his work—breach-of-promise suits, often with a dash of blackmail—was necessarily done in private, usually in his office.[11] This contained a brazier to burn incriminating evidence. But he was also front and center in a number of high-profile cases—the obscenity charge against the play *Sapho*, the prosecution of a greedy spiritualist, the defense of a cat-killing philanthropist. As a regular first-nighter on Broadway and a habitué at Delmonico's, the great restaurant of the era, Hummel was a man about town.

One of the partnership's notable opponents, Arthur Train, said of the big-headed lawyer in 1908, "Of law, he knew and knows nothing."[12] That was unfair. Hummel's formal legal training was sketchy and quite possibly nonexistent. But he learned enough on the job to annoy Train and other district attorneys, and he was masterful at teasing out legal inconsistencies. He was an acknowledged expert in theatrical and matrimonial law.

Howe was the more self-consciously outrageous character. An amateur Shakespearean, he loved the theater of the courtroom. He used his voice as an instrument, going up and down the scale from low whisper to angry roar. Violent death was his specialty; he defended an estimated 650 defendants charged with murder or manslaughter.[13] Howe didn't get all the great murders, but for 30 years, he got more of them than anyone else: Billy Forrester, the chief suspect in the murder of Benjamin Nathan, a locked-room mystery of a famous financier that riveted the city; Ella Nelson, the spurned mistress with the smoking gun; Carlyle Harris, the medical student who killed his child bride; Martin Thorn, who dismembered his love rival; Edward Unger, another body chopper; cop killer "Handsome Harry" Carlton.

Howe liked cases that looked hopeless, and he particularly liked making closing arguments of such spirit and profound lack of logic that the jury could hardly fail to be moved. He was so often driven to tears by his own oratory that other lawyers suspected him of keeping an onion in his handkerchief.[14]

By the 1880s, no account of a trial featuring Howe failed to mention his girth (which kept expanding) and his dress, which ran to technicolor waistcoats and dollops of precious stones. Rubies and emeralds sometimes appeared, but it was diamonds, glorious diamonds, that became his trademark. Why? "I like diamonds," he said simply. "I love their glitter and sparkle."[15] But the man had a tougher side, too. When burglars had the gall to break into his home, Howe seized a revolver and blazed away, coolly letting the criminal fraternity know that he had a gun in every room. "I don't object to burglars as clients—they are pretty good clients he said, "But I seriously object to them operating at my house."[16]

Howe became so famous, and notorious, that in 1890 when his dog Rover got loose in Central Park, the trivial incident made the papers.[17] A few years later, a would-be juror admitted to prejudice on the basis that Howe appeared for the defense: "My impression has always been that Mr. Howe never appears in a case except it is a desperate one."[18] Although, like Hummel, Howe might never have set foot in a law school, his criminal expertise was respected enough that he was part of the team that revised the state penal code in 1882,[19] perhaps on the fox-guarding-henhouse principle.

Between them, Howe and Hummel covered the landscape of 19th-century society. That took some doing. New York City in their heyday was incredibly stratified. The notorious Mulberry Bend, made famous by writer Jacob Riis, was the worst part of America's worst neighborhood, the notorious Five Points. The three-acre area, an elbow-shaped excrescence sited three minutes' walk from police headquarters and five from Howe & Hummel, was the most densely populated patch of land in the world. In this spider web of lanes with names like Bandits' Roost and Blind Man's Alley,[20] multiple families might share a single basement room, bereft of water or light. The area was vermin-ridden, smelly, and crime-wracked; Riis described it as "a vast human pig-sty."[21]

Just a few miles away, but worlds apart, splendid mansions rose along Fifth Avenue, home to the robber barons who were importing European masterworks by the boatload and hosting parties that made Roman excess look like a Shaker picnic. The era in which Howe & Hummel thrived is sometimes known as the Gilded Age; the gilt, however, covered a tiny fraction of the population. Language, culture, and economics, moreover, kept different groups apart. The poor might never leave their neighborhoods, and except for the occasional slumming expedition, the rich had no reason to visit the likes of Mulberry Bend.

In between was a burgeoning, energetic middle class, whose desire for self-improvement and something like stability would, over time, with many fits and starts, come to define the city. In the same way that the 20th-century welfare state cut the knees out from under the personalized politics of the 19th-century Tammany political machine, the drive to create a more ordered city took a toll on a legal firm that won many of its customers by exploiting the unofficial law of the lower class, the contradictions of the respectable middle, and the power structures of the upper.

When Howe & Hummel was in its prime, though, it thrived by connecting across the entire social spectrum. New York's destitute could hardly afford the partners' fees, but the people who made their livings off the teeming masses, such as Danny Driscoll, leader of the Whyos gang that ruled the Irish underground, found their way to Howe & Hummel as regularly as high-society rakes, for whom a summons to that address was the worst kind of news. Here is how one contemporary described a typical scene at 89 Centre Street, circa 1890.

The waiting room benches were always filled, and filled with the damnedest collection of people you ever saw. I've seen [actress] Lillian Russell in there surrounded by pickpockets, Tammany heelers, and bunco men. [Republican] Boss Platt was there quite a bit and so was [Democratic Tammany leader Richard] Croker, and Hungry Joe, the card shark. There were dope peddlers, green-goods men, bookmakers, and any number of queer-looking murder witnesses. There was enough there for a couple of wax museums and a freak show.[22]

The offices of Howe & Hummel were an embarrassing place to be seen. Once a prominent businessman met a friend in the tatty reception room,[23] an ugly place in which to ponder one's sins, whether social or criminal. "So you are here, too? Hope she was a pretty girl and you didn't have to pay too high for your little experience," the businessman joked with bleak bravado. His companion shrugged, "There are two things that no one who enjoys life can escape—death and Howe & Hummel!"[24]

The lawyers knew too much to be invited to the best parties, and they would never forsake their private table in the back room at Pontin's restaurant for the worst dives, but they flitted across social distinctions with unique facility. It takes only one or two degrees of separation to link Howe & Hummel to almost anyone who was anyone in Gilded Age Manhattan—from Kit Burns, who ran a famous dog-fighting establishment, to Mark Twain, whom they represented in a contract dispute, to the likes of Stanford White, the patrician architect whose murder in 1906 by a demented Pittsburgh playboy was a sensation.

Considering Hummel's extensive theatrical practice, it makes sense that the firm had dealings with Lillian Russell, P. T. Barnum, and Buffalo Bill Cody. But it is by no means obvious that minister Henry Ward Beecher, boxer John L. Sullivan, stockbroker Hetty Green, anarchist Emma Goldman, animal rights pioneer Henry Bergh, and, at least in spirit, the courtesan Lola Montez, would all make appearances in the Howe & Hummel epic. Even a young Winston Churchill had a walk-on. During a visit to the United States, he sat at the judge's side during a case in which the firm was involved.[25] And it was a Churchill cousin, William Travers Jerome, who eventually took Hummel down.

Their criminal clients were a fascinating bunch, too. There was George Leonidas Leslie, the gentleman bank robber who ended up murdered in a ditch. The saloonkeeper known as the "wickedest man in New York," John Allen, was a client, of course. So was Fredericka "Marm" Mandelbaum, the city's biggest fence, who laundered money and disposed of goods for all the top crooks, including Adam Worth, who went on to fame and occasional fortune as the thief who stole, and fell in love with, Gainsborough's portrait of the Duchess of Devonshire.[26] Howe and Hummel also played a major role—not that they intended to—in the events that led up to the creation of the Lexow Committee, which investigated police corruption in the mid-1890s.

Their office displayed none of this eminence. Sited in a neighborhood of warehouses and tenements where the air smelled of too many people and not enough plumbing, 89 Centre Street fit in. The building could generously be described as modest. The partners wasted no money on décor, or even on washing the windows, whose dusting of grunge afforded some privacy to the unfortunates within. The reception room in front featured a large safe, stuffed with coal to feed the pot-bellied stove. There were also a few cheap chairs and benches, a permanent collection of litter, and random piles of books. In the back, there was a warren of small rooms. Each partner had his own office, and when the telephone arrived, they invested in that useful implement. Hummel had a special phone under his desk. When a client asked if he knew a judge, he would make a show of picking it up and hold an imaginary conversation. The subtext, of course, was that victory was assured.[27]

When the money was good, and sometimes just for the hell of it, Howe and Hummel were happy to take up the kind of marginal cases and unpopular causes that other lawyers avoided—cop killers and anarchists, for example. On more than one occasion, the partners forced the legislature to rewrite laws in which they had found loopholes, one of them big enough to release hundreds of people from jail. Howe once got a charge against a thief dismissed because the complaint accused him of stealing a "draw" not a "drawer." The judge had to agree that the charge "is not worth the paper it is written upon."[28] The police clerks were more careful after that.

Any lawyer who takes high-profile, controversial cases will make enemies. Neither Howe nor Hummel suffered fools gladly, even when the fool was on the bench, and they had long-running feuds with several of the more incompetent judges. Those pesky anti-sin reformers, Charles Parkhurst and Anthony Comstock, couldn't stand the two, whose business would have gone under in a society that took the Ten Commandments— or even the liquor laws—seriously. In general, though, the partners were widely liked. Howe simply radiated bonhomie and good humor, an important element in his ability to seduce juries, and Hummel was the pet of Broadway. One district attorney, DeLancey Nicoll, defended Hummel in his last case, and another, Arthur Train, had a soft spot for the duo.

Though Train came up against the firm only a couple of times late in their career, he was fascinated by the pair, featuring them prominently in his nonfiction accounts of crime and punishment. It was not enough. Eventually, Train purged the partners from his system by writing a novel, *The Confessions of Artemis Quibble,*[29] a humorous roman à clef about the firm of Gottlieb & Quibble. *Confessions* is broadly fictional, but it includes so much detail that is known to accord with the facts of life at Howe & Hummel that it really deserves to be seen as source material. Here for example is Quibble (i.e., Hummel) on his partner, who was "singularly successful" in murder cases: "Gottlieb (i.e., Howe) could, I believe, have wrung tears from a lump of pig iron, and his own capacity to open the floodgates of emotion was phenomenal."[30] And here is Quibble/Hummel on what made the practice go 'round: "We made money, and that was what we were out for—and we made it every day—every hour; and as we made it we divided it up and put it in our pockets."[31]

One of Train's predecessors in the DA's office, Francis Wellman, couldn't stand Hummel, but he liked and admired Howe as both a first-rate "verdict getter" and an opponent who schooled him in the legal arts. "The great and only William F. Howe,"[32] Wellman wrote, was "a genius in just the kind of work he had chosen for himself."[33] In the middle of one of their most famous tilts, Wellman referred to his corpulent opponent as a "bully good fellow."[34] The newspapers of the time were similarly kind to the partners, who were always good for a story or at least a quip; they might also have had a pet reporter or three on the payroll.

• • •

Howe & Hummel did not spring out of a void. The firm was the creature of a particular time and place. Immediately after the Civil War, New York grew at a rate never seen before or since. In the early 1870s, parts of the city were still rural enough that an ordinance was passed to restrict the movement of goats; by the time the Howe & Hummel shingle came down, there were subways and automobile traffic. The city got bigger, busier, faster, more crowded, and more interesting. New York had more of everything good and bad—more wealth and more poverty, more charity and more greed, more optimism and more despair. A slew of late 19th-century books about the city all explored the same theme. Their titles tell the story: *Sunshine and Shadows; Darkness and Daylight; Mysteries and Miseries; Light and Shadows.*

It was also the era of Tammany Hall, the corrupt Democratic political machine that ran the city, with occasional interruptions, for the better part of 50 years. New York was nominally democratic in this era. Men were certainly free to vote—repeatedly, for that matter—but the public played a trivial role in determining what did, and did not, get done. True political power was in the hands of a few disreputable pros, who pushed the levers of the machine.

The most enduring, beautiful, and notorious monument to Tammany excess sits just a couple blocks north of the side of Howe & Hummel's offices, in the form of the New York County Courthouse—known more familiarly, then and now, as the Tweed Courthouse. William Marcy Tweed bossed Tammany for years; for him, the construction of the courthouse was a personal savings plan. It ended up costing about $12 million, a good fifty times the original estimates, and featured such brilliantly creative accounting as a $41,000 bill for a single broom.[35] When Tweed failed to spread the graft around widely enough, though, an associate squealed. In late 1871, Tweed was arrested. Asked his occupation by the prison keeper, he purred: "statesman." Eventually, Tweed was tried and convicted in the basement of the building that was his downfall; he died before it was finished. But Tammany lived, a force in the city well into the 20th century and essential context for the world in which Howe & Hummel operated.

Swelled by industrialization and immigration, the city became an ideal petri dish for the growth of a professional criminal class. This, in turn, was greatly helped in its nefarious doings by the decidedly unprofessional state of the police. At the same time, the legal profession was a mess. As one law historian put it, Howe & Hummel was "perfectly suited to a time when the criminal bar consisted mainly of de-frocked priests, drunkards, ex-police magistrates, and political riff-raff of all sorts."[36]

Between 1846 and 1871, becoming a lawyer in New York was a simple matter: be male, over 21, of "good moral standing," and with "requisite qualifications." These requirements were never spelled out,[37] and the quality of the bar began to sink to the level "next below that of patent mongering,"[38] according to a lawyer of the old school. Judges were pawns of the political system, which was itself spattered through with corruption. Under the circumstances, a firm like Howe & Hummel was bound to happen. If the partners showed contempt for the law, there was reason for that contempt.

That is an excuse, not a justification; better men behaved better. Reading through the boisterous press of the era, the charisma of Howe and Hummel emerges with a clarity that time cannot weaken. It is tempting, while in their company, to see them simply as valiant advocates for their clients. Aggressive defense, even of the nasty, is a necessary part of the justice system. But Howe and Hummel went well beyond that. They bribed judges. They suborned witnesses. They lied and cheated. They slandered victims, maligned the innocent, and helped seriously awful people slither back onto the streets. The representation of gangsters paid well, for example, and no doubt brought a picaresque thrill. But such representation also released vicious people who went back to preying on their poor and struggling neighbors. Howe and Hummel were fascinating and skilled and likable and sometimes they fought the good fight. They were far short of nobility.

When Hummel was being sentenced, prosecutor William Travers Jerome asked for the maximum, calling him "a menace to the community for 20 years."[39] Granted, Hummel was to Jerome what the white whale was to Ahab, but the DA had a point. Running an office that was, by one's account, a "cesspool of perjury"[40] is not an avocation worthy of praise. But however one adds up the ledger of Howe & Hummel's career, one thing can be said: There was never a dull moment.

This is their story.

SCOUNDRELS
IN LAW

ONE

The Legend Begins

William Howe and Abraham Hummel were public men, conducting their business in open court and appearing regularly in the press. Occasionally, they would even write for a favored paper. "Is Marriage a Failure?" asked Hummel in one article. No, concluded the divorce lawyer and life-long bachelor.[1] "Can Lawyers Be Honest?" he asked in another.[2] Yes, said the blackmailer disbarred once for bribery and again for conspiracy. Their offices were one of the sights of the city, featuring a 25-foot-long[3] sign in blaring capitals: "HOWE & HUMMEL'S LAW OFFICES." Illuminated at night, the sign cocked a massive snook at the prohibition against advertising for lawyers.

But for all their notoriety, the two were elusive, their inner lives a blank. They never talked about their ambitions or their legal philosophy or even their favorite baseball teams; they didn't weigh in on the great issues of the time. Howe's daughter did not go to the parties that made the news, and Hummel's private life was a cipher. In fact, the two went out of their way to shield their secrets. The great scandal sheet of the day, *Town Topics,* revealed that they were on the short list of people deemed "immune from criticism."[4] Presumably, this privilege came at a price. The point is that Howe and Hummel were willing to pay it. The key to their success was their ability to keep a secret; high profile notwithstanding, they practiced this skill on themselves first of all, and forever.

So there are gaps in their story—two of them of significance. The first is that little is known of their lives before they became famous. One of Howe's legal contemporaries, Theron Strong, said that "it was impossible to induce him to dwell on the experiences of his early years."[5] That wasn't quite true. Howe did give a general account of his life in the introduction to the book he coauthored with Hummel, *In Danger, or Life in New York: A True History of a Great City's Wiles and Temptations* (1888). This curious volume was written in the kind of baroque prose favored by Victorian moralists. A blackmailer was "a licensed fiend in human form," and houses of prostitution were invariably "dens of iniquity." One particularly unlikable roué was described as having "hyacinthine locks and lustrous black eyes." Lurking beneath the schmaltz, though, was a dandy guide to the Manhattan demimonde, offering directions to low saloons and a veritable how-to manual of theft and burglary. For female shoplifters, the authors recommended a specially designed hand muff, with wire instead of stuffing; jewelry is slipped into the space, and then a special slide drops it to the bottom. "With one of these muffs, shoplifting is so easy as to be successfully practiced by novices," they encouraged. In the summer, they suggested that the well-dressed shoplifter should hang a bag from a corset; this sits beneath a dress with a slit. Cover the gap with a shawl; then drop the goodies down the hole and out you go.[6]

Howe offered a short autobiography in his introduction to *In Danger.* He said he was born in Massachusetts, the son of an Episcopal clergyman, but spent most of his boyhood in England, where he went to King's College London, then practiced at the London bar.[7] He returned to the United States in the 1850s and began practicing law in "1857 or 1859."[8]

There is no documentary evidence to support this account, however, and the chronology is tricky. An alternative version has it that Howe did spend part of his youth in England, but hardly a prosperous one, as there was a hint of Cockney in his speech. He might have had some kind of medical training, and his re-entry into the United States could have been a hurried one—as a parolee (or "ticket of leave" man) a step ahead of the law. Or maybe he wasn't born in the United States at all. In an 1874 case in which the operators of a bawdy house sued the firm, Howe referred to becoming a naturalized citizen.[9] For the purposes of our story, it's best simply to see Howe as a man who washed up in New York to make his fortune—as so many others did, and do.

There is less muddle about Hummel's background, but not much more information. By all accounts, he was born in Boston, came to New York as a young boy, and grew up on the Lower East Side, where he went to public schools. That is about all that is known. The only glimpse of his young life he ever offered was a curious article he wrote in 1892 about his "pleasantest Christmas surprise": his mother redecorated his room "from a plain everyday affair into an Aladdin bower," giving particular attention to his collection of owls.[10] Why a Jewish mother is giving out Christmas surprises, or why Hummel bothered to write about it, was left unsaid. Still, the owls were a nice touch. Hummel was a devoted brother to two sisters and an attentive uncle, but nothing is known of his parents, their occupations, his education, or how he came to 89 Centre Street in the first place.

One would like to know how a teenaged Hummel went from making fires and doing odd jobs to becoming so valuable to Howe that he was made a partner before he was old enough to vote. How did he learn his craft? Was there a particular case that tipped Howe to the younger man's interesting qualities? A moment of silent recognition between the two? If anyone ever asked, the answers have vanished.

The second big gap is how they became famous. Few reputations are made overnight, but it's not unreasonable to expect to be able to look back and say: Here is the turning point. Or here. Or there. Not in this case. Rather, there was a period of obscurity, a gradual increase in prominence—and then Howe and Hummel were everywhere.

Howe's distinctive sense of drama revealed itself early, and many classic Howe & Hummel strategies were tested before the partnership became famous. There was, for example, the inversion of an obvious, damning fact into something else entirely. The pair would perfect this tactic in later years, but Howe first took it out for a walk in 1860, when he got a pickpocket released on the basis that just because a cop saw the prisoner put his hands into pockets not his own, that "did not prove the prisoner's attempt to steal to be an act of picking pockets."[11] In 1862, Howe had his first murder—a squalid domestic affair in which the murder weapon was gin. He might have also done a brief stint as a military lawyer that year. He made more of a name out of uniform, though, getting enlistees out of military service on the basis that they were drunk when they signed up. For this, he became known as "Habeas Corpus Howe."[12] Other incidents pop up—the defense of a man accused of stealing a pistol, more pick-pockets, the occasional madam. One imagines Howe hanging around the Tombs with the other small-timers, hustling for cases. He got a lot of them, but it was all decidedly trivial.

Perhaps Howe's charisma began to pay off as he accumulated connections around the courthouse. Perhaps Hummel's entrance into the partnership made a difference. Perhaps the timing was simply right for their kind of law. It certainly helped that after the Civil War, crime in New York got more organized and more ambitious—and there was more of it. By the early 1870s, there were 30,000 thieves, 2,000 gambling dens,[13] thousands of prostitutes, and a critical mass of highly skilled bank robbers and con artists. There were enough criminals to create a distinct subculture, complete with its own language. "Blue ruin" was bad gin;[14] "yeggs" were bank burglars; and "kirk buzzers" specialized in working around churches.

By the time Hummel got his name on the sign in 1869, the firm was acknowledged as one of the biggest criminal practices in New York.[15] It didn't hurt that the partners had developed excellent relationships with the officials at the Tombs, which they entered at will. For each client a keeper sent their way, Howe & Hummel returned a percentage of the fee.[16] Quantity led to quality. In the following decade, the partnership began to attract a distinctly better grade of crime.

The partners also had most of the better whorehouses in their pocket by the early 1870s; this was a lucrative business, with many repeat customers. They got $3,200 to defend one such case—asking for a few hundred, then $1,000 more, then another $500, and so on.[17] Those particular clients, the Beaumonts, believed that Howe & Hummel had diddled them. They were quite right, of course, and the case was settled out of court. From then on, the partners acted with more discretion. They cultivated a reputation as honest rascals, taking a lot of money all at one time, rather than squeezing the same lemon repeatedly, as they had with the Beaumonts. This was not a matter of ethics, but efficiency. "Frightening people, innocent or guilty, became to a very large extent our regular business," mused the invaluable Quibble, Hummel's fictional counterpart. "Our reputation grew, and in the course of a few years, the terror of us stalked abroad through the city."[18]

Not that it was all smooth sailing. Hummel was disbarred in 1872 for a few years for a bit of careless bribery upstate,[19] and Howe went bankrupt in 1875. (One of his major creditors, unsurprisingly, was a jewelry firm.[20]) But all in all, when the two waxed nostalgic over the old days, they must have looked back on the 1870s with fondness. It was during this decade that Howe & Hummel began to be noticed.

For that, much of the credit must go to the tale of the blonde, the botched abortion, and the trunk. But first, there was Jack Reynolds.

An illiterate drifter, Reynolds entered a basement grocery on January 29, 1870, informed the owner, William Townsend, that they were brothers, and demanded a place to sleep. Townsend demurred, noting there was barely enough room for his wife and six children. So Reynolds stabbed Townsend dead, in full view of two of the victem's daughters and sundry neighbors. As the cops dragged Reynolds away, followed by an angry crowd baying for his blood, he cried out defiantly, "Hanging is played out." At the station he gave his occupation as "thief."[21]

Assigned to the case, whose peculiar futility made it a natural draw for the press, Howe defended his unsympathetic client with zeal. There was no doubt that Reynolds had killed the man; the only hope was that an insanity defense might save his life. When he went to trial three weeks after the event—a delay considered unconscionably long—the case drew a large crowd, including such a noticeable complement of pickpockets that the judge issued a warning (a few spectators had their wallets lifted anyway).[22]

Howe labored to establish a pattern of mad behavior—the defendant's "frenzied" resistance; his "wild and incoherent" speech; a suggestion of epilepsy (a term used interchangeably with mental illness); the idea that his client's less than keen mind was driven mad by the sight of a knife.[23] Each side brought in experts. The doctors' duel did not go Howe's way, though, as even some of his own medical witnesses decided that on the whole, Reynolds might have been nuts but he was not legally insane.

So Howe changed tack, arguing that just because Reynolds seemed sane when the doctors examined him did not mean that he was at the time of the crime. Besides, there might be insanity that showed no symptoms and that the experts simply could not see; raving maniacs could look normal on occasion, after all. Howe even flirted with the philosophical, getting a physician to admit that "no man will be able to say positively where sanity ends and insanity begins."[24] Reynolds's madness, Howe argued, was proved by the act: "Would any sane man," he asked, "without revenge, without malice, without gain, without notice, have committed so horrible a crime?"

The lawyer strung together the shaky links of his defense in a 90-minute closing argument of wonderful ingenuity and not a little insult. There can be few examples of an advocate disparaging his client with such florid enthusiasm. Reynolds was a "poor, miserable, dirty, filthy, half-savage, half-idiotic wretch"[25] with a lopsided skull; a "vacant, dejected imbecile"; "this poor, demented, God-forsaken wretch, knowing nothing, [is] entirely oblivious to all the senses and faculties of the human mind." And Howe closed with a bang, urging the jury:

> Oh, gentlemen, to violate the living temple which the Lord hath made—to quench the human flame within a human being's breast— is an awful and a terrible responsibility. And I tell you, that if you improperly condemn this wretched man, and consign him to an ignominious death, and a post-mortem examination shall hereafter reveal

his brain diseased; then, gentlemen, the recollection of this day *will never die within you*. Your crime, for so it will be—will pursue you with remorse, like a shadow through your crowded walks. It will hover beside you on your pillow. It will sit at your table. It will ever be present through the remainder of your lives; and at the *"Great Last,"* taking the form of this man's spirit, it will rise to sink and condemn you before the Judgment Seat of God!!![26]

A brave try, but a fruitless one; Reynolds was convicted of murder in the first degree. On appeal, Howe argued instead that the murderer was too stupid to be executed—"of such an extremely low order of intellect as to justify his classification with idiots."[27] That failed. So he went on to contend that the judge's instruction to the jury was inappropriate, because it was so hostile to the idea of insanity. But Judge Ingraham, who had heard the case, was also in charge of the appeal; he was not inclined to overrule himself. A request to the governor for clemency also failed. On April 9, 1870, Jack Reynolds was hanged in the dank courtyard of the Tombs.

Throughout their career, when faced with a bad case, Howe and Hummel were quick to invoke insanity. Just a few weeks after Reynolds's death, for instance, the plea worked for one William Chambers, who shot Dominicus Voorhees during a night of drinking in Brooklyn. Voorhees made the mistake of asserting that George B. McClellan was a Scotsman: "God damn him, then," cried Chambers as he fired. "I'm an Irishman and a Fenian!"[28] Then he called for another glass of ale.

At first, Howe tried to get the case tossed; the indictment, he said, was defective because it never named Voorhees as the victim. The judge didn't care. Then Howe trotted out a similar defense—an instant of epileptic mania—and the same doctor, Gonzalez Echeverria, as in the Reynolds case. There was a good deal of evidence of something like creeping paranoia, as Chambers began to think people were trying to spit on him. Other witnesses, however, described him as a steady and inoffensive man, attentive to his business.[29] The single difference: In this case, Howe made sure that Chambers looked like what the public expected to see in a lunatic. His clothes were shabby, his head swaddled in bandages, and he wore an appearance of dazed suffering,[30] broken by the occasional "wolfish glare."[31]

The mind of a jury is notoriously difficult to read, but something worked. Chambers escaped the hangman—and on leaving the court, told the officers accompanying him, "I've cheated the gallows!"[32] Then he took off his bandages.[33] He spent ten years in an asylum.

Never one to forget a good angle, Howe brought out the Chambers defense in 1891. He was defending a rotten young man named Alphonse Stephani, who killed his lawyer in order to get at his father's estate. Known for his fine figure and natty sense of style, Stephani showed up in court unkempt and filthy. He had not shaved, bathed, or changed his clothes for weeks and refused to say a word, instead staring at the jury with a strange intensity. An insanity decision saved his neck.[34]

Reynolds was not so fortunate. It's ridiculous to try to judge a man's mental health 140 years after the fact on the basis of newspaper articles. What can be said is that he never appeared to understand what was happening around him. Even when he was being sentenced to death, he couldn't be bothered to pay attention.[35] A week before his execution, a newspaper reporter on a visit—and Death Row, for the record, was as easy to get into as a Bowery saloon—described Reynolds as "indifferent and careless." Asked how he was, Reynolds managed, "Pretty well, sir. I can't complain." His prison keepers thought him more than a little odd.[36] But however ably defended—and Howe had played a bad hand skillfully—Reynolds was poor, friendless, and despised. The moment the two little Townsend girls told the court how their daddy was killed before their eyes, Reynolds was doomed.

When the client ends up on the scaffold, there is no way to declare victory. But Howe & Hummel benefited from its association with the case. Shortly after the trial, Hummel published a cheap pamphlet about it. Between the press coverage and the pamphlet, poor Reynolds helped Howe & Hummel to raise its profile. It couldn't have hurt that the lawyers were willing to let reporters tag along when visiting their client, even to the interview in which Howe told Reynolds he would be dead in two days.

The Reynolds case was the first time the firm of Howe & Hummel got any kind of sustained coverage, and Howe had acquitted himself well. By 1871, the *New York Times* was referring to him as "the well-known criminal lawyer."[37] He probably liked being acknowledged by the respectable press, but he didn't really need its approval. He was already a popular figure among the lower class of villains. This we know because of the investigations of the Association of the Bar of the City of New York.

Lawyers have long been ubiquitous in American life, but they have rarely been popular and perhaps never less so than in New York in this era. Almost anyone could set up shop as a lawyer—in 1870, only one in four of those admitted to the bar had gone to law school[38]—and city judges got their appointments from Boss Tweed. Suffice it to say that the Boss was not particularly interested in their judicial temperament or qualifications. Loyalty was another matter. Tweed's judges were expected to stay bought, and they had no trouble with that. But the whole system had begun to stink a little too much. One veteran lawyer complained that when he had joined the bar in the 1830s, "it was an honor to be a lawyer or a judge; now it is almost a disgrace."[39] The Bar Association was founded in 1870 to restore some luster to the profession.

When the Democratic machine known as Tammany Hall lost the 1871 elections, in the wak of the revelations about the Tweed courthouse and other malfeasance the Bar Association was emboldened enough to investigate what was common knowledge—corrupt judges. It asked the state government to examine four in particular: D. P. Ingraham, who had presided over the Reynolds trial; George Barnard, John McCunn, and Albert Cardozo. Ingraham was given a pass because he was about to retire. But beginning in February 1872, the state legislature's Judiciary Committee drilled into the allegations about the other three. Initially, the trio was unconcerned. Barnard was heard to say that anyone with $100,000 in his pocket did not need to fear impeachment;[40] the willingness of the people's representatives in Albany to respond to persuasion of the pecuniary kind was well known.

But the politicians were no dummies. In their trade, they needed to have a sense of the moment, and this was a moment in which the public was well and truly roused. So the committee did a thorough job of it, setting up in a

Manhattan hotel and examining 239 witnesses over two months, eventually compiling 2,400 pages of testimony.[41] Even allowing for honest disagreements and the ambiguity of the law, the results were embarrassing.

Barnard was the most egregious character. He was a Tammany hack, and he acted like one, whittling, drinking, and telling off-color jokes from the bench. Sometimes he held court in the home of his mistress, Josie Mansfield, the showgirl over whom Ned Stokes would later kill Jim Fisk.[42] Barnard had admitted Tweed to the practice of law, a profession for which the Boss had even less training than, say, Abe Hummel.[43]

McCunn also came in for his share of derision, in particular for his desire to mint new Americans—2,000 naturalizations in a day was his personal record. (Cardozo could only manage 800.)[44] Tammany workers drew up the papers, and McCunn initialed them without the least scrutiny. The editorial writers of the *New York Tribune,* one of the city's snobbier papers, speculated that McCunn "has issued an order naturalizing all the lower counties of Ireland, beginning at Tipperary and running down to Cork."[45]

Cardozo was less easy to mock. He had a sound legal education, was in court by 9:30,[46] and was generally dignified. In 1868, he was elected to the Supreme Court, the top trial court for the state, on the Tammany ticket. Here he showed himself eager to pay his political debts. Cardozo was a Tammany hack with good manners. And he, too, had his quirks— for example, sometimes trying cases in No. 13, a private, locked room.[47]

The secrecy is easily explained: Some of his actions were better off not noticed. Specifically, over a four-year period (1868–1871), Cardozo sold writs of habeas corpus to Howe & Hummel, sometimes without seeing the prisoners or hearing arguments. These get-out-of-jail-for-a-fee cards released at least 19 muggers, 215 thieves, and 21 people convicted of assault, plus various prostitutes, pickpockets, and prizefighters. Howe himself estimated that the total was between 300 and 400; of these, he could recall only three who ever returned to court.[48] "Nearly all this habeas corpus business has been transacted by Howe," noted the *New York Times,* "who seems to possess a mysterious influence among our magistrates and judges."[49]

One beneficiary of the system explained how it worked. James Carlisle was charged with assault. His father went to 89 Centre Street, where Hummel assured him that for $300 his son would shortly be home. Mr. Carlisle protested he could not afford anything like that sum, which was equivalent to a year's pay for a low-level servant; Hummel agreed to take the case anyway. At trial, he made no defense, allowing his client to be convicted. Not to worry, Hummel assured the worried father; the boy just needed to wait things out for a couple of days so that the lawyer could "get before a particular judge."[50] Once the judge was in, Carlisle would be out—for $200. And so it passed. Cardozo was the judge.

To put it baldly, Cardozo and what the Bar Association dryly referred to as "the somewhat noted firm of Howe & Hummel,"[51] were in each other's pockets. The Judiciary Committee used more judicious language, but its conclusion was no more complimentary:

> [Cardozo] did wickedly and corruptly discharge such prisoner without just, legal or any cause, as was then and there well known by the said Albert Cardozo, thereby not only permitting the unlawful release from imprisonment of persons legally imprisoned on final conviction, but cooperating with the said Messrs. Howe and Hummel to enable them to coerce large sums of money from such persons.[52]

That was not the end of it, either. Cardozo was also charged with intervening in the gold conspiracy on behalf of Jay Gould and James Fisk. The robber barons had tried to corner the gold market in 1869; when they failed, they went to court to cut their losses. Cardozo was sympathetic (as Barnard had been).[53] Moreover, Cardozo frequently named his nephew, Gratz Nathan, as a receiver in cases before his court. A curious pattern of bank deposits indicated that they then split the fees—to the tune of about $30,000.[54] That was grist for yet another charge. All told, the committee found five grounds for impeachment.

Rather than face trial, Cardozo resigned on May 1, 1872, and returned to private practice. The other two judges were convicted and removed from office. Cardozo's son, Benjamin, was an infant at the time of his father's disgrace. His own stellar legal career, which peaked when he became a justice on the U.S. Supreme Court, was in part an expiation of the sins of his father.[55]

As for Howe and Hummel, their role in the general corruption was noted, but they escaped even the lightest formal rebuke. Other than a few awkward moments before the interrogators, they suffered no consequences. If anything, the whole mess helped. Being rascally was a job recommendation in itself for a Tammany-era lawyer; being rascally and getting away with it was free advertising. If Howe's lowball estimate of 300 writs purchased was anywhere near the mark, then hundreds of minor to middling miscreants had reason to wish him well—and to spread the word to their neighbors who might need the Howe & Hummel style of law someday.

TWO

The Ghastly Trunk

✳

Someone, for example, like Jacob Rosenzweig, a Polish immigrant who arrived in New York in 1865 with, he said, a medical degree. Before long, he opened a medical office for "ladies in trouble." He practiced, by his own account, in five different places in lower Manhattan—the same general area where most of Howe & Hummel's clients lived. After a few years, he prospered enough to move his family to an uptown townhouse, but he still kept at least one downtown office, as "Dr. Ascher." It was under that name that he shilled for business in the newspapers, offering women unspecified, but well understood, "relief."

Rosenzweig was hardly alone in offering abortion services so openly. Beginning in the 1840s, classified ads featured products that offered "relief for female complaints" or pills that restored "female regularity."[1] In one arch approach, pregnant women were warned against Dr. Peter's French Renovating Pills "as they invariably produce a miscarriage."[2] By 1870, a medical journal estimated that abortion advertising brought in $150,000 a year, just in New York City.[3]

No one publicly defended abortion, which in 1846 was made illegal after "quickening," or when the baby's movements could be felt. But no one did anything about it either.[4] There was no reliable birth control and little knowledge of reproductive dynamics; and while abortion was dangerous, so was pregnancy. (A mother in New York, circa 1870, was as likely to die in childbirth as a woman today in Eritrea or Papua New Guinea.) Like prostitution and Sunday drinking, abortion was a business that paid its way. With perhaps one termination for every five births, the economics were decidedly nontrivial. The industry bought off politicians and police and was a staple source of revenue for the newspapers, particularly the *New York Herald*. That was one of the reasons that Walt Whitman, who hated abortion, hated the *Herald*. In a phrase that does justice to his reputation as a poet, Whitman called its editor, James Gordon Bennett, a "reptile marking his path with slime wherever he goes and breathing mildew at everything fresh and fragrant."[5]

It's impossible to estimate how many people in New York were performing abortions in the 1870s. What can be said is that a woman who wanted to terminate a pregnancy could easily find someone willing to do so; prices started at $10.[6] Abortion was, in short, a service industry of sizeable proportions.

Consider Ann Lohman, an English immigrant who styled herself "Madame Restell" on the grounds that when it came to sex, a French inflection always sold. Known as "the wickedest woman in New York," the former seamstress was a shrewd entrepreneur in her chosen field. At one point, she had six retail outlets for her pills; a private hospital; a mail-order business; a corps of traveling salesmen; and branches in Newark, Philadelphia, and Boston.[7]

Restell was the city's richest self-made woman—rich enough that in 1862, she and her husband bought a building site on Fifth Avenue, the city's toniest address.[8] (In a nice irony, Restell outbid the Catholic Archdiocese of New York for the plot, which was a block from St. Patrick's Cathedral, then under construction.[9]) She could not have announced her pretensions more loudly. For more than forty blocks, Fifth Avenue was lined with mansions. Most of these were brownstone hulks of dubious architectural merit; the sheer weight of them, though, was impressive. James McCabe, a fairly waspish chronicler of the city, said that this stretch of edifice complexes had no equal in the world for "the great and unbroken extent of its splendor."[10] He might have been right.

Fifth Avenue could deal with parvenus like A. T. Stewart, who built the city's biggest house on the profits of his department store.[11] (Naturally, the Vanderbilts quickly one-upped him.) But a notorious abortionist was going to be hell on property values. So Restell's neighbors-to-be tried to buy her out. She turned them down flat and started building. When it was completed in 1865, the Restell mansion had a gallery, a ballroom, frescoed ceilings, and 30 hand-painted window shades that were said to have cost $1,000 each.[12] Even the servants' quarters were lined with mahogany and furnished with Brussels carpets.[13] Tchotchkes abounded. To her critics, rivals, and social superiors, it all reeked of a blaring vulgarity begotten by new money. No question, though, there was a ton of it.

Restell was of the never-apologize, never-explain school of business, and abortion was her business. But she was not hypocritical about it. She believed in what she was doing. Her ads not only offered her services but a justification for them. Is it desirable, she asked in one, "for parents to increase their families, regardless of consequences to themselves, or the well-being of their offspring, when a simple, easy, healthy and certain remedy is within our control?"[14]

In the case for which she was convicted, in 1846, one of her patients, Maria Bodine, under pressure from the police, brought charges against her. (Or, as Howe put it in *In Danger*, when "a minion of justice invaded [Restell's] Gehenna.") The trial was one of the most famous of its time, lasting 18 days, much of it occupied in abusing poor Bodine's character. Still, in her testimony, a weepy Bodine described someone rather different than a "Madame Killer," as Restell was often called. Bodine's pregnancy was around six months along,[15] making an abortion more painful and more dangerous—and also illegal.[16] According to Bodine, Restell slept with her as she recovered, attended her several times a day, paid for her journey home, gave her a kiss and warned her, maternally, to be more careful in the future. (Of course, Restell also made Bodine wait until she could come up with $75.) Restell was convicted on a misdemeanor charge of inducing a miscarriage and sentenced to a year in prison.

When she got out, she resumed business; her husband, who operated as "Dr. Mauriceau," also prospered. By the time they moved to Fifth Avenue, Restell was wealthy enough to afford discretion, and she chose to work with fewer, richer women. Even with a less busy practice, she easily took in $30,000 in 1869, charging as much as $2,000 for her services. Some of New York's richer rakes, who needed her on a regular basis, put her on retainer.[17] With the rest of her time, she occupied herself with her real estate speculations and her grandchildren. She could never escape her notoriety, though. On her daily carriage ride, urchins would chase after her yelling, "Your house is built on babies' skulls!"[18]

And the tide was changing around her. Restell bought political protection in bulk, and she knew many a disgraceful secret about the city's most prominent families. Despite these defensive bulwarks, she had to have noticed when Dr. Edward Browne was convicted of manslaughter in 1863 for doing abortions—the first such trial since her own.[19] In 1869, the New York legislature passed a law making all abortions illegal. On the ground, or even in the classified ad columns, nothing changed. Abortion was as available as ever.

Anti-abortion campaigners, a group that included most doctors and women's groups, were disappointed at the ineffectiveness of the law. The New York Times, in particular, began to stir. The newspaper had played a significant role in bringing down Boss Tweed and was looking for a new crusade. It chose abortion, running a regular series of editorials and reports on the subject. Its most ambitious effort was "The Evil of the Age," an undercover project published on August 23, 1871, in which one of its reporters, accompanied by an unnamed woman, made the rounds of some of the city's more notable abortionists: Madame Restell (who offered the couple powders but not surgery); Dr. Grindle, a former cobbler; Dr. Franklin, a former barber with a $40 diploma; Jacob Rosenzweig (alias Dr. Ascher, whose voice has "a twang of the German Jew"); Madame Van Busik of "equivocal reputation." The reporters' conclusion: "There is a systematic business in wholesale murder conducted by men and women in this City, that is seldom detected, rarely interfered with, and scarcely ever punished by law."[20]

All very true, and all very old news. A crusade needs a story, and just days after the exposé, the Times got one. For its purposes, the story of the very naked, very blond, very dead, very young woman in the shipping trunk was made to order.

AUGUST 26, 1871, 1:25 P.M[21]

The one-horse cab pulled up to the Hudson River Railroad Depot on 30th Street, and a 12-year-old lad known as Paddy helped her out. Paddy, whose real name was Alexander Potts, worked around the station selling candy and carrying light luggage. Quick-witted and observant, he noted that the woman wore a calico dress and an alpaca shawl; her hands showed signs of labor. She was also clueless, not knowing that she had to get a ticket if she wanted to check her luggage through. Paddy showed her to the ticket office, where the lady took out two $20 bills, and bought a one-way ticket to Chicago, taking $18 in change.

A few minutes later, a cart pulled up; it carried the lady's luggage—a single trunk, 2½ feet long, and heavy for its size. The boy and the driver, an elderly man in blue workmen's overalls, lugged down the trunk, carefully securing it with an extra strap. Be gentle with it, the woman warned; there was glass inside. They checked the trunk into the baggage room. The cart man drove away, while Paddy accompanied the woman a couple of blocks to a restaurant, where they parted, not entirely amicably. The woman wanted to give him a nickel for his efforts; affronted, Paddy held out for a dime. A simple enough transaction all around.

Back in the baggage room, the handlers either did not know or did not care that there was glass in the red-striped trunk. So it was thrown around with the abandon suspected by travelers of all eras, then tossed onto the platform. But the jostling had opened the lid; a waft of stench began to leak out. Notified by a porter of the disgusting odor, the baggage master took a sniff, gagged, and ordered the trunk opened. The strap was sliced, the flimsy lock cut. Steeling their nerves, the workers opened the lid—and saw a quilt. Lifting that up, they saw a blanket. Lifting that up, they saw a few more cloths. Clearing those away, they saw what they had feared—the body of a pretty young woman, doubled up into the fetal position, her head jammed into the left corner, her golden hair hanging loose around her shoulders.

The police came around 3:00 p.m.; they agreed that yes, she was certainly dead, and yup, this sure looked like foul play. The coroner was called, but did not arrive for almost six hours. Indignity was added to injury; hundreds of people, burdened with more curiosity than decency, were allowed to gawp at the girl. She was lovely and petite; anyone who knew her would have been able to recognize her.

Finally taken to the dead house at Bellevue Hospital around 10:00 p.m., the remains of the young woman were placed in a plain pine coffin. No attempt was made to preserve her; no one even took a photograph or made a drawing. Instead, nature took its inexorable course. By the following morning, the girl's clear complexion and delicate features were gone, replaced by a swollen and putrefied black mass of decay. Stifling his revulsion, the deputy coroner determined the cause of death: acute peritonitis, as a result of a mangled abortion.

The failure to put the body on ice complicated the case, apparently ruining any chance of identifying the corpse. Again, it became an object of curiosity. Hundreds more people trooped through the morgue, all of them saying that they wished to see if it was a missing loved one, most of them just seeking a gruesome titter as they gazed at the remains, the smell of decay inartfully masked by cloths soaked with carbolic acid.

On Monday, August 28, three days after the body was found, the police got a break. William Pickett, the man who had driven the trunk to the station, came forward. He hadn't come sooner, he said, because he hadn't seen a newspaper for several days. When he finally read of the affair, he thought he might be the man the cops were looking for.

His was a simple story. He was at a cab stand when a woman asked him to go to 687 Second Avenue (near 37th Street), ring the bell for the basement, pick up a trunk, and bring it to the station, where she would meet him. They dickered over the price (he asked $1.50, she bargained him down to $1—the woman was clearly a skinflint). After she signed Pickett's log under the name Julia Simmons, he drove to the address. Watched by a couple of women, a stout, dark, fleshy man helped Pickett load the trunk. Escorted to 687 Second Avenue by the police, Pickett confirmed that this was the place from which he had taken the trunk.

A local cop, Sergeant Rooney, put the pieces together, and named the fleshy man as Jacob Rosenzweig, a doctor who lived there with his family. Rooney changed into civilian clothes and waited nearby for the doctor to return; other cops kept watch on the house. Around 4:00 p.m., Rosenzweig entered a nearby saloon for a beer. Rooney followed. When Rosenzweig saw him and tried to bolt, cops descended from everywhere. A crowd quickly gathered. As the cops escorted Rosenzweig to the precinct house, the crowd followed them down the street, crying "Lynch him!" and "Hang him from the lamppost!" Back at the station, Paddy identified Pickett as the cart man, and Pickett identified Rosenzweig as the man who had given him the trunk. To which the doctor replied: "What trunk?" He would never waver from his flat denial that he knew nothing about trunks or abortions or girls.

No one believed him. Rosenzweig's work downtown as "Dr. Ascher" was well known; he advertised widely. His uptown neighborhood also had a shrewd idea of what kind of medicine he practiced—and didn't like it. The *Times* had a particular insight. Its exposé, "The Evil of the Age," had devoted a paragraph to Ascher (i.e., "Rosenzweig"), and on August 30, the reporter, Augustus St. Clair, emptied his notebook.

The account is improbably dramatic in its dénouement—St. Clair said he pulled out a gun as the doctor, suspecting the reporter was a spy, blocked the door. But St. Clair's recounting of his two interviews had the ring of credibility. They included details as to cost ($200), practicalities (Rosenzweig would dispose of the "result"), and accurate description of the layout and interior of the building. And in each of the two interviews, St. Clair said that he saw in passing a slender young woman with blond curls and a clear complexion—the exact description of the girl in the trunk.

The notion of a man whom the papers described as a sensual, coarse-featured, cunning Jew butchering a lovely young blonde did not evoke New Yorkers' finer feelings. Rosenzweig's home and his downtown office were besieged. In saloons and streetcars, the talk was of little else.

And then James F. Boyle walked into a police station with the following story. On the morning of August 26, Boyle said, a man came to his funeral home and asked how much it would cost to bury a woman. A servant, the man said, had died suddenly and without family; he wanted her buried as cheaply as possible and would like Boyle to pick up the body right away. This Boyle refused to do; he would need a certificate of death from a doctor, then a permit from the Board of Health. The stranger went away, but Boyle recalled the incident when he read about the great trunk mystery, as it was beginning to be called. Brought into the cells, he looked at Rosenzweig. That is the man, Boyle told the police.

A few hours later, the police found yet more evidence—a heap of blood-sodden female undergarments wrapped in newspaper and buried under dirt in the cellar on Second Avenue. Letters and other documents confirmed that Rosenzweig and Dr. Ascher were one and the same.

Between the *Times*, the undertaker's story, and the police search, August 29 had been a very bad day for Rosenzweig. That evening, he chatted with a reporter from the *Sun*, another instance of reporters getting astonishing jail access. In this interview, Rosenzweig repeated his strategy of deny, deny, deny. The visit to Boyle's had been a case of "make one hand tickle the other"; that is, a business call. No girl had been staying in his house. Pickett was mistaken. He knew a Dr. Ascher, but only casually.

Rosenzweig's wife, described by the *Herald* as a "low-sized Jewess, thin and vulgar looking," realized the limits of her husband's defiance. They needed help. Bearing a $3,000 retainer, she called in Howe & Hummel. And still, the body was nameless. And still, it continued to deteriorate. One more day, the authorities agreed, and it would have to go to potter's field. The smell, the decay, and the risk of disease were too much.

Then a doctor and a dentist visited the dead house. It was a second trip for the doctor, who suspected the woman might be the missing Alice Augusta Bowlsby of Paterson, New Jersey, whom he had known for five years. On August 30, he returned with the family dentist. Prior to viewing the body, the dentist described the work he had done on Miss Bowlsby. On examination, the girl's teeth fit his description precisely, from the two fillings on the upper teeth to an extracted molar to a scar on her right jaw. The doctor confirmed that the body had a vaccination scar beneath the left elbow and a mole on her neck, distinctive marks that Alice Bowlsby also featured. The girl's aunt, Harriet Williams, confirmed the identification.

Any doubt disappeared when the police, poking into a washtub that had been sitting in the basement kitchen, not far from where the clothing had been found two days before, fished out a lady's handkerchief with the name, "A. A. Bowlsby." Why did it take several days for the servant, Jane Johnston, to wash the dead girl's clothes? Why weren't these items thrown away? And finally, why didn't the police, who had been in the house for days, notice the laundry sooner?[22] All these things are unknowable. Clearly, we are not dealing with either master criminals or masterful detective work here. Young Paddy Potts would have done a far better job. At the end of another bad day, Rosenzweig had only this to say: "I am perfectly innocent."

But Walter Conklin of Paterson had a more troubled conscience. Handsome and personable, the 25-year-old was the son of an alderman and worked as a timekeeper in a silk mill. He had courted Alice Bowlsby—and a few other women, too. When the awful truth came out, after a week of escalating anxiety, he couldn't live with it. He slipped into a back room of the mill on his lunch break and shot himself in the head. The tragedy was complete—father, mother, and unborn child all gone.

"And so, word by word and hour by hour the history of the crime, of which that trunk at the Hudson Railroad Depot told the first sickening syllable, is being inscribed in characters of fire upon the moral conscience," the *Herald* sermonized on September 1, 1871. The paper's morality was not so offended, though, that it refused to run an ad for "Madam Grindle, female physician, [who] guarantees relief for all female complaints." Or one for Dr. Mauriceau [Madame Restell's husband] whose Portuguese Female pills provided "a great and sure remedy for married ladies." There were 10 such ads that day, and about that many every day. The *Herald* was hypocritical; it was also typical.

The inquest on September 1—justice moved briskly in 1871— brought out the evidence. Potts and Picketts, the doctor and the dentist, Boyle and the cops: All repeated the events of the previous week. The one new bit of information came from Jane Johnston, the Rosenzweigs' servant. Nine months pregnant, she had been arrested as a witness; she said little, but left the impression that there was more. Eventually, she said it: A girl had arrived on August 23, and gone upstairs, never to be seen again. Johnston also identified some of the items taken from the trunk as belonging to the Rosenzweigs. The chain of evidence appeared complete.

William Howe didn't see it that way, of course. He hauled himself to his feet, and addressed the inquest:

> The prisoner desires to say that he has a perfect answer to these accusations, and that in the profound deliberations of a legal tribunal he will give a perfect defense. He feels that a great deal of the testimony taken before you was illegally admitted (but with that you have nothing to do) and as regards any atrocities or abortion produced on the body of this woman, he gives an emphatic denial. He says he is not guilty.

Maybe Howe convinced himself, but the locals saw it differently; hundreds of them followed the carriage taking Rosenzweig back to his cell at the Tombs, hissing and screaming. The doctor, if he was one, was charged with second-degree manslaughter.

A week later, Howe offered a glimpse of the proposed defense. In making a plea for bail, he argued that the identity of the deceased was not known; that there was no evidence that this unknown woman had ever been in the Rosenzweig house; or that she had undergone an abortion. The usually amenable Judge Cardozo turned him down. It was one thing to take payola to release hundreds of minor criminals; but no man looking to be re-elected was about to free New York's most hated man.

To anyone except Howe & Hummel, the evidence looked anything but weak. In fact, it looked overwhelming. The trunk, crammed with articles from the house, had been traced from the Rosenzweig residence to the train station. Rosenzweig was a known abortionist; the girl had died from a botched abortion. Two medical men had identified the body as Alice A. Bowlsby, who was last seen in a white dress. A handkerchief with that name was found in the house, and a girl in a white dress had disappeared from it. The "fiend of Second Avenue"[23] was in a lot of trouble.

For that, however, the police could take little credit. They had been energetic, but essentially incompetent. In addition to allowing the body to deteriorate and the flawed search, they had also arrested Rosenzweig's 14-year-old daughter for no apparent reason. They had not even tracked the ticket to Chicago, although they had plenty of time—the train left hours after the body was discovered, and someone used the ticket as far as Albany. They never found the tightfisted woman in the cab. Exhausted by his efforts, Police Chief George Walling left town before the inquest. This was not the finest hour for New York's Finest.

Not that it mattered; the story was no longer simply a criminal matter. It was a morality tale, and New York, which was just about to expel Tammany from power (for a few years anyway), was in the mood for morality. Like nothing else, the blonde in the trunk stirred the public against "the evil of the age." There were three more abortion-related deaths in the city between August 30 and September 4; prosecutions were sought in each of them. And when a judge told a grand jury that was hearing one of these indictments "that from this hour the authorities, one and all, shall put forth every effort and shall strain every nerve until these professional abortionists, these traffickers in human life, shall be exterminated and driven from existence," the crowd in the courtroom cheered.[24]

A single public voice of dissent piped up against this refrain of dudgeon. That came from the pages of *Woodhull & Claflin's Weekly*, a magazine founded by two sisters, Victoria Woodhull and Tennessee Claflin. Not only had the two set up shop as Wall Street's first female brokers (backed by Cornelius Vanderbilt), but they also preached free love and votes for women. They were marginal but fascinating figures. And they saw the whole issue differently—not as a matter of evil doctors and fallen women, but of rigid mores and hypocrisy.

We say that society itself is the patron of abortionists, that society's present laws make their occupation excusable, nay, a necessity; that the very men who are so loud in their denunciations of Rosenzweig and his class have, nine out of every ten of them, paid for his assistance, and, among women, nine out of ten would act as Alice Bowlsby did, if placed in the same position.[25]

It would not be the last time the sisters said something undoubtedly true that no one wanted to hear. But it hardly helped Rosenzweig that the only people willing to come to his defense (to the extent that they did) were the likes of Woodhull and Claflin.

When the trial opened in late October, the atmosphere was somewhat less charged. In the middle of it, Boss Tweed would be arrested, pushing the fiend of Second Avenue off the front pages. There were two bits of new evidence. The police found yet another item belonging to Alice Bowlsby—a false bosom made out of material she had also used in a dress. And a young woman named Nellie Willis testified that in 1869, she had gone to Rosenzweig, whom she knew as Dr. Ascher, for an abortion. Otherwise, the prosecution rolled out the same lineup that had appeared before the coroner, in an efficient and compelling presentation that took about a day.

Then it was Howe's turn. He rolled out many of the rhetorical weapons that made him one of the great courtroom advocates of his time.

There was, for example, obfuscation. When the facts are against you, Howe believed, make them confusing. So he spent the better part of two days thumbing through a stack of gynecological texts in an effort to get the coroner to admit that he couldn't be sure that there had been an abortion. The press, at least, was unconvinced. In a phrase that summed up the general opinion, the *New York Sun* dismissed Howe's line of questioning as "a medical quibble here and a legal quibble there."

Then there was nit-picking. In his opening remarks, Howe promised that he "would dispel, link by link, the chain of evidence." He certainly tried. For almost every damning circumstance, he provided a different explanation. The girl in the white dress? That was a visitor, Netta Fox. The visit to the undertaker? Done at the behest of a charitable society. The girl herself? There was no proof she was ever at the Rosenzweig home. The damning handkerchief? He dug up one Cornelia Bowlsby of Brooklyn who swore that she and her daughter Anna had known the

Rosenzweigs for years and had left the handkerchief behind one day. (It is probably best to consider the second Bowlsby as a drop in the cesspool of perjury. The firm was known to have a stable of witnesses on demand; in this case, it appears they went out and bought one.)

And then there was attack. The various marks and molars were hardly conclusive evidence of Alice Bowlsby's identity, Howe argued. Only a mother's eyes could tell for certain—and Mrs. Bowlsby had refused to come to the morgue. This decision not to be an eyewitness to the mutilated and putrefying remains of her daughter Howe presented as an abdication of maternal love, leaving it, he said scornfully, to "a hired dentist and an hireling physician." And even if the body was the unfortunate Alice, mightn't Walter Conklin have been responsible for her death in New Jersey, and then had her body sent to New York, taking his "worthless life to save himself" when it was found? Prove that it wasn't! Maligning a dead man and insulting a mother—this was not pretty. But shamelessness in defense of a client was a tool neither Howe nor Hummel blushed to employ.

Taking the stand, Rosenzweig did the usual, denying everything— the undertaker lied; Pickett was mistaken; the bloody clothes were those of his wife, who had given birth five weeks before; he had never performed an abortion in his life. Urged by Howe, he walked from the stand, opened the trunk, which had been sitting in the court from day one, and examined it closely. No, it wasn't his.

Howe made several motions to dismiss the case. Even if there had been an abortion, and even if the woman in the case was Alice Bowlsby—and he did not concede either point—there was no proof that the operation was not necessary to save her life. And where was the evidence that young Alice had ever been in New York? Once the court swatted away these motions, Howe made his closing arguments, always his favorite part of the case.

After delivering a few more rhetorical kicks in the direction of Conklin, he advised the jury that suspicion was not proof. All the evidence could be looked at from a different perspective. There were numerous cases of false identification even of live people, much less dead ones; the woman in white could have been anyone. Pickett was stupid and impulsive. And then, he turned to Rosenzweig, remarking on the unflinching manner with which the defendant had examined the trunk: "Had he packed the body in that trunk, could he, without a tremor, have opened it?" Howe was stretching a thin line here, but in a bad case, he used what he had. There was enough ambiguity, he concluded, not to send a "generous, honest, and upright" husband and father to prison. (On cue, wife and daughter wept.) The spectators were moved.

But the jury, at least, got over it, finding Rosenzweig guilty. The judge was not inclined to mercy, telling him: "You sent two human beings to their last account, deliberately, willfully, murderously." If he could, he would like to sentence him to death. But because the charge was manslaughter, he would have to settle for the maximum: seven years at hard labor. Two days later, Rosenzweig was on his way to Sing Sing Prison, sent off by a jeering crowd—the last spectacle associated with this awful chain of events.

A reporter from the *Sun* accompanied the prisoner on the ride upstate. "I was convicted before I was tried," Rosenzweig complained, in between moaning about how he would never survive prison, what with his bad leg and his weak heart. He was innocent, railroaded by a hostile press. Two months later, Rosenzweig was transferred to Auburn, a gentler prison, where his work was to serve meals to his fellow prisoners— a slush of boiled cod and potatoes on the day a reporter visited. "I'm damned sorry I had a lawyer at all," Rosenzweig told him. "Howe didn't do a damned thing for me."[26] The bitterness suggests that the doctor had borne the full brunt of the partnership's three golden rules, as expressed by Quibble: First, "thoroughly terrify your client. Second, find out how much money he has and where it is. Third, get it."[27]

But Rosenzweig was being too hard on his portly counsel. Howe was not finished. Ironically, it was anti-abortion activism that got his client out of prison. In the wake of the Rosenzweig trial and the other abortion cases, in April 1872, New York State made all abortions illegal, with a maximum penalty of 20 years.[28]

Howe was best known for his courtroom presence, but he had subtler legal skills, too. Right around this time, he deployed them to engineer a mass breakout from Blackwell's Island, the city jail for short-termers.

Not with chisels or sledgehammers, but with the far more effective tool of legal scrutiny.

The question Howe raised had to do with the Court of Special Sessions, which heard minor criminal cases. According to the 1870 statute that created the Special Sessions, two judges were supposed to preside. Typically, though, there was only one. Howe argued that the court was therefore illegally constituted and any convictions heard by a single judge must be set aside. His client, James Miskel, a petty thief convicted of attempting to escape from jail, should therefore be released. In fact, since the court that convicted him was unconstitutional, his subsequent escape was no offense at all. Though the District Attorney's office sputtered that "it is due to a patient public that the thorough-going thieves and pickpockets famous in the annals of the Tombs should not be allowed to escape,"[29] the Court of Appeals reluctantly agreed the law was the law. Howe & Hummel did a roaring business, getting hundreds of men out of jail. There was, said the *Herald,* "jubilation among the slums."

Howe used a similarly keen legal discernment on behalf of Rosenzweig. First, he asked for a new trial, on the basis that the testimony of Nellie Willis should not have been allowed, as it charged a separate felony against the accused. It was unfair, in effect, to try the doctor on two cases at once. The prosecution had been sure that her story would doom Rosenzweig; instead, it turned out to be overreach. The appeals court agreed with Howe and ordered a new trial, scheduled for November 1872.

Rosenzweig was brought back to the Tombs to wait for his next day in court. In a snapshot that shows the many connections the law firm was making with the criminal world, the doctor shared a cell with Dutch Heinrichs, a Howe & Hummel client who once stole $1 million in bonds.[30] The "Flying Dutchman," as Heinrichs was known, often fenced his loot through the good offices of the Greenthal and Mandelbaum families, who were also Howe & Hummel clients. Abraham Greenthal, the patriarch of his criminal clan, had waited tables with Rosenzweig at Auburn Prison.[31] New York's criminal culture was a tangled web of rivalries and loyalties; Howe & Hummel operated in the middle of it.

There was no reason to believe that a new trial would have a different outcome from the first. The better bet was not to have a trial at all. Howe found a way. The April 1872 abortion act, he argued, had repealed the previous abortion law; there was therefore no statute in existence under which Rosenzweig could be tried. Think about it: The bloody trunk was discovered before the 1872 law, so the offense could not be subject to it; but the older law had ceased to exist when the new one repealed it. In effect, there was no law under which his act could be prosecuted. The court, reluctantly, agreed. Rosenzweig was discharged.

The partners were happy to be rid of him. In custody, their client had been rude about his lawyers, whining that if they had done their job right, he would not have been in prison at all. And they probably didn't like the man. Few people seemed to.

So Howe and Hummel took a belated revenge in the pages of *In Danger*. No waffling here about whether there had been an abortion, or if the identification had been sufficient or the rest of it. No mention, either, of Brooklyn's Mrs. Bowlsby or the alleged callousness of the mother. Nor did they find room to mention how the Rosenzweig case had made Howe & Hummel the favored practitioner for abortionists, a job the firm performed well. Thomas "Lookup" Evans, known as the "ghoul of Chatham Street" for the squalid condition of his clinic, was released after conviction when the lawyers challenged the judge's faulty instructions. Howe & Hummel performed a similar service for Ann Burns, a female "physician" who lived in a Long Island mansion but did business downtown. When a young woman gave a deathbed statement that Burns had performed an abortion gone wrong, the police picked her up. It was in the middle of the Rosenzweig hysteria, and Howe lost the case, rather emphatically. Hummel, though, saw an opening. In the appeal, he argued that Burns was tried in December and the jury had been impaneled for November only—a violation of statute that called for a new trial. The court had to agree. When a new trial was called, the key witness had disappeared. Burns went back home to Long Island.

In Danger mentioned none of this. No, in a passage that could have been written by the prosecutor, Howe and Hummel convicted Rosenzweig scornfully, and dismissed the sentence of seven years as "obviously out of proportion to the enormity of the crime."[32]

• • •

But abortion was really a subspecialty. Murder was still job one. The firm's reputation in this area was affirmed when it got the call in the second-biggest murder of the era.[33] Benjamin Nathan—banker, philanthropist, and uncle of the infant Benjamin Nathan Cardozo—was in a locked room in the early morning of July 29, 1870, looking over papers and pondering the first anniversary of his mother's death. He would never see the second. When his son Frederick came to wake him to go to synagogue, he found his father dead, lying in a pool of blood, his head bashed in with a carpenter's dog—an iron bar, turned down and sharpened at each end. The cash box was empty and some jewelry had disappeared.

It was summer and Nathan was rich; the headlines were big and dark, pushing the Franco-Prussian War off the front page. On the next trading day, the New York Stock Exchange flew its flag at half-mast to honor Nathan, who had been both powerful and popular, not a universal combination in the halls of finance. His townhouse on 23rd Street, right across the street from that of Samuel F. B. Morse, the inventor of the telegraph, became a tourist attraction.

The sons were quickly exonerated, though not without some embarrassment. Washington Nathan had to admit that "he had been in company which could not even be called doubtful."[34] In short, he had been at a whorehouse. He would never quite shake free from a miasma of suspicion. A few people came forward who had seen something or other, almost all of it irrelevant. In the weeks that followed, the investigation went nowhere, except for tips from the usual cranks, clairvoyants, and confessors, drawn by $45,000 in reward money.

A break came in March 1871, when a burglar residing in Sing Sing Prison, George Ellis, claimed that he knew who had done it. Let's make a deal. But when Ellis was brought down to the city to do just that, he couldn't bring himself to talk. He went back to Sing Sing. A few weeks later, he changed his mind again. This time, Ellis said that he and a colleague, Billy Forrester, had done a burglary in New York, taking a carpenter's dog, among other things. Billy had subsequently talked about robbing the Nathans over the summer, when they were usually at their country home. Ellis's story made Forrester a greatly wanted man, but the career criminal who had escaped prison half a dozen times was elusive. He was not picked up until more than a year later, in September 1872.

An expert safecracker, Forrester had contacts all over the criminal underworld, and on his arrest, he wasted no time: He called in Howe & Hummel. The first benefit the firm provided was to persuade the authorities to keep him at police headquarters; Forrester thus escaped the dank atmosphere and terrible food of the Tombs. He had been such a wanted man for so long that he was a celebrity, and the cops treated him as such, providing him cigars and brandy.[35] Howe and Hummel were also attentive, consulting with him at length. When the time came for the hearing that would decide whether to go to trial, they were ready.

The key moment was the cross-examination of Annie Keenan, a music teacher who had been on her way to church in the early evening when she saw a strange man with something up his sleeve skulking outside the Nathan home. Forrester, she swore, was that man. She stood up well to Howe, gently contradicting him when he asked, "You didn't stop, did you?"[36] She had stopped, she said, because the figure she saw appeared so strange. But as a whole, the interrogation screams "reasonable doubt."

> HOWE: What color coat was the person you saw wearing that night?
> KEENAN: Light brown. [The coat in custody was dark gray.]
> HOWE: What color were his eyes?
> KEENAN: A brownish gray. [They were black.]
> HOWE: Any facial hair?
> KEENAN: A bit beneath the chin. [Last known with a black mustache.]
> HOWE: Are you near-sighted?
> KEENAN: A little. [Actually, a lot.]

Keenan was "morally certain" that Forrester was the man she saw. Except he wasn't; she had described a private watchman who worked in the area. And the second eyewitness called refused to be morally certain; Forrester looked like the man he had seen, but he couldn't be sure.[37]

After more than two years, the evidence came down to the word of a jailhouse snitch (who, as a convict, would not be allowed to testify) and the flawed eyesight of Miss Keenan. The police, who had been pursuing Forrester for 17 months, were unable even to prove that he was in New York at the time of the murder. Nor did they ever trace any of the stolen goods back to him.

The prosecution dropped the case. While the DA said that he, too, was morally convinced that Forrester was their man, "the technical facts fall far short of making out a case against him." The judge had to agree that the testimony "will not bear cross examination." Howe and Hummel must have preened at the unintentional praise.

Then they did one last service for their client, hustling over to the Supreme Court to get a writ ordering Forrester's release the next day. If the requisition from Illinois, which requested the pleasure of Forrester's company in Joliet State Prison for the next 13 years, was incorrect in any way, he could be discharged, as there would be no legal ground to hold him.[38] A nice point, but a moot one: Illinois officials did their work flawlessly. Forrester went to Joliet; never was a man happier to see the inside of a state prison.

Years later, Hummel would hint that he, too, was morally certain that Forrester was the man. "I cannot speak fully without violating professional honor, for the man was a client of my office, but I can say this, that from what I learned from him Washington Nathan had no more to do with the killing of his father than I."[39]

THREE

Sisters in Law

One of the fascinations of life at the criminal bar was the variety of it. Howe and Hummel were happy to chalk up wins with unsavory types like Rosenzweig, the abortionists, and Forrester—none of them appealing and only Forrester remotely likable. In November 1872, they turned their attention to two women who could not have been a bigger contrast to the likes of Rosenzweig, the surly weakling of Second Avenue.

Victoria Woodhull and Tennessee Claflin were, for a start, discernibly female. Both were beautiful, intelligent, and possessed of charm mixed with a forthright willingness to speak their minds about things like sex and politics that made them notorious. Nice women didn't talk about such things, and if they did, they were supposed to repeat the conventional wisdom. In that sense, the sisters were emphatically not nice.

Born in Homer, Ohio, to a family that was so unpopular that their neighbors actually paid them to leave town, Victoria and Tennessee (or "Tennie C.") were the cream of their ghastly parents' crop of ten children. Their father, Buck, "was worthless," concluded one historian, and their mother, Roxy, "was worthless in spades."[1] From an early age, Victoria and Tennie supported the family as spiritualists, mesmerists, and general-practice occultists (a brother chipped in by selling quack cures for cancer). Tired of riding the second-class circuit, the sisters led their family to New York in 1868. More poetically, Victoria said she had a vision from her personal seer, Demosthenes, advising the move.

The sisters drew the attention of Cornelius Vanderbilt, whose advancing age had given him a keen interest in the next life. He found Victoria's thoughts on the subject congenial. For earthier reasons, he also enjoyed the company of the stunning and sexually matter-of-fact Tennie.[2] In February 1870 Vanderbilt set the sisters up in their own brokerage office, where they greeted customers and curiosity seekers in daring ankle-length skirts and mannish jackets with ties.[3] The "bewitching brokers," as they became known, did fairly well—Vanderbilt was a useful ally, and Woodhull repaid the favor by passing on stock tips from the spirit world—achieving a solid celebrity that allowed them to feed their freeloading relatives.

This motley crew included Woodhull's daughter, Zulu; her mentally handicapped son, Byron; her parents; an elderly anarchist named Stephen Pearl Andrews; three divorced sisters;[4] her second husband, Colonel James Blood, whose sanguinary sobriquet belied his colorless character; and her first husband, who was busy drinking and doping himself to death. (Claflin had also married someone or other, but he seems to have vanished along the way.) There were 20 or so when everyone was in town, all living together in a mansion in Manhattan's high-rent Murray Hill district.

It was a stability the sisters had never known before—and it was not enough. Among other things, Victoria and Tennie wanted to end traditional marriage; repeal the law of supply and demand; and usher in pantarchy, or universal government based on reason, which would be conducted in "Alwate," an early version of Esperanto.[5] To promote all this, in May 1870 they founded, with Vanderbilt's help, *Woodhull & Claflin's Weekly*, a 16-page newspaper with the slogan "Progress! Free Thought! Untrammeled Lives!"

It was, from the start, a curious publication, a mélange of Victoria's speeches, Tennie's antimarriage screeds, reports from various newspapers, and personal attacks on people they didn't like. It comes as no surprise that the *Weekly* was the first U.S. paper to publish Marx's "Communist Manifesto."[6] Vanderbilt eventually withdrew his support from the sisters (maybe dud tips from the "other side"). As a result, their brokerage faltered and the magazine struggled.

Woodhull hit the lecture trail, where she was always able to attract a good audience. It no doubt helped that she was a striking woman, slim with short hair, usually dressed in black, complemented with a single red rose.[7] But it was her willingness to say the unsayable that packed lecture halls. And there was curiosity value, too: In May 1872, the Equal Rights Party formally nominated Woodhull for the presidency.

Her views were eccentric for the times, but they were sometimes serious, too. In January 1871, she was the first woman to testify before Congress, making a cogent case to the House Judiciary Committee that the 15th Amendment, which promised the vote to all citizens, could be interpreted to include women.

The lectures, although popular, didn't pay enough to keep 20 people living in style. So the sisters turned to an asset, in the form of a secret. They knew that Henry Ward Beecher, the famous minister who had made Plymouth Church in Brooklyn one of the richest in the country, had had an extended affair with Elizabeth Tilton, his best friend's wife. Woodhull had heard the story from two separate sources, one of them Elizabeth Cady Stanton, a friend and suffragist colleague, and she subsequently confirmed it during her fling with the cuckolded husband, Theodore Tilton. (Her advice to the anguished Tilton when he told her about the affair: Stop this "babyish whining"; he was no "vestal virgin after all."[8])

In September 1872, she fired a shot across Beecher's bow, detailing to an audience of spiritualists in Boston the whole seamy Beecher-Tilton connection. If the sisters were hoping for a discreet payoff, they didn't get it. Beecher stayed silent. Meanwhile, with all those feckless relatives to feed, they were getting desperate. Woodhull told a court around this time that she did not own "the clothes on my back."[9] Outing America's most revered man of God would sell a lot newspapers. And it would humiliate Tilton, too, who had earned Woodhull's wrath when he refused to support her bid for the presidency.

It was the end of what had been a passionate relationship.[10] Tilton had even written a short biography of Woodhull that compared her to Joan of Arc, praised her classic profile, complimented her athleticism, and on and on. The thing was so smarmy that Julia Ward Howe issued this classic review, worthy of Dorothy Parker in her prime: "Such a book is a tomb from which no author rises."[11]

In the issue of the *Weekly* dated November 2, 1872, the sisters went for it, publishing what they called, correctly, an account of "one of the most stupendous scandals which has ever occurred in any community." The spirits, Woodhull wrote, demanded it. (One wishes they had also demanded an editor; the article ran almost 12,000 words.) Woodhull was not, she wrote sincerely, bothered by the adultery. A man like Beecher needed more than one woman, and it was only society's stupid laws that prevented a man of his "immense physical potency" from openly finding what he needed. "Passional starvation, enforced on such a nature, so richly endowed, by the ignorance and prejudice of the past, is a horrid cruelty." But if that was the case, he should say so. Instead, Beecher preached the opposite of what he practiced: "He has, in a word, consented, and still consents, to be a hypocrite." Woodhull was equally unsparing of Mrs. Tilton: "I conceive that Mrs. Tilton's love for Mr. Beecher was her true marriage and that her marriage to Mr. Tilton is prostitution."

In another article in the same issue, Claflin took her own turn at the topic of sexual hypocrisy, telling of an incident she said she had witnessed in 1869, when a Wall Street man named Luther Challis and a friend got two teenagers drunk and then seduced them. Challis was so proud of himself that for the next couple of days he showed off his bloodstained fingertip, the "red token" of his victim's virginity.

When the *Weekly* hit the newsstands on October 28, it sold out immediately. Crowds surrounded the downtown offices to score a copy, and a brisk secondary market developed. The paper, which cost 10 cents, changed hands for many times that price. Eventually, it sold perhaps 150,000 copies, 10 times the usual number, and was rented out for a dollar a day.[12]

To most New Yorkers, the Beecher and Challis stories were delicious scandals, and they read them with the same avidity Americans display today toward celebrity peccadilloes. To one man, though, they were something more. They were Sin. Indecent. Obscene. And he was going to do something about it. His name was Anthony Comstock, and he was just beginning to carve out a career as a scourge of all that was unclean.

Comstock's standards were extraordinarily high, and vanishingly narrow. Any mention of sex, any sight of nudity—well, it was disgusting. The November 2 edition of the *Weekly* combined elements of everything Comstock loathed: assertive women, ridicule of authority, and mentions of nonmarital sex. Comstock was not going to stand for it. When the DA's office, despite his pleas, declined to prosecute, he went to the feds, charging that the magazine violated laws against the use of the mail to transmit obscene publications. He found a fellow prig to agree, and on November 1, the sisters were arrested.

What followed were 17 extremely unpleasant months for the sisters. Woodhull had long had an audience for her lectures, but she didn't really have a following. In her hours and days of need, she found very few allies. One was George Francis Train, who made a fortune in shipping, banking, and railroads, and then retired to vent his feelings on things like Irish rebellion (he was for it) and to indulge in such whims as going around the world in 72 days. He, too, had declared for the presidency. Train liked lost causes, and this looked like one.

Train was a gadfly, but no idiot. When he read the Beecher article, his analysis was that "This may be libel, but it is not obscenity,"[13] which was exactly right. There was nothing remotely pornographic or even titillating in the 12,000 words. One wishes there were; sexual freedom becomes tedious when defended a dozen different ways. Another ally was William Howe, who offered his services.[14] It was a meeting of true minds. Woodhull, Claflin, Howe (and Beecher, for that matter) all believed that the ends justified the means. All were passionate in their pursuits but elastic in their principles. All were good at what they did. But someone was going to get hurt.

At the initial arraignment, the prosecutor made it clear that whether the paper was "vulgar and obscene" was only part of the problem. The larger offense was the "abominable and unjust charge against one of the purest and best citizens of this State"—i.e., Beecher. Of course, if Beecher had been offended, he didn't need Comstock to make a federal case of it. He could simply sue for libel, as Challis was doing. The preacher never did.

The sisters lost the argument that this was supposed to be an obscenity case and had nothing to do with Beecher. Be that as it may, the judge decided, he didn't like them. His entirely injudicious comment: "An example is needed and we propose to make one of these women!" He set bail at $8,000 each, an astonishingly high figure for a misdemeanor, and packed them off to Ludlow Street Jail until they could pay it. (They turned down Train's offer to pay the sum, preferring to stay independent. They later changed their minds, allowing a variety of people to pay their bail, which eventually reached more than $60,000.) Back at the office, their equipment was either seized or destroyed.[15]

Ludlow Street was the jail for county and federal prisoners. Originally stuffed mostly with debtors,[16] it was a homey type of jail, run by a warden, William Tracy, who liked the sisters enormously. On their first day, he even read them excerpts from Alexander Pope's poems, laughing that these were a lot racier than anything the *Weekly* ever managed.[17]

Still, it was a boring life. They were awakened at 6:00 a.m., and other than meals at 7:00 a.m., noon, and 5:30 p.m., there was little to do; the only break in the routine was a church service every Sunday, with a billiard table serving as the altar.[18] But it was not a harsh place. All the officers, Woodhull would record, were polite and civil, with nary a swear word heard.

There was a caste system at Ludlow Street. The riffraff on the vermin-infested upper two floors had a nasty time of it; the cells were smaller, the bedding dirty, and bedbugs rife. There was one tap for the 32 cells and people could go months without bathing.[19] The food was bad and there was not much of it—bread and coffee for breakfast, which the prisoners ate standing in their cells; soup, bread, and some meat or fish at midday; and then another standing-room meal of bread and tea in the evening. No utensils were allowed, except a soupspoon.[20]

The "boarders," in the fresher air on the ground floor, paid extra and got something like a self-furnished hotel. For about $15 a week, the sisters used the same bathroom as the warden's family and ate the same food; this was served to them in their room, complete with linen and utensils.[21] Eventually, they even had a rug on the floor and their own bedding on the cots.[22]

The sisters would not leave Ludlow Street for a month, and they would return to it often, as they bounced between the federal indictment and the libel case. (Colonel Blood was in a different jail on the libel charge.) Woodhull had said that she wanted her article on Beecher to "burst like a bomb-shell into the ranks of the moralistic social camp." What she did not anticipate was that the blowback would almost destroy her. That it didn't was thanks largely to William Howe and Abraham Hummel. Together they figured out a legal strategy that saved Woodhull from herself. Call it the Bible-Shakespeare defense.

Howe introduced the idea on November 5, the day the sisters were indicted. Hinting that "private malice" from certain persons was the real source of the case (he might have meant Comstock, Beecher, or any number of people who couldn't stand the two), Howe argued that if the *Weekly* was found to be obscene, "then the transmission through the mails of the Holy Bible, Lord Byron's Poems, and Shakespeare's works should be stopped, for they are open to the same objection." Indeed, the Bible Society should be prosecuted for shipping Bibles to pagans overseas. And incidentally, if the articles were so obscene, why wasn't the *Herald* prosecuted for reprinting them?[23] A good question, that one. The next day, though, there was more bad news: Ulysses Grant had beaten Woodhull for the presidency, and no, it wasn't close.

The libel strategy was different. Here Howe aimed to show that Challis was exactly the kind of man who might have gotten a teenager drunk so that he could have his way with her. Unfortunately for the reader, then and now, this required the lawyer to ask questions that, according to the *Times*, "elicited facts totally unfit for publication." The *Herald*, which had been happy enough to republish the entire article relating to Challis, covered its moral tracks by scorning the testimony's "filthiness of detail" and ridiculing the sisters' funny-looking supporters. These were apparently youngish men, with greasy hair parted in the middle, whose faces combined insipidity with passion—altogether "bearing the signs of the peculiar lunacy that guides the doubtful fortunes of the ism of free love."[24]

The *Herald* would later become Howe & Hummel's greatest friend in the press. At this point, the paper was ambivalent. A subhead was intriguing, but uncomplimentary: "The Agonized Attempts of a Criminal Lawyer to Wring More Filth Out of an Already Filthy Scandal," but the article itself Howe would not have objected to. It showed his quickness afoot, his humor, and his willingness to go as far as he could for the sake of a client. And for the first time, he got public credit for his dress sense—a green plush vest stretched tight across his ample stomach.

Howe put Challis through the wringer for two days (on the second, he switched to a vest of Scotch plaid, set off by a diamond pin), asking him about a gift of undergarments, his acquaintance with a well-known brothel-keeper named Molly, and whether he had ever kissed Tennie C. Claflin. His more daring gambits the judge, who was apparently of the Comstock school of sex, would not allow.

Challis tried to throw the mud back, saying Claflin had tried to blackmail him and then offered to recant for money. This was not beyond the realm of possibility —but it also did not mean that the original story was untrue. Woodhull's testimony, and that of James Maxwell, who had been at the notorious ball with Challis, ended the first round. Challis could not have been happy that it looked, as so many libel cases do, as if this would turn into a he-said, she-said affair in which things would be made public that he would much prefer remain buried.

Comstock also had an uncomfortable time of it, coming across, quite accurately, as an officious ass. Unlike Challis, though, he was able to hit back. In early January 1873, realizing that the allegedly obscene issue of the *Weekly* was still being sold, he arranged to have a copy sent to a friend's address in Connecticut—and swore out new warrants for interstate trafficking in obscenity. He went to the *Weekly*'s offices to arrest the sisters, where he spotted "six or eight of the hardest kind of free-lovers, judging by their looks, to be found anywhere."[25] It was left to the reader to imagine what hardened free-lovers looked like. But he did not find the sisters; Claflin was out of town, and Woodhull was a step ahead of Comstock and the U.S. marshals.

Scheduled to give a talk, mischievously titled "The Naked Truth," on January 9, 1873, in New York's Cooper Union, Woodhull arrived disguised as a Quaker, bent with age. Then she hobbled to the stage (closely followed by Hummel), tore off her accoutrements, and gave one of her usual toe-curling speeches, in which she confidently predicted that the U.S. government would never go through with the prosecution and took a few shots at "the zealot, Comstock."[26] Perhaps the marshals shared her view of Comstock; they let her rip for a good 90 minutes. When she finished, she dramatically—Woodhull was incapable of not milking such a moment—ran toward the officers, throwing her arms out in a gesture of crucifixion.[27] They escorted her back to her home away from home, the Ludlow Street Jail.

All told, Woodhull and Claflin faced four charges for the same offense: one for using the mails; one for sending the newspaper across state lines; one for criminal libel; one on a civil charge. George Train was also arrested for obscenity, for publishing in sympathy a journal called *The Train Ligue,* in which he copied out the naughtier bits of the Bible,[28] punctuated by headings from the *National Police Gazette* and extracts from the Catholic catechism.[29] His point was to prove how absurd the obscenity charges were; his counsel was Howe & Hummel. And Colonel Blood was sitting in the Jefferson Market Court, also on the libel charge, also defended by Howe & Hummel.

The month in jail without trial—this in a time when murderers were often before a judge in a matter of weeks—the accumulating charges, the extraordinary amount of bail, and the opaqueness of the case, began to modify public opinion. Sure, the sisters' views on sex and politics were wrong and probably immoral, but people began to wonder if all this wasn't going a bit too far. The day after Woodhull was hauled off the Cooper Union stage, for example, the first obscenity trial started. She was dunned for more bail during the trial and arrested yet again a week after its conclusion, this time on the libel charge. The sisters never changed or even softened their positions—rather the opposite. But despite themselves, they began to win some sympathy against the tactics of the decency Javerts. New York's *Sunday Mercury* was derisive of the whole case, editorializing that it had "all the elements of a mockery, gratifying to no one but him [Comstock] who, 'solitary and alone,' has set it in motion."[30]

A classic Howe & Hummel defense came in layers. The first was often technical. So on the obscenity charge, for example, the initial argument was that no one could prove that any of the accused had actually mailed the newspaper. That failed.

Time for the second layer—usually the most important one. Howe set up this defense when he finally had Comstock in his sights during an examination of whether the charge should be taken to trial. The lawyer read line after line of the offending newspaper and asked: Is this obscene? "No," the scourge of indecency was forced to answer. What about this sentence? "No." Or this one? "No."

Eventually, both Comstock and the prosecutor had to concede that their original premise that the whole newspaper was obscene was wrong. The charge then came down to a single three-line sentence in the article about Challis: "And this scoundrel, to prove that he has seduced a maiden, carried for days on his finger exhibiting in triumph the red trophy of her virginity." The trap laid, Howe sprung it. He opened the Bible to Deuteronomy 22:15, and read: "Then shall the father of the damsel, and her mother, take and bring forth the tokens of the damsel's virginity unto the elders of the city in the gate."

Is this portion of Holy Scripture obscene, he asked Comstock? No, he didn't think so. Well, then, Howe concluded, "No Pharisee would think of prosecuting a man for sending the Holy Scriptures through the mail." Surely the Congress never intended that Comstock be the de facto arbiter of obscenity, Howe argued, and thus of press liberty. Comstock modestly declined to speculate.

It was a sweet moment for the defense, and vindication for Howe. A few months earlier, he had lost a case brought by Comstock; apparently the books and photographs involved, including such classics as *The Confessions of a Voluptuous Young Lady*, made any plea of innocence ridiculous.[31] Losing to someone like Comstock was not an experience he wanted to repeat.

The day was a disaster for the prosecution. But with the willful blindness that was a hallmark of his career, Comstock didn't see it. "Their counsels [Howe and Hummel] were very anxious to break down my testimony," he wrote in his diary that evening, "but utterly failed. Truth was too much for them. They do not take stock very largely in that commodity."[32]

In his closing argument, Howe sent rhetorical reinforcements to his first two layers of defense and then went to the third—effrontery. If the sisters were guilty of sending obscenity through the mail, then so was Comstock. He, after all, had induced someone to send him the copies on which he made his claim. Comstock whined in his diary of the defense: "They still continue to abuse me, but they are beneath my notice."[33]

Two weeks later, the judge decided that the precedents were conflicting enough that the case should go to trial. But he showed little enthusiasm for it. When the case opened in June 1873, Comstock barely had time to testily correct his name—let it be "distinctly understood" that there was no middle initial "J"[34]—before the case was shut down. The sisters won, on a technicality. The judge ruled that the act that they were said to have violated did not cover newspapers. To read the judge's tortured interpretation of the legislation is to understand that he was looking to get rid of the case without giving the sisters a victory or the prosecution a defeat. Howe & Hummel had eviscerated the government's case. A retreat with some semblance of dignity was the only option left. "An Inglorious Failure," crowed Beecher's home paper, the *Brooklyn Daily Eagle*.

That left the libel case, which finally came to trial in March 1874. At this point, Howe had moved on to other things, leaving matters in the hands of his co-counsel. The sisters won again. It took eight days of testimony, and could have lasted much longer—many of Challis's Wall Street friends, called to testify as to his character and pleasures, failed to show up. The jury drew the appropriate conclusion; they were also signally unimpressed by Challis, who revealed himself to be a cad. When a

Challis friend and a local madam broadly supported the account in the *Weekly,* the jurors gave Woodhull and Claflin the benefit of the doubt, while making an unusual statement that the verdict did not mean that they approved of the sisters' beliefs. The judge was not as judicious. He called the verdict "shameful and infamous." But so what? Being called names was nothing new for the sisters. They left court with a spring in their step. It was over.

Not quite; as they left the courthouse, they were arrested, yet again, on a civil suit that Challis had initiated. In the end, Challis was wise enough not to go through with it. Now it really was over.[35]

For all the principals, the Beecher-Tilton-Woodhull-Comstock-Challis mess resonated for years. In a convincing proof that justice does not always prevail, the two with the most to apologize for were hurt least.

The first was Comstock, who should have been embarrassed but wasn't. People who possess absolute moral certainty never are. This was the first big case of his career. Howe, it turned out, was wrong when he asserted that Congress did not intend Comstock to be the arbiter of decency. That is exactly what he became in 1873, when he pushed through a federal obscenity statute that became known as the "Comstock Law." The federal government had, almost without debate, decided to become a censor, and named Comstock as its chief enforcer.[36] By his own account, by 1875 he had destroyed 67 tons of obscene books, 194,000 lewd pictures, 60,300 contraceptives, and several trainloads of aphrodisiacs.[37] Comstock would tilt against Howe & Hummel several more times. He always came off second-best, and he never knew it.

The states followed with a blizzard of mini–Comstock Laws; within a few years, any printed mention of sex or contraception was liable to prosecution. In a very real sense, Comstock was the big winner of the whole mess, silencing not only pornographers, but sex educators and social reformers who wanted to improve the rights of married women. Even Horatio Alger fell foul of the Comstock lodestar.[38]

Comstock had the same effect on abortion. In January 1878, he visited Madame Restell's mansion, pretending to be inquiring on behalf of a lover. When she sold him some powders and a syringe for $20,[39] he had her arrested on a charge of selling abortifacients. Restell,

67, went to the Tombs again. Facing ruin, she revised her will, and on March 31, filled a bath with warm water, then slit her throat with an eight-inch carving knife.[40] Comstock rejoiced.[41]

As for Beecher, the other person with much to apologize for, he survived a well-cooked investigation by Plymouth Church. A few years later, however he was not able to maintain his lofty silence when Tilton sued him in 1875 for alienation of his wife's affections. It's hard to overstate how big a case this was. Regularly, entire pages of the newspapers were filled with dense extracts of that day's doings in court. The trial ended in a hung jury, and Beecher went back to the pulpit. One piece of doggerel from the era goes like this:

> *Beecher, Beecher is my name*
> *Beecher 'till I die!*
> *I never kissed Mis' Tilton,*
> *I never told a lie.*[42]

The great man never would have been laughed at like this before the scandal broke. But he kept his job and most of his reputation. That could not be said of the Tiltons. They were forced to leave Plymouth Church and were ruined, financially and socially.

George Francis Train was charged—at Comstock's behest—with obscenity in December 1872 and sent to the Tombs. Bleak and damp, the Tombs afflicted its keepers with rheumatism and tuberculosis and seemed perpetually darkened by its own shadow. It was an awful place to live, or to die, but thanks to lax notions of security and order, it could be surprisingly convivial. In this environment, Train was a hit, promptly winning election as president of the Murderers' Club.[43] His next-door neighbor was another Howe & Hummel client, William Sharkey. That may be less of a coincidence that it seems at first blush. Around this time, *Woodhull & Claflin's Weekly* noted in a long article that can only be called a hagiography of their lawyers, that Howe & Hummel represented 23 of the 25 alleged murderers in the Tombs and were consulting on the other two.[44] The *Weekly* provided no evidence to back this up, and it is possible that the article was payment in kind for Howe's services; the sisters were running out of money. But the figures are not impossible, either.

Sharkey was a particularly interesting neighbor. A gang leader, he did yeoman's work for Tammany, once being nominated for alderman.[45] Through some freak of nature, he lost a bid for reelection and went back to his natural métier. Known for his dress sense and his ruthlessness, Sharkey was an entrepreneur of crime. He and a couple of colleagues started a firm, W. E. Gray and Company, which was a front for forgery and fencing stolen stock certificates. When they gave up the lease to their office, Woodhull and Claflin picked it up to start their brokerage.[46]

A couple of years later, in a rare miscalculation, Sharkey lent a fellow lowlife, Bob Dunn, $600 to start a gambling game in Buffalo. Dunn lost the lot. He was drowning his difficulties in a saloon in September 1872 when Sharkey came in and asked for his money. Dunn said, honestly, that he didn't have it. Sharkey shouted, "You'd better pay me now!" Then he made it impossible for Dunn to do so by pulling out his Derringer and shooting his debtor. Sharkey quickly apologized—"I did not mean to shoot you"—but Dunn was past caring. Sentenced to death, Sharkey sat in the Tombs to await the outcome of his various appeals.

This was nice for him, because young Maggie Jourdan, a girl of quasi-respectable origins who had developed an unfortunate predilection for rough trade, was able to visit him every day. Sharkey was described as having the eyes of a rattlesnake, the mouth of a wolf, and the jaws of an assassin.[47] But Jourdan, who adored him, considered him the "most beautiful man in New York." She was a popular girl, pretty, modest, and amiable, while Sharkey was a pain in the neck, getting liquored up and then amusing himself by spitting and swearing at the staff.[48]

Considered the purest example of ancient Egyptian architecture outside Egypt, and constructed in part from stones of Bridewell, the previous jail,[49] the Tombs occupied an entire city block. Not just a hanging place or a jail, the Tombs was a veritable emporium of crime. In addition to the cells, there were several courtrooms, special accommodations for the well-heeled, a women's prison, a workhouse, offices, and the teeming Bummers' Hall, a massive space about 60 feet by 20, crammed with dozens of men doing short stints for drunkenness, vagrancy, and the like.[50]

The Tombs was where people waiting for trial, for shipment to prison upstate, or for execution spent their time. Pity, in particular, the poor folks who were accused of nothing but being in the wrong place at the wrong time; witnesses could be held indefinitely pending trial. It was not unknown, or even unusual, for a criminal to be released on bail while the witness against him stayed behind bars.

Despite its size and pretension, the Tombs was a mess from the day it opened, because it was built over the inadequately filled-in remains of the old Collect Pond.[51] This body of water, fed by underground springs, had been a romantic trysting place during the colonial era (except for the gibbet on the island in the middle) and had floated the first steam-boat in America in 1796. Then it became a pestilential and smelly dumping ground for industrial and animal waste. The city recognized that it was becoming a health hazard, and drained it in 1811. The job was done poorly, leaving behind soft, damp ground. Though the Collect has been buried for centuries, the topographical contours remain. Stand in the un-inspired area known as Foley Square and look around in a broad circle. The smaller buildings describe the perimeter of the Collect; beyond them, the structures are abruptly, and noticeably, taller.

There are more sobering connections as well, between Manhattan's past and present in the area. When a new courthouse was being built near Foley Square in 1991, archaeologists unearthed almost a million[52] artifacts from the old Five Points neighborhood, which was also built on the moist remains of the Collect. These ranged from the remains of a stone-lined privy to bottles, pipes, dishware, a spittoon, inkwells, even the skeletal remains of a monkey, probably the companion to an Italian organ grinder.[53] The collection was stored for safekeeping in the basement of 6 World Trade Center. On 9/11, one of the twin towers fell on the building, and all but 18 items were destroyed. There is an awful symmetry in the remains of New York's worst neighborhood being lost on its worst day.

As for the Tombs, it still exists and still serves as the city jail; but it is the third building to be known by that name. The original Tombs was replaced in 1902, Egyptian pretension giving way to Victorian Gothic. The current version, opened in 1941 just down the street, is Art Deco in inspiration; it nods to its history with two pillars that echo the design of the original.

In Sharkey's time, the Tombs had four tiers of cells; the lowest (and dampest) was for lunatics, drunks, and those waiting to be shipped elsewhere; the third tier was for thieves; and the fourth for minor villains and the chapel, which held Protestant services on Sunday that almost all of the prisoners found easy to resist.[54] Sharkey lived on the second tier, which was home to the most serious criminals, including those on Murderers' Row.

The typical cell had a cement floor, an iron bed, and a chamber pot. Thanks to Maggie Jourdan, Sharkey's was considerably more comfortable. She provided such civilities as flowers, a walnut table, a carpet, a canary, a magazine rack, and a dressing gown and velvet slippers.[55] Cell 40 took on the air of a middle-class living room.[56] Jourdan became such a familiar figure, coming every day and spending all of it at the door of Sharkey's cell, that the guards began to wave her in without searching her.

On November 19, 1873, she came as usual, and as usual, the guards sent her on her way, no doubt with a sympathetic smile. A few hours later, Sarah Allen entered. She was the wife of Wes Allen, a career criminal whose address was Sing Sing, and the sister-in-law of John Allen, known to his great pride as "the wickedest man in New York," a sobriquet he had printed on his business cards. Two other brothers were burglars and Theodore "The" Allen ran one of the city's sleaziest saloons. The Allen brothers were, naturally, Howe & Hummel clients; and when they needed bail, they went to Marm Mandelbaum, another client.[57]

At the gate, Mrs. Allen got the red ticket that conferred permission to visit. She stopped to say hello to Sharkey and Jourdan, then went up to the third tier to visit her friend. Jourdan left around 1:00 p.m., a little earlier than usual. Half an hour later, an ungainly female attired in a heavy green veil also left, depositing a red ticket with the guard before boarding a street car. When Mrs. Allen tried to leave, though, things got interesting. She had no ticket. Patting herself theatrically, she declared, "I must have lost it."

Even the dim-witted guards thought this was not quite right. They searched the cells, and lo and behold, Sharkey was gone. He had left behind all the little things his lover had brought him—and also his clothes and mustache, the latter neatly shaved off and still wet with lather.[58] The biggish female, whom everyone now remembered as being peculiar looking, was Sharkey; Jourdan had smuggled in female clothing under her dress. He was gone. (Rumor had it that he dropped off the clothes he escaped in at Howe & Hummel's office.)[59]

Mrs. Allen protested that the loss of the ticket was a simple mistake. Then she hired Hummel.[60] Maggie Jourdan, arrested at her mother's house, was in soaring spirits—"I am the happiest woman in New York," she told a reporter. "I am sure I cannot be punished. My lawyer says so."[61] That lawyer was Howe. Mrs. Allen never stood trial, and Jourdan got off; the argument that she was a victim of her devotion worked. The jury was not entirely convinced, but a hung jury was enough. She walked, eventually joining her man in Havana. But Sharkey was not actually a very nice person; he abused her and she dumped him. She came back to New York.[62] He never did.

How well Train knew his next-door neighbor Sharkey is not known, but it is likely he did. The evidence that came out after the escape made it clear that prisoners in the Tombs wandered about at will, and Train was a gregarious man. Moreover, because the Tombs was overcrowded and the kitchen inadequate, it was common practice for visitors to bring in food. Edward ("Ned") Stokes, who murdered Jim Fisk in 1872 over the affections of a showgirl, even had a personal servant; the latter fetched in food from a local restaurant.[63] Everything was for sale in the Tombs—from conjugal visits to clean sheets to cigars and booze. The latter was not strictly allowed, but prisoners managed, one by having a flask of whiskey incarcerated in the belly of chicken.[64] Vendors moved among the prison tiers hawking their goods in exactly the same way a sidewalk vendor would outside. It is intriguing to imagine Train, the courtly gadfly, chatting with the ingenuous Maggie and her man over a quiet meal from Delmonico's in Sharkey's well-appointed cell.

Train's own story would not end well. The judge practically begged him to plead not guilty by reason of insanity; there was a wink and a nod that his stay in the asylum would be short. But Train could be as unbending as Comstock. He would only plead guilty to "publishing an obscene paper composed of Bible quotations."[65] He wanted his trial to be a test case, and he stayed in his dank cell for five months in an effort to get one. He kept refusing bail and drawing attention to the unhealthy conditions in the Tombs, singling out the distress of Rosenzweig, the infamous abortionist.[66] In Train's judgment, the Tombs was the worst of the 14 prisons he had been in. "My chief purpose in jail was not to get out," he wrote, "but to be tried on the charge of obscenity. I had been arrested for that offense, and determined that I would be either acquitted or convicted."[67]

He was never allowed to make his stand. By March 1873, his suit was regarded as a white elephant. Everyone official wanted him to go away.[68] The unofficial verdict was different; the proceedings in court became known as the "Train matinee" and always drew a raucously appreciative crowd. But it went on and on, with various fakirs, reformers, acquaintances, and faux Polish nobleman weighing in on their old friend's virtues. Finally, the jurors rebelled. "We're tired out," said the foreman, "and don't think it's right to force us to listen day after day to the same old story."[69]

At the trial in May 1873, Howe argued, again, that quoting from the Bible could not be obscenity, and discoursed at some length about the wonders of religious freedom, even Train's, whose tenets were "peculiarly his own."[70] Howe should have stopped there, but didn't, going on to say that even if *The Train Light* was obscene (and it wasn't, honest!), Train was insane when he published it. The judge leaped at the opening, instructing the jury to acquit on the basis of insanity, which it did.[71]

Train was furious that his big moment was denied, and immediately moved for the impeachment of the judge.[72] Of more consequence, though, was that though he was judged sane now and sane at almost every hour of his life, except when he was publishing *The Train Ligue*, on the basis of this momentary insanity, the state confiscated his fortune. He never spent a night in an asylum. In later life, Train lived, literally, on peanuts in a small hotel room, feeding pigeons and speaking only to children.

FOUR

Gangsters of New York

Here, too, are lanes and alleys paved with mud knee deep; underground
chambers where they dance and game; ruined houses open to the street,
whence through wide gaps in the walls other ruins loom upon the eye,
as though the world of vice and misery had nothing else to show; hid-
eous tenements which take their names from robbery and murder; all
that is loathsome, drooping and decayed is here.[1]

If that sounds like a scene from Charles Dickens, it is. But, the novelist was not describing a fictional London, but real life in New York,
circa 1841. Specifically, he was describing the area known as the Five
Points—a name derived from the five-pointed intersection of Worth,
Baxter, and Mosco streets[2] that was the heart of the neighborhood.
Urban poverty that could appall Dickens had to be something special,
and the Five Points was. The area's fame made it a deliciously dangerous
tourist haunt; visitors to New York, including Abraham Lincoln, swung
by for a look and a shudder.

Also part of the moist landmass that had replaced the Collect Pond,
the area was never intended to be a slum, but it quickly became one.

It was sodden and smelly, and residents who could afford to moved out; the poor moved in. Expelled by the famine, the Irish in particular swarmed into the area, cramming the buildings with their dreams and their poverty. In 1855, two-thirds of the adult residents of the Five Points were born in Ireland.[3] There were also free blacks, poor immigrants from other countries, and a few native-born whites.

But the Five Points became associated with the Irish, and the Irish became associated with crime. This was not an entirely fair characterization. Most of the immigrants did what immigrants of all generations have done—worked at nasty jobs in the hope that they could improve their lives and give their children a better chance.[4] A year after Dickens's damning description, Walt Whitman visited the Five Points, and saw it differently, describing the residents not as "paupers and criminals, but the Republic's most needed asset, the wealth of stout poor men who will work."

That said, there was desperation and crime in the Five Points; lots of it, in fact. Prostitution and violence and saloons were ubiquitous: By the 1850s, a network of gangs claimed specific territories and defended them with determination—as well as brass knuckles, bare fists, bludgeons, and teeth.[5] These gangs claimed to protect their own against a hostile culture, and to coax a few benefits as well. The rise of Tammany to political power helped. The Tammany machine needed votes, and it encouraged gangs to deliver them. They reliably delivered the Sixth Ward, in which the Five Points was located, and the adjacent Fourth, which touched the East River. For their work, the gangs were generally untroubled by the forces of justice, although murder and disturbing the gentry might bring down the law.

By 1880, the Five Points was almost as Italian as Irish,[6] but the Irish gang culture endured. Of the various groups, the most powerful were the Whyos, whose name came from the birdlike call they used to communicate with each other: The first syllable was high, rising almost to a falsetto, and the second fell to a baritone.[7] The Whyos did not pretend to be protectors; they were strictly criminal, and like most gangs, their victims tended to be their own kind. Through intimidation and shrewd marketing, they took over many a smaller gang, and dominated professional crime in lower Manhattan. Among the members were such notables as Hoggy Walsh, Googy Corcoran, and Baboon Connolly.[8] One Whyo was found with a price list in his pocket: The services offered ranged from punching ($2) to "ear chawed off" ($15) to "doing the big job" ($100 and up).[9]

By the mid-1880s, the Whyos were notorious. Their spiritual home was the groggeries and tenements of Bottle Alley, which the reformer and journalist Jacob Riis christened "the foulest spot in all the city." The Whyos fit right in. Any villain with an Irish name was apt to be called a Whyo, and the gang probably got blamed for more than its share of dirty deeds. But these were filthy enough. One member invented an eye gouger;[10] another was acclaimed for his technique in biting off the tails of barroom cats.[11] The Whyos were also early practitioners in the art of systematic extortion. Still, powerful as they were, the Whyos were not as powerful as they thought they were. They made a couple of mistakes, or rather the same mistake four times—killings that left a trail of evidence. After the gang lost four leaders in a row to murder convictions, it never recovered its influence. It was finished by the mid-1890s.[12]

The first leader to go, Felix Lavelle, was not represented by Howe & Hummel; perhaps the lawyers were affronted that in 1878 Lavelle had killed his erstwhile lover, Sarah Hayden, almost literally on their door-step.[13] They did represent the next two, though, and turned down the fourth because he did not follow their advice.

Their first client was Michael McGloin, who shot and killed a French-born wine dealer named Louis Hanier on December 30, 1881.[14] McGloin and three confederates had gone to the wineshop and tried by a ruse to get Hanier to leave the till. He was not taken in, and the four left. But they came back after midnight "to clean it out and get some cigars," McGloin testified. They were rifling the place when Hanier's wife heard them. She woke her husband. As the wine dealer rushed down the steps, McGloin spied him and shot. Hanier managed to stumble back to the bedroom. *"L'assassin!"* he cried, then reeled back to his bed and died.

It was a pointless, brutal death by brutal men who lived pointless lives. When a friend saw McGloin the next morning and asked him about the killing, the Whyo was at first cagey, but managed this *bon mot*, which became the unofficial slogan of his gang: "A man ain't tough until he knocks his man out." As the two walked and talked, McGloin admitted to the killing but said it was in self-defense—he thought he saw a gun. (Hanier was unarmed.)

The police took an interest in the case. If one gang member killed another and didn't leave a body hanging around carelessly, that might go uninvestigated. But this was another matter: Hanier was a law-abiding father of seven. Police Captain Thomas Byrnes swore he would get his man—and by this time, when Byrnes said something like that, the bad guys had reason to fear.

A strapping six-footer with a magnificent mustache, Byrnes had joined the force in 1863 and was named chief of detectives in 1880. At the time, the post was little more than a title and a salary boost. He took it seriously. Byrnes's big insight was that in order to compete against the worst criminals, he needed two things: competent men and information. He got the first by firing all but three of the over-the-hill gang he inherited and then, in a bureaucratic coup d'état, making the Detective Bureau answerable only to himself.

As for information, the bureau got daily newspapers from most of the major cities[15] and developed contacts with police departments around the country and overseas.[16] This allowed Byrnes to make arrangements with rascals on the move. It was common practice for a city detective to meet a known criminal as the latter arrived in New York and advise him that he could stay—but do no business. Surprisingly often, it worked. Byrnes also expanded the Rogues' Gallery—photographs of suspects that could be used to identify them. By the mid-1880s, there was a collection of 7,000 criminal worthies.[17] Copies of these, with basic information on the back, were sent to each precinct, as well as to other jurisdictions when necessary. Byrnes tracked arrests and developed a network of snitches: "There is no honor among thieves" was one of his favorite sayings. When there was a big event in town, such as the funeral of President Grant in 1885, Byrnes would order the arrest of all known pickpockets on suspicion, even sending officers to railway stations to welcome traveling rascals.[18] Police magistrates would hold them until the event was over and the crowds dispersed—or, basically, until Byrnes told them to.[19] This casual disregard of constitutional trivia was highly thought of.

He and his men knew by sight all the pros in the city, as well as their skills and techniques. When journalist Lincoln Steffens was relieved of his paycheck one day, he complained to Byrnes, who asked what streetcar line he was on and at what time. From that, the detectives figured out what pickpockets were at work and tracked down the evildoer. Informed that he had robbed a friend of the chief of detectives, the thief made instant restitution.[20]

Steffens was grateful but not altogether a fan. Byrnes, he said "would buy you or beat you, as you might choose, but get you he would."[21] Indeed, Byrnes bragged of refining the third degree and while he argued that the best interrogations were more psychological than physical, he employed the latter technique at will.[22] The *New York Tribune* wrote of Byrnes in 1893 that he dealt with criminals on the "principle of fear." The paper heartily approved.

But then, Byrnes made time for the writers. He cooperated with Julian Hawthorne (son of Nathaniel) on five potboilers said to be based on the detective's diary. *A Tragic Mystery* (1887), for example, is a fictional retelling of the Hanier murder, and *The Great Bank Robbery* (1888) does the same for the safecracking at the Manhattan Savings Institution (Chapter 5). Byrnes could only have been pleased with this brisk-selling drivel, which depicted him as brave, bold, smart, imaginative, charismatic, generous, sly, and not a little handsome. Howe and Hummel, moonlighting as literary critics, also approved of this tripe, which was far superior, they believed, to the "blasé, frowsy, overgeometrical Gallic detective romance."[23]

Byrnes's own literary effort, *Professional Criminals of America* (1886) was much better, a straightforward summary of the deeds of the best crooks, with pictures from the Rogues' Gallery, all supplemented by Byrnes's occasionally waspish, and always well-informed, commentary. His description of Billy Forrester, the man who probably murdered Benjamin Nathan, for example, not only listed 10 aliases but carried a description of remarkable detail, from Forrester's "small, narrow feet" to the tattoo of a full-rigged ship on his breast to a small scar below his right eye to a one-tooth gap in his upper jaw. Of "Hungry Joe" Lewis, Byrnes noted that he was a "terrible talker" who has "victimized more people by the bunco [i.e., con] game than any other five men in the profession." Any reader with a normal share of curiosity must regret never having made the acquaintance of Colonel Alexander Branscom, a swindler and forger of Florida bonds whose "expertness with the pen is a marvel, in view of his being obliged to write with his left hand, his right arm having been cut off at the elbow." And what exactly did Byrnes mean when he said of George Bell, a pickpocket and forger, that he "affects a staid and religious air during his operations"?[24]

As for the daily press, Byrnes would let reporters accompany his men on high-profile arrests and allowed reporters to interview famous prisoners. He was not averse to making himself available for the occasional fawning profile. He liked to show reporters a museum of crime, New York style, that his men had put together. Among the items: loaded dice and marked cards, forged banknotes, a jimmy used in the Manhattan Savings job, bogus gold bricks,[25] even the black hood that covered Chastine Cox's head on the gallows and the rope that broke his neck.[26] The exhibit was meant to impress, and it did.

Realizing where the power in New York was, Byrnes took special care of the rich, sending men in evening dress or fancy costume to society balls to watch for pickpockets.[27] Wall Street was a particular interest. On the day Byrnes was appointed to lead the Detective Bureau, March 12, 1880, he set up an office at 17 Wall Street and stationed ten men there. The financiers were so delighted with the attention—robbery of their messengers had become something of a rite of passage for the aspiring hoodlum[28]—that they gave the police an office in the Stock Exchange itself, connecting it by telephone to every bank and finance house in the city.

Violating all kinds of civil liberties, Byrnes drew a notional boundary across the financial district of lower Manhattan. Any known thief or pickpocket found south of this "dead line" on Fulton Street who could not prove he had legitimate business could be jailed overnight. Wall Street crime, at least of the nonfinancial type, dropped precipitously. According to Byrnes's own estimation, made in 1884, from the time he set up shop, "they have not lost a 10-cent stamp on Wall Street by a professional thief; not a penny, not a cent."[29]

This did not mean that criminals reformed their ways. They were allowed to operate elsewhere in a series of arrangements that, in effect, regulated the practice of crime. The keeper of a stale beer dive on the Bowery was on his own, but Byrnes's methods certainly worked well on Wall Street, and the Street paid him back handsomely, in the form of stock tips.[30]

The people most in tune with Byrnes were those he was trying to arrest, and they admitted that the town changed after he took charge. Frank McCoy, a thief and bank burglar of some distinction—Byrnes estimated Big Frank had filched $2 million in his career—knew everyone who was anyone in the criminal underworld of the 1860s and 1870s. In 1893, back in New York after being pardoned from a Delaware jail, McCoy was in a mood to reminisce. "Byrnes has driven out or jugged" the best criminals, he told a reporter. "The old, organized, first-class gangs of bank burglars, bunco steerers, bank sneaks, and forgers are no longer at work in New York . . . A crook's life nowadays is a short one."[31]

Byrnes was not, however, universally celebrated. Lincoln Steffens was grateful that he got his paycheck back, but he realized that Byrnes's men were able to recover it so readily because the ruffian who took it was being allowed to operate. The whorehouses, gambling dens, fences, forgers, and con men who stayed within bounds—which meant paying fees to the cops and not disturbing their betters—had little to fear. Steffens put it this way: "The detective's trade consists not in pursuing but in forming friendships with criminals."[32]

In 1884, hearings before a state legislative committee chaired by a young Theodore Roosevelt corroborated the suspicion that cops and robbers were entirely too close. But this created less of a stir than might be expected. The police had in fact become more professional and more competent in many ways, and the city was not quite the cutthroat oasis it had been a decade before. Influential New Yorkers were inclined to give the cops a pass.

A decade later, that view would change, and Byrnes would be forced to retire, his reputation besmirched (Chapter 7). But in 1881, he could pretty much do what he wanted—and he wanted to solve the murder of Louis Hanier. It was the kind of high-profile case the Detective Bureau was made for.

McGloin helped out. The Whyo leader realized that he needed to get rid of the gun, but instead of simply throwing it into the river, or an outhouse, or any number of other obvious places, he pawned it for $2. The cops tracked it down easily. The pawnbroker also described McGloin, who at 19 was well known to the police (convictions for larceny and assault). The 32-caliber bullet from Hanier's body was matched to the gun, which was traced to a saloon where McGloin had stored it.

The police had other help too—from an informer, who told them of a saloon favored by McGloin. Byrnes was not quite ready to make an arrest, but he wanted to keep up the pressure. So he posted a cop there, posing as a customer. One day, Officer Max Schmittberger went into the saloon and coolly hung a circular offering a reward for the wanted man on the wall above where McGloin was sitting. The idea was to see if McGloin would betray himself. Equally cool, he did not react. When Schmittberger left, the cop on duty heard McGloin ask, "Did I turn white when he hung that up?" His companion answered, "No, and you've got a nerve."

Nerve McGloin had to spare, but brains, not so much; a wiser man would have left town. McGloin didn't, and a few days later, a posse of police, led by Byrnes, snatched him from another saloon, then rounded up the confederates. It was a model police operation, one that William Howe later compared favorably to the best efforts of Eugene Vidocq, the French criminal who became a renowned detective (and the inspiration for Edgar Allan Poe's Auguste Dupin).

At the police station, Byrnes put McGloin in a chair by his office window and his accomplices in an airless, windowless room where they got some form of the third degree. Looking out the window, McGloin saw his colleagues depart, one by one. "Squealed," Byrnes murmured.[33] With that, and on seeing the gun and the bullet, McGloin caved: "This will break my mother's heart!" he cried in the best tradition of Irish gangsters in the hands of the law. But he also said that it was self-defense: "I thought the bloke coming down the stairs had something in his hand." Then he called Howe & Hummel.

Howe got a separate trial for his man and did an energetic cross-examination of the witnesses. But he presented no evidence, other than to claim that McGloin thought his life was in peril and that his confession was coerced. The latter was not impossible, but the fact that McGloin had made his confession to the coroner, and signed a statement saying it was voluntary, cost him what might have been, quite literally, breathing room. The police work tracing the path of the gun, the day-after comments to the friend, the overheard snippet at the saloon, the accounts of the three confederates, and McGloin's own confession didn't leave much room for reasonable doubt.

So Howe opted for the cigar defense. McGloin and his friends, he argued, got in through an open door (prove it was locked!). All they wanted to do was to steal a few cigars. The distinction mattered—killing in the commission of a felony such as burglary, carried the death penalty. If they had sauntered in through an open door for the sake of a few cigars, the killing would have occurred during a misdemeanor. It was the difference between murder one and manslaughter one—and between life and death.

The jury didn't buy it. The pictures of the Whyos in the Rogues' Gallery show an unsavory lot. With their hooded eyes and sullen expressions, they looked the part of young toughs. The jury saw them that way, too, judging it unlikely that the four were strictly after cigars. It took the 12 men just enough time to walk down the hall, take a vote, and walk back, to convict McGloin of murder in the first degree.

He received the verdict with a contemptuous sneer, and, appropriately enough, accepted a cigar. At the entrance to the Tombs, McGloin shifted his manacled hands, and extracted two silk handkerchiefs from his pocket; these he presented to two admiring maidens. Then he went inside, to cell number 3 on Murderers' Row. A year and a week later, he was hanged.

Howe shared a cigar with the murderer on his last night and witnessed his farewell to his sobbing parents. Howe was also with McGloin on his last morning, and watched as the Whyo walked to the gallows and covered the proffered crucifix with fervent kisses. At 8:12 a.m., the weights fell, and McGloin swung. Startled, a flock of birds took flight, alerting the waiting crowds of his doom.[34] He was the fortieth man to hang in the courtyard of the Tombs.

When the coffin was delivered to the McGloin family home, one cop observed of the chastened and decidedly rough-looking crowd that accompanied it, "I tell you what—this is a lesson that these ruffians won't forget very soon. I think some of them have learned more in the last half hour than they ever knew before."

Danny Lyons and Danny Driscoll were not among the enlightened. They took over leadership of the band of thieves, pickpockets, bullies, and vote-getter-outers that McGloin left behind. Lyons was the first among equals until he got locked up in 1884 for robbing a bird store, stealing or releasing all the feathered stock. Two of the parrots he gave to a girl-friend; the cops made the connection, and picked him up.

With Lyons resting in Sing Sing, Driscoll took over. Danny Driscoll had a square, regular face with pleasant features and a dashing cleft in his chin. He was well spoken and could be charming; he clearly had charisma, attracting loyalty from men and devotion from women. "There was an awful halo of successful criminality around his head," noted one contemporary, "which made the vicious of both sexes fall down and worship."[35]

Born and raised in the Five Points, Driscoll never strayed far from the area except for a brief sojourn in San Antonio that ended badly—another bullet wound and a suggestion that he get out of town. He decided not to mess with Texas and came back to New York in 1886 to become the unofficial, but widely acknowledged, king of the Whyos.

It is best to think of the Whyos as disorganized crime. They had the usual rackets, and their influence extended well beyond their immediate neighborhood, a fact that gave them a notoriety they relished. But they were unsystematic and crude. What distinguished someone like Driscoll was not his flair or intelligence, though he had a touch of both, but his willingness to hurt people. Here is how he was described at the height of his fame:

> [Driscoll is] the toughest of the tough, the readiest with knife or re-
> volver, the most reckless in threats against all who thwarted him, the
> steadiest in drink, the most industrious in thievery, the most learned
> in the science of picking pockets, the bravest and most skillful in
> slipping steel into an adversary's back without exposing himself to
> danger, the most venomous, worthless, sneaking, drunken, quarrel-
> some and murderous reprobate known in the city.[36]

Though he did three brief prison stints for larceny, Driscoll mostly got away with his thuggery—thanks in large part to his alliance with Thomas "Fatty" Walsh, whose saloon/gambling den on Mulberry Street was a favored haunt of local pols and tough guys. Driscoll, who liked a drink, probably knew the place. He certainly knew Walsh, who was a figure of consequence in the Sixth Ward.

Walsh had come to prominence for his part in the Fourth of July riots in 1857. Besides heat, booze, Protestant-Catholic animosity, and general gang dynamics, the whys and wherefores of what sparked the violence are murky. But it certainly didn't help that New York at that moment had two competing police forces, which in effect meant none. Seeking to undercut Tammany Mayor Fernando Wood, the state legis-lature had passed a bill to create the Metropolitan Police Force, which would serve all of greater New York and answer to Albany. Wood wanted to keep the current operation, known as the Municipal Force, under his own authority. The men in both outfits had their own alle-giances. When a warrant was sworn out for Wood's arrest for defying Albany's order, the two police forces battled on the steps of City Hall. It took the Seventh Regiment to calm things down. (Wood lost the battle when the Supreme Court upheld the law, but Tammany won the war, regaining control of the police in 1870.)

With both police forces effectively stymied, the young bloods of the Sixth Ward felt frisky; it was time to crack some heads. They thrashed a couple of cops[37] and then went at each other. The affray lasted for days; a dozen people were killed. Walsh, a member of the predominantly Irish-Catholic Dead Rabbits gang, managed to shoot himself in the leg, rather than the Protestant Bowery Boy he was aiming at, but to the

Sixth Ward at least he was fighting the good fight. The scar was one of honor and Walsh became an institution, and a political force.[38] He served a term as a state legislator and one as a city alderman, but his real power was of the behind-the-scenes variety, a matter of personal connections and leverage.

Walsh's influence was one of the keys to Driscoll's career. The other was his reputation for violence. Complainants, fearful of retribution, would fail to show up in court; if they did, he would ask Walsh to make any charges disappear. Once Driscoll got into a barroom fracas in which all four combatants had revolvers and started firing; Driscoll both delivered and received a wound. No one pressed charges. Drunk, he went after a couple of Italian peddlers. Walsh made the charges go away. Driscoll had a duel with his landlord; both got winged and all was forgiven.[39] He robbed a paunchy, sleeping German, then commandeered a streetcar for his getaway. No charge. Refused entry to a saloon, he shot the bouncer, snatched a passing dray, and when a boy identified him, broke the lad's jaw with the butt of his gun. No charge.[40]

Driscoll's ability to escape punishment made him a minor legend, and the Whyos prospered. At their peak, the gang counted perhaps 150 men and assorted women. "They were not first-class people," was the assessment of one police captain. "They were not cracksmen"—the aristocrats of crime—"but sneaks who would go through a drunken man or ring [take] a man's watch." Pickpocketing was an important source of income, and the gangsters also ran a few women for fun and profit. They liked to drop bricks from buildings on passing policemen, and Driscoll himself assaulted several officers.

Used to doing as he pleased, Driscoll failed to recognize that he had made enemies who were in a position to hurt him. The cops were not likely to miss a chance to get even. When John McCullagh became captain in 1884, he stated baldly, "Either I or the Whyos must go from this precinct."[41] And he backed up his rhetoric by raiding a Whyo dance; about half of those picked up had charges pending, which McCullagh had the nerve to pursue. The cops began to arrest Driscoll on petty charges and even delivered a sound beating via that useful implement, the club, that laid him up for days.[42] Even the clubbing, though, did not get it through Driscoll's skull that the days of impunity were closing. In his mind, the only question was: Could he get away with murder?[43]

That question became more than academic on the night of June 26, 1886. Driscoll was on bad terms with one Jack McCarthy, another career criminal. In mid-June, McCarthy had thrown Driscoll out of the bawdy house he ran, and the two exchanged shots a few days later. Driscoll did not forgive such slights, and after a night of drinking, he and a couple of friends met up with Bridget "Beezy" Garrity, a female of little virtue but great affection. Beezy liked to describe herself as "the gamest and nerviest girl in the [Sixth] Ward." At a young age, she developed a fatal attraction to the Whyos and proved her loyalty when she refused to peach on the gang members who threw a friend off a rooftop.[44] Beezy became not only a good little earner, but also a boon companion in her off-hours.

After another half-dozen saloons, the crew washed up outside McCarthy's premises, a shabby building on Hester Street. The front door was always open, so they entered easily enough. Then, knowing that Driscoll would not be allowed in, Beezy knocked on the locked door of the front parlor. McCarthy, who was playing cards, opened the door a crack and let her in; Driscoll tried to follow, but McCarthy spotted him and pushed against the door. As they struggled, each man drew a gun. McCarthy, encumbered by the flailing Beezy, couldn't shoot. But Driscoll could; jamming the snout of his weapon into the crack in the door, he fired, hitting a wall.

At this point, McCarthy chose flight over fight. He threw Beezy off, slammed the door shut, then followed the other cardplayers out a window. Beezy ran to the rear door to let in her lover. When Driscoll saw the door begin to open, he thought it was McCarthy trying to sneak out. He fired; Beezy caught the bullet in her abdomen. It shredded her intestines and settled in her stomach.

Without pausing to check on his mistress, Driscoll ran. He managed to get rid of his gun, but was found hiding at his mother's, where he said he had been all night. McCarthy returned to his own establishment and handed over his gun to the waiting cops. Both men were arrested.

The next day, dozens of Whyos were on hand to greet Driscoll as he left the police station. "It will be all right," he told them with characteristic bravado. "I've never worked in my life, except on Election Day, and I don't intend to now." Then he was packed off to the Tombs.

That afternoon, Beezy died. But while she was still conscious, she talked to her mother, Margaret Sullivan. With her daughter expiring by inches in front of her, Mrs. Sullivan could not resist one last opportunity to nag. "Beezy," she moaned, "I always said you would come to this." Her daughter was not interested, "Don't talk of that now, Mama. I'm going to die." Her loving mother changed the subject: "Who did it?" she asked. Beezy drew in a breath and murmured, "Danny Driscoll."

At the inquest a week later, McCarthy was cleared. The cops had examined his gun and found that it had not been fired; it was also of a different caliber from the bullets recovered from Beezy's body. That left Driscoll. Charged with murder, he called Howe & Hummel.

Driscoll was confident in his lawyers, but he had his own ideas about freedom. The day the trial opened, September 28, 1886, the warden searched his cell. He found a heap of mortar and stones under the bed, and a hole near the drain pipe that ran halfway through the wall and was stuffed with a screwdriver and twine. The idea was to create a small hole, drop down the twine outside his window and haul up more effective tools for a breakout.

Inside the court, Plan B began to unfold. Driscoll's wife was there, with the essential accompaniment of a small child. (Howe and Hummel were known to supply babies to childless defendants; in this case, Driscoll had his own curly-haired little daughter.) The jury selection took a little more than a day, but there was an unusual snappishness to the proceedings that continued throughout the five-day trial. During the questioning, for example, one candidate for the jury said he understood that the defense conceded that Driscoll had fired the shot.

"Quite the reverse," said Howe.

"No," agreed the judge. "Mr. Howe never admits anything." True, but hardly necessary to point out.

The trial started briskly. One damning witness was Carrie Wilson, described as a "Bowery maiden with an evil reputation and a bad face." It can be taken for granted that Wilson was no maiden. But was she a liar? Her story was that she went to the fateful house at 3:00 in the morning, after leaving a wake, to pick up a bundle of old clothing. While there, she saw Driscoll fire the fatal shot. It was a thin story, but she stuck to it, and it was corroborated by some of the cardplayers, who swore that McCarthy was halfway out the window when they heard the second shot; he could not have fired it.

When Beezy's mother told the story of her daughter's dying words, there wasn't a dry eye in the place. Howe, wisely, did not question her. McCarthy admitted he hated Driscoll, but swore he never fired his gun that evening; he was too busy running away. Officer Monahan backed him up. He had confiscated McCarthy's gun, and brought it into court as evidence, still fully loaded.

"Don't let Colonel Fellows [the prosecutor] have it," cried Howe, in mock alarm.

"I will have it," said Fellows, who was short and plump and almost as dapper and emotional as Howe.[45]

"Then I'll leave the room," said Howe.

"Go ahead; that will entirely satisfy the people."

The gun stayed. So did Howe.

Hummel opened for the defense, which was simple: McCarthy did it. There was a chance it would work. For a start, while Beezy told one thing to her mother, on two other occasions, to a cop and to a doctor, she had fingered McCarthy for the shooting. In addition, McCarthy was a three-time loser who admitted he had shot at Driscoll a few weeks earlier. But there wasn't much more to offer. One of Driscoll's companions that night, Owen Bruen, swore that "Dan had no pistol and didn't fire no shot." But the limited credibility of a drinking buddy of Danny Driscoll was seriously impaired when he couldn't explain how McCarthy fired a bullet into a wall when he was facing the door. "Dat's too much for me," admitted Bruen, forsaking perjury just this once. "I give it up."

Then it was Driscoll's turn to take the stand. The prisoner made a good impression, with his composure, fine features, and well-modulated voice. Under Howe's gentle questioning, Driscoll's account was straightforward, if unheroic. He had been passed out drunk in the back of a cab, he said, when it pulled up at McCarthy's. He didn't even know where he was until he heard the shot. Then "I got sobered pretty quick," and bolted, leaving Beezy bleeding on the floor. When the police picked him up, he had lied about his whereabouts because he wanted to avoid trouble and the cops were intimidating: "All seemed anxious to club me; all were eager to club me; all were ambitious to club me."

As for McCarthy, Driscoll said he had forgiven him long before, and wanted to be pals. Another bitchy moment passed between the lawyers at this point. Driscoll began to get mixed up recounting his history with McCarthy, and when Howe tried to help him out, he, too, tumbled over his rhetorical feet and acknowledged as much to the court: "I made a mistake."

Fellows was not gracious: "No one doubts your ability to make mistakes."

"And no one doubts your ability to indulge in tomfoolery at a murder trial," replied a nettled Howe.

In his summation, Howe made a simple case: Beezy had said twice that McCarthy had shot her. And since Carrie Wilson was a liar and Jack McCarthy "one of the vilest miscreants" in New York, there was more than enough room to acquit. "Is not the testimony fatally conflicting?" he asked. "Is there not in your minds, gentlemen, a reasonable, a terrible doubt?"

Well, no. The jury took just 29 minutes to convict Driscoll of first-degree murder. The testimony *was* conflicting, but all those involved in this affair were lowlifes to some degree, with perjury shooting in every direction. So the jury plumped for the side whose liars had at least some corroboration. There was surely also an element of convicting Driscoll on general principles. He might have been a hero to the rough trade in the Sixth Ward; to respectable New York, a death at the end of a noose looked like simple justice, much delayed.

But the verdict took Driscoll by surprise. So certain was he that he would not be going back to his cell that he had dressed in his best outfit, complete with gold watch and chain; he had even packed up his toiletries into a little bundle. He kept his cool, shaking Howe's hand. "You'll get me out of this," he told the lawyer. "I ain't a bit afraid. I ain't fazed." He spent the night in Cell No. 5 on Murderers' Row and was sentenced to death a month later.

The story would take a long time to play out, through appeals, claims of new evidence (probably manufactured), and more appeals. But at least Driscoll had some congenial company as he waited for the legal system to free him.

His old friend Danny Lyons didn't spend long in Sing Sing for the bird caper, and when he got out, he returned to his usual pursuits—drinking, idling, and pimping. He had a number of mistresses-cum-employees. Unfortunately, one of them, Kitty McGowan, was also the beloved of Joseph Quinn. The two men quarreled over pretty Kitty, and Lyons threatened to kill his rival. This was no idle threat. Borrowing a gun from a friend, he began to hunt. A few days later, on July 5, 1887, Lyons spotted his prey and shot him in the groin. Quinn died. Lyons fled New York; his parents hired Howe & Hummel.

And his remaining girlfriends quarreled. The story goes that Gentle Maggie and Lizzie the Dove were sharing a drink in a Bowery dive when they had the following Socratic dialogue.

"You're nothing but a filthy whore," said Gentle Maggie.

"You bet I am," replied Lizzie, "but at least I'm not a *diseased* filthy whore."

So Gentle Maggie stabbed her in the throat. As Lizzie died, she swore that she would meet her killer in hell—and scratch her eyes out.[46]

Lyons was picked up in Pittsburgh and brought back to New York a few weeks later. Howe met him at police headquarters but refused to act for him, because Lyons had not followed his advice to turn himself in. He was quickly convicted, sentenced to death, and sent to Murderers' Row. His next-door neighbor was Danny Driscoll.

The Tombs dated back to 1841, and one might think that over time, a certain expertise would have developed as to how to run a jail. One would be wrong. Right from the beginning, positions at the Tombs, from cook to warden, were political. What that meant was that toadies with no background or even interest in penology could spend years there, putting in time until they could collect a pension. Take, for example, Thomas "Fatty" Walsh. Walsh took over from the capable Warden Finn in late 1886 as part of a deal for not contesting the Democratic nomination for Congress.

Yes, this was the same Fatty who had once been a protector of the Whyos. In his new position, though, he didn't much care for the gang—and vice versa. He was also grossly incompetent.

Shortly after Thanksgiving, on November 29, Lyons and Driscoll began a hunger strike, protesting what they said was disgusting food. They stuck it out for several days; as punishment, they were not allowed to leave their cells. Driscoll began to eat again shortly before heading for court on December 2, where he was to hear the result of an appeal.

No one who looked like a Whyo was allowed in the court. Still, Driscoll might have been reassured at the sight of Howe, ablaze in diamonds, rubies, and emeralds.[47] But the news was bad: The death sentence was affirmed. The judge advised Driscoll to spend his remaining weeks in repentance and prayer. Driscoll's reply: "I'm taking McCarthy's medicine, by God!" He was disappointed, of course, but probably not crushed. He had a Plan C in the works. But when he was taken to Cell 6, rather than to his usual digs in Number 5, he knew Plan C was done for.

While Driscoll was in court, Warden Walsh had taken a look at his cell—for the first time in months, as he later acknowledged. What he found in the ten-foot-by-five-foot space was a well-developed escape plot. Using a fine saw, Driscoll had cut the crossbar from the foot of his bedstead, then hid it beneath his mattress. The bar had clawed away a cast-iron plate that protected an embrasure that led to the narrow window; using soap as a glue, he had disguised the effect with a piece of white muslin. With the masonry exposed, it would have been short work with the sharpened bar to widen a hole big enough to crawl through.

Even Walsh realized the implications. He moved on to the home of Danny Lyons in Cell 3. Lyons was still on a hunger strike and failed to play the part of pleasant host. He had gone a bit further than Driscoll, cutting away the heavy bar at the window and ripping apart the iron lining of the embrasure. The tool he had worked with, also from his bed, was bent; this combination crowbar and jimmy would have completed the necessary work in a couple of hours. He was moved to Cell 13.

Driscoll did not take the discovery well, cursing Walsh and the keepers in foully creative terms. A few hours later, he had recovered a fair approximation of cool. "It came pretty near to being a fine job," he told a reporter from the *World*. "I can't tell youse gentlemen how we cut our way through the walls, but we come right near fixin' ourselves. I ain't kicking, though."

The idea had been to create an opening big enough to crawl through, jump down, and then go to a designated spot where outside helpers would toss a rope. Any keepers in the way would have been taken care of. The hunger strike was a ruse. Confinement to their cell allowed them to work in peace. How did the prisoners get their tools? Fatty Walsh had no idea, and not much interest. Maybe it was the toughs who visited Lyons; maybe it was Driscoll's wife. As for the longshoreman's hook, perhaps it came from Cell 2, where such implements were stored. Cell 2, Walsh said casually, was often unlocked, and Driscoll could have filched the hook during his daily exercise. The two men communicated, he speculated, via the sewer pipes. Considering two convicted murderers had come within a couple of hours of escape, Walsh was remarkably offhand about it all.

But then that was the way he worked. It later turned out that Mrs. Driscoll had for months had easy entry to the cell. Equipped with her own key, she would visit with her husband at length. She returned from one of these visits, in late January 1887, with the ultimate souvenir—she became pregnant with their second child, a son, born while his father was on Death Row. On another occasion, Driscoll got a fake beard and a knife.

For all this, Walsh got something like a free pass; the papers never made an issue of it, and to be fair, Walsh did learn from his mistakes and tighten security. But he could not be other than what he was—a creature of politics. He confiscated and then sold contraband that visitors tried to smuggle in, and made more money by selling sundries to the prisoners (candle, 5 cents; roast beef and coffee, 50 cents). Such minor fiddles were a way of life in the Tombs, but Walsh took it too far. He was also in way over his head; he would be gone by early 1888.

With the implosion of his escape plan, and now under much closer guard, Driscoll turned to the courts for one last try. Howe asked for a new trial, on the basis that Carrie Wilson had perjured herself. It was at least a little queer, he noted, that on Beezy's last night, Wilson had apparently left the killing zone, walked past several policemen, and gone home to chat with her mother, never saying a word about the shooting, an event that even in her neighborhood counted as important news. Wilson had made up the story to protect McCarthy, Howe claimed on January 13, and he had the affidavits to prove it. One was from Driscoll and one was from his wife, each claiming that Wilson, remorseful, had admitted her perfidy; these did not carry much weight. Two others were more intriguing. Patrick Foster, a keeper at the Tombs, swore that he overheard Wilson confessing she had committed perjury; and one Margaret Gubbins stated that Wilson had been at her home at the time of the murder.

Prosecutor John Fellows, who had appeared against Howe in almost 50 previous murder cases—and lost too many to be entirely happy about their relationship—was not impressed. These recollections had come very late in the day, Fellows noted, broadly hinting that the motives of the witnesses might have been of a more tangible nature than a disinterested pursuit of the truth. Besides, Wilson was not budging and Driscoll had not "led a simple Christian life."

While the judge considered the request for a new trial, Howe traveled to Albany to make the same case to the state's highest court. If that failed, he was prepared to argue that the original appeal had been heard in the wrong court. If that failed, he had two petitions for pardon in his pocket. If they failed, he had yet another petition, asking for two weeks' delay to allow Driscoll to consult with his spiritual advisers. "I feel cheerful and will use every effort," he telegraphed back to the office. Told of all this, Driscoll took hope. "I know Mr. Howe will save me," he told Hummel. "He will do everything he can for me. He is my friend. God bless him."

The state did not. Other than getting the execution delayed by three days, Howe lost on all counts. "All is over," he cabled to the condemned man on January 18. Driscoll must hang on January 23. He probably did not appreciate the irony, but he had a new neighbor in the Tombs. Carrie Wilson had been picked up for streetwalking and was in the women's wing.

Driscoll's last days were not serene. He smuggled out an angry letter accusing Fatty Walsh of being a "licensed ruffian," who reveled in extortion, petty tyranny, and casual cruelty. The condemned man also had to mediate a dispute between his mother and his wife about who would have the responsibility for his body. He tried to settle the matter by saying he would donate it to science for dissection; he thought the doctors would be interested in a form that was studded, he figured, with five or six bullets.

Other than his irritation over the kvetching women, who argued that his body would go to science over *their* dead bodies, Driscoll maintained something like aplomb in the shadow of the noose, sleeping well and impressing the keepers with his calm. On his last night, he was considerably less emotional than his family, who sobbed and wailed. The last women he saw on his last full day on earth were four Sisters of Charity; the last men (other than the guards), two priests. His last lunch was roast chicken with celery and potatoes; his last supper beef, potatoes, bread, and butter. All this he had to eat with his hands, not being allowed utensils. His last reading consisted of accounts of his pending demise in the newspapers; his last luxury, cigar after cigar.

Driscoll slept well that evening, and was awakened at 4:00 in the morning. He dressed in clothes supplied by the Tombs—a cutaway coat with black cravat—and made his confession. A very late convert to the comforts of religion, Driscoll seems to have rather enjoyed the Sisters of Charity who made it their mission to attend to the doomed, even writing a poem to one of them:

> *Sweet Sister Mary Z.,*
> *Your influence over me*
> *Has saved me from temptation*
> *And if I am saved,*
> *To God and thee,*
> *I owe my salvation.*
>
> *I may not be a poet*
> *Or an eminent divine*
> *But I know goodness when I see it*
> *And feel kindness such as thine.*

Life to me was but a burden
All was dark and drear.
But like a ray of sunshine,
You came—and all was clear.

Not good, but not bad for a man with hours to live. The Sisters would have been pleased to see him, on his final morning, quietly reading the Bible. Then Driscoll wrote last letters to his family and to his old pal, Owen Bruen, who had lied so ineffectively on his behalf. He attended Mass, took communion, and had breakfast back in his cell—toast and coffee.

His last walk beckoned. The gallows had been placed near the exit to his cell; he would only need to make a journey of 40 feet to reach it. Police were everywhere, creating a cordon around the Tombs and even on surrounding rooftops, lest the remaining Whyos make a scene. But these were scarce on the day, just a clump or two of hard-looking young men and women. To the gang, Driscoll was already history.

Then the witnesses began to arrive—Elbridge Gerry, who was on a commission to examine forms of capital punishment, Police Inspector Alexander Williams, the coroner, and ten reporters. Finally, there was the sheriff, wielding a rosewood stave. Following him, marching two by two, were 14 deputies, all dressed in black, with tall silk hats and gold badges, carrying staves with bits of black crepe knotted at the ends. They looked imposing. By contrast, the executioner was a stumpy little man in a shabby coat and cap. But Joe Atkinson was expert at his job—he had hanged McGloin and had recently brought his gallows to Pennsylvania to do a job there.[48] He now gave his instrument a final once-over, tugging at the new white rope of fine Italian hemp. The undertaker arrived, bearing a casket.

Inside, Driscoll gave away his last possessions—a ring to his brother, a religious token to one of the keepers, his brown derby to Owen Bruen, thus symbolically handing over leadership of the Whyos.[49] At 7:20, Driscoll received his last delegation of visitors—the sheriff, a deputy, and the hangman himself. The sheriff read the death warrant; and then came the touch of the hangman. Atkinson pinned Driscoll's arms behind him, and slipped a noose around his neck, with a length hanging down his back.

The day was raw and damp, tinged with a yellow fog. As Driscoll stepped through the doorway he looked around—and shuddered as he spotted the gallows. A minute later, flanked by two priests, he reached the foot of the instrument. He was a diminished figure, "transformed from the bully of the Bloody Sixth to a shrunken, pale and mild-looking youth," according to the *Sun*. But he also maintained a quiet dignity. "Jesus, have mercy on me," he murmured as the black hood was lowered over his head, its silk streamers dancing down his neck.

Atkinson adjusted the noose, then struck a piece of wood three times. This was the signal for the ax to cut the rope that released the 400-pound weight. Driscoll's body shot up into the air; his neck broke instantly, but his hands clutched and his legs spasmed as the breath was squeezed out of him. The time was 7:32 a.m.

Seven months later, on August 21, 1888, Lyons, too, would march into the yard of the Tombs, wear the black hood—perhaps the same one worn by his friend and colleague—and be carried out. The Whyos went on, but a combination of carelessness and lack of political protection made them more vulnerable, and dozens of them ended up in prison or forced to flee the city. Owen Bruen would be convicted of armed robbery a few months after receiving the brown derby and sentenced to nine years.[50] The gang lost the critical mass that had been its strength, becoming just one more of the many gangs of New York and frittering into irrelevance by the mid-1890s.

Driscoll and Lyons were not the last men to be hanged in the Tombs. That distinction would go to "Handsome Harry" Carlton, a run-of-the-mill Whyo.[51] A genuinely nasty piece of work, the 26-year-old Carlton, after a night in the saloons, was rousting a drunk around 5:00 in the morning when a cop interfered. So Carlton shot Patrolman James Brennan in the jaw and temple. When Brennan fell, Carlton stood over him, and shot twice more. Brennan died in Bellevue Hospital around

7:00, at just about the time his wife was putting his breakfast on the table.

In the police station, Carlton denied knowing anything about the death of Brennan. Given his own condition—his head was bleeding and his face swollen from rough handling—perhaps he was not inclined to cooperate.

The trial opened on December 10, 1888. Fellows prosecuted; acting for the defense was, in the words of the *Tribune*, "both the wily 'Little Abe' Hummel and his belligerent partner, the redoubtable William F. Howe."

The case looked hopeless. Fleeing the shooting, Carlton had literally run into three cops. The drunk he was trying to rob, Julius Roesler, saw the shooting. So did a woman looking out a window. And he was a thoroughly bad lot whose first recorded crime came when he was 14; he had graduated from larceny to robbery to assault and highway robbery. Carlton might not have even been that handsome. His reddish mustache was lush, but the newspapers also reported a weak chin, beetle brows, cold eyes, cadaverous features, and thin lips. All in all, reported the *Tribune*, his visage "bore the unmistakable stamp of so much cruelty and badness." Cop killers, then and now, do not get a good press. And this time the babe in arms would be carried by the widow of the victim. She showed up in court in deep mourning with her 15-month-old.

But at least Carlton had Howe & Hummel on his side, an advantage the paper admitted: "His counsel, it is universally admitted, stand the first among their peers for unsurpassed ability, great legal acumen and eloquence which it is indeed difficult to resist." Not that the paper gave the man a chance because, "even these high and ennobling attributes of mind must occasionally give way and yield to the majesty of the truth."[52]

The truth, said Howe, was that Carlton was in fear for his life; he had shot Brennan because the officer had raised his club. In the reaction of a moment, there could be no premeditation; the charge, if any, should be second-degree murder. As for Roesler's testimony, the man had admitted to 10 or 11 beers—how could he be believed? Roesler had his own explanation. "Of course I was not sober like them temperance people who drink nothing," he explained in a thick German accent, "but I was not drunk."

The testimony took a little more than a day. It presented a coherent, simple, and damning story. Carlton took the stand on December 14. His version of events was a simple one, too. He and a couple of friends had given Roesler a hard time at the saloon, and when they ran into him later, he called them names. Carlton wasn't going to take this kind of thing, and he slapped him. The wimpy German called for the cops. When Brennan appeared, he grabbed Carlton by the lapel and hit him with his nightstick, swearing, "I will kill you." When he raised his club again, Carlton fired and fired and fired and fired.

"You felt you were in great bodily danger—in danger of your life?" asked Howe.

"Yes, sir," replied Carlton.

"You did not intend to kill this officer when you fired?"

"Certainly not, sir. I shot in self-defense."

That was also the theme of Howe's closing remarks. As he spoke, he held a policeman's nightstick, using it to gesture and making the silent point that being on the wrong end of such a club might well put a man in fear for his life. Fellows, who had already played the baby card so deftly, one-upped Howe here, too, by waving around the killing pistol during his own summation.

After three ballots and 50 minutes, the jury made its own opinion known, convicting Carlton of first-degree murder. A week later, he was sentenced to death. And that's when things got interesting.

Even in the 1870s, there was a lively debate over the death penalty; jurors were routinely canvassed on the subject. Thirty-six of the first 73 men (and jurors were all men) queried for the Carlton trial, for example, reported qualms about imposing the death penalty and were excused on that basis.

Of course, they might have been trying to escape; jury service was as popular then as it is now. One humorist for the *Herald* told of his own experience. He joined 75 other good men—"dudes from Fifth

Avenue, Hebrews from Baxter Street, Ethiops from Thompson Street," and so on. When the clerk asked if anyone had legal reasons to be excused, 74 of them stood up. They were "all prepared to commit perjury rather than be incarcerated in that palladium of our liberties, the jury box."[53] The man from the *Herald* chose a different strategy. Asked if he had scruples about inflicting the ultimate penalty, he declared himself delighted at the prospect of sending someone to perdition. The defense quickly excused him.

By and large, capital punishment was politically acceptable; it was the means of it that provoked controversy. Specifically, there was concern that hanging was a bad choice of termination. And there was considerable evidence to back this up. Hanging a man took skill. When it went wrong, the result was not a quick snap of the neck, but a lingering death from strangulation that revolted witnesses. This was not uncommon. Unlike Europe, which had trained executioners, in New York, each jail or prison was responsible for providing its own. Lacking experience or training, they got it wrong distressingly often.

Alexander Jefferson, for example, was condemned for killing two people by firing a shotgun into a shack where a party was going on. He thought his brother, Celestial, was moving in on his girlfriend. They both survived the assault; the two people killed were uninvolved in the romantic triangle, if there was one. Jefferson then tried, and failed, to kill himself. The City of Brooklyn agreed to complete the task.

On his last day, August 1, 1884, Jefferson was reasonably composed, distributing his goods and writing a few words of wisdom on the wall of his cell: "I now trust in God, but I wish you would all let drink alone." He left his clothes to another inmate, and his brain to his lawyer. After breakfast and a religious service in which he sang his favorite hymn, "Beulah Land," for the last time, Jefferson made the walk to the hanging ground—in this case, the corridor between tiers of cells in Brooklyn's Raymond Street Jail. The noose was visible to the 600 prisoners. There were dozens of invited onlookers inside—including, for some odd reason, O'Donovan Rossa, Irish revolutionary and a Howe & Hummel client. The spectators smoked and joked as they awaited the fateful hour.

One last prayer, and the executioner—the son of a former hangman at the Tombs—placed a black cloth over Jefferson's face, fixed the noose, and then stepped out of sight. Brooklyn had almost no experience in administering capital punishment; neither, it turned out, did the man it brought in. Hanging is a learned skill, not a hereditary one.

A few moments later, the chop of an ax cutting the rope was heard, and Jefferson's body jerked up and then down, as intended. But the noose had not been applied correctly; it slipped under the condemned man's chin. As he struggled against the slow-killing rope, Jefferson managed to throw off the black cap. His face contorted, his legs swinging wildly, he gurgled in agony. The Raymond Street Jail never saw a more horrible three minutes until the inevitable blessedly arrived. Some of the spectators got sick; others fainted. It was awful. No one was laughing anymore.[54]

Scenes like these led authorities to consider other forms of capital punishment. Those with the keenest interest in the subject—Death Row inmates—agreed that they would prefer not to be hanged. In 1879, the *Herald* sent a reporter to the Tombs to canvass 12 convicted murderers on the subject.[55] "Hanging is too ignominious and uncertain," said William Burke, who described himself as anti–death penalty on principle. All things considered, though—and Burke had clearly spent some time pondering the subject—he would rather be drowned or suffocated. Patrick McCormack also plumped for drowning, preferably in whiskey, while George Smith opted for shooting: "I don't want to be hung like a dog. Stand me against a wall and put a bullet through my heart." Chastine Cox, a Howe & Hummel client, gave a learned disquisition on forms of hanging in Europe; he, too, preferred a "rifle ball through head or heart." And one Italian, Frank Bello, noting correctly that "My country no hang. Bad for poor Bello," simulated a knife thrust to make his preference known.

In 1886, the New York state legislature put together a three-man commission to study whether to replace hanging. One of them, Elbridge Gerry, attended Danny Driscoll's hanging and came away impressed with its efficiency and dignity. Gerry still thought there must be a better way, though. The commission went on to describe 34 different methods of capital punishment, ranging from beheading (French-, Chinese-, and Japanese-style) to boiling in oil, to being blown from a cannon ("no interval for suffering," it noted) to crucifixion, flaying, flogging, garroting, poisoning, pounding, the rack, stoning, and strangling.[56] At the end of this ghoulish litany, the commission recommended electrocution as a swifter, surer, and more humane alternative. The legislature agreed, and on June 4, 1888, New York became the first state to replace hanging with electrocution, starting January 1, 1889.[57]

And that, argued Howe, was the point. Carlton could not be put to death because there was no legal method to do so. Hanging had been outlawed in June and since electrocution was not to start until January, there was no form of execution available to do the job. "I say, therefore," he concluded, "that Your Honor has no lawful right to pass any sentence of death upon this prisoner." In fact, because there was no punishment legislated, law and logic dictated that Carlton should be freed. "I contend," Howe told a reporter, "that Judge Martine had no power either to say that Carlton should be hanged or that he should be killed by electricity."

The argument created a sensation. "I have to express my belief," Judge Martine told Howe in an unusual compliment from the bench, "that you have most ably defended the prisoner. Everything that skill, legal ingenuity and eloquence could suggest has been done for him." Then he kicked the question upstairs, to the Court of Appeals.

Would this mean that the dozen or so murderers in the Tombs who had been sentenced since June 4 would be freed if Carlton was? No, explained Abe Hummel; they had not raised the objection, and could not benefit from it after the fact. But Carlton could. To bolster his point, Hummel brought up the case of Jacob Rosenzweig, who had been released on exactly that point—that there was no punishment on the books for the crime of which he had been convicted.

But it would not work this time. Technically, Howe had a point, but the authorities were not about to give even a single convicted murderer—and a cop killer at that—a free pass. The Court of Appeals rejected the argument. Carlton did get a few more months of life as appeals and requests for new trials wound their way through the system, but on December 5,

1889, Joe Atkinson did his usual efficient job. Handsome Harry Carlton was the forty-fifth, and last, man to be hanged in the Tombs.

Twenty months later, the first man to be electrocuted in the United States took his unwilling place in history.

The reluctant pioneer was William Kemmler, who had murdered his wife with a hatchet. He was arrested at the saloon where he had gone for a beer after his bloody deed. Sent to Auburn Prison in upstate New York, Kemmler appealed his punishment, arguing that electrocution was cruel and unusual. For Kemmler, the appeal of an appeal was to buy some time; even if he won, he would be hanged. And he was a poor man. His legal bills were probably paid by George Westinghouse, who did not want his alternating-current (AC) electrical system used, lest the public associate AC with killing.

In the event, AC *was* used, to the grim satisfaction of Thomas Edison, who thought capital punishment was wrong, but if it was going to happen, did not want his preferred method of direct current (DC) associated with it. So, in one of the nastier moments of his career, Edison quietly but effectively began to promote electrocution. He wrote a letter to the death penalty commission in favor of electrical execution[58] (using AC, of course) and much of the research was done in the Edison lab in New Jersey. This consisted of electrocuting dogs, calves, and horses. The lab worked on a prototype of the electric chair, and Edison himself testified to the efficacy of electrocution in Kemmler's appeals, going so far as to recommend a preferred technique— he thought the electrodes should be attached to the hands. Finally, it was an Edison associate who came up with a verb to describe this innovative punishment: to "westinghouse."[59] The word never took, but it was a cheap shot all the same.

For his part, Westinghouse didn't want any part of electrocution, even refusing to sell his generators to the state if they were to be used for that purpose.[60] But the government got them anyway and after more experiments with four-legged innocents, the authorities were sure that they had perfected the most humane and dignified method of capital punishment yet.

Kemmler might have disputed that opinion, if he could have. His execution, in August 1890, "was so terrible," the *Times* decided, "that the word fails to convey the idea." The first jolt of electricity was turned off after 17 seconds. He was dead. Or was he? One of the official spectators saw the prisoner's chest rising and falling and called out, "Great God! He is alive!" It might have been an involuntary muscle reflex, but no one was inclined to take chances. Alerted, the technicians pumped in another blast of current, lasting more than a minute. Kemmler's face began to break out in spots of blood as capillaries burst; his hair and flesh smoked, filling the room with a acrid stench. The skin on his back burned all the way through to the spine.

The witnesses were shocked. "I would rather see 10 hangings than one such execution as that," said Deputy Coroner Jenkins. "It was fearful." The district attorney was in tears. The *Times* was certain that this would be the last such execution and called for the prompt repeal of the law that brought this disgusting innovation to the state.[61] William Howe thought the stories were grisly enough that jurors would be loath to impose the death penalty: "I believe that the recent attempt at electrocution in Auburn has practically abolished the death penalty for some time to come."[62]

On consideration, though, the official view was that death had indeed been quick and painless, if an affront to the senses. A botched hanging was much worse. So New York stuck with it, deciding that electrocution might be the worst form of execution, except for all the others. Joe Atkinson was out of a job; he retired, bringing home with him a souvenir of his life's work—the crossbeam of the Tombs gallows.[63]

The state was confident enough that it had mastered the new technique that it scheduled four executions for the same day in Sing Sing in July 1891. At the death of each man in the earliest hours of the morning, a colored flag was raised, indicating to people outside which of the four had breathed his last—white for James Slocum, who beat his wife to death, blue for Harris Smiler (a mistress killer),[64] and so on. Young men even bet on which flag would fly next.[65] The Sing Sing authorities used the same chair that had killed Kemmler, but they had learned from Auburn's mistakes. They made sure the required voltage (about 1,500 volts) was flowing, a problem in Kemmler's case, and they tested their apparatus on a horse.[66]

The quadruple execution took less than two hours. The chair had made its case.

FIVE

Murder, Inc.

When it comes to murder, even the best, least principled, and highest-priced lawyer—and that is a precise definition of Big Bill Howe in his prime—can't win 'em all. Sometimes the client is dead guilty, the jury is too intelligent, and the opposition is on its game.

Those were the prevailing conditions in the trial of Carlyle Harris, a handsome, young, and personable student at Columbia Medical School. On February 8, 1890, Harris secretly married 18-year-old Mary Helen Potts in order to sleep with her, and with the firm intention of forgetting the whole matter when it was time to move on. The marriage certificate, No. 2062, still exists, under the names "Charles Harris" and "Helen Neilson"—the crinkling paper a mute and decaying witness to a forgotten tragedy.

After the marriage, the young lovers went back to their respective schools in the city, getting together when they could. When Helen got pregnant, Carlyle himself tried to do the abortion but botched the job. She was sent to her uncle, a doctor who cleaned up Harris's work. When Mrs. Potts learned of all this, she was, naturally, upset and outraged. She saw only one way out: Carlyle Harris must marry her girl before a minister and acknowledge the connection publicly. Mrs. Potts set a deadline of February 8, 1891, the one-year anniversary of the City Hall ceremony done under false names. If Carlyle balked, she threatened, she would tell his mother—a very minor celebrity who lectured about temperance and child-raising under the name "Hope Ledyard."[1] His uncle would disinherit him, and he would certainly lose any breach-of-promise suit.

Still he resisted. Just 22, Carlyle Harris was not interested in settling down. Besides, when it came to a permanent wife, he was looking for more wealth and status. But he was cornered. In a graceless letter to Mama Potts sent on January 20, 1891, he submitted to her demands, "provided no other way can be found to satisfy your scruples."[2] All the while, Helen was safe and happy at a boarding school in New York, where she was proud to talk of her darling Carlyle to the other girls. Her only problem was that she occasionally suffered from headaches. On January 20, the same day Harris had sent his grudging promise of remarriage, he got a prescription to help her—a mixture of a little morphine and a lot of quinine. "One before retiring," the instructions read. He kept two capsules and gave her the other four.

Three times, Helen took a capsule, but didn't like the reaction it caused, writing her lover an amusing note that he must not be much of a doctor. She told her mother she was going to throw the last one away, Mrs. Potts recalled, "but I—I—advised her to take them."[3] Helen took the last one, and fell into a deep sleep punctuated by odd dreams. When her roommates returned from an evening out, she woke up and told them she felt funny. Then she went into a coma. Doctors were called in but they couldn't do much, or at least not enough. Less than 12 hours after she swallowed the last capsule, Helen was dead. Carlyle Harris was at her bedside. The first words of the grieving husband: "Is this going to get me in trouble?"[4]

The whole thing was a little off, enough to warrant an inquest that delivered a verdict of accidental morphine poisoning. Harris handed over one of the capsules he had kept for himself (the other was lost); it was properly filled with one-sixth of a grain of morphine and 4.5 grains of quinine. So the tragic and beautiful Helen Potts Harris was buried.

Unfaithful unto death, Harris demurred at his name appearing on his child bride's gravestone.[5]

But the story never quite died. Columbia Medical School began investigating its scholar, and of course Mrs. Potts had her suspicions. Almost two months after her death, Helen's body was exhumed. The results of the autopsy were curious: There were traces of morphine, but none of quinine—the opposite of what would be expected given that there was supposed to be 27 times as much quinine as morphine in the capsule.

On May 13, 1891, Carlyle Harris was charged with first-degree murder. Harris, the prosecution charged, had opened one of the capsules and substituted morphine for quinine. Then he kept two in a misguided attempt at self-protection and gave the rest to Helen. All he had to do was wait. On taking the doctored capsule, she would kill herself, which she did.

The trial, which began on January 14, 1892, was the sensation of the day. Middle-class readers could identify with the handsome medical student and his young wife; the unique killing method gave the case a certain something extra. It also meant the trial was as much a science lesson as a legal tribunal.

Harris had three lawyers, of whom the most important was William Travers Jerome, a former prosecutor who would later return to that side of the aisle. It was a sophisticated defense. The symptoms of uremic poisoning, a kidney disease, were identical to those of morphine poisoning, Jerome argued. Therefore, no cause of death could be definitively established. Harris must be given the benefit of the doubt.

The prosecution, led by Francis Wellman, had a word for that: piffle. If the capsule was innocent, there should have been no traces of morphine in the remains, since the pill was supposed to contain only a sixth of a grain. The fact that any was left proved that the poor girl was crammed with the stuff.

The defining moment came on January 30. The defense appeared to get off to a good start, bringing out its chief expert witness, Dr. Horatio Wood, chairman of nervous diseases at the University Hospital in Philadelphia. Wood concluded that the cause of death could not be established. The autopsy was too late, and the poisoning symptoms were ambiguous. "My own belief is that in the present state of medical science no accurate opinion could be passed upon it; the symptoms are compatible with various conditions other than that of morphine poisoning." At this, reported the man from the *World*, the jury looked impressed and the defense "pretty cheerful."

The smiles lasted a New York minute. Wellman recognized that this could be a career-making case—as did Jerome, for that matter. Both had become fairly expert chemists and knew more about poisoning at this point than was strictly comfortable. As Wellman paced toward the witness box, he had the supreme feeling that a courtroom lawyer might get once or twice in a lifetime: He was going to win in the next few minutes.

Wellman approached the box so closely that Wood shrank back. Lobbing questions like explosive projectiles, the prosecutor forced Wood to admit that he had seen a single case of morphine poisoning in the last 20 years, compared to the dozens the New York doctors had treated: "Will you, with one experience in 20 years, come here and say that you don't believe that they can tell what she died of?"[6]

Wood could only affirm that, yes, that's what he meant, but his composure was eroding before the jury's gaze. It would soon disappear entirely. The one difference between uremic and morphine poisoning, both sides agreed, was that in the latter the pupils of the eyes dilated symmetrically, as Helen Potts's physicians swore had been the case. (In uremic poisoning, the pupils stay normal.) Wood had testified, though, that he knew of a morphine poisoning case in which only one eye had dilated. In fact, he was struck enough by this event, which had occurred in the practice of a Dr. Taylor, that he included the incident in one of his own books. Wellman kindly read out the paragraph.

The detail mattered because if there was a case of morphine poisoning without the distinctive dilation, then the possibility that Helen Potts had died of something else was strengthened considerably. Wellman also knew the Taylor case. In fact, he knew it better than Dr. Wood. And in his next question, he offered Wood a single fact that changed everything: In the Taylor case, the patient had a glass eye.[7] No wonder, then, that it had not dilated. The jury caught the point immediately: The uremic defense was destroyed.

> The courtroom had the hush of death. The whole room seemed trembling and vibrating with the intensity of the strain. It became frightful. People looked around with wild eyes and gasped. Some hurried to seek the air. Others sat as dazed. . . .[8]

So where were Howe & Hummel in all this excitement? On the sidelines—interested, but irrelevant spectators. Perhaps Howe was irritated at not being invited into the biggest case in town, or maybe he was trying to soften up a future opponent in the DA's office. He might have just been feeling mischievous. At any rate, he wrote an extraordinary letter to Wellman[9] during the trial, touching on his favorite part of any trial: the closing argument.

In the letter, Howe suggested that Wellman paint a word picture for the jury, inviting them to accompany him in mind to the grave of Helen Potts, then turn to Harris and declare: "You dare not go to that spot. You put your victim there, she whom you swore to love, cherish, and protect; and you would hear through the sod which covers her remains her cry of 'Murderer! Murderer!'" And sure enough, the last couple of paragraphs of Wellman's final argument closely followed the template suggested by the Bard of Centre Street. It took the jury just 80 minutes to find Harris guilty of first-degree murder. His execution was scheduled for March 21.

Now, finally, it was Howe & Hummel time. Mrs. Harris, perhaps guided by the wisdom of the Tomb habitués she was getting to know so well, hired the pair to take the case to the Court of Appeals. But, she told Jerome, if the original defense team wanted to assist, she would be happy to have them. Thanks but no thanks, they replied stiffly. They could not associate with the likes of Howe & Hummel. Mrs. Harris was sad but resigned; "Lawyer Howe said he thought that was just what you would say."[10]

Howe went to work and appealed on 11 different points, including the fact that the district attorney hadn't signed the indictment. More substantively, he argued that the cause of death was a guess, based on an exam done on the body after embalming and 56 days underground.[11] In January 1893, the court turned the defense down flat. Howe delivered the bad news to Harris in his home in Cell 8 on Murderers' Row, where he kept busy by writing essays on topics like prison reform, which he favored, and vivisection, which he regarded as justifiable homicide. Harris also wrote poetry, of a kind:

> Miss Lucy we used to call her,
> And I tell you, boss, she was neat!
> The street dogs perked when she went by,
> She looked that cute an' sweet.[12]

With the appeal decisively rejected, it was time for something new. In an abrupt change of strategy, Howe and Hummel abandoned the defense that Helen had died of something else. She had died of morphine poisoning, they said, but she took it herself: Helen Potts was a secret morphine addict who died of an overdose. And they managed to drum up a few people who signed affidavits to this effect.

These were singularly unconvincing. One was from a druggist who had once been arrested for keeping a disorderly house; an acquaintance swore that he later bragged of getting $500 for his testimony.[13] Two were from a mother and daughter with dubious reputations who could not prove they had even known Helen. Another was from an acquaintance who said he sometimes sort of thought that she might have been on something. Helen slept a lot in the afternoon and was restless— symptoms also synonymous with adolescence.

The prosecution countered with an entire book of testimony from people who actually knew Helen. On March 16, Judge Smyth decided that nothing in the "so-called newly-discovered evidence" would have changed the original verdict. There would be no new trial. Four days later, Smyth set a new date for execution: May 8.

Considering that the year before Howe had done his bit to get Harris hanged, it is worth noting that he ended up liking the handsome killer. Harris returned the affection. He had nothing but praise for Howe's failed efforts. Allowed to address the court on the day of sentencing, he singled out his counsel for praise:

> I know it is not usual for a defendant unsuccessful in his cause to eulogize the counsel that have defended him; but I feel so proud of having won the esteem, the confidence and respect of Mr. Howe, I feel so grateful to him for what he has done for her who is dearer to me than myself . . .[14]

Then, in a moment that was surely scripted, Howe handed Harris a flask of whiskey and Harris presented Howe with a black-bordered envelope. Inside were diamond cufflinks. Howe's hand shook as he accepted the gift from the condemned man. "This was the last gift from Helen to me," Harris told his ally. "I ask you to take it with her love and mine."[15] Howe wept.

Sent to Sing Sing to await execution, Harris had only one avenue left—a pardon from the governor. Mrs. Harris began a petition campaign to save her boy; she eventually gathered 60,000 signatures. That was enough public spirit for the governor to appoint a referee to take a dispassionate look at the case. Nothing worked. Harris must die.

On May 8, pale but composed, the condemned man ate a light breakfast and worked on his farewell message. At 12:36 p.m., he stepped into the death chamber. His last words: "I am absolutely innocent." The prison barber shaved his scalp; his pants were slit up the leg,[16] and the leads applied. At 12:40, his body absorbed 1,700 volts of electricity; at 12:43 he was declared dead.[17]

Carlyle Harris's mother was faithful after death. Into her beloved son's coffin, she dropped one of the affidavits alleging that Helen Potts was a morphine abuser. And on top of the coffin, she affixed a plaque engraved:

CARLYLE W. HARRIS

MURDERED MAY 8, 1893

As for Howe, the big man had known hundreds of murderers. But Carlyle Harris was special. "My feelings for that noble and much persecuted youth could not have been deeper had he been my own son," Howe would say of the poisoner. He wore the diamond cufflinks for the rest of his life.[18]

Not that he thought the much-persecuted youth was innocent. In 1900, Howe would write, with friendly indulgence, that he considered Harris "one of the cleverest of all the murderers I have known."[19]

Howe had no such sentiment for another notorious killer, Martin Thorn. Along with his lover, Augusta Nack, Thorn carried out a thorough murder that included shooting, stabbing, and decapitating his victim before chopping the body into four chunks and disposing of the pieces in four different locations. Despite the painstaking premeditation, the first remnant of the unfortunate victim—shoulders, arms, and flayed chest—bobbed up in the East River on June 26, 1897, just 15 minutes after it was dunked. Only the head, which had been encased in plaster, never surfaced.

The police swung into action; so did the tabloids. In the next few days, both the *Journal* and the *World* charged into the investigation. The *Journal* would declare on June 30: SOLVED BY THE JOURNAL. The ostentatious self-congratulation was vulgar, but not far off the mark. *Journal* reporters uncovered at least as much evidence as the police. Of course, the papers also filled dozens of columns with speculation, fabrications, and such useful tidbits as the views of clairvoyants.

The big break came when a reporter for the *Journal,* working hard at an East Side saloon, overheard a couple of men talking about the disappearance of a colleague. This was one William Guldensuppe, a masseur at the Murray Street Baths. Brought to the morgue to look at the recovered torso, six different employees, all of whom had seen Guldensuppe dress and undress for his work, were convinced. The scar on the left index finger; the crossed toe; the mole on the shoulder—all just like Willie's. Then there was the shield-shaped cut in the chest, right where Guldensuppe had a tattoo of a woman.

The identification led police to Augusta Nack, a fellow German immigrant with whom Guldensuppe lived, in the euphemism of the day, on intimate terms. On June 30, the police paid their first visit to Nack, a large, muscular woman with massive hands and a bossy manner who was no one's idea of a femme fatale. Her story was that she hadn't seen Willie for several days, but the cops were unconvinced. They arrested her when she was caught packing for a quick exit to Germany. Nack hired a lawyer, the estimable Emmanuel "Manny" Friend, and stayed busy keeping her mouth shut. But she could not do the same for her neighbors, who revealed that her previous roommate was a barber named Martin Thorn, whom Guldensuppe had thrashed over the fair Nack's favors.

On July 3—tipped off by the *Journal*—police investigated the killing ground, a small frame house in Woodside, Long Island. The place was clean, the kind of cleanliness characteristic of the best efforts of a German hausfrau. But there was one curious thing. The water meter showed that thousands of gallons had been used since the last inspection—though the house had only been occupied for a few days.[20] And then there was the duck. The bloody water had formed a puddle in which a nearby duck wallowed, coating its white feathers a suspicious pink.[21] A chemist also determined that there was blood in the drainpipe—an example of the increased sophistication of police techniques. [22]

Bit by bit, more and more evidence surfaced. Police traced the purchase of the plaster that had wrapped the head back to Thorn and found a bullet imbedded in the baseboard. But Nack still kept mum, and Thorn stayed out of sight. He did not stay quiet, though, confessing to a fellow barber, John Gotha, on July 5. The story he told was that after Guldensuppe had displaced Thorn, the fair Augusta had changed her mind. She would rather live with Thorn, she told him, but Guldensuppe might get violent. So they spent weeks plotting to kill him.

Nack lured him to Woodside the morning of June 26, clicking the gate twice to signal to Thorn that their victim was on his way into the house. Thorn, dressed only in his underwear, hid in an upstairs closet. When Willie came into view, Thorn shot him, then stabbed him with his razor. "It's done," he reported to Nack.

But they were only half-finished. It took Thorn several hours to cut up his victim; then he and Nack simply carried Guldensuppe's upper body, wrapped in a plastic cloth, onto a streetcar, boarded a ferry, and dropped it overboard. This was the piece found 15 minutes later. The next day, they disposed of the other three packages of body parts; they also pawned Guldensuppe's clothes and watch.[23] Did Thorn regret anything? Of course, he told Gotha. They should have found a house with a sewer connection, and weighted all the remains.

Gotha might have been a friend, but he did not like being the man who knew too much. He snitched. On July 9, Nack and Thorn were reunited, in court, where they were indicted for murder. When their eyes met, Nack had two words for her lover: "*Schweig still!*" she hissed. Say nothing. He reached out with his unmanacled hand and squeezed her arm.[24] Nack's lawyer was on hand, but Thorn told the judge he couldn't afford one.

Fortunately, William F. Howe happened to be in the courtroom. He was never easy to miss and in this case, he was front and center, fairly panting to get involved. The judge, perhaps bemused, appointed him as Thorn's counsel. In a matter of minutes, Howe was telling reporters that there was no chance Thorn could be convicted.[25]

It would be four months before the trial started, and the only thing of note that happened in the interim was that it was transferred to the courts in Long Island City in Queens County, where the Woodside cottage was located. Neither Thorn nor Nack squealed. Perhaps there was no honor among thieves, but these co-killers were true to each other. And in that they had hope.

When the trial finally started, Howe, 71, was dressed to impress in a black yachting cap with gold buttons in the form of his initials. There were so many diamonds on his scarf and turquoises and rubies scattered about that he fairly sparkled.[26] A massive chrysanthemum completed the outfit.[27] He breathed assurance, and he passed his confidence on to Thorn, who seemed self-satisfied and even rather pleased at being the center of attention.

Jury selection took only a day. Long Island City was just across the East River from Manhattan—the courtroom was no more than two miles from Central Park. But it was on a different planet from its big-city neighbor: Half the jury were farmers and oystermen.[28] They were the most important audience, of course, but hardly the only one. There were 63 reporters and 10 telegraphers on hand[29] to send every disgusting detail back to a national readership that could not get enough of the case. There were even carrier pigeons to wing sketches from the courtroom to the presses.[30]

Howe had prepared a three-part defense.

1. No corpus delicti. Eighty percent of a body was not enough; murder could not be proved.
2. If murder had been done, there was no proof that the remains were those of Willie Guldensuppe. Howe had even rounded up a businessman from Virginia who swore that the pieces sure looked like those of a wandering, and vanished, photographer named William Edwards.[31] By this time, Howe said, Guldensuppe was probably in Germany.[32]
3. She done it.

Howe appeared to be making some headway on the basis of the forward and fallback defenses, but at the end of the first day of trial, he was abruptly forced into the final option: Nack confessed.

Blame a lisping little brat of a boy, the four-year-old son of a minister who had been visiting the accused murderess for months, urging her to make her peace with God. When his wee boy climbed into her lap and kissed her as the minister read from the Bible, she broke down in remorse.[33] That's one story, anyway.

The fact is, Nack found herself not just in the middle of a trial, but in the middle of a classic problem in game theory known as the prisoner's dilemma. In this construct, two people are charged with the same crime; kept apart, each is offered a deal that mitigates his own sentence but hurts the accomplice more. Whatever the other person does, the individual prisoner is better off being the first to confess; if both confess, the outcome is worse than if both remain silent. Depending on the conditions attached to the deal, the optimum result is to say nothing. The nature of the game is to make the certainty of immediate self-interest more compelling than the possibility of cooperation. Philosophers have used the prisoners' dilemma as a way to talk about the nature of morality and the utility of altruism. Nack was not that deep a thinker. She simply measured up her options and decided she would be better off betraying her former lover.

Howe got the message later that evening. He put up an excellent front: "Two minutes reflection dismissed my doubt and perturbation," he told the press. "I came to the conclusion that if Lady Macbeth killed Duncan she had a perfect right to say so, but she lied about it when she said her husband committed the crime."[34] The response, while brave, was short of both legal and literary logic; after all, it *was* Macbeth who killed Duncan, not his lady. But mostly, Howe was furious at Emmanuel Friend, whom he felt was not playing cricket. "You! You insignificant little imp!" he accosted his fellow lawyer. "You insect! I ought not to notice you. You are not worthy of being considered a respectable rival of Howe & Hummel!"[35]

The next day, Nack told all in a cool and collected manner "as if she were relating a little argument in the market over a pair of chickens."[36] She loved Thorn but feared him, too, she told the court in a bland, German-accented monotone; she had no choice but to do his bidding. Her testimony confirmed Gotha's tale and matched all the physical evidence. Only at the end did her composure falter. Weeping into her handkerchief, she blubbered, "I want to make my peace with the people and with God."

But first, she would have to face Howe, who lit into her with merciless aggression. He charged that she was not only the mastermind— something that everyone believed—but that she also did the rough work, using the medical skills she had acquired as a midwife. Thorn was the cat's paw of a woman whose unfathomable sexual allure had drawn him into a situation beyond his control. All the poor fool had done was to help clean up Nack's mess.

Nack stood up to the red-faced, looming lawyer with a phlegmatic composure that might have been admirable under other circumstances, even viewing the gory photographs of the various body parts without expression. All she did, she told Howe, was tie up one bundle.

And then, the trial stopped. A juror got appendicitis and had to be excused; the whole thing had to be done again, starting a week later. This time, Howe went straight for she-done-it defense. He also wowed the new jury pool with a spectacular outfit: a fist-sized moonstone in the form of Medusa, surrounded by diamonds, placed artfully in the center of a red silk scarf.[37] The oystermen of Queens had never seen anything like it.

During the second trial, Nack did not testify. In a nod to Howe's effectiveness, the prosecution did not want to expose her to cross-examination again.[38] There was enough evidence to convict Thorn without her. Thorn, however, did take the stand. Coached by Howe, who on that day was somberly dressed in black, with a dusting of diamonds, Thorn blamed Nack for everything. She thought up the plan; she lured Guldensuppe; she shot him; and she hacked him to pieces. All Thorn did was fall in love with her. And hold the body while she cut it up. And wrap the head in plaster. And dispose of it. And pawn Guldensuppe's belongings.[39] And hide. And lie to the police. But really, that was it.

It was enough. Though the reviews of Howe's closing argument were kindly, the evidence was stronger than the rhetoric. Martin Thorn was convicted of first-degree murder. The judge praised Howe's work, telling Thorn that no "counsel could have done more for you."[40] Then he sentenced him to death. The body of Guldensuppe, which had been pickled since its discovery, was finally released for burial. Some 10,000 people filed by his coffin, thrilled to see the headless body, dressed neck to toe in basic black.[41]

Howe was greatly disappointed. Until Nack's confession, he thought he had a real shot with the "no head, no foul" defense. He wrote to Hummel, who was in Paris at the time: "Dear Abe, I had the prettiest case and here is all my work shattered. I can still prove that they couldn't identify Willie's body and that it wasn't cut up in the Woodside cottage. Now all my roses"—Howe had a soft spot for roses, which he raised on the grounds of his home in the Bronx—"are frosted in the night and my grapes withered on the vine." [42]

Of course, it was no fun for Thorn, either. He was shipped to Sing Sing, where he occupied the same cell that had once housed Carlyle Harris.[43] On August 1, 1898, Thorn shared the poisoner's fate in the electric chair. Augusta Nack, by virtue of her confession and her sex, was convicted of manslaughter and sentenced to 15 years.[44] She served nine. Released in July 1907, a mob greeted her as she stepped off the train in Grand Central Terminal. Always an entrepreneur, and rather more talented along those lines than the men in her life, she went into the deli business. The image of her spending her days slicing up meat is not a pretty one.

Such high-profile defeats aside, there was a reason that Howe & Hummel became known for murder—or, rather, that Big Bill did. Hummel played a supporting role in the criminal practice; he was busier with blackmail and Broadway. But Howe, well, he adored a killing, the grislier the better, to a degree that makes one wonder about his mental makeup. He never seemed bothered by a client who had done a perfectly decent person in, and he never shrank from maligning some poor corpse, as he did with Helen Potts. No, Howe relished everything about a high-profile murder. And he really was rather good at it.

There was the fortunate George Evans, for example, sentenced in 1886 to 15 years for killing Thomas Currie, who had taken his janitorial job. The sole evidence against Evans were Currie's dying words, in which he named Evans as his killer. In law, such end-of-life statements carry particular force on the grounds that individuals on the brink of death are considered unlikely to lie. To make a dying declaration legally bulletproof, there were a series of questions that victims were required to answer; the answers were written down in the grimly named "Ante-Mortem Inquisition." Asked if he believed he was about to die, Currie had answered, "Yes." In the follow-up question, "Have you any hope of recovery from the effects of the injury you have received?" he answered, "It is hard for me to say." He then related his story: Evans, who had not been told he had been replaced, ordered Currie off the premises. When the latter refused, Evans called him a son of a bitch and threatened to "blow my black head off." Then he drew out his gun. So did Currie, but only Evans fired a shot. Currie signed the statement with his mark, a shaky "X."

On appeal, Howe argued that the fact that the victim did, in fact, die, did not make his words a dying declaration because Currie was not sure he was doomed. Somehow two appeals courts thought that made sense. With no other evidence to consider, the DA gave up.[45] Evans walked.

Michael Considine also had reason to thank Howe. The saloon keeper shot and killed John Malone, a friend who owed him money, in a case so problematic that four times Howe offered to plead to manslaughter. The district attorney's office refused, meanwhile bouncing the case around to so many courts—nine transfers, by one count[46]— that it was more than a year before it came to trial. When it finally did, in 1896, Howe was ready. The key moment came when he took the cane with which Considine said he had been threatened, then suddenly crashed it down on the table. *Thwack!* When the prosecutor flinched, Howe jumped in. Now, he lectured, the jury could appreciate Considine's fear.[47] It was enough; Considine was acquitted.

Then there was Philip Lohges. When his much-abused sister told him that her husband, John Hester, had threatened her, Lohges said he would talk to him. Before initiating this chat, though, he stopped by a store, bought a gun, and had the shopkeeper load it. At his brother-in-law's workplace on December 4, 1884, the two exchanged a very few words, whereupon Lohges shot Hester five times, "as long as he was standing," in his words. When Hester was safely down—and there was no way he was still standing after the first couple of shots—Lohges walked to the nearest police station and calmly gave himself up.

This was no murder, Howe said, but self-defense during an act of brotherly love. Hester, a tailor, had come at Lohges with his shears. To emphasize the point, Howe picked up the said shears, displayed them to the jury, dropped them on the defense table with a thud, then opened and closed them with a vicious snap. Deploying confusion, Howe was able to tie the police in knots, getting them to contradict each other on the stand. And he also employed another favorite tool—tears—with particular deftness. Lohges's sister, the widow Hester, defended her brother's honor and spent most of the trial crying. When she testified, she wept—over her husband's perfidy, her love for him, her brother's loyalty, her poor innocent child (inexplicably left home).

Howe was also greatly moved. When he began his closing argument, he had an audible quaver in his voice, a glint in his eye (and a massive diamond on his tie). "If you convict him of this crime, the recollection of this day's deed will never leave you," he warned the jury, gesturing to Lohges, who was now also in tears. "It will follow you to your places of business, to your homestead, and will make your deathbed one of horror."[48] Some of the jury wept, too.

Result: Lohges was convicted, but on the lowest charge possible and with "a strong recommendation to mercy." He was sentenced to seven years, a short term for what sure looked like a cold-blooded killing. This was Howe in his prime—a force of nature so compelling that even Judge Gildersleeve recognized it. He told Lohges, when the jury reported its lenient verdict: "You owe this result largely to the remarkable ability with which your defense was conducted. You have been defended by one of the ablest criminal lawyers in this city, aye, in this country or any other country."[49]

Blaming the victim is not a pleasant thing, particularly when the victim is dead. To Howe, it was simply business. He certainly seemed to take an unholy glee in maligning Charles Goodwin, a part-time salesman and full-time man about town who was shot by his neighbor, a bookmaker named Burton C. Webster,[50] on August 2, 1891. Goodwin had made a habit of tossing provocative comments in the direction of Webster's resident girlfriend, a wild child turned failed actress named Evelyn Granville, and might have given her a spontaneous squeeze once or twice. Granville could not have been all that shocked; she had a colorful, not to say sluttish, past on two continents. While never quite a professional, she certainly lived off her relationships with men. She was also known for lounging around the Percival Flats in something less than full dress. Granville had every right to resent Goodwin's advances, of course, and to tell Webster about them. But she was begging for trouble.

On the fatal evening, Goodwin came to the Webster/Granville apartment, perhaps after one or two too many. He knocked, and when Webster opened the door, Goodwin was surprised. He mumbled something to the effect of, "Oh, it's you," and went back to his own rooms. Webster, who also had been drinking, followed him a few moments later, to remonstrate against his attentions. The argument ended with a bullet in Goodwin's brain, his body bleeding near a broken cuspidor.

There was no question that Goodwin was dead and that Webster had done the deed. So in the months before trial, deftly abetted by the defense, Goodwin's reputation was shredded in the press. He had had a long-running affair with a married woman, who was in South Dakota getting a divorce at the time of his death. Her husband didn't seem to mind; invited to abuse Goodwin at the trial, he instead defended the dead man. But the seeds were planted for the defense: Goodwin deserved what he got.

And then there was the broken cuspidor. Goodwin had assaulted poor Webster with the sinister spit-holder, Howe charged. This was no piece of crockery; with evil intent, it was a killing machine. Webster therefore had had no choice but to shoot his assailant in the head to save his own life. Evelyn Granville, now his lawfully wedded wife, accompanied by her seven-week-old infant, born (sob!) while Webster was in jail, confirmed that the cuspidor was about to crash down on her husband's head when he shot. She was at a loss to explain why the story she gave to police immediately after the shooting was quite different—that she had seen and heard nothing.[51]

But character assassination was really the heart of the defense. If Howe could get the jury to dislike Goodwin enough, then Webster might walk. So in his closing statement on March 3, 1892, Howe lit into the dead man with venomous contempt. The shooting, he said, was the impulse of a moment, provoked by a sneak attack with a deadly weapon from a "dastard, a libertine, and a drunken coward when he attempted to debauch this little woman, his wife." Getting into his stride, Howe went on, "This poor little woman," he said, gesturing to Evelyn,

> had her life made wretched by this lecherous devil, Goodwin. He walked about attired so disgustingly and acted so like a beast that, as there is a God above us, I say he ought to have been shot there and then. . . .
>
> He [Goodwin] was a libidinous, lecherous man. Who lived like a beast and died like a beast. He deserved to die; such a man should have been wiped off the face of the earth!

And it damn near worked; eight jurors wanted to acquit, but could not convince the holdouts. With no one budging, the jury gave up. "There were two sides," a juror later explained. "One would not admit Goodwin's testimony at all because he was a beast. The other side followed facts." It looked as if Webster might get a free pass. Hung juries often meant the end of matters, particularly when, as in this case, there were more votes for acquittal. This time, the authorities decided to try again.

When Webster went back to trial nine months later, the conditions were markedly different. There was a tougher prosecutor, Francis Wellman, before a sterner jurist, Judge D. P. Ingraham. The latter kept a tighter grip on the proceedings, limiting the degree of postmortem character assassination.

Wellman had considerable respect for Howe's talents, enough that he was not thrilled to be in charge of the retrial. "By this time I had become convinced that in every trial in which I had been opposed to Howe, his defense had been simply a tissue of lies, with just enough foundation of fact to make the perjury fit in naturally in the eyes of the jury."[52] But Wellman was not afraid to fight Howe on his own territory—that is, in the use of theatrics. It was Wellman who provided the most dramatic moment of the second trial. Cross-examining Webster, he raised one of the pieces of the famous cuspidor over his head. Frozen in position, Wellman asked Webster if he could really pull his revolver from his pocket and prepare and shoot it before being hit. Webster stuck to his story, but the demonstration was a palpable hit.

For his closing argument, Howe, appeared before the jury dressed in a dark suit, with a little black bow tie. Thus garbed like a Puritan divine, he launched again into an attack on Goodwin, whose attack on fair womanhood, he said, was the real crime. But even his sartorial seriousness was not as impressive as the charge of Judge Ingraham, who rebutted Howe's essential points directly: "The law does not allow a man to be killed for an insult to a woman. The law provides for the punishment for that—and it is not in any case death." As for self-defense, the judge's words stopped just short of scorn: "You will judge, gentlemen, whether this man, going there with his pistol in his pocket, or the other man, standing there with the cuspidor in his hand, was the assailant." Though the jury appeared favorably impressed by the couple's visible devotion to their squalling little son, brought in for a cameo appearance, it was not enough to get the father off. Webster was convicted of manslaughter and sentenced to 19 years.[53] Under the circumstances, Howe had done well to save his client's life; the means he chose, however, were ugly. Goodwin was an imperfect man; he was also very dead.

Howe used the same technique, with even greater success, in the trial of Edward Hahn. On June 2, 1887, Hahn had spent all day at the policeman's picnic, then had a few drinks with Captain Jack Hussey, the gatekeeper at Castle Garden, the spot on the toe of Manhattan that received immigrants before Ellis Island opened. Hahn got into a huff about the bar bill; as he left the saloon, he turned and growled, "Come on out, you big cur." Hussey, however, was fully occupied with his whiskey and stayed seated. Frustrated, Hahn fired a shot, which did no harm.

Hussey finished his drink, and finally began to head for home, a few blocks away, bereft of hat, coat, and shoes. He paused to steady himself on a wagon; Hahn, standing across the street, spotted him and fired another shot, missing again. His judgment impaired by a hard day's drinking, and naturally irritated at being shot at twice, shoeless Hussey gave chase. Hahn fled down Jackson Street, turned and shot again, from 15 feet away. This time, the bullet found flesh, burying itself in Hussey's ribs. That was the story told in court by five different people—two bystanders, the saloonkeeper, and two acquaintances of the victim. When Captain Jack died in the hospital 19 days later, Hahn was charged with first-degree murder.

Howe and Hummel devised a three-part strategy. First, they argued self-defense, rolling out three perjurers who swore that a small mob had been chasing Hahn. This unimpressive trio was poorly chosen. Notable mostly for stupidity, they were promptly confused and impugned and rendered completely unbelievable. They said, for example, that the crowd was hurling stones picked up from a building site; in fact, work had not begun on the site until some days after the killing. Whoops.

Second, Howe argued that Hussey died because of bad medical care, not the bullet in the ribs. But this fell short, too, as even the defense doctors agreed that it was the bullet that caused the deadly complications. And the patient who swore he saw Hussey walking around half-naked on a diet of whiskey and beef? He remembered it perfectly, because it was the day of a political picnic—which took place a month after Hussey died. Whoops again.[54]

So that left the third option: Malign the accused. Slandering a dead man in front of his loved ones is not for the squeamish; Howe didn't seem to mind. So he suggested, without any corroboration, that Hussey was one of the leaders of the 1863 Draft Riots. These were the worst civil disturbances in New York history; a five-day reign of terror in which mobs rampaged around the city. The hordes took particular pleasure in maiming and killing the black population, culminating in the burning of the Colored Orphans Asylum. It took hardened combat veterans returning from the Battle of Gettysburg to finally quell the violence, which left more than a thousand dead. The suppression of the Draft Riots was also one of the finest hours for New York's finest, who fought the mobs bravely. Howe was peripherally involved—he defended a number of rioters.[55]

It had not escaped Howe's attention that the father of one of the jurors, Cleveland Dodge, had led a committee that gave the police force a flag in honor of their riot service.[56] Subtly but certainly, the idea was planted that Hahn, as a policeman, was a protector of order, something that was a matter of great concern in the wake of the Haymarket affair (see Chapter 7) and highly publicized anarchist rumblings. He should get the benefit of the doubt against a bruiser of a drunk with a history of rioting.

That was a gross caricature of Hussey, a father of four who went on a bender about once a year and was known as the "Castle Garden life saver" for his record in pulling men, women, children, and animals out of the drink. The U.S. Congress gave him a medal and the vaudevillians, Harrigan and Hart, mentioned him in a song. At 58, Hussey was also no physical match for 26-year-old Hahn, who admitted he knew the Castle Garden lifesaver was unarmed. But a thick blue line of cops testified that Hussey was a well-known rogue whom Hahn had every reason to fear.

Or, as Howe managed to put it to one cop, "Did you know him [Hussey] to be a violent, ferocious and turbulent man?" Officer McSherry swiftly answered, "Yes."

The question was an example of the enormous latitude Judge Cowing gave the defense during the five-day trial, allowing every derogatory reference to the dead man as a rogue and a cur, an outlaw and a ruffian, a rioter who should have found a bullet in his belly back in 1863. Even Hussey's record—he had saved dozens of people and seven horses from drowning—attracted nothing but scorn from the defense table. A trained dog, Howe said, would have done the same. At one point, the prosecutor, Colonel John Fellows, was seething at yet another pro-defense ruling, when Howe slipped behind him and lightly put his hands on his opponent's shoulders. Nettled, Fellows shrugged off the touch, and snapped, "I cannot stand Mr. Howe's caresses."

Everyone who wasn't wearing blue or obviously lying told a consistent story—that Hahn had stirred up a conflict and then shot his man for no good reason. In his closing, even Howe hinted that a verdict of manslaughter might serve the ends of justice. But not before planting this image: "Hahn, in drinking with Hussey, saw Hussey's eyes dilate as the lion tamer beholds the change in the aspect of his beast, and he heard the incipient growl of the savage under the breath of the man."

As the jury filed out, Howe wandered over to the reporters to get their judgment on the outcome. "Murder in the second" was his guess.[57] He was wrong.

An hour later, the jury returned: "Not guilty," the foreman announced.

The verdict on the verdict was almost unanimous: "Astonishing," said Judge Cowing. "Simply astounding," said District Attorney Randolph Martine. "Staggered," said the defendant,[58] who promptly went to police headquarters to get his job back. "Justice cheated, again" the *Tribune* deplored, thanks to "deliberately manufactured" testimony. "One of my greatest victories," bragged Howe,[59] as he relaxed with a cigar and soaked in the congratulations in his grungy throne room at 89 Centre Street.

• • •

In the case of the dissected lodger, the victim was so bland as to be impervious to invective. So Howe blamed the killer's affectionate little daughter instead. No one gave Edward Unger a hope of escaping the gallows. But he did.

Pity the poor clerk who first detected the whiff coming from the brown trunk, sent from New York to John A. Wilson of Baltimore, to be kept until called for. The trunk sat in the freight depot for days. When the stench became overpowering, and Mr. Wilson failed to show, it was opened. Inside was a headless torso, the legs and feet cut off and piled inside. Foul play was suspected.

Because the trunk (in both senses) came from New York, the police in Manhattan took up the case. In a display of efficient detective work that did Thomas Byrnes proud, two days later, the perp—or perhaps "the fiend in human shape," as the *Herald* put it—was in custody. The police had traced the journey of the trunk, and then traced the trunk back to its owner—Edward Unger. Going to Unger's two-room apartment on the top floor of a tenement on 22 Ridge Street, detectives saw traces of blood everywhere—on the walls, the carpets, the chairs, the floor, and inside two buckets. There was also a knife, a hammer and, most ominously, a saw. The headless torso, they discerned, belonged to August Bohle, a recent German immigrant who had lived in Unger's front room.

In death penalty cases, there was a tradition to assign counsel to indigent clients; Howe and Hummel got the call this time. Under their instruction, Unger should have known enough to say nothing. But he buckled under some masterly psychological maneuvering by Byrnes. First, the great detective brought in, one by one, a string of people who could implicate Unger—the keeper of the saloon where he stored the trunk, the neighbor who saw him carrying out buckets, the hardware dealer who sold him the saw, the storekeeper from whom he bought the rubber that wrapped the body. They said nothing, just let Unger look at them.

Then Byrnes displayed the hammer, bloody to the handle; the saw, with blood between its teeth; and the blood-soaked rubber wrapping. How much did you pay for this item? Byrnes asked three times. Unger denied the purchases three times. Later that same afternoon, Byrnes ratcheted up the pressure further. He had the bloody trunk placed outside Unger's cell and the sofa on which Bohle died placed in the detective's waiting room. Called to Byrnes's office, Unger saw the trunk as he left his cell. Byrnes appeared, and took out each bloody article of clothing. Do you know anything about this? Or this? Or this? Unger knew nothing.

Unger then walked to the waiting room, where he was invited to sit on the fateful sofa. He sat, then jumped up when he realized what it was. "When you get ready to tell the truth," Byrnes told his thoroughly rattled prisoner, "send for me."[60] It was a textbook example of Byrnes's belief that "It is not remorse that makes the criminal confess; it is anxiety, mental strain."[61]

Two hours later, back in his cell, his mind full of those awful sights, Unger broke. He admitted killing Bohle, but in self-defense. During a quarrel over money, Bohle had come at him with a poker. Unger struck with a hammer, twice, imbedding it deep into his victim's scalp. When he realized he had killed the man, he hid the body because his son was due home shortly. The next day, when his son went to work, Unger ingested a quart of whiskey, dismembered the remains and packed them off to Baltimore. The head he carried onto a ferry and splashed into the East River.

Justice could move briskly in 1887; two weeks later, Unger was on trial for his life. The details of the case were so disgusting that few gave Unger a chance. But he made an unexpectedly good impression. A former seaman who had served in the Union navy during the Civil War, he had a bluff, manly presence, and when he told his story, he had the courtroom riveted. In an account that reads like a theater review, the *Herald* said of Unger, "He cried, he laughed, he sighed, he whispered, he shouted. He exemplified the emotions of love, hate, fear, remorse, terror, despair, hope. And he did all this where it should be done and with telling effect. He held his audience spellbound from beginning to end." He even acted out the battle of Ridge Street, rising from his chair to show how he fended off Bohle's attack. The only details Unger added were of his guilt and remorse. He saw the ghost of Bohle at night, and concluded simply, "I am a miserable, miserable man."[62]

The other assets the defense had going for it were the Unger daughters, 18-year-old Anna and little Emily, who was around eight. Though they did not live with their father, they loved him dearly and came to court every day, flanking him at the defense table. Emily was a charmer, snuggling up to Unger during jury selection and being generally adorable. Everyone knew that the children's presence was a calculated bid for sympathy. "But no amount of dragooning by counsel could bring the genuine lovelight into Emily's upturned eyes," concluded the *Herald*.[63] "These things are beyond the art of even Howe & Hummel."

In his closing remarks, Howe conceded all the facts, but justified it all as self-defense; the grisly dissection was beside the point. "Did you leave your homes," he asked the jury, "to hang a man upon inference? Would you take the defendant away from his children and lock him up for life in a living tomb?" A sailor who had served his country; a loving father; a good man pushed to violence because violence was being done unto him. This was the tragedy of 22 Ridge Street.

If anything, the sheer, unremitting toil required to carve up Bohle proved Unger's paternal love, argued Howe. In a very real sense, it was not his fault: "Gentlemen, Unger did not cut off the head of the dead man. Unger did not mutilate and dismember him. Unger did not pack the limbs in different boxes and send them away. Unger did not throw the head from the ferryboat into the water." A pause here as the spectators gasped: Unger had admitted to doing all these things. Now Howe went for the big finish. Blame Emily!

> Gentlemen, it was that little child, now unconscious of the nature of these proceedings and sitting on her father's knee—'twas she who hacked and mutilated and hid the body of Bohle. For when Unger in self-defense had slain the man, this beauteous little creature's face came before him. He expected her foot to come to his room and to hide from her innocent gaze the awful spectacle, his mind set in motion by the recollection of the child, commanded these horrible acts.[64]

The children of Unger wept loudly as they cuddled their stricken father during Howe's powerful, if absurd, argument. And they kept it up. When DA DeLancey Nicoll read a passage from *Richard III* to prove Unger's consciousness of his guilt—a nice touch, thoroughly in keeping with the theatricality of the proceedings—little Emily upstaged him, jumping into her father's lap and nuzzling his mustache.

It is a good rule of thumb for people who desire to dispose of troublesome roommates not to chop them into seven pieces. No jury, even one consisting of New Yorkers, can overlook that entirely. But when Unger was convicted only of manslaughter, the verdict was considered a triumph. Howe's fellow lawyers gave him credit: "It was nothing but Howe's intensity and power as an actor," Theron Strong would later write, "playing upon the sympathies of the jury through the medium of the little girl, that saved Unger's life." Wellman, who attended the production, called Howe's performance "the finest piece of acting I ever heard of in a murder trial." In fact, Wellman continued, the whole thing "was well mounted, well costumed, and magnificently acted."[65]

These were all good results, adding a few more leaves to the laurels of Howe's reputation. But when Howe died in his bed in 1902, all the obituaries pointed to one case as the glory of his career in murder. That was the matter of the middle-class mistress, the *femme* who was truly *fatale*— Ella Nelson, who shot her lover and got away with it. This was a classic case of sex and death, and one that illustrated the Howe & Hummel precept that the best chance to win the worst case was to tell the most unlikely story, with maximum brio.

Ella Nelson was, perhaps, no better than she should be. But then, neither was Samuel Post. The young widow had met Post at Manhattan Beach in 1886; a few months later, he set her up in a small apartment. There they lived happily enough, except when Post was with his wife, whose existence he neglected to mention for a year. Nelson was not amused when he finally admitted to having committed matrimony, but they continued on for another four years. When yet another woman made an entrance into Post's life, Nelson let him know that adding a girlfriend to his already complicated romantic life of wife and mistress was asking too much.

On the evening of February 18, 1891, she snapped. Four shots were fired, and Post died of his wounds. Nelson was unscathed, and Nathan Michaels, a friend of the couple, saw it all. According to Michaels, the three of them were chatting amicably when Nelson mentioned Post's new room, which she said was just a bolthole to which he brought women. He disagreed, the two quarreled, and Post decided to leave. Nelson followed him into the bedroom, where the bickering continued. Then a single shot sounded. Post came stumbling into the parlor crying out, "Oh my God, I'm shot!" Ella Nelson, gun in hand, followed close behind. In the parlor, where Michaels was perched no more than six feet away on a piano stool, she fired three more times, then shouted, "Now, damn you, I have got you now." Michaels fled to find a cop or a doctor or both. When he came back, Nelson was standing over Post's bleeding body, gun still in her hand.[66]

To the doctor who had been summoned, Post was able to make a feeble joke: "I guess she [Nelson] made a bulls-eye this time." He named Nelson as the shooter to two different cops. At the hospital, asked about the circumstances of the injury, he was able to explain, "When I told her [I was leaving] she said to me, 'You're not going away.' I said, 'Yes, I am going away.' Then I heard the pistol—bang! bang!—and felt a pain in my abdomen." He also made a formal Ante-Mortem Inquisition to the coroner, in which he said that he "wanted to go back to the wife I had wronged and lead a better life." When he and Nelson argued about this, she shot him.[67]

Cops use the term "smoking gun" to describe a murder that is simple to solve. Rarely is it an exact description of a case. But it was this time. Even Howe and Hummel seemed to think so. They offered to have Nelson plead guilty to manslaughter. Prosecutor Francis Wellman refused. He was looking for second-degree murder at least. And he felt that the defense was in no position to bargain. Not only did he have a pile of evidence, he also had Frederick Smyth on the bench. Smyth, a former prosecutor who could make lawyers quake like schoolboys,[68] was not so much a hanging judge as a convicting one. In the subtlest of ways, he could and would put his judicial thumb on the scales of justice, generally to the benefit of the prosecution. "He's a good judge, a foine judge," said one Irish-born lawyer of Smyth, "but he thinks ivery man ought to go to prison at least wance."[69]

Fridays, when Smyth pronounced sentences, were gloomy days in his court. Each convict would walk forward, hear his fate, then turn to another court officer to provide personal information. These questions were routine, but comedy occasionally broke out, such as the bigamist who answered "yes" when asked if he was married. On another occasion, a court officer named Flaherty, apparently a proud Catholic, conducted the following interrogation:

FLAHERTY TO DEFENDANT: Say, me friend, where was ye born?
DEFENDANT: Lowell, Mass.
FLAHERTY REPEATS TO THE CLERK: Lowell, Mass.
FLAHERTY TO DEFENDANT: Where de yez hang out?
DEFENDANT: Nowhere.
FLAHERTY TO CLERK: Ain't got none.
FLAHERTY TO DEFENDANT: Are you married?
DEFENDANT: No, thank God.
FLAHERTY TO CLERK: He says, no, thank God!
FLAHERTY TO DEFENDANT: Ever receive any religious instruction?
DEFENDANT: How's that?
FLAHERTY REPEATS: What's your religion?
DEFENDANT: Don't believe in nothin'.
FLAHERTY TO CLERK: Protestant![70]

Howe knew what he was facing in Smyth's court, so when he opened for the defense, he immediately took the offense. He challenged Post's statements, ridiculed Michaels, insulted the victim as a "double-dyed scoundrel," and appealed to the all-male jury's sense of chivalry to this "respectable widow" entrapped into concubinage by a "base wife deserter."[71] In the course of the struggle, Howe argued (as Nelson sobbed, continuously and copiously) she had accidentally pulled the trigger on the man she loved—indeed, still loved! It could happen to anyone—even if it did happen four times. "Who shall dare to say whether it was the hand of that man or the hand of this poor, unfortunate woman that pulled the fatal trigger?" Ella Nelson, dressed in a faded black dress that set off her reddened eyes, wept with quiet dignity.

When it came time for her to tell her story, she played the pathos card. Between snuffles, she recounted the argument, whimpering that she was upset because she suspected that Post had yet another woman on a string. "I told him that he had ruined his wife's life and my life and now he wanted to ruin another woman's life." It was Post who drew the pistol: "We had a scuffle over the pistol and it went off."[72] And then what happened? She didn't know. "I was sort of crazy and when I come to my senses, he was lying on the floor with his head in my lap."[73] Under Wellman's cross-examination, she continued to weep, but managed to stick to the basics—a struggle, some shots, and then nothing. "I don't know how that pistol went off. I didn't know anything about it. I never had the pistol in my hand."[74]

In his closing remarks, Howe brought all his passion, all his dramatic flair, and all his oratorical will to bear. And these were considerable. Theron Strong, a contemporary who admired Howe but didn't trust him, recalled that in one defense, Howe was so overcome that, with great effort, he lowered his considerable weight, and on his knees implored the jury to acquit. They did.[75] For the girl with the smoking gun, Howe stayed on his feet, but otherwise pulled out all the stops.

Michaels could not be believed, he asserted; Post was a seducer who deserved to die; the testimony conflicted; and it was a fearsome thing to send a woman to the electric chair. In short, the usual stuff. Then he strode over to the sobbing Nelson. "Can you live with the specter of this woman haunting you all your days? Can you? Look at her face!" This was not possible because, as usual, it was buried. So Howe tore her hands away, simultaneously digging his long nails into the soft skin at her wrists. As Nelson's head jerked up, revealing her tormented visage to the court, she shrieked in unexpected pain. Howe roared, "Can you say, 'I sent her to a felon's doom?'"

Wellman remembered the moment vividly.

It would be impossible to describe the effect this unearthly shriek had upon me, steeled as I was to the manufactured defense that Howe was attempting to foister upon the jury. It was as if someone had suddenly put a lump of ice down my back. The jury seemed completely petrified by it, and I saw the case was over from that moment.[76]

Wellman did a brisk, rational summation, but as he suspected, Howe had turned the tide. After three hours of deliberation, including a leisurely dinner break, the jury came back with a verdict: "Not guilty." It was a surprise to everyone except themselves. Nelson herself was astonished, swooning into Howe's arms.[77] The 12 men said that, sure, they had considered Post's statements. The problem was that in his dying declaration Post had only said that he "heard the pistol—bang! bang!—and felt a pain in my abdomen." But he didn't say that it was Nelson who produced the bangs. Who else it could have been was a matter to which they did not lend their wisdom. Then, for no apparent reason, they decided not to believe Nathan Michaels. Once the dead man's testimony was dismissed, and then that of the only eyewitness, there was reasonable doubt galore. Somehow it made sense to 12 good men.

For the prosecution, the verdict was hard to take. The next day, Wellman kept to his office in anguish; 33 years later, when he wrote his memoirs, the defeat still rankled. But it was a glorious win for Howe—not that he had much time to enjoy it. He had to disentangle himself from Ella Nelson's tear-sodden grasp to hustle to another courtroom, where Johann Most (see Chapter 7) was fighting a last-ditch effort to stay out of jail. The great lawyer was a busy man.[78]

The next afternoon, though, he was almost certainly at Pontin's restaurant, a short walk from the office and the unofficial headquarters of the more prosperous members of the New York criminal bar. That's where he and Little Abie were most lunchtimes. After a famous victory like the acquittal of Ella Nelson, Howe would have wanted to waddle through the dining room, basking in the congratulations of his peers and bestowing mock sympathy on the prosecution.[79] Then he and Hummel would have gone to the rear, to a private dining room that was their second office. Settling in, the partners would have ordered the excellent, if overpriced, cuisine (including the best roast beef in the city)[80] and raised a glass to the majestic legal institution that they loved so well—the jury that could be bamboozled.

SIX

The Mandelbaum Salon

At the four corners of Clinton and Rivington Street today are a Mexican restaurant, a Greek bakery, a brick oven pizzeria, and a diner with pretensions. Go a block in any direction, and the pattern—a multiethnic blend of classes—is confirmed. There are 99-cent stores and boutiques that sell $100 T-shirts; a Chinese flower shop and Dominican beauty salons; pawnshops and an organic dry cleaner; a homeless shelter and luxury condos; a health food store and one of those storefronts that sells an unlikely combination of things—in this case plaster saints and ice cream.

This part of New York's Lower East Side is dominated by six-story redbrick structures, built a century and more ago as tenements for the poor and near-poor. Today the area is home to a vigorous immigrant population, largely Hispanic and Chinese, leavened by upper-class migrants looking for a quasi-bohemian urban edge.

In Howe & Hummel's prime, the area was also mostly modest and mostly immigrant. But the immigrants then were predominantly German, many of them Jewish, giving the area its nicknames of "Kleines Deutschland" or "New Israel."[1] Today, except for Rothstein's hardware store and a tiny concrete-and-cobblestone park named for Nathan Straus, there is little hint remaining of this not-too-distant past. The Jews have moved on, and so have the Germans, in the perpetual recycling of humanity that is the hallmark of a living city.

The neighborhood features no world-class art or monumental buildings. But for the historian of Howe & Hummel, 79 Clinton Street, at the corner of Rivington, is a landmark site. For that address was the home of one of New York's great criminal minds—Fredericka "Marm" Mandelbaum, a German Jewish immigrant who was banker, ally, bondswoman, mentor, and mother figure to an entire generation of criminals. The building is long gone, replaced by the ubiquitous brick. It seems a pity that there is not at least a plaque to the memory of Mandelbaum; at her peak, she was a woman of fame and stature. In a unique way, she was both an exemplar of the American dream and a pioneering businesswoman. But mostly she was a crook.

The skilled bank robber never had it so good as in the 1870s and '80s. Banks were stuffed with the products of a modernizing financial system, such as stocks and bonds, but without the security to match. This made robbing them, more often than not, a low-risk proposition. As long as no one got seriously hurt—and sometimes that proviso went out the window—there was a well-established etiquette.

The bad guys could not cash the commercial paper, unless they really wanted to be caught; but their owners could not, either. So the dance would begin. A go-between would get in touch with the bank officials and, in effect, hold the paper to ransom. For a percentage of the value, the robbers would return the loot. Even if the police were brought in, they usually accepted the arrangement. Depositors were more concerned with getting their savings back than with principles of abstract justice, and the bankers were typically among the most influential men in town.

Sneaking into a bank and penetrating its vault was, of course, a crime, and not a victimless one. But it required such skill, daring, technical knowledge and a certain *je ne sais quoi* that bank burglars were universally regarded as the "cream of the crime world," according to Nell

Kimball, a madam who spent her entire life among the non–law-abiding classes and then wrote a lively book about her experiences.[2] Nor was it strictly among criminals that safecrackers were regarded as a natural nobility. "The successful bank robber is a king among thieves," stated George Walling, chief of police from 1874 to 1885, "and so far as the skill and cunning which he exercises are concerned, he undoubtedly earns his reputation."[3]

Consider, for example, John "Red" Leary, a burglar by vocation and avocation. It's hard to assess how good he was, because most of what is known about him comes from his failures. But he was well regarded by his peers—Marm Mandelbaum fenced his takings, a service she provided only to those she trusted—and the man did indeed have the nerve of a safecracker. One of his first big acknowledged jobs was the robbery of the Northampton Bank in central Massachusetts in January 1876. Five men forced their way into the home of the cashier, beating him until he told them how to open the vault. But there was no way they could get further, the cashier said, as he had only one key and three others were required to enter the safe, which had a patented double-dial combination. "We know about bank locks better than you do," the thieves assured him. Around $1.5 million later—including $14 taken from the pockets of the cashier—they had proved the point.

True to the usual protocol, the gang sent two stolen stock certificates to Northampton with a note: "You can make a proposition to us, the holders, and if you are liberal, we may be able to do business with you."[4] The fee: $150,000. This time, though, the bankers seemed to want to catch the villains. They brought in the Pinkerton National Detective Agency, whose motto "We never sleep" and logo of a perpetually open eye were a fair reflection of the cool tenacity the agency brought to its work. (The logo was the origin of the term "private eye.")

The detective agency, founded by Allan Pinkerton in Chicago in 1850, was famously honest. More to the point, its espionage service during the Civil War and its roster of national clients, such as railroads and messenger services, gave it an unrivaled knowledge of the American criminal element. Pinkerton detectives identified the team led by James Dunlap and Robert Scott as the most likely perpetrators of the Northampton burglary. The Dunlap gang was suspected of similar burglaries in Kentucky, Illinois, and Pennsylvania over the previous five years, as well as a few unfinished jobs in New York. The gang was the envy of the criminal fraternity because it appeared to have inside help. It did: William Edson, an expert in safe design and manufacture, worked for the company that made Northampton's supposedly impregnable safe.

Edson had been selling his skills to the bad guys for years. Now he suspected, correctly, that they were preparing to do him out of his share. So he was ready to listen when the Pinkertons gave him a choice. Edson could be prosecuted with his fellows or get immunity and an award for turning them in. He took about three seconds to name names, starting with Robert Scott and James Dunlap,[5] whom the Pinkertons had been trailing for weeks.

Much to their surprise, the two robbers were arrested, prosecuted, found guilty, and sentenced to 20 years. Not at all pleased with this, they refused to tell where the booty was. Neither did their friend and colleague, Billy Connors, who was picked up in New York, where he was residing in $100-a-week splendor in rooms above Solari's restaurant. Connors was sent to the Ludlow Street Jail, the former home of Victoria Woodhull and Tennie C. Claflin, but found its environs uncongenial. So he got a copy of the keys, and walked out after lunch in June 1877.

Leary, too, was arrested—briefly. He was with his wife, "Red Kate," a pickpocket, shoplifter, and con woman of some renown, at their country residence in Brooklyn in early August 1877. Armed with a warrant for Leary's arrest in connection with the Northampton robbery, several cops showed up; Leary agreed to go quietly. All he asked was to get his overcoat and say a private good-bye to Red Kate. As a gesture of good faith, he even left the door to the back room partly open. Then he dashed out another door, scaled a fence, and hopped into a waiting horse and buggy. "Good-bye," he called gaily to the infuriated cops, who shot fruitlessly at the laughing bandit.[6]

Leary was not seen, officially, for some time, but cops suspected his presence at the penetration of the Manhattan Savings Institution on

October 26, 1878, the greatest bank robbery in an era of great bank robberies. The genius behind the caper was George Leonidas Leslie. A longtime Howe & Hummel client, Leslie was no ordinary villain. Born in Ohio to a more than respectable family, he was cultured and genteel, a reader of good books, a lover of good food, a patron of the arts, and a boon companion in a number of prestigious men's clubs.[7] He might also have been the best bank robber in history. He toiled in his chosen field for almost two decades, roughly 1860–1878; over that period, Chief of Police George Walling figured that Leslie played a role in 80 percent of all bank robberies in the United States, taking in some $7 million. Those numbers are, at best, semieducated guesses. The point is that New York's top cop believed them.[8]

What set Leslie apart was his professionalism. Thomas Byrnes, the preeminent detective of the era, might have been describing Leslie when he wrote: "The professional bank-burglar must have patience, intelligence, mechanical knowledge, industry, determination, fertility of resource, and courage."[9] Leslie had all this; he was also a good personnel manager, recruiting a set of intelligent men, like Leary, "Sheeny" Mike Kurtz, Johnny Dobbs, Big Frank McCoy, and Banjo Pete Emerson, with complementary skills, and keeping them cohesive for years. Handsome and debonair, Leslie was a real-life precursor to the fictional Raffles. He was, in short, a skilled craftsman—and recognized as such. Criminals in other cities and states hired him as a consultant to look over their plans.[10]

For the Manhattan Savings job, Leslie invested three years in planning. He and his men, in various guises, surveyed every inch of the premises, and determined who did what and when. Learning the brand and make of the vault, he ordered an exact copy for himself. Then he set out to learn its strengths and, more important, its weaknesses. It took months, but he finally figured out how he could tumble the tumblers. With that mission accomplished, a freelance member of the troupe got a job at the bank. This man allowed Leslie in one night to prepare the vault for future action. But Leslie misjudged, and the bank noticed that something was wrong—and changed the lock. That meant more months of work; Leslie settled down to it, even designing some specific tools for the job.[11] Two more attempts fell short, but the group still felt that the bank was a "pudding," or soft target. Leslie certainly never gave up on it.

In his varied and colorful criminal career, however, Leslie must have done someone (or several) wrong. Perhaps it was over a woman; perhaps there were problems over the division of the spoils of a job in Dexter, Maine, in which the cashier had died after being locked in the vault. The death might have spooked Leslie, who did not like violence. Perhaps the troops were restless for new leadership. The undeniable fact is that on June 4, 1878, Leslie's body was found dumped near Tramp's Rock, just over the New York City border in Yonkers. He had been shot twice in the back of the head.

Marm Mandelbaum mourned. She had been a close friend of Leslie's and had financed many of his operations. In her sorrow, she paid for Leslie's funeral and supported his widow for a time.[12] "Poor Shorge, he vas such a nais man!"[13] was her epitaph for the stylish cracksman. But she was also a businesswoman; she had put up $2,500 for the Manhattan Savings job.[14] Though the king was dead, there was still a pudding waiting for a touch.

In the same vein, Leslie's colleagues decided that he would have wanted the work to go on; on October 26, 1878, the gang struck. At 6:00 in the morning, they entered the premises and tied up and gagged the janitor, Louis Werckle, and his family. After getting the combination to the vault from a terrified Werckle, they forced open the main door of the safe, which was easily done since the watchman, Patrick Shevelin, had let in one of the gang, Jimmy Hope, several times to drill the lock in preparation.[15] Once inside, some of the gang went through the safe; others began prying open safe deposit boxes. There was one truly frightening moment, when a cop looked in the basement window. It was not a normal time for anyone to be at work, but his suspicions dimmed when the man he saw, Abe Coakley (another friend of Mandelbaum's), nodded and dusted vigorously. The cop figured he was just getting an early start.

In about three hours, the gang got away with $2.7 million. To their disappointment, about 90 percent of this was in nonnegotiable bonds.[16] Even so, a haul of some $250,000 in liquid assets was a good night's work. The list of stolen goods takes a full, single-spaced page in the official affidavit, ranging from gold eagle coins to promissory notes to "three keys of the value of fifty cents each."[17]

This was the case that provided Howe & Hummel with their largest single payoff—$90,000 when all was said and done, according to Hummel.[18] It would also make the career of Thomas Byrnes, who would become chief of detectives in 1880 and eventually chief of police. In 1878, however, he was a new captain, and a bank in his jurisdiction had just been violated. He dug in and was able to get a lead, probably through an informer, on who was involved. The heist was sophisticated enough that there was a limited pool of suspects, and the cops noticed Shevelin was spending money with a new liberality.

One thing led to another, and in December, Leary was the first to be arrested for the heist. The police were delighted to get their hands on the man who had humiliated them by his brazen escape. "Leary is in the front rank of bank burglars," said one. "I tell you, when that fellow crooks his finger, the other burglars take their seats." The thinking was that if Leary could not get done for the Manhattan job—it all depended on whether Werckle could identify him—Pinkerton could haul him back to Massachusetts for the Northampton one. Leary was in trouble, and he knew it.

But he was not without friends. For some reason, people nicknamed "Red" generally seem to be well-liked, affable sorts. That was certainly true for both Leary and his bride. He had fought bravely for the Union during the Civil War, then migrated to Paris to work as a pickpocket during the 1867 Exposition Universelle. He got caught, escaped jail, and returned to his natural habitat in New York. Red-bearded, red-mustached, and with a bad eye disfigured by some careless dynamite, Leary was a large man for the time—about six feet tall and weighing 200 pounds. With his broad chest and muscle-packed frame, he was considered one of the strongest men in New York.

He had wit and warmth, too. When he had money, he was generous with it; he was loyal to his friends and not too vindictive to his enemies. Kate Leary was also tall, broad, and charismatic; she possessed a "rude culture," according to Frank Moss, a reforming lawyer who couldn't help admiring her, and "delved into esoteric Buddhism."[19] Together, Red John and Red Kate made a magnificent couple.

More important, they had an energy and a charm that drew others to them. They were natural leaders, much admired and trusted among their own kind. One of Kate's best friends (and occasional partner), for example, was Sophie Lyons, an accomplished pickpocket. William Howe had a soft spot for the fair Sophie and wrote a two-part series about her for the *National Police Gazette* in 1897 in which he said, with unmistakable pride, that she "has stolen more money than any other woman in the world."[20]

Lyons would not have disputed the accolade. In her autobiography, written when she was a matronly do-gooder, she titled her younger self "the Queen of the Underworld." Like any queen, she was proud of her ancestry, which featured criminals of note on both sides. Her grandfather, she bragged, "was a cracksmen to whom Scotland Yard took off its cap."[21] Her father, Sam Levy, made his first fortune as a bounty jumper, joining the Union army all over the United States, then moving on. Sophie herself was born in prison (her mother was in for shoplifting) and began in the family profession as a child, being arrested for the first time, she claimed, at age three.[22] Both brothers were pickpockets and her sister was a shoplifter.[23]

Introduced by Marm Mandelbaum, Sophie Levy married burglar Ned Lyons—the wedding must have been a sight—and for a time all went well. Ned helped George Leslie relieve the Ocean Bank of almost $800,000 in 1869, and worked with Johnny Hope (son of Jimmy) to rob the Philadelphia Navy Yard of $150,000.[24] With a substantial nest egg in hand, Ned bought a house on Long Island to settle in for a period of cozy domesticity. Sophie joined in the spirit of things: She got pregnant, giving birth to a son who would take up the family business and die in Auburn Prison. So sad, she mourned, "He was cut off in his promise."

But she was not a woman for whom the delights of suburban bliss could long endure. A criminal both born and made, she missed the action. When her son was a few months old, she began going into New York for a bit of five-finger discounting.[25] One day, she spied a pudding of a jeweler's shop and felt the itch. Flirting outrageously with the smitten clerk, Lyons had abstracted two diamonds and was working on a third when she was caught. Convicted, she went to jail on Blackwell's Island.

Perhaps no place in New York has changed more since Howe & Hummel's time than this cigar-shaped 147-acre topographic eruption in the middle of the East River. When Sophie Lyons took what was known as the "ferry of despair" to Blackwell's, it was the island of the unwanted, home to 7,000 people who occupied grim, convict-built[26] structures for New York's diseased, insane, indigent, and mildly criminal. Renamed Welfare Island in 1921 and then Roosevelt Island in 1973, today it is a pleasant, if bland, middle-class enclave. Only a few ghostly ruins, such as those of the smallpox hospital, exist as reminders that this was once New York's saddest place.

On Blackwell's, Sophie repented her sin of carelessness. Then Ned got nicked, too. Sophie got out first but before long, perhaps because she was out of practice, she was picked up for a botched bit of shoplifting. The upshot was that the couple was reunited, this time at Sing Sing. They both managed to escape—he in 1871, with the help of Red Leary, and she in late 1872—and went back to work.

The next few years were good ones for the Lyons clan, with steady work, no arrests, and three more children. But in 1876, they both got done again. This time, Sophie got out first. Sensing that Ned's best days were behind him, she took up with a better burglar and began to develop her own specialties—con games and artful thieving from banks. When Ned got out, nothing really went right for him. He tried to kill Sophie's lover, but instead caught two bullets himself (resulting in the only known photo of the famous thief, in his hospital bed). He would go to jail a couple more times and died a poor and bitter man.

Sophie, too, spent more time behind bars in the 1880s, but it marred neither her beauty nor her confidence. On each release, she went back to her craft with new energy and imagination—the badger game here, a bit of fraud there.[27] One profitable ploy was to follow the circus through small towns. When the parade came through, bank employees would naturally rush to the door to see it. Meanwhile, Lyons or her faithful sidekick (and lover) Billy Burke would enter through the back and rifle the till.[28] It worked a treat.

In her mid-20s, Lyons had finally learned to read—education had not been a priority chez Levy—and she steadily schooled herself in the finer things so that she could pass for genuine quality. Confident in her acquired gentility, in the late 1880s she went to Paris, and became Madame de Varney, a minor but much-admired ornament to society. That lasted until a nuisance of a gendarme saw her coaxing a watch out of a gentleman's pocket. The expatriate community rallied to her cause, particularly when the chief of police said he suspected her of being Sophie Lyons. *Quel absurdité!*[29] But perhaps Paris was not quite the right venue for her skills anyway. As one colleague said of the French, "If you rob them of anything, they squeal worse than a pen full of pigs."[30] New Yorkers were more sanguine.

The key to Sophie's success was that she was both a proficient technician and a convincing actress. She combined the two skills in a successful stint as a jewel smuggler, perhaps inventing the hollowed-out shoe heel.[31] Picked up for a diamond theft in St. Louis in 1895, and accused of being Sophie Lyons, she retorted, "Sophie Lyons is a hardened criminal, and too smart to be caught like this."[32] The locals were not entirely convinced by this argument, but they escorted her out of town without further ado.

By this time, Lyons realized that the odds were beginning to turn against her. A nice little blackmail went awry for her in late 1894 when a cop spotted her as she was heading to the bank to cash the $20,000 check of the naïve and sentimental gentleman she had traduced.[33] Lyons escaped prosecution, but the incident was emblematic of a larger problem. After more than 20 years of work, she was too well known, and as she got older, it was going to be more difficult to flirt her way out of trouble. Given her record, another conviction would mean doing real time in a manner to which she was no longer accustomed. So in the late 1890s, she turned legit, making another fortune in commercial real estate, marrying Billy Burke, and becoming a society columnist for the *New York World*. She also wrote a series of pamphlets urging criminals to repent and reform, as she said she had.

In 1913 she wrote her winsomely misnamed autobiography, *Why Crime Does Not Pay*. Lyons tried to tell a moral tale, salting the thing with hymns to the honest life. But it only really sings when she is telling of her nefarious deeds, like the time she stole $500,000 in diamonds from an American socialite.[34] That said, it seems likely that Lyons really did go straight; she even used her fortune to fund things like prison libraries and homes for juvenile delinquents.[35] She died in 1924—ironically, at the hands of thieves, who had heard rumors of her wealth. They broke into her home and beat her up so badly that she lived only a few more painful days. Sophie Lyons left an estate of almost $1 million. The "Queen of the Underworld" had done all right.

Was Sophie Lyons's good friend and fellow traveler in the Mandelbaum troupe, Red Leary, part of the Manhattan Savings crew? It's not clear. It was certainly his kind of thing, and he knew everyone who was. But there was no hard evidence, as even the police had to concede. When the janitor, Louis Werckle, was unable to identify him, Leary walked.

Things might have been different if the cops had played their hand more deliberately. By picking up Leary so quickly, they did not have their best card to play—the watchman, Patrick Shevelin, who turned informant and spent the next year testifying against his former partners in crime. Largely on Shevelin's say, three men were convicted of the Manhattan Savings job; others who were suspected of involvement but who had been fortunate enough not to come face-to-face with the faithless watchman won acquittals. One of these, Johnny Dobbs, took a hiatus from direct criminal work, using his earnings to buy a saloon a few doors away from a police station. Some questioned his location, considering that he was counting on his criminal fraternity brothers to be regular clients. Would they want to spend their leisure hours so close to the cops? Dobbs, however, knew what he was about: "The nearer to church, the closer to God," he replied.[36] The saloon thrived.

There was one only one man whom Shevelin specifically accused, and who got off anyway. He was a policeman, John Nugent—and his lawyers were Howe & Hummel.

The evidence against Nugent looked strong. Shevelin said that Nugent had been recruited to act as a "crow" or watcher outside the bank while the burglars toiled inside; Nugent later told Shevelin that he had carried away the swag, "and oh, what a pile of stuff it was!" A bartender, Patrick Ryan, said that he had seen Nugent in the company of two of the burglars and had heard that remark. A bystander testified that he had seen Nugent lingering outside the bank, wearing an eye patch, during the crucial hours. And then there was Nugent's interesting record. Joining the police force in 1872 after a short career as a gambler, he was charged with burglary in 1875 (acquitted); accused of robbery in 1876 (never charged); promoted the same year for his heroism in rescuing several people from a fire; suspected of another burglary in 1877 (never charged); accused of writing abusive anonymous letters about his captain (convicted), and demoted in 1878.[37] In addition, he had been fined 11 times for neglect of duty.[38]

Indicted in June, Nugent did not come to trial for seven months. Howe prepared two lines of defense, the first audacious and the second less so. Line number one was to ridicule the prosecution. He tried to shred Shevelin, who by this time was such an experienced witness that he was stirred but not shaken, even as Howe forced him to admit to acquaintance with criminal after criminal. Ryan, a bartender with a past, also caught the rough edge of Big Bill's tongue. "It would be manifestly unsafe," Howe argued, "to convict Nugent on the evidence of self-confessed criminals like Shevelin and Ryan." But then, this was a case notable for a complete absence of innocents—except perhaps Nugent's infant son, who did his job well, looking cute and vulnerable.

On to the second line: It was all a "foul conspiracy" to convict an innocent man. Besides, Nugent had an alibi for the night in question. Cue a Brooklyn florist, Andrew Lyon, who said he had seen the prisoner sick in bed the night of the burglary. Nugent's sister-in-law, Maggie Mulligan, agreed. Finally, a cop named James Goldrick said he had run into Nugent during the time the robbery was taking place; Nugent had said he was on his way to the doctor. Well, maybe. But the stories of Lyon and Mulligan didn't fit, and Goldrick was forced to admit that he had recently received a letter from Nugent. The prosecutor was decidedly suspicious: "Is it not true, Officer," he charged Goldrick, "that you have done all the running around in putting up this alibi?"

Howe was shocked and appalled: His witnesses, he proclaimed, with some justice, "were just as respectable as those of the prosecution or Captain Byrnes." The dozens of rakes in the gallery who knew Byrnes rather too well cheered the sally. Nugent, though, was depressed. The jury wasn't buying it, he told his wife: "Tomorrow will wind me up. They snickered at her [Mulligan] as she gave her evidence."

Nugent was right to be pessimistic. At the first ballot, the papers reported that the jury voted seven to five for conviction. How could they know? Because the partitions to the jury room were usefully thin; court officers could overhear the proceedings without strain and pass on such nuggets.[39] But then things stuck. The judge ordered the twelve to be locked up all night. Exhausted, at 11:00 the following morning, they delivered the verdict: "Not guilty."

Silence in the court. Astonished, astounded, stunned, incredulous silence. And then cheers from the peanut gallery. Stilling the rabble, the judge addressed Nugent: "I have sat on this bench now for over a year, and this is the first time justice has, in my opinion, miscarried in that time. I believe you a guilty man." He went on to deliver a prim lecture about breach of trust and all that. Nugent listened with manifest indifference. Turning to the jury, he thanked them and blasted the "manufactured evidence I have had to contend against." Then he picked up wife, mother, and child and walked out a free man. At Howe's suggestion, that afternoon he went to his precinct house, reporting for duty. He also wanted his back pay. Nugent eventually got the money, but he lost his job.[40]

It was a great victory for Howe, but not one he particularly enjoyed. Nugent had kept interrupting him and offering suggestions and generally being a pest. In 1883, Nugent and two allies were caught trying to relieve the cashier of a New Jersey bank of a satchel containing $12,000 as he sat in a train. Despite being clubbed with a lead pipe, the cashier clung to the money. When the trio fled, the entire train pursued. After a chase that featured random gunshots (from both sides), a wild horse, and a foot race, all three men were caught. Howe did not represent Nugent, who got ten years for highway robbery.[41]

. . .

As for Leary, getting out from under the Manhattan Savings charge was a start, but Robert Pinkerton was right there to take him back to Massachusetts for the Northampton job. Not so fast, argued his lawyer—who was, naturally, from Howe & Hummel.[42] Show me a writ of habeas corpus. Pinkerton did not have one, so instead of a quick trip to Northampton, Leary went back to the Ludlow Street Jail. Not without incident: A gang of 15 men tried to storm the posse leading him to the carriage in which he was to be transported. Pinkerton and the guards beat them back. In a pause in the action, Pinkerton established a position on the top step and cried out, "Gentlemen, I'll shoot the first man that comes an inch this way." Then he cocked his gun and leveled it at the leader of the pack. Leary had many friends, but being shot at point-blank range—and no one doubted that Pinkerton would do exactly what he threatened—was testing affection too far. They paused, and Leary was hustled back inside the courthouse. Pinkerton relished the chance to get in the last word. "Next time you put up a job to beat me out of my prisoner, put it up better," he told the throng. "I'll take him with me, dead or alive."

When the writ came through a few days later, Howe & Hummel disputed it. The man named in the writ was not their John Leary; it must have referred to some other six-foot, red-bearded professional burglar with a bad eye. Besides, the governor of Massachusetts lacked the authority to issue an extradition warrant. Pinkerton defended the warrant and swore it was the right Leary, but it was not to be that easy. There would be months of legal wrangling over these issues. Delay, delay, delay—something might come up—was a key Howe & Hummel precept.

In the meantime, Leary lived quietly at Ludlow Street, on excellent terms with the keepers. For a burglar, he was a nice bloke, they thought, and they cut him considerable slack. He was allowed to stay out of his cell all day, to walk anywhere in the jail, and to entertain visitors freely. He even had his dog for company.

Leary's geniality was an end to a means, which became clear on the evening of May 7, 1879. The wall on the north side of the jail abutted a new five-story tenement building at 76 Ludlow Street. Noticing this,

Red Kate saw the possibilities. She rented rooms on the top floor of the tenement, and moved in a few bits of furniture as if she intended to live there. A few days later a couple of men joined her; tongues wagged that they were not seen to leave. Well, they were busy.

The men cut a hole through the fireplace in the hall bedroom of Red Kate's new home. They worked meticulously, using drills to make the first break, then special tools to quietly scrape out the mortar between and behind the bricks. These were removed and hidden. Once they got through the tenement walls, they had access to the wall of the third-floor toilet at Ludlow Street Jail. With mallets padded for quiet, they went to work. When they were about halfway through, they slipped in a thin steel probe. This served as notice to Leary that the tunnelers were getting close.

On May 7, Leary had a long visit with Red Kate and his friend Butch McCarthy. They left around 8:00 that evening,[43] taking the dog with them. Leary commenced his nightly constitutional; around 9:15 he wandered into the bathroom, as he had done for months. This evening, though, he punched through the single line of bricks remaining. Then his friends on the other end threaded a rope through the opening; Leary looped this around himself, squeezed into the hole, and was pulled through to the fifth-floor apartment, where he dusted himself off and greeted his pals. They left the equipment behind—everything from the rope to leather gloves to pillows to pepper to toss at any intruder— and walked out, locking the door behind them to delay the inevitable pursuit. When the Ludlow guards came by Leary's cell for the 10:30 bed check, he was gone.[44]

The escape was a sensation but, not for the first time, the Ludlow Street staff proved impervious to embarrassment.[45] It was no one's fault, the sheriff said; the tenement never should have been built. The fact that the jail was so loosely run that there was a saloon on the premises was not the problem at all.[46] The next day, many of the Ludlow Street residents were allowed to take a look at Leary's bolthole. One of them decided to explore it further, to see if there was anything worth stealing in the apartment. He came back of his own accord, but the mind boggles at the fact that the hole was simply left open for jailbirds to appreciate at their leisure.[47] Meanwhile, the caretakers of the tenement made a nice bit on the side, charging 10-cent admission to see the famous hole in the wall, before the city blocked it up again, with a layer of iron to prevent a repeat performance.[48]

No one at Ludlow Street was punished or even reprimanded for allowing yet another burglar to escape. The unstated assumption was that lowly guards could not be expected to match wits with these aristocrats of crime. Robert Pinkerton saw it differently. Now two members of the Northampton gang—Connors and Leary—had gone absent without leave from Ludlow. The detective suspected collusion but could prove nothing. "If you ask me no questions, I'll tell you no lies," was Red Kate's tart response to the sheriff's request for information. She lived a quiet life, and kept her sense of humor, adorning her daughter's coat with buttons in the shape of keys.[49] Leary was not heard from for 21 months; he had escaped overseas, living mostly in London. But New York was where he belonged, and he returned in early 1881. On February 4, Pinkerton arrested him.

It was a curiously restrained affair. Leary was riding in a sleigh in Brooklyn when one of Pinkerton's men jumped out, grabbed the horse, and ordered him down. To which Leary is said to have replied cheerfully, "All right Bob, I give up." Such deference to authority was out of character. "There is some reason to believe," noted the *Times* dryly, that the incident "was not very much of a surprise to him."[50] Leary certainly didn't seem at all bothered that his liberty was threatened. At the Brooklyn police station, he compared the officers to Britain's elite Coldstream Guards, joked that it was quite a "surprise party" that stopped his sleigh jaunt, and asserted that Ludlow Street was like being "locked in a hardware store" because it was so easy to get out.[51]

Taken to court, Leary said he was more than happy to accompany Pinkerton to Northampton, "and if you have no objection, I'll bid you good day, Judge." After the judge agreed, Pinkerton and Leary, apparently the best of friends, went to a saloon and had wine and cigars. Leaving that place of refreshment, they climbed into a carriage and headed to New York. Leary was not handcuffed, no doubt the better to buy more drinks at more saloons. A boozy air of bonhomie accompanied the unlikely couple on the train to Northampton. By a marvelous coincidence, Billy Connors was arrested the same day in Philadelphia.

A month later, a Massachusetts grand jury refused to indict Leary, Connors, or a third gang member, Thomas "Shang" Draper. And yes, the bank got back most of the securities at about the same time. The deal did no good for Dunlap and Scott, though, who were already locked up. Dunlap served his whole sentence, minus time off for good behavior, and Scott died in prison. It was certainly a case in which justice delayed meant that equal justice was denied. Had Scott and Dunlap been able to stay free longer, they too might have been able to work out a deal. But they didn't, so they paid the price while their associates got paid off.

No one, except Scott's widow, who was understandably bitter, was heard to complain. The depositors got most of their paper back; the Pinkertons notched up another success; and Leary kept enough of the proceeds to live quietly and arrest-free for the next several years. Then in April 1888, after a night of drinking, one of his companions, a con man named Billy Train, heaved a brick, shouting, "Look out for your heads, boys!" Or maybe they were having a fight over dividing some swag. The fatal brick didn't care: It hit Leary on the back of his head, and he went down. He died a few days later. Train was charged but acquitted, the jury ruling that it was an accident. That might have been true. Train and Leary were old friends. The story goes that young Billy even provided the wedding breakfast for the Learys by mugging a man and spending the proceeds on chicken and champagne.[52]

The corner of Clinton and Rivington is relevant to all these stories, because that was the nerve center for Marm Mandelbaum's operations as the city's most prominent receiver of stolen goods. More than that, though, 79 Clinton was a criminal salon. Weighing in at something like 250 pounds, Marm obviously believed in keeping a good table, and with the pick of a great deal of stolen furniture, her rooms were elegant. But the biggest appeal was the company—all the really good crooks, plus, she averred, "the department boys in blue and yes, yes, judges and others."[53]

For a time, Marm also ran a school for promising young sneak thieves. "I hadda give it up," she told Nell Kimball ruefully. "One day who sashays in but the son of the highest police guy, and asking me for lessons."[54]

Sophie Lyons, who was neither humble nor stupid, called Marm Mandelbaum "the greatest crime promoter of modern times."[55] Everyone who was anyone in the criminal world yearned for a seat at the Mandelbaum table. Consider the following connections:

- Billy Connors, the colleague of Red Leary who walked out of Ludlow Street Jail, was a regular diner chez Mandelbaum. So were Butch McCarthy, who helped tunnel Leary out of prison, and Billy Train, who brained Leary with a brick.
- One of the men arrested with ex-cop John Nugent for the highway robbery attempt was Banjo Pete. He was part of the Leslie/Mandelbaum crew.
- She also did business with Johnny Irving and Billy Porter, burglars and close friends who were widely suspected of being involved in Leslie's death. They both favored the saloon owned by Shang Draper, which he had bought with the earnings from the Manhattan Savings job. In October 1883, Draper's dive was the site of a gunfight between Irving and John Walsh, another burglar. Porter was also armed and in the vicinity. The sequence of events is unclear, but the results were unambiguous: Irving and Walsh dead, revolvers at their sides, their bodies making an L, their feet almost touching in deathly intimacy. How incestuous was the criminal elite at this time? Well, Red Leary was eating oysters next door when the shooting occurred; the bartender on duty when Irving rushed in was Harry Hope—son of Jimmy, brother of Johnny. And the attorney for Porter, when he was eventually charged with first-degree murder? William Howe, of course. The verdict: not guilty.[56]
- Another of Marm Mandelbaum's clients was "Black Lena" Kleinschmidt, who was in the same league as Red Kate and Sophie Lyons as an artful female dodger. In middle age, Black Lena decided it was time for a more conventional existence. She moved to Hackensack, New Jersey, and bought local popularity by hosting excellent parties. She financed her

life as a respectable matron by commuting into New York a couple of days a week to steal. This satisfactory life came to a crashing halt when she wore a stolen jewel to a neighborhood soiree—and the original owner recognized it. "It just goes to show," sniffed Marm, "that it takes brains to be a real lady."[57]

- Marm Mandelbaum guided the professional development of "Piano Charley" Bullard, a gifted musician who was born to wealth but not wise about it. Once he drank his way through his inheritance, he worked as a butcher. But that was a lot of work. So he dabbled in highway robbery instead; he was once being sprung from prison by Billy Forrester, the burglar who probably murdered Benjamin Nathan.[58] Bullard found his true vocation in more sophisticated crime as the lifelong partner of . . .

- Adam Worth, one of Mandelbaum's favorites. The regard was mutual. Like Marm, Worth favored guile over brawn, with a pinch of élan. But he got nabbed in 1869 during an ambitious effort to rob the cash box off an express wagon, his only U.S. arrest. He did a little time in Sing Sing before escaping (truly, it begins to seem those who didn't leave that alleged fortress simply lacked ambition). Partnering with Piano Charlie to tunnel into Boston's Boylston Bank in 1869, he exited with $1 million in cash and securities. Worth dropped the securities off (possibly with Howe & Hummel),[59] then shipped out to Europe.

Worth's most famous job there was the theft of Thomas Gainsborough's portrait of the Duchess of Devonshire from a London art gallery in 1876. Then the unexpected happened. Worth fell in love with the painting; he couldn't bear to part with the canvas, often tucking it under his bed. In 1901, worn down by age, a tough stint in a Belgian jail, the insanity of his wife, and the relentless pursuit of the Pinkertons, he sold the Duchess back to the gallery for $25,000. (J. P. Morgan then bought it.) A year later, separated forever from his beloved Duchess, Adam Worth died. But he had at least reconciled with his children—one of whom became a Pinkerton agent.

. . .

A woman of Marm's profession obviously needed legal counsel. She chose Howe & Hummel, reportedly paying a retainer of $5,000 a year.[60] The firm would help any small fry who were careless enough to get arrested and pay off police clerks to lose paperwork. The main job was to keep Marm out of trouble. The partners did their work well. The evidence for this is the absence of evidence: From 1862–1884, the most famous fence in New York was never charged with a crime.

Mandelbaum came to the United States from Germany in 1850 and started out as a peddler.[61] She prospered—by 1873, she reported a net worth of $5,000[62]—and began to operate out of a dry goods store, which did a less than roaring business. She lived above the shop, but the real work took place in the back, where pickpockets, burglars, and shoplifters would bring their bounty. Silks were a particular specialty. Over time, Marm made her business less conspicuous; she would instead have the goods taken to various warehouses or off-site premises,[63] where she would dicker over the merchandise and have her staff remove any telltale marks. Sometimes she would conduct business through third parties or by letter, creating a degree of separation from the criminal transaction.

Mandelbaum was not, by any conventional standard, a woman who would draw admiring attention. Besides unusual height—almost six feet—and girth, she had small, close-set eyes, a massive nose, fat cheeks, bushy brows, thick lips and a pointed chin.[64] In the image of her that all the papers used, she wore a bonnet, adorned with black ostrich feathers, of astonishing ugliness. Still, something about Fredericka pleased one Wolf Mandelbaum, who married her and then had the wisdom to retreat to her substantial shadow. "He reminded me," remembered Nell Kimball, "of the talk about a whorehouse piano player who was 'so dumb he didn't know what they did upstairs.' "[65] He died in 1875.

Criminals of every ilk knew about Mandelbaum's operations; as early as 1871, she fenced a good deal of the loot from the Chicago Fire. But her renown went beyond simply being known. She was a tough bargainer, but an honest one: she was "honorable and reliable among the businessmen with whom she had a professional relationship," was the assessment of a local German-language newspaper. "Her word was good as gold."[66]

Autocratic but generous, she enjoyed, according to Harry Hill, a dive keeper (and Howe & Hummel client) on the periphery of the criminal element, "the perfect confidence of every thief."[67] She was quick to bail out a friend or client, purchase an alibi, or send Howe & Hummel. These were not charitable contributions; she expected to be repaid, with interest.[68] But the service was an essential one. Police Chief Walling called her establishment the "Bureau for the Prevention of Conviction."

Mandelbaum operated so long and in such a variety of ways that her fame spread well beyond the circle of criminals that comprised her extended family. To call her business an open secret is wrong because it was no secret at all. From 1862, when she made a rare appearance in the police records, to 1884, she handled as much as $10 million in stolen goods.[69] Estimates of her personal fortune start at $500,000.[70]

How could she get away with it? For a start, the Mandelbaum business was not strictly among criminals; she frequently sold the goods on to more or less legitimate retailers. Typically, she would pay about 20 percent of value;[71] even when she added a substantial markup, her buyers, who ranged from as far away as Cincinnati, Canada, and Mexico,[72] still got a discount.[73] If stolen goods were traced to an establishment—and the cops had a pretty good idea of the secondary market—the usual recourse was to negotiate a price to sell them to the original supplier. That created an unvirtuous circle, in which police, retailers, thieves, and fences all got a piece of the action.[74]

In addition, while the law was not exactly on the side of the fences, it might as well have been, because it was so difficult to get a conviction. The prosecution not only had to prove that the property in question was stolen, but that the receiver knew it to be so. Even if an accomplice squealed, that was not enough; the evidence had to be corroborated by a third party. No wonder Mandelbaum and her colleagues operated with confidence. Only the original purchasers suffered, either swallowing the loss or paying twice for the same goods.[75] Considering the legal and practical obstacles lined up against them, they shrugged it off as a tax on doing business in New York.

• • •

Boston was the home not only of the bean and the cod, but of a class of merchants less willing to grin and bear it. In early 1884, one of them, James Scott, brought a civil suit in New York against Marm Mandelbaum, alleging that she had knowingly received and then sold the fruits of a burglary at his store in 1877. Three burglars were involved, according to the suit. Two of them, including George Leslie, were dead; but the third, "Sheeny" Mike Kurtz, was picked up, convicted, and then induced to blab. After being released from prison on grounds of ill health, he signed an affidavit that stated that he had sold the goods—2,000 yards of silk and 20 cashmere shawls—to Marm for $1,000. Kurtz could not be found to testify at the trial—with good reason, for he might have preferred to avoid the glowering looks of Marm's friends, including Red Leary, who filled the back rows of the courtroom.[76]

But another minor character, James Hoey, was on hand. He was once a close friend of Mandelbaum's, he told the court, and had discussed the transaction at length with her. She definitely knew that the goods were stolen and had supervised the removal of identifying marks. The jury was persuaded, ordering Mandelbaum to pay $6,660 in costs and interest. It was the first time since 1862 that Marm had had to defend herself, and the first time she lost.

Let us establish here, once and forever, that, as Thomas Byrnes was wont to say, there was no honor among thieves. Sheeny Mike had dished on Mandelbaum; later, he would do the same to Billy Porter. Sophie Lyons was accused of peaching on her colleagues in Europe and got done in later in her career by another informer. Johnny Irving went after John Walsh because he thought Walsh had squealed. Irving himself turned in some colleagues in a bonded warehouse robbery. James Hoey testified against Marm in the Boston case; his wife Molly would later do the same—and would be pardoned by New York governor Grover Cleveland for her help. As for Marm, according to an assistant district attorney, she was willing to turn in some underlings to the police in exchange for the quiet life she certainly enjoyed.[77] No less than in other forms of capitalism, self-preservation was the golden rule for the business of crime. Romantics need not apply.

"I am glad that for once the old lady has been outwitted and made to suffer for her violation of the law," remarked Chief Walling of the successful civil prosecution. But the comment still begged the question of why a Boston merchant acting on a Boston burglary had succeeded in New York where Gotham had failed for decades. Sure, Kurtz and Hoey had been persuaded to testify against Marm, but couldn't New York have exerted such pressure? Walling and Byrnes both insisted that despite unwavering and determined efforts, the law just hadn't been able to get the goods on her. There might have been a more sinister reason—"that her intimacy with the detectives of the police force was only less close and confidential than her intimacy with the thieves," as the *Times* charged.[78]

Mandelbaum's victims—chiefly wholesale dealers and department stores—came away from the case with a new perspective. They began to believe that they could get a conviction if they could get the evidence. But the New York cops were not going to get that evidence. District Attorney Peter Olney, who had his own issues with the police, agreed with that assessment. Together, they agreed on a plan: Call in the Pinkertons.

It took five months for the famous private eyes to do what New York's Finest had been unable to do for almost a quarter of a century. Robert Pinkerton gave $1,000 in capital to an operative named Gustav Frank, a German immigrant who had once worked in a dry goods store. His task was to infiltrate the operation. First, Frank underwent an intense tutorial with silk buyers, who drilled him on prices, quality, and other basics of the business. Then he and a number of other Pinkertonians rented rooms in New Israel, and spent a month watching 79 Clinton. Their most important conclusion was that Mandelbaum was both careful and popular. The neighborhood looked out for her, reporting the presence of police or suspicious strangers. So they took their time and blended in.

With an idea of how the place worked, Frank was ready to bluff his way in. Every business needs customers; he would use his $1,000 stake to become one. Calling himself Stein, in March 1884, Frank went to Marm's store, introduced himself as a friend of an unnamed (and unavailable) crook, and said he wanted to buy silks—cheap silks, really cheap. Perhaps he winked. Marm sent him away. He came back again and again. She tested him, citing outrageous prices. He spurned her, showing a keen grasp of the business. Finally, he was allowed to buy a few rolls. When these disappeared without repercussions, the ice broke. Frank/Stein then revealed what already was obvious to Marm, her son Julius, and her associate, Herman Stoude. He was a crook, he told them, and he wanted to buy stolen goods that he would sell on his own terms.

On June 16, 1884, they decided to give this nice German a try, selling him a roll of stolen silk; Frank promptly took it to the Pinkerton offices. Examined, it showed the private mark of a dealer named Simpson, Crawford & Simpson. (The major silk merchants had agreed to create new, hard-to-find marks to allow the goods to be identified.) Less than a week later, Frank/Stein purchased more Simpson silk, plus a roll from James A. Hearn & Son, also marked. "Don't sell this piece in New York," Mandelbaum told her new friend, "because it came from one of the big stores here." Over a period of three months, Frank/Stein bought some 12,000 yards of silk. Other Pinkerton detectives were able to trace back much of that, via the hidden marks, to the original owners. The unidentifiable, unmarked silks were sold via auction; Pinkerton actually made a profit on this part of the operation.

On the basis of this evidence, the Pinkertons applied to Justice Henry Murray of the Harlem Police Court, almost a dozen miles away on the other end of Manhattan, for a warrant for Marm's arrest. As the geography suggests, the choice was a deliberate one. Murray had made a stir six months earlier for some notably caustic comments about the police force. "Police affairs in this City were never more rotten than at present,"[79] he charged in private comments that became public. Pressed to clarify, he was happy to. "Vice flaunts defiance in the public eye, and it could not become such a shame to the city if no dues were paid for its protection." Who was doing the protecting? Murray would not name names, but he did point out that "[Police] Captains upon a salary of $2,000 a year live extravagantly and become rich."[80]

Of course, the police courts were no models of justice, either. Political appointees all, the judges were not required to have any legal training. As the fictional Artemis Quibble observed, any student who believed a career on the bench "is lighted by the midnight oil of study, let him disabuse himself of that idea, but seek rather the district leader."[81] The

CHARLES H. PARKHURST, D.D.

WILLIAM TRAVERS JEROME

DE LANCEY NICOLL

ABRAHAM HUMMEL

Images from an era: George Train (LOWER RIGHT, FACING PAGE), the man
who might have inspired Jules Verne's *Around the World in Eighty Days*,
was a disgruntled Howe & Hummel client. The other men on these pag
were disgruntled opponents. Charles Parkhurst and Anthony Comstoc

THE DAILY
AN ILLUSTRATED EVENING
VOL. 1—NO. 74.
NEW YORK, WEDNESDAY, MAY 28,

GRAPHIC STATUES, NO. 15—A THREE-DECKER AND TENDER.

REV.

Big, bluff Bill Howe and short, savvy Abe Hummel (LOW
were irresistible fodder for New York cartoonists. (New York
Library)

WILLIAM FREDERICK HOWE

THOMAS BYRNES

ANTHONY COMSTOCK

GEORGE FRANCIS TRAIN

were anti-vice campaigners; William Jerome and DeLancy Nicoll were prosecutors; and Thomas Byrnes, an earnest practitioner of the third-degree who retired rich, was one of New York's most famous cops. (*Notable New Yorkers of 1896–1899*, by Moses King, 1889)

READING-ROOM IN LUDLOW STREET JAIL.

EXTERIOR OF LUDLOW STREET JAIL.

The Tombs (TOP), conveniently located across the street from Howe &
Hummel's office, was the country's most famous jail. Designed in imitation
of an Egyptian mausoleum, this building lasted from 1838–1902.
The Tombs was dark, dank, and unwholesome, but there was also an
improbable sociability to the place, with prisoners and vendors wandering
about during the day. The Ludlow Street jail (BOTTOM), where Boss Tweed
and Victoria Woodhull spent far more time than they would have liked,
was for county prisoners. It was also a social kind of place (LOWER LEFT), so
much so that it earned the nickname "Hotel Ludlow." (New York Public Library)

THE FORMER OFFICES OF HOWE & HUMMEL, CENTER AND LEONARD

Howe and Hummel were so famous that their offices were sometimes a stop on tours of the city. This is a rare and possibly unique photo of the premises. Tough and sometimes fair Recorder Smyth (ON THE BENCH, BOTTOM) presides over a day in court in this illustration. Bill Howe can be seen standing to the left. (New York Public Library)

WESLY ALLEN,
ALIAS WES ALLEN,
PICKPOCKET AND BURGLAR.

SOPHIE LYONS,
ALIAS LEVY,
PICKPOCKET AND BLACKMAILER.

LENA KLEINSCHMIDT,
ALIAS RICE and BLACK LENA,
SHOP LIFTER.

MICHAEL KURTZ,
ALIAS SHEENY MIKE,
BURGLAR.

BILLY FORRESTER,
ALIAS CONRAD FOLTZ,
BURGLAR AND SNEAK.

JOHN HOPE,
ALIAS WATSON,
MANHATTAN BANK BURGLAR.

Members of the Mandelbaum salon: All the best crooks knew Fredericka "Marm" Mandelbaum (FAR RIGHT, FACING PAGE), and did business with her. Wes Allen (TOP LEFT) ran a notorious downtown dive; Sophie Lyons was an esteemed con woman; Lena Kleinschmidt a pickpocket with pretensions; and Billy Forrester a burglar who might have committed one of the great murders of the era, the killing of financier Benjamin Nathan. The rest were bank burglars and sneak thieves. (*Professional Criminals of America*, by Thomas Byrnes, 1884)

JOHN IRVING,
ALIAS OLD JACK.
BURGLAR.

JAMES HOPE,
ALIAS OLD MAN HOPE,

A German immigrant who combined
a maternal sensibility with a shrewd
criminal instinct, Marm Mandelbaum was
the premier female crook of the era. Over
the course of her career, she handled an
estimated $10 million in stolen goods.
(New York Public Library)

Abe Hummel had the country's biggest and most sophisticated theatrical practice. Among his clients were Little Egypt (TOP LEFT), who brought the coochee-coochee to New York; Lillian Russell (TOP RIGHT), whose various marriages and contract disputes were a steady earner for the partnership; and Olga Nethersole (BOTTOM), the British actress whose production of the play *Sapho* became a cause célèbre. (New York Public Library)

police court judges worked part-time for a generous salary of $8,000 a year and were notoriously arbitrary in their rulings.

Murray was, however, serious about justice and therefore a good bet to allow the Pinkertons to skip the police and to make arrests themselves. On July 22, 1884, they did just that. Warrant in hand, the detectives searched 79 Clinton, taking away more stolen silks. They also got into the family safe, where they were startled to find a veritable museum of jewelry—"diamonds as big as peas," according to Pinkerton, "bracelets with rare stone settings, heaps of gold watches, chains, rings, scarf pins. . . ." Then they arrested the Mandelbaums, mother and son, as well as Herman Stoude. As the agents and their charges took the tram uptown to Murray's court, Frank/Stein revealed his true identify to Marm. In reply, she punched him in the face, shouting, "You wretch, you!"

But his boss, Robert Pinkerton, was pleased. His men had caught a big one. There might have been another source of satisfaction. Byrnes's success in cleaning up Wall Street had cut into the agency's business there; showing the police up so blatantly had to feel good.[82] But mostly, Pinkerton was proud to catch a thief whom he regarded with something like wonder. He would later describe Marm's operations this way:

All the noted thieves—burglars, sneak thieves, shoplifters, second-story climbers—have been connected with her at one time or another—that is, all first-class thieves in their special branches. Whenever thieves wanted ready money, they applied to her, for she always had it. She had rooms for storing goods in New York, Brooklyn, Hoboken, Passaic and other towns. Often she would pay the rent of an entire flat for a man and wife to have the use of one or two rooms. Many women whose husbands were serving terms in prison for burglaries were secured to occupy these places.[83]

To the police, the case was a painful embarrassment. The private arrest of the famous fence was, as the *World* put it, "the most effective snub which the municipal police have probably ever received. It shows that the District Attorney had no confidence in them." The fact that private agents had made a case, brought charges, and then actually arrested the trio, was highly unusual—in fact, unusual enough that it might just provide a defense. Mandelbaum called her lawyers.

It's impossible to know if Howe matched his attire to the stature of a case; the papers did not report every minor engagement. What can be said is that when the stakes were big, he dressed big. And though the proceedings in the Harlem Police Court were only to decide whether Mandelbaum should be brought to trial, the fact that the woman was in any kind of court made it a big deal. Here is how Howe's favorite paper, the *New York Herald,* described him in all his sartorial glory:

> He wore a big white vest and a rolling collar. In his collar button was a large diamond and another diamond was set in a massive cravat ring, below which was a diamond stud as big as a hazelnut. From a ponderous gold chain depended a huge gold locket set with diamonds. The third finger of his right hand was encircled by a ring in which were set nine very large diamonds and a Masonic ring set with diamonds adorned his left hand. From his cuffs hung two enormous solid gold handcuffs. A sky blue umbrella leaned against his dovecolored lapels. The lawyer blazed and twinkled and sparkled from head to foot with jeweled splendor.

The proceedings didn't take long. Murray heard enough during the bail discussion on July 23 to decide he wanted to hear more. So he set a date for further testimony, and then assigned bail—$10,000 for Marm, $5,000 each for the others. Volubly incredulous at what he called the "simply tremendous" sum, Howe hinted at a possible defense. Marm had never even been indicted before, but here she was in jail not "upon the evidence of the police, but upon the word of a detective about whom there are rumors that he was her accomplice." As for Julius, receiving stolen goods was not an offense; there had to be guilty knowledge, and the poor boy was just doing as Mama asked, as any son would. Julius was 24, the prosecution noted, hardly a boy. "Why, you're a boy," retorted Howe, "an old boy."

Murray appeared amused at the antics of the bejeweled behemoth, but nevertheless declined to release the prisoners, lower their bail, or allow Marm Mandelbaum to pay it. Howe was impatient: "She is as good bail as ever you took," he told the uncooperative jurist. "She will never disappear, rest assured, till her case is disposed of." Eventually, everyone got bailed, but it was clear that this case would not die an easy death in Murray's court.

The testimony so far, Pinkerton's cagey but pointed remarks to the press, and the timely leak of an affidavit from a Leary associate named Molly Hoey, all pointed to something more than police incompetence. Miss Molly, then resident at Blackwell's Island on a pickpocketing charge (but shortly to be pardoned),[84] said that a detective sergeant named Dusenbury was "almost a daily visitor" to 79 Clinton Street, even guarding the movement of stolen goods. On one occasion, Dusenbury said that his wife required some good black silk. Molly Hoey, chagrined, had to admit she had nothing of that kind on hand.

"You must get it," said the detective.

"We can't except by stealing it."

"I don't care how you get it, but I must have it."

He got it.

There was more, much more, along these lines, leading to a dandy snit between the Detective Bureau and the DA's office. The DA's men said that the police force was full of rotten apples; the cops fired back that the DA's office was packed with political cronies. We couldn't trust the cops to get Mandelbaum, zinged DA Olney; you just don't like me, retorted Byrnes. Probably, said Olney, because you're "trashy." So's your mother, snapped Byrnes. This is not an exact transcript, but that was the gist of this very public, very nasty fight. Wisely, the two sides stopped after a couple of such free and frank exchanges of views. No good to their reputations could come of this circular firing squad. They needed each other.

Beginning on July 28, the testimony took two full days. This was astonishing. The city's seven police courts were responsible for minor cases—drunkenness, vagrancy, unlicensed vending, and the like. There was no jury, and though defendants had the right to appeal, few did. Due process rarely peeked out from the bench. Typically, a queue would form in the morning. When the judge arrived, he would call up the first defendant in line, ask a few questions of cop and prisoner, make a decision, and move on to the next. After a couple of hours of this, there would be a break for lunch, then the process would be resumed for another few hours in the afternoon.

Given the volume of cases, multitasking was common. Judges might be hearing evidence, signing over a prisoner to jail, and tossing off vulgar comments pretty much simultaneously—all this in a room crowded with the ill-behaved, and often drunk, effluvia of urban life.[85]

A typical case was an exercise in summary, and exceedingly swift, justice—often decided in less than five minutes.[86] If the judge did not get to the end of the line, the prisoners would be returned for another uncomfortable night in the Tombs. Since it was legal to arrest on suspicion, many an innocent spent days waiting for his four minutes in court. Pity the cops, too. If they were not present with whomever they arrested, the charge would be dismissed. That meant coming in even during their off-hours, which were erratic.[87]

In this context, Mandelbaum's two-day trial was an eternity. The question at hand was whether the case was strong enough, and serious enough, to be transferred to the Court of General Sessions, which heard felonies. Murray was in no rush to make a decision; the case was a treat compared to his usual lineup of pathetic nonentities.

Gustav Frank started things off, telling of his different transactions, particularly his dealings with Herman Stoude. Business was not so good these days, the assistant had told him. The civil suit had made Marm cautious: "Burned children shy the fire." But no, Stoude had never done anything illegal in Frank's presence, or told him the silks were stolen. If that was the case, Howe argued, why is Stoude in court? "Law is just like laudanum," he said, obscurely. "It is far more easy to use it as a quack than apply it as a physician." Justice Murray declined to take the hint. Stoude was Marm's confidential clerk, which provided more than enough reason to keep him around. When it was Stoude's time to be heard, he told the court that he had been employed as a jack-of-all-trades for the last six years, cleaning, dusting, and delivering goods. He was paid $8 a week and had no knowledge of any stolen goods.

On that testimony, Howe heaved himself to his hind legs[88] and suggested that since, yet again, no one knew anything, surely Mrs. Mandelbaum could be released. The request was sheer impudence and was never going to be granted. But Howe used it to make what were, in fact, serious arguments. To wit: Where was the proof that anyone knew the silks were stolen? Even Gustav Frank had said he didn't know if the silks he bought were legit. How could it be assumed that Marm knew? So where was the larceny? Motion denied.

Then, in the guise of questioning Gustav Frank—whom he derided as a "paid spy, a professional witness"—concerning how he went about his business, Howe ventured into delicate territory. The temper tantrums between the detectives and the DA's office were all over the papers. Howe sought to show that the prosecution of this hardworking widow was really a political stitch-up. "Were you ever told," he asked Frank, "that it was necessary to get Mrs. Mandelbaum arrested in order that Inspector Byrnes and the Police Commissioners might be attacked?"

The question was a Howe & Hummel special—introducing an idea for which there was no foundation but that was unfavorable to the prosecution. It was an attempt to create reasonable doubt, or at least reasonable cynicism, out of rumor. He kept it going: Did the DA's office "tell you there was a feud with Inspector Byrnes?" "Did you ever see any of the municipal police at Mrs. Mandelbaum's?" At that, the prosecution finally lost patience, objecting to the question. Howe commented, assuming a pious mien, that he was simply showing that "This slander upon the Police Department is unfounded." Let's move on, Murry suggested.

Four more merchants identified their merchandise as stolen; four more times, Howe suggested dismissing the whole thing. Four more times, Murray turned him down. Then they all went home.

The defense would get its turn on July 30, an occasion that Howe honored with a particularly startling outfit—a bright green suit, with indigo accents and a pink-and-green checked shirt, slathered with diamonds. "Mr. Howe looked," according to one fashion critic, "like a Maypole of more than ordinary circumference."

The cynosure of all eyes, he proceeded to read a statement from Mrs. Marm, authored by Hummel. The most important sentences were, "I have never, never, stolen in my life" (Howe's voice quavered); "I never gave money to any person whatsoever to bribe or influence any official, so help me God (a demi-semi quaver); and "I will not be a cat's-paw to suffer because there is a feud and a fight between the police and other officials" (with righteous scorn). Murray refused to allow the last sentence into the record—this was not the time or place for a "stump speech," he cautioned, a comment that provoked Howe to anguish. "Your remark is very disgusting. It is very indecent. It is very unjudicial." Murray was unmoved. But of course the cat's-paw remark, and similar ones, made it into the newspapers and thus into the court of public opinion, which was the point. If this case was to go to trial, Howe was looking to plant a few seeds in the jury pool.

The prosecution kept it simple: Given the testimony of the Pinkerton agent and the various merchants, wasn't there enough evidence to justify a trial by jury? Yes, there was. Seven counts of second-degree grand larceny, and one of receiving stolen goods, would go to trial in the Court of General Sessions. Howe, Hummel, Mandelbaum, and company trooped out.

The indictment came down in August, with the case scheduled to go to trial on September 22. But the defense had a question. Shouldn't Gustav Frank's character be thoroughly investigated? They suggested the appointment of a commission to examine the Chief Magistrate of Cologne, Germany, Frank's hometown. To bolster this, Hummel offered his translation of a letter from that office that implied Frank was a fugitive from justice. Hummel was fluent in the language; unfortunately, so were several court officers, whose own translation of the communication was considerably less damning. There was no need to go to Germany, the court ruled.

Okay, then, said the indefatigable duo, let's at least go up to the Court of Oyer and Terminer because they would be arguing "intricate, novel and perplexing questions of law." Bah, humbug, said DA Olney; the only reason they wanted to change venues was to delay matters. That was true, of course, but it worked. After two months of consideration, the judge sent it on. What took so long? Maybe the judge, Charles

Donahue, had an incentive to take his time. (Remember the Howe & Hummel principle: Delay, delay, delay.) Two years later, Donahue was investigated and eventually censured by the Bar Association for, among other things, postponing the Mandelbaum trial, to unfortunate effect.[89] Eventually, the new court set a new trial date: December 2. Olney was primed and ready, with 14 witnesses and three assistants raring to go. Howe demurred; the indictment had two charges on it (grand larceny and receiving stolen goods). Under the legal code, there could be only one. If this little matter could be taken care of, he'd be happy to come back tomorrow. Olney practically wept.

On December 4, all was ready. The inventive genius of Howe & Hummel had run out of motions, objections, and quibbles. Olney was champing at the bit; Pinkerton hardly less so. In the gallery, bankers jostled next to bank burglars. The 14 witnesses were in order. At the defense table, Howe was seated, serene and plumed. By his side was Hummel, who hummed a show tune.

At 11:00 a.m., the court clerk called out: "Fredericka Mandelbaum!" No answer. As required, the clerk called the name three times. When the echo of the last syllable faded, Howe rose and told the judge, "The District Attorney must, in the words of Shakespeare, 'have the due and forfeit of his bond.' Mrs. Mandelbaum is not here." Neither was Julius, or Herman Stoude.

In the event, the DA didn't even get the forfeit. George Speckhardt, who had posted bail for Marm, had transferred the deeds to a relative who then transferred them to Mrs. Speckhardt. The other bondsmen had made similar arrangements. Like the defendants, the bail had vanished.

Howe was unblushingly cheerful about it all. No, he didn't know where the defendents had gone, he told reporters, and if he had known they were going, he would not have said. It was up to the DA, not the defense, to keep tabs on people. "I believe Mrs. Mandelbaum acted upon Mark Twain's theory that absence of body is often better than presence of mind," he mused. "Fredericka the Great," Hummel murmured approvingly.

They could afford to be expansive. For all the legal fluff Howe had thrown in Harlem, he knew a loser when he saw one, and Mandelbaum was likely to lose if she came to trial. But what about their fees, a reporter asked? Had the defendants burned them, too? In a rare insight into the business side of the practice, Howe jiggled some coins, while Hummel grinned and hummed. A paper left artlessly visible was full of figures with a few words like "fair divvy," "my share," and "whack up the real estate" plainly legible. "When we take a case," Howe explained, "we secure fees covering even an appeal to the Court of Appeals. If our client is hanged before the appeal is made, he will never need the money, and we might as well have it. If it goes to the higher court, we are secured for our trouble. We look very far ahead—much farther, I would remark, than the District Attorney." Hummel smiled at his partner and added, "We would not get left." Then they laughed.

The mercenary element of Howe and Hummel's characters might not have been news to the reporter. Their love of money was sufficiently well known to their contemporaries to be a source of satire. The comic novel *The Sinister History of Ambrose Hinkle* (1929) featured a wispily disguised version of the pair. In it, a safeblower is defended by the petite, Broadway-loving Abraham Hinkle, of the firm Hope & Helwell, whose offices happen to be across the street from the Tombs. The thief remarks of his counsel, "Yeah, he sprung me; I give him that. But I had ten grand from the job when I went to Little Amby, and I got out of his hands naked."[90]

There was also laughter at police headquarters at the disappearance of the famous fence. The DA's office, after all their snide comments on police incompetence, had lost their woman. Schadenfreude reigned. As usual, no one took responsibility. The Pinkertons said they had been brought in too late to watch, which was true. The police said that they had never been asked, and Olney said that once the defendants were out on bail, it was the court's job to keep them in town. He tried to put a brave face on it, saying, "I think we effectually floored the old girl and broke her business up in fragments."

In a service economy like receiving stolen goods, it is knowledge and contacts that matter. Marm still had both. But it would be Canada's problem from now on. For that is where they washed up, in Hamilton, an upscale suburb of Toronto. (Canada did not have an extradition treaty for grand larceny.)

Hummel had to dash up there briefly, to take care of a ridiculous vagrancy charge and a slightly more troublesome one of bringing in stolen property. The latter referred to a six-inch lump of melted gold and gobs of jewelry secreted on Marm's ample person—mostly diamonds, with a few emeralds for color, probably from a jewelry heist in Troy, New York, by her old pals, Billy Porter and Michael Kurtz. That landed the absconding trio in a Canadian jail. Showing a distinctly puckish sense of humor, Marm's local counsel brought her a copy of Allan Pinkerton's memoirs when she asked for something to read to help pass the time. A note from Hummel made for happier reading. "Cheer up," he telegraphed. "Done nothing can hold you in Canada and have good lawyers." He was right on both counts. The matters were easily disposed of, and Marm, Julius, and Herman settled down to life in the north.

As far as is known, Marm only left once, to attend the funeral of her daughter, Annie, who died of pneumonia in 1885. She came and went without attracting any official attention. On her return to Canada, she went back into business. In 1886, she opened a dry goods shop in Hamilton. But first, she needed stock, so she sent a letter to the United States.

Dear ___,

I beg to announce to you that I have opened my new emporium, in every respect the equal of my late New York establishment. I shall be pleased to continue our former pleasant business relations, promising not alone to pay the best prices for the articles which you may have for sale, but also in carefully protecting all my customers, no matter at what expense. With my present facilities, I am able to dispose of all commodities forwarded to me with dispatch and security. Trusting to hear from you soon and assuring you that a renewal of past favors will be greatly appreciated.

I am, yours faithfully,

F. Mandelbaum[91]

When a reporter visited, he found that all the goods were from New York, at startlingly low prices. None had any trademarks or labels.[92]

SEVEN

The Accidental Reformers

Given the breadth of Howe & Hummel's practice in the 1880s and 1890s, they were bound to run into people entirely unlike themselves—that is, altruists and reformers. The work paid, and the publicity was terrific.

Besides, New York was lousy with do-gooders and civic worthies and crusaders. There were women's rights and labor activists and anti-vice campaigners galore, of course. But there were also movements afoot to build playgrounds and change the marriage laws and license dogs and feed newsboys and build public baths and send flowers to the poor[1] and loosen corsets.

Some of them even worked. Thanks to the patriotic nudging of Joseph Pulitzer's *New York World*, the public eventually ponied up enough pennies to pay for the pedestal for the Statue of Liberty; the massive lady emigrated to the United States in 1885. After almost a decade of effort, sparked in part by Jacob Riis's haunting photos in *How the Other Half Lives*, Mulberry Bend was razed in 1895 and converted into a little park[2] that is today a hub for the nearby Chinese community. And in a daring departure from tradition, George Waring, named commissioner of street cleaning in 1895, actually cleaned Manhattan's streets—most of them twice a day, and the busiest ones as many as four times.[3]

Howe & Hummel had nothing to do with these matters. But in the decades that nursed the impulses that would bloom into what became known as the Progressive Era, they couldn't help being drawn into a couple of causes.

One was the effort to ban prizefighting from New York. Boxing was legal; indeed, the manly art was practiced at all the best gentlemen's clubs and was even part of the Harvard curriculum. But such sparring was for amateurs and was thus guided by a set of rules no less profound for being unspoken. Prizefighting was different. It was professional; the aim was to knock the other man out; and it became associated with criminals and gangsters. Theodore Roosevelt, for one, loved boxing but disdained prizefighting as a "brutal and degrading" spectacle that fed all the worst impulses of the lower orders.[4]

Though prizefighting was illegal almost everywhere in the United States (and had been banned in New York in 1859), it thrived. Bouts would be held on barges to evade the law, or moved from place to place. Somehow the newspapers and the fans—and not just those of the loutish variety, either—always caught up. In 1877, the *Times* reported on what it called a "brutal prize fight" at Red Leary's that the police failed to stop, either through "connivance or incompetence."[5] Connivance and incompetence were widely available.

In the early 1880s, a boxer emerged who became the first modern superstar of the sport. He liked to introduce himself this way: "My name's John L. Sullivan and I can lick any son-of-a-bitch alive." He could, too. Sullivan became recognized as the heavyweight champ in February 1882, when he beat Patrick Ryan in Mississippi City in a $5,000 bareknuckle bout. Sullivan embarked on a victory tour of sorts, stopping in New York to pick up his money from saloonkeeper Harry Hill before arriving in Boston to a hero's welcome.[6] He began to cash in.

What Sullivan didn't do was expose himself to real competition. Instead, he favored exhibitions under the rules published by the Marquess of Queensberry in 1867: gloves; three-minute rounds; no wrestling; and a fighter counted out after ten seconds down. These bouts were perfectly legal; they also introduced hordes of people to the sport, a large number of them rich, worldly, and influential. Sullivan began to insist that any challenger withstand a Queensberry four-rounder before the champ would grant a shot at the title, which would still be an illegal bare-knuckle fight to the finish.

As a result, these "exhibitions" became thoroughly professionalized, with real money (through betting) and consequences (a shot at the title) at stake. In May 1883, for example, New York Police Captain Alexander Williams stopped a fight against Charlie Mitchell, a Briton who had come to the United States to knock out Sullivan.[7] At the rematch 13 months later, a crowd of 6,000 people packed Madison Square Garden. Among them, according to the *National Police Gazette*: the Reverends Henry Ward Beecher and DeWitt Talmadge, seven aldermen, five judges, two police commissioners, four police inspectors, one Vanderbilt, plus various magnates of business, both legitimate and otherwise.

The *Gazette* didn't like Sullivan one bit; the big Irishman had snubbed its proprietor, Richard K. Fox, at Harry Hill's a few years before, and Fox had made it his mission to find someone to knock John L. off his perch. This quest was so well known that it became the stuff of music-hall derision:

> The Fox may go to England
> And the Fox may go to France,
> But to beat John L., he can go to Hell,
> And then he won't have a chance.[8]

Fox believed in boxing. He had built up the pink-tinted *Gazette* from near failure to a tabloid institution with a national circulation of 150,000. "Be as truthful as possible," Fox advised his staff, "but a story's a story."[9] The *Gazette* filled its pages with sex, murder, and boxing, and it had no use at all for the pieties of the time. It once ran a full-page picture of a family with a sick child, with the caption: "The Fiends of Religion:

How the Brooklyn hypocrites torture the sick and dying with the hellish clangor of their Sunday church bells."[10] In the pages of the *Gazette*, Fox argued that if people like Beecher showed up for "sparring exhibitions," how bad could actual prizefighting be?

Sullivan, however, showed up late for the scheduled bout against Mitchell, and impaired. He reeled through the ropes and announced to the crowd: "Gentlemen, I am sick and not able to box. The doctor is here and this is the first time I disappointed yer." He punctuated the sentence with strategic hiccups, then crawled back to his bottle, completing an impressive 48-hour bender.

With a reputation to restore, Sullivan accepted a challenge from Richard K. Fox's latest hope, Alf Greenfield, the self-proclaimed champion of England. Sullivan got rid of some of his blubber and fought a tune-up exhibition on November 10, 1884, to raise money for flood victims in Ohio. He won easily but was huffing in the second round. As the date of the fight neared, the question swirled: Could he keep it up against a real fighter?

That question, however, was superseded by a more pressing concern: Would the fight even take place?[11] New York Mayor Franklin Edson, who was not at the fight and knew nothing about boxing, did not like what he had heard. He ordered the police to prevent any recurrence of an activity he considered "disgraceful . . . and demoralizing to young men." On November 15, two days before the big fight, Captain Williams arrested Sullivan, Greenfield, and their backers on the charge of conspiracy to commit a prizefight.

The following day, Judge Barrett grilled the pugilists on their intentions. They were not going to hurt each other, really, just try to pile up points—sort of like fencing, but without the weapons; it was to be a scientific exhibition of boxing. Sullivan and Greenfield confirmed that they had nothing against the other fellow and didn't expect any blood to be spilled. Then the two signed a deposition—Greenfield could only make a mark, and the act of writing did not come readily to Sullivan either—and were allowed to go.

Barrett excused himself for an hour, then made his decision. The question, as he saw it, was whether the proposed contest was a "friendly sparring match not calculated to injure either party, or a serious physical contention." It seemed to Barrett that if the contestants did as they proposed to do, there would be no problem. But, he concluded, "If severe blows are struck, which are likely to cause injury to the parties or to inflame their passions or the passions of the bystanders," the police would have to stop it.[12] The pugilistic scientists could take the ring.

They were back in business: four rounds, Queensberry rules, on November 18, 1884, at Madison Square Garden. Among the 2,000 spectators: William Howe, Abraham Hummel, Henry Flagler (John D. Rockefeller's right-hand man), Charles Tiffany, Isidor Straus, and a number of people who had gone to the Astor wedding that afternoon.[13] Plus, of course, the rough trade that had given the sport its reputation—and more than 100 cops, just in case. Captain Williams and Chief George Walling had ringside seats, the former armed with the much-used nightstick that gave him his nickname, "Clubber." Walling brought only his total ignorance of the manly art.

At 10:15, the pugilists entered the ring. Both wore white tights; Sullivan accented his with a green, shamrock-speckled sash, Greenfield with a red one. After a little strutting and posturing, the bell rang to start the fight. The first round went by without incident, though Sullivan had much the better of it. Greenfield could barely land a blow and at one point, escaped into a clinch of such desperate longing that a wag shouted, "Kiss 'im, Alf!"[14] Sullivan broke free and managed to land a couple more examples of scientific self-defense before the bell tolled.

But it was the second round that would become a point of contention. Greenfield kept whiffing, Sullivan kept connecting, and the two of them kept ending up in each other's arms. Finally, the challenger managed to land two shots in a row, a success he would regret because, in the words of the *Herald*, "This made Sullivan wicked." A right and a left opened a cut over Greenfield's eye; as the blood began to flow, the crowd bayed in approval. Backed against the ropes, the Englishman took more blows to his body "of the sledgehammer description," while his own gloves waved feebly and hit with the force of a tired butterfly.

At ringside, Walling did not like what he was seeing. "This has gone far enough," he told Captain Williams. Seconds later, Clubber cried "Stop!" and crawled through the ropes to end the fight. "I'm sorry to interfere," Walling explained, "but the second round was a slugging match."

After dressing, the boxers led a procession of hundreds on a snowy walk of three blocks to the nearest police station. Sullivan, Greenfield, Fox, and five others were indicted the next day for "instigating, aiding, encouraging, and furthering a contention and fight without weapons between two persons."

Greenfield was disgusted. "'Ere I've been a fortnight in this blasted country, and I've spent three days in the police courts, and 'eaven only knows 'ow many times I've been asked if I could read or write." Sullivan, who looked as healthy and unmarked as if he had spent the evening at home with the wife and baby—a ludicrous idea—was also chagrined. "If I get out of this," he said, "I think I'll steer clear of New York. Things are getting a little too-too in this town."[15]

But could he get out of it? Well, he had a good shot. First, public opinion was swinging behind a more expansive view of boxing. And second, Howe & Hummel had stepped into the ring. Howe represented Greenfield, and one of the firm's associates, Peter Mitchell, appeared for Sullivan, following in Howe's slipstream throughout the proceedings.

Howe liked to brag that he was confident enough in his skills that he didn't give a toss about the jury. This was bravado. He dipped with purpose into the jury pool, skimming off men who showed unfortunate prosecutorial inclinations. He once turned down a juror because he did business in Jersey City. "We don't want any Jersey influence here," Howe sniffed.[16]

In this case, Howe wanted manly men of libertarian sensibilities, not earnest souls with sensitive consciences. So, for example, Henry Kraus, who admitted he didn't like boxing, scientific or otherwise, was sent home. So was William McBride, who admitted, "I dissipate, I do." How? Playing checkers at night. Not what Howe was looking for. But Thomas Brennan, a merchant whose hobby was Roman history and who liked gladiators, was warmly welcomed.

When the trial opened on December 18, the court was graced by a truly remarkable number of flattened noses and large-checked trousers.

The city's pugilists had come to sit by their men. The first witness was Chief Walling, who gave a straightforward account of his night at ringside. For Walling, the tipping point came when Greenfield was bleeding, and Sullivan was still pounding him. At that moment, the chief said, the pair had crossed the line from boxing to slugging.

Passing the blood-flecked gloves for inspection, Howe asked, "Is there as much blood on these gloves as would come from a bloody nose?" Walling wasn't sure. Don't the police have a boxing club? Walling thought so. And doesn't that club sometimes have sparring matches at Madison Square Garden? Well, yes. "And the men dressed the same way and wore the same gloves?" Pretty much. "That will do," Howe concluded.

Things got no better for the prosecution when Walling stepped down, because not even his fellow cops shared his perspective. Captain Williams, who was an amateur boxer and a regular spectator at the fights, denied any untoward violence. So did Inspector Thorne, adding that the clinches that Walling saw as evidence of slugging were just a matter of technique. Look, he offered to Howe, let me show you. Thorne left his seat and attempted to put the defense lawyer in a clinch; but the two of them were both so fat, all they managed to do was to rub paunches, much to the edification of judge and jury. Taking advantage of the now-jocular mood of the court, Howe pointed out that clouts that looked hard to Walling might not be to the participants. "A blow given by such men" as Sullivan, Greenfield, and even Williams, "all of them finely developed, muscular men, would have more effect than one dealt by my partner, Mr. Hummel," who looked up from his papers to join in the general laughter at his expense.

Greenfield and Sullivan both proved that while they lacked education, they were eminently teachable. They stayed on point during their testimony, Greenfield noting that he hit Sullivan no harder than the young gentlemen back in England whom he schooled in the manly art. He bore no ill will toward his opponent.

"We had a friendly set-to," Sullivan agreed, noting that of course he wanted to live up to the spirit and letter of Judge Barrett's prefight strictures. As for the blood, that was just an accident. He could have hit a good deal harder.

What it came down to was the testimony of Chief Walling, who had never seen a boxing match before, against everyone else. A little after 4:00, the jury retired. Less than 10 minutes later, they were back: not guilty. But it was an expensive win. Sullivan later said he had paid his entire share of the Greenfield fight to Howe & Hummel.[17]

In the aftermath of the Sullivan-Greenfield affray, the conventional wisdom was that Howe's victory had settled the matter: As long as the fighters used gloves and nodded at the legal formalities, they would be allowed to go at it. The *Gazette* could not resist patting itself on its pink back. "Thanks to this just judge and the energy and resolution of Richard K. Fox," it concluded in its first issue after the trial, "the cause of manly sport has won a substantial and final victory."[18]

Not quite: Like many social changes, the gradual reform and then legalization of boxing was a process, not an event. Howe & Hummel played a role in that process—though the firm didn't give a damn for the cause.[19]

After Sullivan's technical knockout against the New York authorities, he continued as undisputed heavyweight champ for another eight years, winning the last bare-knuckle championship in a 75-round brawl (for which he and his challenger were arrested and later convicted). Then he became the first champion to lose his title wearing gloves, to "Gentleman Jim" Corbett in 1892.

But Corbett was no gentleman, at least not according to his wife, Olive, who objected to sharing his attentions with a young lady named Vera, in particular, and other women in general. When Olive sued for divorce in 1895, she hired Howe & Hummel. Corbett had met his match this time. Olive got the divorce, $100 a week for life, and her name back.[20]

Calculated indifference to the deepest values of their clients also marked Howe & Hummel's defense of anarchism. There were three great figures in 19th-century American anarchism—Justus Schwab, Johann Most, and Emma Goldman. Howe & Hummel would defend Schwab and Most. Goldman was a close friend of Schwab's, and one of her roommates would marry Most.[21]

The anarchists were, of course, more than a little bit odd, and their ideas were a mix of gibberish, unreality, and insight. A world run according to anarchistic lines—and these were uncertain, given the ideological splintering that was one of the movement's most characteristic features— would have been a chaotic disaster. No one would want to live in a city where anarchists were in charge of, say, maintaining the sewers.

That said, they were shrewd social observers, seeing more keenly than most of their contemporaries the racial, sexual, and economic fault lines that were, particularly in retrospect, so glaring a feature of 19th-century America. And the anarchists were sincere—desperately, even comically so. Goldman told the story, for example, of being taken aside by a young colleague during a gathering and reprimanded for her joyous dancing. The party disintegrated into a fierce debate between those who would allow dancing and those who saw it as egotistic indulgence that diverted energy and betrayed their deepest beliefs. Being an anarchist must often have been a wearisome thing.

Anarchists tended to believe that a formal legal system blasted the spontaneous expression of human genius. Howe and Hummel, of course, needed a formal legal system, if only to express their own genius in wriggling around it. The partners saw little further than their own self-interest and were cheerfully insincere about everything. When it came to working with the anarchists, though, such differences didn't matter. The anarchists wanted to stay out of prison; Howe & Hummel wanted to win. That was enough common ground to forge an enduring connection.

Justus Schwab was the first anarchist to avail himself of the Howe & Hummel treatment. A German immigrant, Schwab owned a saloon in the basement of a tenement on First Street that was patronized by all the best radicals. Lined with images of the French Revolution and stuffed with books on politics, the place was so popular that Schwab became embarrassingly prosperous. But he was also a true believer—generous with his wealth and loyal to the cause. As one contemporary said of him, "A more amiable and better-informed man than Schwab never trod carpet slippers."[22]

He got into trouble in February 1885, though, when he and other German anarchists crashed a meeting of the Social Labor Party, another German group, which had convened to condemn the recent dynamitings in London by Irish nationalists, a denunciation Schwab considered a capitulation to the ruling class.

The two groups were literally fighting over the gavel when Police Captain John McCullagh—a protégé of Walling, and sometimes as clueless—announced his presence and ordered the fighting to stop. Schwab's response, according to the captain, was to call on the crowd to kill the captain.[23] A riot ensued, and by the time police reinforcements came, Schwab was gone. McCullagh ordered his men to go to the saloon and arrest him.

Schwab scoffed at this account. Then he called in Howe & Hummel. The first ploy was to try to get the more serious charge thrown out on a technicality. Incitement to riot required the participation of three or more people, Hummel told the police court. On McCullagh's own account, only Schwab had done any inciting; therefore, there was no case to answer. A clever idea, but it failed.

At the trial three months later, the defense was more straightforward: Prove it. The police, Howe and Hummel said, did as much as anyone to turn the affair into a riot, if there was a riot. Their man Schwab was no communist—he even had a bank account. If he was guilty of anything, and they weren't saying he was, it was of nothing more than having unpopular opinions. And in this great land of ours, that was no crime.

At the trial, McCullagh retold his story in greater, but not more convincing, detail. In this version, Schwab had shouted: "Captain Mc-Cullagh! Police! Murder him, kill him and fire him out!"—a level of redundancy that judge, jury, and courtroom all found damn funny. And a number of defense witnesses flatly contradicted him. The trouble began when the police reinforcements arrived, a reporter for the *Herald* told the court: "The clubbing was very thoroughly done."

When Schwab's time to testify came, Hummel introduced his client, with a touch of defensiveness, as an "estimable citizen with theories and pronouncements abreast of the able thought of the age." The mute witness of petite wife and sleeping child bolstered the idea that Schwab was just another bloke with funny political ideas, sort of like being a Republican in the Sixth Ward.

Although Schwab, an atheist, refused to swear on the Bible, he managed to play along with Howe's gentle questions, describing himself as a saloon keeper, importer, and news dealer, who had gone to the meeting strictly as an interested citizen. He had tried to calm the disturbance, not provoke it. Articulate and well-groomed—in marked contrast to his scruffy allies in the courtroom—Schwab made a good impression.

Under cross-examination, however, the radical within could not be suppressed. Yes, Schwab said proudly, he was a revolutionary socialist, and when the masses were educated enough, he would "certainly urge them to revolution and annihilation." Schwab dug himself in deeper with every phrase, until, mercifully, a juror stepped in. The trial was about an alleged riot, not the definition of socialism; "It is cruelty to animals to make us sit here to listen to this debate."

All that was left were the closing arguments, always Howe's specialty. Red in the face, his voice throbbing in passion, he played the patriotism card. Our own founders were revolutionaries, he pointed out, and the Constitution they wrote guaranteed liberty of speech and religion to all. The only question to consider was what happened at Concordia Hall the night of February 2, not Schwab's atheism (granted) or political beliefs (peculiar, but protected). Schwab was a scapegoat for poor policing, nothing more, and deserved acquittal.

After the prosecution made its case, the judge made some pointed remarks about the difficulty of believing a man who did not believe in God, and a little before 3:30 the jury retired. They gave up, pale and haggard, at 3:00 p.m. the next day. The voting was 8–4 for conviction, but they were never going to agree on a unanimous verdict. Schwab was free to go; there would be no second trial. In victory, he was generous: "Mr. Howe and Mr. Hummel," he said with relief, "have been brave and loyal, and I am very thankful to them."

But Schwab did not get away scot-free. In his absence, his saloon had been robbed. He did not call the police.[24]

. . .

Johann Most was a more consequential, and controversial, figure than the sociable Schwab. Born in Germany, Most was scarred for life when an operation for an infected jaw left his face permanently twisted. The disfigurement did nothing to soothe a combustible temperament; at the age of 12, he organized his first strike, against an unpopular teacher, and was expelled from school. It would become a pattern. He bounced around northern Europe, wearing out his welcome first in Austria, and then in Germany, where he was arrested for a speech that was overenthusiastic about the utility of explosions as a form of political discourse. Moving to London, he started a newspaper, *Freiheit* (Freedom), that was extreme enough to get him expelled from the Social Democratic Party. It was about this time that he picked up the nickname of "General Boom Boom."

Most might have been able to beaver away indefinitely on the margins, if *Freiheit* had not gloated over the assassination of Alexander II in 1881. "At last he died like a dog," Most concluded of the czar. It was too much for Britain, which had its own royal family and problems with bomb throwers. He did another stint in jail.

On his release, he took up Schwab's invitation to come to the United States, arriving in late 1882. Taking up the reins of *Freiheit* again, Most quickly established himself as the face of anarchism, which at the time was regarded as something of an inside joke that Europeans played on each other. Most was a ferocious and stirring presence, by all accounts, who favored what he called the *attentat*, or "propaganda of the deed." The practicalities of this he addressed in 1885, with the publication of his most famous work: *The Science of Revolutionary Warfare: A Little Handbook of Instruction in the Use and Preparation of Nitroglycerine, Dynamite, Gun-Cotton, Fulminating Mercury, Bombs, Fuses, Poisons, Etc., Etc.* The book won a devoted following among arsonists and insurance scammers, but it cost Most his friendship with Schwab, who failed to see arson-for-hire as an appropriate revolutionary tool.

America's bemused tolerance of the anarchists expired in the bloody chaos of Haymarket Square in Chicago on May 4, 1886. An anarchist-organized rally for the eight-hour workday began peacefully. Police moved in to break it up around 10:30; a pipe bomb was thrown, and police fired into the crowd. When the smoke cleared, eight policeman and four protesters were dead, and scores injured. It was a terrible day, but how the blame should be apportioned was impossible to determine.

At the time, though, the immediate reaction was to blame the radicals for everything. "The villainous teachings of the Anarchists bore bloody fruit in Chicago tonight," began the *New York Times* account of the tragedy, "and before daylight at least a dozen stalwart men will have laid down their lives as a tribute to the doctrine of Herr Johann Most."

Most wasn't even in Chicago, and he couldn't have cared less about the eight-hour day.[25] But as the most high-profile anarchist in America, he was going to pay for Haymarket. New York authorities did not have to look very hard to find a reason to arrest him. In fact, they had an indictment all ready. On April 23, he had given a speech to a meeting of anarchists in which he brandished a rifle and said:

> You can make bombs out of glass tubes and old iron pipe which you can load with dynamite or gunpowder and fasten with caps at both ends. And when you see any of the rascals, throw them under their feet and kill them. . . . Then when we are all armed we can rise at a given moment, and take possession of all the armories and arsenals in the city. In one year, 100,000 men could be armed and then we should seize the capitalists by the throat.

And so on. This was, on one level, gas-baggery of the kind Most had been venting for years. But however incapable Most was of turning his rhetoric into rivers of blood, the sensibility was creepy. A grand jury quickly handed down indictments for incitement to riot and unlawful assembly. On May 11, Most was arrested. The police said they found him half-dressed and hiding under the bed in the tenement apartment of an 18-year-old acolyte. It was his first night in an American jail—and time, of course, for Howe & Hummel.

Most was released on bail a few days later, complaining of the filth and vermin of the Tombs, the calumny of the press—the hiding under the bed story infuriated him—and the theft of $180 from his belongings. At the trial, the prosecution was brisk. Colonel Fellows described the meeting, and read out extracts of Most's remarks. Fellows was all for free speech, he asserted, but not to speech that "leads to acts of blood and violence." Then half a dozen witnesses, a mix of cops and civilians, told what they saw, all broadly corroborative.

Most was panting to be heard, but he did not want to face questions. So he, rather than Howe, delivered the closing remarks, to the latter's visible disapproval. Most did his cause no good. He again denied being found under the bed, accused the witnesses of misrepresenting the nuances of his argument, and closed by shrieking, "My conviction means the downfall of free speech! Then will be the downfall of the press and the end of the Republic." The one thing Most could never be accused of was not taking himself seriously.

The jury decided to risk the death of liberty and convicted him promptly. The judge chipped in a rousing commentary, telling Most, "A more wicked and atrocious scoundrel than you are does not disgrace the face of this earth." Most got the max, a year at Blackwell's, and was shipped over to the island of misfits and petty criminals a few hours later. His full beard was shaved off, exposing the dented left side of his face. Now he really looked like the vicious murderer the *Times*, for one, considered him. "If ever a man earned death on the gallows," that newspaper editorialized, "Most has earned it."[26]

By any measure, that was an extreme view, a sign of post-Haymarket fury more than any reasoned consideration of the man's deeds. Howe & Hummel's performance had been lackluster. But then, they didn't have much to work with. Waving a rifle while urging the masses to take up arms to kill, kill, kill is not protected speech anywhere. When Most took away Howe's best shot—the closing address, in which he had confused many a jury into letting real villains free—Most sent himself to jail.

He didn't see it that way. "I did not expect anything else from a jury of capitalists," he sniffed. "They were not my peers." That the 12 small businessmen, bartenders, and clerks were not of the same world as Most was surely true—and entirely irrelevant. They were far more representative of the society he had chosen to live in than his not-very-merry band of anarchists.

. . .

With time off for good behavior, Most was off Blackwell's in 10 months; he had even been allowed to regrow his beard before release. He had not, however, been rehabilitated.

Back on the platform, he picked up where he'd left off, telling a crowd in Philadelphia, for example, "It is no crime to kill the policemen such as Chicago employs." And he repeated his affection for the *attentat*: "Yes, bombs! Bombs are far better." It was only a matter of time before he would have to answer again for his words.

That time duly came in the wake of the execution on November 11, 1887, of four anarchists for their alleged role in the Haymarket tragedy.[27] It was natural for New York's anarchists to mourn these deaths; and considering the preponderance of Germans in the movement, it was natural for them to do so in a beer hall. When Most came in, it was inevitable that he would speak. What did he say? Well, according to the *New York World*, which hated Most, he began by addressing the 100 or so people in the back room of the beer hall as "fellow slaves" and went on to threaten "death to the butchers" who were responsible for killing the Haymarket martyrs. Then he renewed the call to arms.

Such words would hardly have been out of character for Most, but he instantly denied the substance of the *World*'s account, threatening to sue the paper for slander. The *New York Sun*, which was of more tempered character than the *World*, had a substantively different account: "Most says Anarchy Lives," was the headline, "But he isn't very wild about it and doesn't dabble in blood," was the subhead. In the *Sun*'s account, Most made no threats and even contradicted a cry for immediate revenge. There was no gun-waving from the platform, and no melee. Nonetheless, Most found himself indicted, again, on the charge of unlawful assembly.

The press had nothing but disdain for the anarchist cause, but even so, Most's arrest gave some of them pause. The *Times*, which had wanted to gibbet Most the year before, now questioned the basis of the prosecution: "Is it wise to prevent his vaporings because he vapors to his own detestable kind?"

This time, then, Most had a real defense; and this time, Howe & Hummel would pull out the stops to defend him.

The trial convened on November 22. Prosecutor DeLancey Nicoll needed only a single day to make his case. He brought in three people to testify to Most's allegedly riot-inciting words. Officer Louis Roth, a veteran of Howe & Hummel's two previous anarchist cases, gave his rendering of Most's speech. He had not taken notes at the time, Roth said, because he would have been attacked, but he wrote it down right after and his German was good.

Not as good as Abe Hummel's, who had grown up speaking German. He whispered to Howe, who had one question to Roth on cross-examination: "Give me the German for 'fate,'" a word Roth had used when testifying. Roth didn't know. Howe waved his hand in dismissal: "You can go, sir." The second cop at the meeting, John Sachs, also ran into trouble with the legal tag team. He, too, said his German was excellent. Again, with Hummel's tutoring, Howe managed to expose some linguistic deficiencies.

When things resumed the next day, Howe's opening remarks were a characteristic mix of brio and calculation. Referring to his client as a "fanatic and a fool," he reminded the jury that they, at least, were solid American citizens and therefore lovers of personal liberties. His voice dropping to a whisper, Howe advised the jury not to "allow your voices or your sympathies to be moved against the sacred right that our glorious Constitution guarantees to us." Then he raised his voice in passion: It was not Johann Most who was on trial, he thundered, but "freedom of speech which is arraigned in this court of justice." A few more flings of purple rhetoric, a scathing reference to Anthony Comstock, and Howe got down to business, calling half a dozen witnesses who gave their own versions of the speech. It was emotional, they all agreed, but less than bloodcurdling. In a nice touch, they all gave their testimony in German, an unstated but well-understood reference to the linguistic shortcomings revealed the previous day.

One of the witnesses, Emil Kosz, provided a dash of comedy—but one that also revealed the anxiety that proximity to anarchists provoked. Kosz took the stand carrying a box, an accessory that the judge eyed suspiciously and that worried Police Captain McCullagh enough that he put his hand on his gun. Asked what had brought him to the meeting that evening, Kosz fingered his box; the crowd rustled as if ready to flee to the exits. He opened it, and revealed—corn plasters. When they did not explode, there were sighs of relief all around. Kosz explained that he was a peddler; he had thought he could sell a few plasters to the gathering. Later, both Howe and Hummel accepted Kosz's kind donation of his wares because, they said, the prosecution had been treading on their corns all day.

From Hartwig the wigmaker, who had been moved to tears at Most's words, to the blowhard who kept referring every question back to the concept of the "philosophical god," to Rosenzweig the cigar maker, who had been studying anarchy for eight years but could not define it, the defense witnesses were not impressive. But their accounts were consistent. Looked at dispassionately, there was little to choose from between them and the questionable testimony of the prosecution's men.

Howe and Hummel should have left it there, but they knew the jury would want to hear from Most himself. Just as surely, he would want to speak. But allowing Most to testify was a gamble that did not pay off. At first, the grim-visaged anarchist performed well, giving a calm and compelling version of events. He even maintained his poise when Nicoll forced him to recount his various arrests and grilled him on his beliefs. But then his luck ran out.

The turning point came when Nicoll asked Most if he was an author. Sensing what was coming, Howe was on his feet, objecting. But the judge ruled that Nicoll could ask Most the names of his works, and Most could decline to reply if he so wished. Most chose to name a few pamphlets and his recent opus, *The Hell of Blackwell's Island*. "Any more?" Nicoll queried. That's enough, said Most. The prosecutor followed up, "Are you not the author of a book entitled *The Science of Revolutionary Warfare*?"

Howe popped to his feet again. This was an outrage! The judge, he sputtered, had ruled several times that the book was immaterial. Nicoll replied that the judge had allowed him to ask about Most's written work. That's all he was doing, he shrugged innocently. The judge agreed that

Nicoll could cite passages from the book, but only to ask if Most had authored them. It was all the prosecution needed. Nicoll paged through the book, reading out some of the more explosive passages. Did you write this? he asked about a reference to ten pounds of dynamite being enough to take down a small building. Most took the Fifth. Then Nicoll turned the page, to a recipe for poisoning arrows. Did Most write that one? He took the Fifth. Finally, Most retorted that he didn't say any of this at the meeting. And took the Fifth again.

In closing, Howe repeated that this was a trial about his client's words and actions on the night of November 12, 1887, in a private room in New York, not about Haymarket or what Most had written years ago. "If the first dangerous encroachment of free speech is made now, how long, think you will it before the *New York Herald*, the *Times*, the *Sun*, the *Tribune* and the *Star* will be arraigned in this court." (Note that he did not mention the *World*.) Nicoll replied that his own witnesses had no reason to lie and were certainly more credible than the atheists who supported Most. The defendant had every right to his opinions, but not to make threats.

The first ballot of the jury was seven to five for acquittal. Four-and-a-half hours and a hot dinner later, they managed to find unanimity: guilty. Most was sentenced to another stretch on Blackwell's, but he wouldn't go for several years. Howe had enjoyed his role as protector of civil liberties, and told Most, who made about $10 a week, not to worry about money.[28] "I was just as certain this time of his innocence as I was before of his guilt," Howe said.[29] "This prosecution was an attack on free speech and a free press." He would take care of the appeal.

And he was as good as his word. In a closely reasoned motion for a new trial, Howe argued that no version of Most's language amounted to a threat; that any mention of *The Science of Revolutionary Warfare* should have been suppressed; and that referring to the defense witnesses' atheism was contrary to the New York Constitution.[30]

He was probably right on all three counts. There was enough to chew on that the appeals went through several courts. But the conviction was eventually confirmed and in June 1891, Most went back to Blackwell's. He got out a couple of months before Emma Goldman's lover, Alexander

Berkman, shot industrialist Henry Clay Frick. Berkman had turned to
guns when an effort to build a bomb from the blueprints in *The Science of
Revolutionary Warfare* failed.

The shooting of Frick was Most's theory of the *attentat* in action. And
yet, Most was not impressed. When he heard of the attempted assassination, his first reaction was to deride it as a fiction to create sympathy
for Frick. And his second thought was to denounce it. Such violence,
he said, was not the answer, because America's revolutionary sensibilities were too immature.[31] This came as news to many of his followers,
considering he had been saying the opposite for years. Emma Goldman,
naturally, was incensed. When Most repeated his criticism at a lecture,
Goldman stormed the stage, horsewhip in hand and, in her own words,
"lashed him across the face and neck, then broke the whip over my knee
and threw the pieces at him."[32]

Most would get in legal trouble one more time. In 1901, he reprinted
a 50-year-old article on the virtues of tyrannicide. Unfortunately, it was
published the same day President McKinley was assassinated by a self-
described anarchist.[33] Most got another year on Blackwell's for that bit
of extraordinarily poor timing. On his release, he went back on the lecture circuit, but he managed to stay out of jail until his death, from natural causes, in March 1906. At his memorial service, a widow of one of
the Haymarket martyrs spoke. So did Emma Goldman, who had long
regretted horsewhipping her hero.[34]

It is America's saving genius to turn extremism into bourgeois re-
spectability in a generation or two. Though the anarchist did not live to
see this outcome, his son John Most Jr. became a dentist, and his grand-
son, Johnny Most, was the beloved sportscaster for the Boston Celtics
for almost 40 years. His famous call—"Havlicek stole the ball!"—during
the 1965 playoffs has achieved an immortality that none of his ancestor's
words ever did.[35]

The anarchists were well outside the realm of polite society, a construct
they believed didn't exist anyway. But they were almost mainstream
compared to a peculiar little group that called itself the Midnight Band

of Mercy. The self-proclaimed mission of the members of the band was to help cats. And they did so by killing them. Howe & Hummel—need it be said?—was not on the side of the kitties.

It was not the first time the firm had been called in on a case related to animal welfare—a concept that was essentially invented by Henry Bergh, who founded the American Society for the Prevention of Cruelty to Animals in 1866. Before Bergh, the abuse of animals was casual, public, and not considered anything worth noticing. Bergh made it his life's mission to change that mindset. In 1867, he managed to nag the New York State legislature into passing the first law against abusing animals. The state attorney general and the city district attorney appointed Bergh their representative in all such cases.[36] He went to work.

The following year, Bergh brought a prosecution against Christopher "Kit" Burns, for holding dogfights and rat-killing contests in Sportsman's Hall in his saloon on Water Street. Sportsman's Hall was thoughtfully designed. To reach it, customers started in the bar, then walked through a labyrinth of narrow passages that could be easily blocked to delay police, reformers, and other riffraff. The hall itself was about 25 feet square; in the center was an oval pit, about 16 feet long by 8 feet wide, ringed by a 2-foot-high fence. The ceiling rose 20 feet above the floor, creating enough space for a rude amphitheater whose benches could hold a couple hundred people. There was a special spot set aside for Kit Burns's pet bear.

The venue had another use. Burns rented it out to Christian revivalists, who implored the Almighty, above the din of the baying dogs housed in the cellar, "to flood Water Street with Divine Grace." Burns took $150 a month to rent the place for an hour a day—"no pay, no preach" was his succinct bargaining position—but he didn't like the company he was keeping. On one occasion, as soon as the irritating Christians left, he called to a colleague: "Them fellows has been a making a pulpit out o' the ratpit and I'm going to purify it after 'em. Jim, say, Jim. Bring out them varmints!"[37]

But dogfighting was the main attraction at Sportsman's Hall. The dogs aimed to kill each other and were specially trained to the purpose. Stray dogs were sacrificed to the cause to develop the champ's jaw muscles and killer instinct. At the highest level, if that term makes any kind of sense, bouts were meticulously organized, with purses of $1,000 or more, huge betting on the side, and detailed contracts.

Henry Bergh thought this was awful, but his was not a universal opinion. One judge threw out a case on the grounds that there was nothing wrong with the "fine sport of dog-fighting."[38] Given the difficulties that many New Yorkers had just getting through the day, being nice to dogs was a low priority. But Bergh kept at it, and after a few failures managed to get Burns charged with cruelty to animals in 1868. The outraged entrepreneur turned to William Howe.

Howe was a slimmer man then, but the oversize personality was already in evidence. He lit into the prosecution with a combination of sarcasm and ridicule. Banning dogfighting or rat-killing contests, he argued, was the thin end of the wedge. He could just see what would be next: People wouldn't be able to open up shells and eat oysters anymore. Or roast clams alive. And what about turtle soup? Was the American way of life to be sacrificed to the whims of a rich dilettante like Bergh? The case was dismissed.[39]

Bergh did not give up, though. In November 1870, he sneaked into Sportsman's Hall accompanied by two cops. A dogfight was in progress when they identified themselves and rounded up all the suspects who had not managed to escape out the windows—34 of them, including Kit Burns.

Perhaps recognizing that the public attitude to dogfighting was darkening, Howe took a different tack when the trial started in February. After Bergh and the two cops testified to what they had seen, Burns's son-in-law, Jack Jennings, spoke for the defense (Kit had died in the meantime). Bergh had it all wrong, Jennings explained. It was supposed to be an evening of dog versus rat when a couple of curs had got loose and started to fight. What was a man to do? To prove his point, Jennings noted that the police had taken away a cage of 150 live rats that were supposed to be the heart of the evening's exhibition.[40] The Water Street 34 went free.

Bergh took the loss in stride and kept up his crusade. By the time he died in 1888, he could look back on far more victories than defeats. He had almost single-handedly made the case that animals, too, had a claim to human kindness. What he could not do, however, was control the actions of those who made his mission their own—people, for example, like the Midnight Band of Mercy.

The first inklings of this curious crew came to public notice in June 1893, when the *Times* reported a conversation with one Mrs. G. G. Devide, president of the Midnight Band of Mercy, which she said had disposed of 8,000 cats over the previous four years. She was defending a colleague who had just been arrested for throwing a freshly killed cat in front of a Brooklyn butcher shop. The butcher objected; Devide objected to the butcher. There was "a perfect right to throw the cat there"; it was up to the city to pick up such carcasses. "Why, there was a time we used to put the dead cats in the best parts of Fifth Avenue because we knew they would be taken away from there quickly."

In a later interview with Nellie Bly, the famous journalist, Mrs. Devide gave more details of the Band's technique. She and her allies would dress in old clothes and toss out catnip to draw the felines. Then they would stuff them into a chloroformed basket, carefully lined with oilcloth to make it airtight, and close the lid. The basket would shake and the cats begin to protest. In the kindest tones, the felines would be reassured: "Hush, kitty," their rescuers would murmur. "You are going to Jesus, kitty. 'Meow!' Kitty, hush, Kitty; your soul is going to the Lord. 'Meow! Meow! Meow!' Kitty has gone to God. Amen, and all was over."[41]

Devide herself was not religious. Still, she respected the beliefs of the members who were, including one who was sure that the cats were unborn children, and the more she chloroformed, the more of her grandchildren she was saving. This particular theological innovator would go so far as to filch pets from her friends and send them heavenward without their consent. Devide thought that was asking for trouble, but "they knew I would never betray them as long as there was a bottle of chloroform and a cat."

The *Herald* picked up the story when clumps of dead cats became a regular sidewalk feature on Waverly Place in Greenwich Village. "There was much dead cat this morning," said a German resident, "but not so much dead cat as yesterday. There was sure 12 dead cat here yesterday. My cat he is not go out now at all."[42] Rumor had it that a veiled lady with a basket was the cause of the precipitous decline in the Village's feline population.

A few weeks later, Policeman Joe Connelly was patrolling West 135th Street around 9:00 in the evening. He saw a woman calling to a cat, and then a flash of a white rag. "There's a good pussy," Sarah Edwards murmured as she held the rag over the animal's head. When Connelly demanded to know what she was doing, she replied loftily, "I'm one of the Midnight Band of Mercy, King's Daughters, Henry Bergh division." Connelly was blank. "Don't you know what that is?" Edwards barked. "Well, you're slow."

At Connelly's request, the lady opened her basket; inside were five chloroformed cats. Asked to explain her actions, Edwards proudly acknowledged her membership in the Midnight Band and maintained that under its rules, any cat on the streets after 8:00 p.m. would be deemed homeless and go into the basket. "The Bergh Society," she said, referring to the ASPCA, "has authorized us to kill cats." (The Berghers were, in fact, aghast.) Connelly tried to inform her that there was no such thing as a right to kill cats, and there was also an ordinance against carrying dead animals through the streets. Edwards was unmoved: "I know my business."

So did the cops, who charged her on five counts of animal cruelty. Frustrated that the forces of law and order did not understand the nobility of her work, Edwards went public, telling a reporter from the *Times*:

> Monday I chloroformed 19 cats, Tuesday 10, yesterday 18. On the last day of July, I chloroformed 53 cats. During the last three years I have painlessly put out of the way over 3,000 suffering animals which certainly would have died of starvation had I not done so.

As for the ASPCA, she had nothing but disdain:

The work is too dirty for them, consequently they leave it to us and simply because we are women and for the sake of suffering animals choose to depart a little from conventional methods, we are ridiculed and criticized. . . .[43]

Edwards had the wit to notice that her actions were unconventional, and it has to be said, the Midnight Band had a point. Many of New York's 400,000 or so cats[44] did live nasty, brutish, and short lives. But what Edwards and the rest of her deadly band entirely missed—the fact that made them both ridiculous and frankly sick—was that their love for cats seemed to be expressed only by the act of killing them.

Edwards, then, was not going to be easy to defend, which made it a case for Howe & Hummel. This time, Hummel took the lead, accompanied by half a dozen young staff eager to see the master at work. A lawyer for the ASPCA prosecuted. The star witness would be Policeman Connelly. Titian-haired and sure of himself, the officer stood up well to Hummel's implication that these were street cats who were better off dead.

HUMMEL: Was [the cat in question] emaciated?
CONNELLY: I don't know.
HUMMEL: Do you understand what I mean?
CONNELLY: No, sir.
HUMMEL: Well, was it thin, like a vagrant?
CONNELLY: It was a good-sized cat.

Not a good moment for the defense. Hummel had made the rookie mistake of asking a question for which he did not know the answer. But perhaps he was distracted. A couple of days before, a woman named Annie Palmer whom he had represented in a divorce went to the papers to accuse Hummel of having married and abandoned her. "Every man must have his crank," he said philosophically, "and I suppose it is my time now."[45] He was able to get rid of Palmer eventually, but not before she ran up hotel and shopping bills in his name.

So Hummel was not at his best in the case of the fanatic cat killer. He faltered again when he questioned the vet who had performed the autopsy on the cat Connelly had brought in. The vet testified that, before the last rites in the fatal basket, the animal had been fat and healthy, with a stomach full of potatoes. Hummel jumped in. "Is it not a fact that cats only eat potatoes when they are at the point of starvation?" Well, no, said the doctor, he had fed potatoes to many a cat. "I mean cats born in this country," Hummel clarified. "I refer to good American cats" was the bemused response.

Edwards took the stand in her own defense. Although she had not been allowed to kill a cat in court to show just how merciful an act it really was, she brought in the famous basket. From this she produced what Hummel called Exhibit A—to wit, a dead cat that she had personally chloroformed to oblivion. Holding it up, she instructed the court with the calm of a professor of anatomy, "See what a calm, peaceful look is on its little face," she lectured. "There was no pain there."[46]

The judges knew their business: guilty on all counts. Edwards was fined $10 per feline and ordered to stop. Considering how committed the cat-killing crew was to their work, it seemed unlikely that they would give it up so readily. But either they did or they got better at hiding it. The Midnight Band was never heard from again.

So no, Howe & Hummel were not always on the side of the angels. But at least once, they did the right thing for the right reason. In the case of the sinister spiritualist, Howe and Hummel were at the height of their powers, and they deployed them all in a good cause.[47]

Luther Marsh, a former law partner of Daniel Webster,[48] was a retired judge and a commissioner of parks. But when his wife died, he became something else, too: a lonely old man. So when a woman approached him and told him she could help him communicate with his beloved, Marsh wanted to believe. And lo, she gave him reason to, revealing holy truths of the next world and creating majestic spirit paintings before his eyes.

The relationship gave Marsh a renewed interest in life. The 72-year-old took to sliding down banisters and invited the muse, Editha Diss Debar, her husband, and two children to live with him. His home was filled again with companionship. Marsh became ever more convinced that spiritualism had solved the mysteries of both life and death. He was happy.

At a public lecture in 1888, he explained his beliefs to a skeptical and not particularly polite audience. "If I am on the side of God"—and the former judge had no doubt of this alliance—"we are in the majority," he told the crowd. When Marsh displayed a portrait of Rembrandt, painted before his eyes by a truculent Raphael, his audience began to titter. When he showed a portrait of Alexander the Great, this one painted by "my friend Appelles," the court painter of Macedon ("Alexander would sit for no other"), the giggles turned into roars. Marsh was unruffled: "I like a hearty laugh," he said complacently. And when he finally introduced his muse, he noted, "If she is a fraud, she is a big one," a reference to her 250 pounds or so of undoubtedly material flesh. It was impossible not to like the man.

But then Marsh gave over his four-story brownstone on Madison Avenue, worth $60,000, to his spiritual guide. She promptly cashed in, mortgaging it for $11,000. Alarmed, his friends acted. A group of lawyers called on Howe & Hummel and asked the firm to bring a private prosecution for fraud against the spiritualist—a sign that if the duo were not entirely trusted, they were respected for their skills. The partners rarely prosecuted, but they took this case gladly. It had the kind of outré character they enjoyed; and they, too, liked the deluded Marsh. On April 11, 1888, on the basis of two affidavits, Madame Diss Debar, her husband, and two helpers, Benjamin Lawrence and his son, Frank, were arrested for fraud.[49]

Who was Editha Diss Debar, alias Princess Editha, alias Loleta Montez, alias Madame Messant, alias the Countess of Langfeldt? Well, it depends on whom you believe. Diss Debar said her mother was Lola Montez and her father the mad King Ludwig of Bavaria. More down-to-earth sources, including government documents and her brother, said that she was born Ann O'Delia Salomon in Kentucky in 1849. At the age of 20, she left home and began a peripatetic life, living on her wits and developing a reputation for boozing and running up debt. She settled down for a time in Philadelphia, where she met a retired general, Joseph Diss Debar; they would be together for nine years.

Like any successful con artist, Diss Debar knew how to read the people she was dealing with. In this case, she understood that neither the court nor the prosecution, in the ample form of William Howe, were sympathetic to her spiritual emanations. After a couple of days in the Tombs, she weakened, deeding the brownstone back to Marsh; Cicero had told her to, she said.[50] If she hoped the transaction would change her circumstances, it didn't. The court would not allow Marsh to pay her bail, and no one else was stepping up.

Because this was a private prosecution, proceedings would start in the police court.[51] Howe & Hummel's task was to show that there was enough evidence to present to a grand jury.

From the start, the partners had two goals. One, of course, was to set the Diss Debars on the road to conviction. The other was to convince Luther Marsh of his folly. This was as much a defense of the kindly lawyer's well-being as a prosecution of his swindlers. And so, Howe and Hummel proceeded methodically.

On the first day, the star witness was George Salomon, who had signed one of the affidavits used to bring the prosecution. Salomon's point was simple—the defendant was not the illegitimate spawn of European royalty, but his sister, born in Kentucky and an irritation all her adult life. The family had disowned her years ago, but she kept popping up, usually to ask for money (Howe read out several letters that backed this up). "She has destroyed the peace of mind of almost everybody who has ever said 'good morning' to her," concluded her brother.

The other affidavit had come from J. W. Randolph, a theatrical manager who was planning to put Diss Debar on stage. Randolph had seen a commercial opportunity; and in his forthright cynicism about the stupidity of the paying public, Diss Debar thought she recognized a kindred spirit. Work with me, she suggested, and we can take the old man for another $150,000. No need to worry about bad publicity: She had told Marsh that she had had a communication from the Angel Gabriel, saying that if he read the papers, "his punishment would be that his soul will be in hell 30,000 years." Then she laughed.

Randolph was no altruist, but this cold-blooded fleecing of a nice old man like Marsh was too much for him. He was also revolted when Diss Debar made a most unwelcome attempt to seduce him. Pressed to explain her romantic technique, he blushed and whispered the specifics to the judge, who gagged and agreed that they were "unfit to be heard."

In the next few days, the trial moved into new, and entertaining, territory. Here the star was genuinely a star—a dapper magician named Carl Hertz, known as the "King of Cards." Hertz said that he could, by trickery, produce the equivalent of spirit writings. He handed a blank piece of paper to his wife, who folded it three times. Taking back the paper, Hertz placed the paper in her other hand, and instructed her to place her hand against her forehead. He waved his arms, then asked the judge to open the paper. On the previously blank sheet were the words: "Luther R. Marsh—Editha." Astonishment in the court, and deep red on the visage of Madame Diss Debar. The performance was intended, in part, to show Marsh how he had been deceived, but he was not in the courtroom at the time.

A few minutes later, he arrived in court to make his own case. Gently questioned by Howe, Marsh described himself as a "reformed lawyer," and he was serenely confident that the gods were on his side. As evidence, he offered three notebooks containing messages from Saints Anthony, Peter, and Paul. What happened, he earnestly explained, was that when Diss Debar felt a communication coming, she would place a blank notebook inside a book or magazine. Then he would take one end, and Madame the other. Spirits willing, they would hear the workings of a quill on the pad. When the sound ceased, they would remove the notebook, and read the wisdom so transmitted. The one from Saint Peter was special. It took 15 minutes to read but had appeared to him in just over two minutes. "Peter was a lively scribbler," remarked an irreverent Howe.

If that wasn't enough evidence that the spirits were communicating through the wondrous medium, Marsh went on to describe how the 75 or so spirit paintings in his possession had appeared. "She suddenly hears spirit voices in the air, and she repeats the words, which I take down on a piece of paper," he explained as if to a dimwitted child. Whenever the spirits promised a painting, a painting came. Why, in December, the spirit of the late great actress Adelaide Nelson had informed him that Rembrandt would paint Marsh's portrait. He could expect it on Christmas. It had not arrived by the time he went to church, so he asked his muse to check with Adelaide. She promised to do so, and when he got back from the service, she had glad tidings: The picture had arrived! Marsh rushed upstairs—and there it was. When he finished this story, Marsh leaned back in a pose of complacency and utter conviction. No one had the heart to laugh.

Hertz came back for his second act, this time with Marsh in the audience. The two sat down across the stenographer's table, and Hertz showed Marsh a notebook exactly like the one Saint Peter had written in. Wrapping it in newspaper, the magician asked Marsh to hold it. He clutched it tight as a crowd began to press against the witness box. He passed it back to the magician, who suggested calmly, "If you wish to tear a corner so as to identify it, I have no objection." Marsh did so, and passed it back: Lo and behold, the tablet was different, covered with writing. Marsh admitted, sadly, that the magician had deceived him.

But none of this disproved the "holy truth of spiritualism," he insisted. There were still the spirit pictures. To prove his point, he brought some to court on the third day. One of these, a portrait of Lola Montez, he recalled, had arrived in February. On seeing it, the general had cried, "My mother-in-law!" Then there was the Rembrandt portrait, which had a fascinating backstory. "Rembrandt had painted Raphael's picture," the old lawyer recalled, "and the latter returned the compliment by painting Rembrandt's. This so pleased Rembrandt that nothing would satisfy him but to paint mine. Of course I acquiesced, and that's how my portrait came to be painted."

In more down-to-earth testimony, Jennie Kellogg, a clerk in an art store, identified both Diss Debars as frequent purchasers of paint and canvas. Once they returned a canvas because it was marked with the store's name. That would never do. Two art critics testified that the spook pictures sure looked like the product of human hands to them, and unskilled ones at that.

There was just one more thing to do before the defense had its day. Could the prosecution produce a spirit picture? On Day 4, it did. David

Carvalho, a photographer, brought with him a blank piece of paper; this Howe unfolded to show the gallery. Two court officers held the paper up, while Carvalho passed a sponge over it. Instantly, Adelaide Nielson appeared. The gallery applauded, except for the coterie of spiritualists, who shifted and looked disapproving at the storm of laughter.

And then the prosecution rested.

The defense was simple. The Diss Debars had never asked for anything; Marsh had invited them to live with him and voluntarily deeded his home. If Marsh did not feel aggrieved, there was no case to answer. And their powers were real. To prove it, the defense lawyers called a parade of distinctly unimpressive witnesses. One was a blithering Harriet Beach, wife of the editor of *Scientific American*, who refused to leave the stand until she could explain her philosophy. As court officers carried her out, she kept talking, waving a picture of an ancient Egyptian astronomer with her right hand and pressing smelling salts to her nose with her left. "Now if you can crack that nut," she tossed off as her last words, "do so."

Another witness told of seeing Madame Diss Debar produce a spirit painting while bathing in the Massachusetts surf. "A watercolor, eh?" Howe asked. By the time the last witness surfaced—and never has a group done less to help its cause—Howe was enjoying himself again. He knew he had this thing won. So when Ezekiel Leonard was called to testify that he too had seen the emergence of a bad painting through the assistance of the spirits, Howe set him up, repeatedly referring to him as "Mr. Gosling." After a couple of iterations, Leonard, nettled, asked the court to correct the lawyer. Howe pretended chagrin at his mistake and shot off his well-prepared witticism: "I ought to have known that so big a goose could not have been a gosling."

It would be up to the Diss Debars to save themselves. They took the stand on the fifth and final day—and got hammered. General Diss Debar had to admit that he had a perfectly serviceable wife and family in Philadelphia, and that yes, he had a background as an artist. Madame continued to insist that she was the daughter of Lola Montez and King Ludwig, and was nonplussed when presented with a copy of the Salomon family Bible, showing the record of Ann O'Delia's birth.

Justice Kilbreth's conclusion was the obvious one: The Diss Debars would have to face the grand jury. As for the Lawrences, all they were really guilty of was freeloading at the Marsh dinner table. They went free. By now, even Marsh realized that the Diss Debars were not his friends. He was shocked that they were not married, and he even began to question whether Madame was the daughter of Lola Montez. They would not be returning to 166 Madison, he told the press; he sent the children packing, too.

In due course, the grand jury had no problems voting an indictment. At the trial in June, there was only one surprise for those who had been following the case. On the second day, in walked George Francis Train, the gadfly with a cause who had bailed out Woodhull and Claflin. "Dear cousin Luther," he greeted Marsh. "You're no more crazy than I am." Despite Train's dubious intervention, the Diss Debars were convicted of conspiracy with intent to defraud and packed off to Blackwell's.

Howe and Hummel could be pleased and proud of their work in the case. Hummel had done much of the detective work, and Howe had managed the courtroom artfully, questioning Marsh without challenging his dignity. This was the partnership at its best.

Still, this was victory with no winners, only an overriding pathos. More than a century later, the image that abides is of an old man hurrying home from church on Christmas Day, as eager as a child, to see if his new spirit painting had arrived. Perhaps there is a sucker born every minute, as Howe & Hummel client P. T. Barnum professed. Or perhaps there are simply broken hearts, willing themselves against all reason into an illusory happiness.[52]

About once a decade during this time, New Yorkers would wake up and decide that all was not as it should be in their fair city. So a committee would be appointed to prove the point. Disgusted, voters would vote in some goo-goos ("good government" types). They would get into trouble, be tossed out, and then everyone would get back to business as usual. The Committee of Seventy in 1871; the Roosevelt Committee of 1884;[53] the

Committee of 15 in 1900[54]—all revealed monumental corruption and malfeasance.

And then, there was the 1894 Lexow Committee. In some ways, Lexow fit this pattern all too well; it ushered in a reform government that lasted only a single term. But in Lexow's genesis (a sermon) and one of its results (the rise of Theodore Roosevelt), it was unique. Howe & Hummel was all over it.

The Lexow Committee was the 19th century's most comprehensive investigation into the operations of the New York City Police Department, and it started, in all places, in the Madison Square Presbyterian Church. On February 14, 1892, the Rev. Charles Parkhurst climbed the steps to his pulpit and delivered a blistering sermon. Tammany, not Scripture, was his subject, specifically the links between the municipal government and the city's vice trade. The result, he thundered, was an "official and administrative criminality that is filthifying our entire municipal life, making New York a very hotbed of knavery, debauchery and bestiality."[55]

The reaction was immediate, and hostile. The mayor denounced him; the grand jury chastised him for making accusations without evidence to back it up; and even the press professed to be dismayed at the minister's audacity. The *World*, quick to exercise its specialty of sanctimony on demand, accused Parkhurst of "the bearing of false witness." The *Sun* thought he should resign. No one, it appeared, would take Parkhurst on faith.

Ticked and more than a little humiliated, the minister set out to get the evidence his critics demanded. He did something it is impossible to imagine the man doing under any other circumstances. He went slumming.

Beginning in the mid-1880s, slumming was a popular form of recreation;[56] by the 1890s, a walk on the semi-wild side was an established part of the tourism industry.[57] A typical slumming expedition would start after dinner at a police station, where the tourists would check out the cells and see such tools of the criminal trade as jimmies and tilted roulette tables. Then, accompanied by a cop, they would head off into the dense and lively streets around the Bowery—visiting a tenement, a flophouse, a concert saloon, with perhaps a peek into an opium den, and a rousing finish at a German beer garden.[58] How the unfortunates at the flophouses felt about having a bunch of middle-class gawkers stare at them went unrecorded—if, indeed, anyone gave it a thought.

Parkhurst, though, went slumming with a purpose. On four evenings in March, he set out in disguise with a private detective, Charles Gardner, and a parishioner, John Langdon Erving, who was so innocent his nickname was "Sunbeam." Gardner paid $6 a night plus expenses,[59] did his job with a will, and Parkhurst, too, went at it with clerical earnestness. As they went to dive after whorehouse, the minister would repeat, "Show me something worse."[60] And Gardner did. An African-American dance house; a German whorehouse; a "French circus," a term whose meaning has been lost but was apparently very naughty indeed; even the basement of Scotch Ann's Golden Rule Pleasure Club, where heavily made-up boys were for sale.[61] At the establishment run by Hattie Adams, a couple of blocks from Madison Square Presbyterian, the unlikely trio saw a nude can-can and a game of leapfrog. Gardner played the frog, while Parkhurst drank beer and watched.[62] God bless him, the things the man endured for his mission!

When Parkhurst ascended the pulpit on March 13, 1892, he chose as his text a line from Psalms: "The wicked walk on every side when the vilest men are exalted."[63] This time, when the minsters said that the city was "rotten with a rottenness that is unspeakable and indescribable,"[64] he knew what he was talking about. He also had affidavits from private detectives hired by Gardner naming hundreds of saloons and whorehouses that had been open the previous Sunday.[65] Parkhurst's critics had demanded particulars, and he had delivered them. Waving the affidavits, he threw down a challenge: "Now what are you going to do with them?"[66]

Well, something clearly had to be done—not much, just enough to make Parkhurst go away, but something. So the powers that be—among them Howe & Hummel—devised a novel strategy. They would actually prosecute one of the places on Parkhurst's tour, choosing the disorderly house run by Hattie Adams. And rather than do the usual—that is plead guilty, pay the fine (plus Howe & Hummel's fee), then go back to work—Madame Adams would contest the charge. If she came to trial, Parkhurst would have to testify against her. There was no way, they figured, that the upright Presbyterian would let himself be grilled.

Thomas Byrnes, the pride of the New York detective force, apparently came up with the idea, but Howe and Hummel were happy to cooperate. Helping Byrnes, who had just been promoted to chief of police, could be useful. Besides, they all agreed that the city was better off without Parkhurst,[67] who clearly had no business in Gotham. But they underestimated the man.

Howe and Hummel did their best to discredit the minister, beginning with jury selection. Lip curled, voice dripping with scorn, Howe asked one man, "Do you know this so-called clergyman?" To another: "Did you ever hear that Parkhurst once played leapfrog?" Poor Sunbeam Erving had to endure Hummel at his most puckish. The lad was mortified at having to recount the awful things he had seen, and almost fainted when ordered to demonstrate how he danced with one of Adams's naked ingénues.[68] Then Parkhurst took the stand.

In a classic courtroom conflict that had New York atwitter, Howe, dressed in "a constellation of diamonds and a wilderness of brilliant dry goods,"[69] took aim at the reverend. But Parkhurst combined the zeal of a missionary with the certainty of a 19th-century reformer. Cool and self-possessed, he simply refused to be embarrassed.

HOWE: Did you tell Mrs. Adams that you were a minister of the
    Gospel?
PARKHURST: No, I did not.
HOWE: Did you remind those poor creatures that they were
    misbehaving?
PARKHURST: No, sir.
HOWE: Did you see them undress?
PARKHURST: I did not. I turned my gaze away.
HOWE: Did you play leapfrog?
PARKHURST: No.
HOWE: But you drank beer?
PARKHURST: Yes.
HOWE: And you are a minister?
PARKHURST: Yes.[70]

Hummel was also upset at the disgraceful behavior of "this nauseating, slimy polluter of the Gospel." Getting himself nicely worked up—no need for Howe to have all the fun—Hummel delivered the closing argument. He imagined Parkhurst saying, "Come to my arms. I am here to suppress vice. On with the dance! Let joy be unconfined." Sure, the women at the Adams residence might be degraded—a significant concession, given that this was supposed to be a prostitution case—but "I hold Hattie Adams's character," Hummel concluded, "against all the Dr. Parkhursts in the universe."[71] Adams wept.

All in a day's work for Howe & Hummel, but to no avail. Adams was convicted and Parkhurst vindicated. "They are truly the devil's advocates," he said of Howe and Hummel. "But they never unsettled me."[72]

But the story did not end when Adams shipped out to Blackwell's. The pressure on Tammany continued to build, and when the state legislature went Republican in the 1893 election, it moved quickly to institute proceedings to embarrass the city's Democratic machinery. The result was a committee to investigate police corruption. State Senator Clarence Lexow would lead it.

It almost died at birth. Democratic Governor Roswell Flower vetoed a bill to fund the committee, saying that New York was the best-governed city in the state, and that the proposed committee was just a partisan effort to shame Democrats. New York's Chamber of Commerce stepped in and agreed to pay the bills.

With that, the Lexow Committee was off. John Goff, an acerbic lawyer who looked like a biblical patriarch, was the chief counsel. A stickler for the law in the United States, the Irish-born Goff was a quasi-revolutionary when it came to the old country. His grandfather had been hanged by the British for his part of the 1798 rising,[73] and Goff himself once organized something called the "Irish Rescue Party," which chartered a whaling ship to go to Ireland to try to rescue some rebels about to be shipped to Australia.[74] For his more prosaic crusade in New York, he had two assistants: William Travers Jerome, a former assistant district attorney and the man who would ruin Hummel, and Frank Moss, the lawyer for Parkhurst's Society for the Prevention of Crime.

Between March and December 1894, the committee interviewed

678 people, almost all of them extremely reluctant. The witness chair, for good reason, became known as "Goff's Gridiron."[75] The man was relentless, sarcastic, and well informed. The published account of the proceedings comprises almost 6,000 appalling pages, and proved Goff's contention that the police force was, "to all intents and purposes, exempt from and above the law of the land."[76]

Witnesses were guaranteed immunity from prosecution for their testimony. On the other hand, they were not allowed to have lawyers with them. Even so, Howe and Hummel were all over the proceedings, on stage and off.

Prostitution, for example, was proved to be a rich source of supplemental income for the cops. (It was also a reliable source of cash flow for Howe & Hummel. When the police for some reason raided a bunch of Tenderloin establishments in 1892, the firm represented almost of the women—and not a few of their clients.[77]) The key witness before the Lexow Committee in this regard was Matilda Herman, known as the French Madame. The prospect of her testimony was considered so dangerous that a group of police chipped in $1,700 and escorted her out of town.[78] She got snagged on an ill-advised visit back.

Nell Kimball, a business rival, described the French Madame as "a monster with the mustaches and whiskers of a horse-car driver" who ran a rough house where "nude women were manhandled, danced the can can and put on gang bangs, circus shows for the customer who demanded wilder and wilder stuff."[79] So we can safely assume that Matilda Herman was no innocent. Nevertheless, the shakedown was extreme. She testified that she had paid more than $30,000 to various police over the previous few years, becoming known to the force as the "French gold mine."

Then there was police brutality, which was so routine that Goff took to referring to police stations as "slaughterhouses."[80] It was also almost never punished. The most telling testimony came from Augustine Costello, a former police reporter who in 1885 had published—at his own expense, and for the benefit of the police pension fund—a ludicrously slavish book, *Our Police Protectors*. After a series of complications regarding a similar hagiography of the Fire Department, Costello found himself at a police station on behalf of two employees. He posted bail, went to dinner, and returned around 7:00 p.m. to retrieve his men. "Like a spider and the fly," he told the Committee, "I walked right into Inspector Williams's arms."

This was terrible timing; Costello had just written an article critical of Williams. Clubber was not amused. He kept Costello on a leash for the next few hours while he sent a few men to ransack the writer's house and terrify his family. This they did. Around midnight, Costello was formally arrested on a charge of destroying evidence in reference to the dispute over the fire department book. Transported to a different police station downtown, he was about to enter when two men came out of the darkness. One, seen clearly in the light of the lamps, was Captain McLaughlin; his fist enveloped in brass knuckles, he punched Costello in the face. The writer fell to the sidewalk, where he was kicked and mauled. Dragged into the station house, he was booked and beaten some more, then sent to the cells, where he was denied water.

The next morning, Costello called in Howe & Hummel. The latter represented him and got the bogus charge dismissed. In his only appearance before Lexow, Hummel confirmed Costello's story. The writer was in a "very badly bruised condition," Hummel told the committee. "He seemed almost unrecognizable to me."[81]

The cops were also directly involved in gambling and other rackets, as the testimony of George Appo made clear. Appo was the son of Quimbo Appo, who came to the city in the late 1840s and may have been the first Chinese immigrant to New York;[82] he was certainly the first one to be convicted of murder. Like his father, George Appo was a career criminal, albeit a nonviolent one. A Howe & Hummel client, as his father had been,[83] Appo gave Lexow what amounted to a tutorial in the green-goods game (also known as the "panel" or "sawdust" game), a con in which people thought they were buying counterfeit currency, but actually got robbed of their own good money. Appo detailed how the police helped to codify the rules of the green-goods game. They would assign territories to different dealers—$500 for exclusive rights to a ward, plus 50 percent of the profits from any sucker who complained[84]— then clear out the competition.[85] Howe & Hummel not only represented

Appo on his numerous days in court, but also acted as counsel for most of the green-goods industry. And it was an industry. James McNally, a Howe & Hummel client, was the J. P. Morgan of the panel game. He had something like 300,000 names and addresses[86] and employed eight writers to compose letters intriguing enough to draw in dupes.[87] In a big operation, 20,000 circulars a day might be sent out,[88] and $8,000 in profits taken in.[89]

Lexow witnesses also proved that shakedowns of legitimate businesses, from bootblacks to sailmakers to peddlers to steamship companies, were routine. One man, short of money, got a helpful suggestion: Pawn your wife.[91] Saloons were assessed a fee to keep their license and to stay open after hours. Harry Hill[91] ran a famous saloon/dancehouse (ladies free all the time, and not-quite ladies too) on Houston Street that was a staple of slumming tours.[92] Hill didn't allow robbing or killing on the premises, and he insisted that the ladies at work there be treated as such.[93] He had always been on cordial terms with the police, opening his wallet without being asked. But when an old friend, Captain Murphy, took over the local precinct, he shook his old pal down for a $1,000 "initiation fee" and insisted on a $50 a month retainer. Hill bristled at the brazen demand and also refused to pay another assessment of $800. Murphy's law struck back. A few weeks later, Hill's place was shut down. Then he was hounded out of Harlem and blackballed in Brooklyn. In his better days, Hill was fat and jolly and wore a diamond on his shirtfront[94] that Howe might have envied. Now he was ruined, reduced to hocking his winter coat. In April 1894, friends sponsored an evening benefit to raise some money to put him back on his feet. Abe Hummel chipped in $50.[95]

For those who are tempted to regard all this with a wink and an indulgent smile, perhaps even feeling warm nostalgia for the naughtiness of Olde New Yorke, consider the story of Caela Urchiteel, a Russian immigrant widow with three children who toiled long hours at a boardinghouse to save $600 to buy a cigar store. On her first day in business, the local bobby demanded a payoff. When she refused, he dragged her through the streets, tossed her in jail, and found a couple of urchins to testify she had sold herself to them for 90 cents. Convicted in a police court that couldn't be bothered to hear testimony as to her respectable character, she went back to jail. Finally able to pay her fine and go home, the widow found her children had been sent to an orphanage, which refused to give them back because she was a convicted prostitute. In short, Mrs. Urchiteel lost everything because she shooed a crooked cop out of her shop with a broom. She pleaded to the court: "My heart craves to have my children with me." On October 19, in a scene that softened even the gruff Goff, the family was reunited.[96]

All of this was terrible, but it could also be dismissed as the actions of a few, or maybe more than a few, rogue cops. But as the Lexow Committee ground on, proving uncomfortably competent, that convenient fiction became increasingly unbelievable. The question became: How far up did the rot go?

Right to the top. That was the bombshell dropped by Captain Max Schmittberger, who had been accused of taking payoffs by an agent of the Cunard shipping line and then accused, even worse, of not sharing the wealth with his juniors. The Police Board charged him with taking bribes.

Why him? At this point, many more disgusting things had been heard, but snatching graft from another cop crossed the blue line. Facing years in state prison for doing what everyone else did, Schmittberger made two decisions. First, he hired Howe & Hummel. And second, he decided that he would be damned if he was the only one who went down.

With pressure bearing down from two directions—the Lexow Committee wanting answers and the Police Board wanting his scalp—his wife made up his mind for him. On the morning of December 21, Frau Schmittberger gathered their eight children in the dining room and asked her husband, "Max, are you going to prison and leave your wife and children to starve in the street?" He broke down at the pathetic sight, and vowed to tell all.[97] Beginning that afternoon, he did, in a confession that *Harper's Magazine* called "astounding in its revelations of the depth and breadth of official degradation and corruption."[98]

Schmittberger told an ugly tale, accusing two of the four serving inspectors of accepting bribes and two of the three commissioners of protecting vice (the third took money for promotions). One of the commissioners, he said, even ordered a patrolman to return to a whorehouse he had investigated to apologize to its keeper, Sadie West, for his lapse of protocol.[99] Link by link, Schmittberger described the chain of systematic blackmail that bound the police to the criminal element. He admitted he was involved from both ends, taking the tribute collected from gamblers, saloonkeepers, pimps, numbers runners, and businesses by his inferiors and then passing it up to Inspector Williams,[100] among others. As for getting on the force or getting promoted, Schmittberger said, there were only two options: "politics or money."[101]

The captain, in truth, told the committee nothing new. But what he said was shocking anyway because he said it. It was possible to doubt the veracity of the Matilda Hermans and Harry Hills of the world, and even to question the motives of patrolmen who had good reason for contempt against their superiors. But when a captain with a record of bravery and 20 years on the job confirmed the worst, implicating himself in the process, there was no more room for doubt. Asked if the police department was rotten, Schmittberger's reply was simple: "to the core."[102]

Howe & Hummel made the criminal indictment against Schmittberger go away, as even the prosecution must have known would happen. The Lexow Committee had repeatedly assured its unwilling witnesses that nothing they said could be used to prosecute them. The rules could not be changed because the police department was angry with a man it regarded as a snitch.

Schmittberger did not get off scot-free. A few weeks after his testimony, he was transferred to an outpost in the Bronx that was so remote it was commonly known as "Goatsville." But he would get the last laugh. A few months later, he came back to civilization;[103] he went on to become chief of detectives and one of Police Commissioner Theodore Roosevelt's favorite officers. Journalist Lincoln Steffens was so fascinated by the handsome German that he tried (and failed) to write a novel about him[104] on the theme of how a good man goes bad. But the captain had lost the respect of much of the force. At the police parade in 1896, the first since Lexow, "Schmittberger the Squealer"[105] was hissed.

• • •

What the Lexow Committee revealed, convincingly and publicly, was what many people suspected—that the police force was not so much the enemy of crime as the regulator of it. This was old news to the bad guys, of course. And to be fair, this system—and it was very much a system—was okay, for a time, with many New Yorkers. But things went too far. Vice became too visible, cops too greedy, the corruption too wide and too deep, the victims, like the widows Urchiteel and Augustine Costello, too innocent. The Lexow Committee used the term "terrorism" to describe the police hold on the city.[106] It had become almost impossible to be an honest cop, which was profoundly demoralizing to the many men who wanted to be just that. Lexow was backlash.

But was it effective? Less than it might have been, given the detailed and convincing evidence. When Lexow ended, the newspapers confidently predicted further investigations into the police courts and the Fire Department, whose operations, as hinted during the hearings, also smelled distinctly rotten. That never happened. And although dozens of men in blue were suspected, only a few were convicted. McLaughlin was one of these—not for crushing Costello, but for bribery. In his ten days in the Tombs, he shared a cell with Michael Considine, a Howe & Hummel client. McLaughlin was able to get the verdict reversed; he would step out of the Tombs, get back on the beat, and retire with an estimated fortune of $1 million.[107] All the other cases were thrown out for lack of evidence.[108]

Many a criminal cop left the hearings to return straight to duty. One of these was Alexander "Clubber" Williams, who once summed up his philosophy of policing this way: "There is more justice at the end of a policeman's nightstick than in any Supreme Court decision." As far back as 1878, the National Police Gazette was saying of him that it was a rare month "in which he does not furnish at least one newspaper item in the way of an assault upon some un-uniformed plebian."[109] By 1887, according to one historian, he was the subject of 358 formal complaints and had been fined 224 times.[110] He barely dodged being expelled from the force. By 1891, though, Williams was so highly regarded that he almost became chief; Byrnes got the job instead.[111] The two had a testy relationship; Byrnes had brought Williams before the Police Board on charges of neglect of duty in 1893. Clubber got off with a talking-to.

Lexow was a sterner test. Forced to testify and at least listen to tough questions, Williams denied everything and displayed a defiant insouciance that affronted the committee but served his own interests well. The 18 charges of assault that had been brought against him? He wasn't sure there were so many. Disorderly houses in his district? He didn't close them because "they were kind of fashionable at the time"[112]—a rare instance of his saying something that approached truth. The charges, from Schmittberger, former Mayor Hewitt, the grand jury, the board of education, Charles Parkhurst, and innumerable merchants and crooks, of corruption? They all lied. What about the many dives operating all around him? He didn't know what was meant by a "dive."

Williams even came up with a dandy explanation for how he managed to own a yacht and a Connecticut mansion on his civil service salary. He had profited from real estate holdings in Japan, he said, where he had traveled as a ship's carpenter. When the Japanese consul explained that foreigners were not allowed to buy or sell land in Japan,[113] Williams simply said, well, he had.

Byrnes was the last witness heard from, on December 29. He made a better impression. Even so, his testimony damned the department. When he took over as chief in 1891, Byrnes said, he found it "honeycombed with abuses." Why that should have been a surprise to a 32-year veteran went unexplained and unexplored. Ditto for the story of his surprising wealth. Byrnes acknowledged a personal fortune of about $350,000; this, he said, was the result of stock tips he got from Commodore Vanderbilt and Jay Gould, who were grateful for his protection of Wall Street.[114] Politics was the root cause of the police problems, he said, not alliances with crooks and certainly not management.

All in all, the committee treated Byrnes with circumspection. Perhaps they wanted to leave the department with one hero; perhaps they were simply tired. Byrnes offered a patently insincere letter of resignation, which the committee declined to accept. He, too, went back to work.

Nonetheless, change was coming. A couple of days after Byrnes testified, New York had a new government, courtesy of the November elections in which voters vomited out Tammany. William Strong, the candidate of the reform coalition, became mayor. John Fellows beat incumbent DeLancey Nicoll to become district attorney, and John Goff replaced Frederick Smyth on the felony court.[115]

Elected in large part because of Lexow, Mayor Strong had a mandate to do something about the police. And he had a man in mind to do it: Theodore Roosevelt, who became president of the revamped Board of Police Commissioners in May 1895. An interested observer of Lexow, TR believed that the Police Department was rotting from the top down, and that the rank and file were forced into corruption by their superiors. "The bulk of the men," he believed, "were highly desirous of being honest."[116] He wanted the scalps of those who felt otherwise.

Less than two weeks after he took office, both Byrnes and Williams were gone. Many dirty cops had already resigned, fearful of prosecution; TR coaxed 200 more to do the same and appointed 1,700 new men,[117] chosen mostly on merit.[118] On Roosevelt's watch, patrolmen were more likely to walk their beats, rather than wait them out in saloons, and morale improved. He also shut down the shelters in many police stations that made them the place of last resort for the homeless, began a bicycle squad, and insisted on firearms training.[119]

Roosevelt picked the wrong battle, though, when he decided to try to enforce the law that forbade the sale of booze on Sundays. He was right that payoffs to cops to stay open on the Sabbath were the source of petty corruption from which much else flowed. In this at least Roosevelt was no prude; he would have preferred a law legalizing Sunday openings. But the law was on the books, and he decided to enforce it, thus enraging the hitherto staunchly Republican German community. It all became a bigger mess than anyone intended. A civic hero in 1895, Roosevelt might have been the most unpopular man in New York in 1896—and the most frustrated one in 1897. He was thrilled to go to Washington that April as assistant secretary of the Navy. And much of New York was glad to see him go. Hummel said of TR: "When they bury him, they can write on his tombstone, 'Here lies all the civic virtue there ever was.'"[120]

The Lexow backlash inevitably wrought backlash of its own. Strong was a one-term mayor as Tammany retook power with the slogan, "To hell with reform!"[121] Boss Richard Croker returned from England. Schmittberger rediscovered the delights of off-the-books income.[122] New York, it appeared, was back to business as usual.

Not quite. The effects of Lexow were less than they should have been. Still, they were more than anyone had anticipated, and they linger to this day. Lexow broke the idea that the way to police New York was to operate hand-in-glove (or pocket) with the criminals. Under Roosevelt, the police began to show that they could, as he put it, "be both honest and efficient."[123] That was a new and refreshing concept for Gotham, and one that has informed the way the city has seen its police ever since.

There are tangible reminders of the Lexow era as well. Back then, reporters worked across the street from the police headquarters on Mulberry Street in apartments known as "shacks." In today's Police Headquarters, a squat brown building of remarkable ugliness, journalists share a warren of rooms known, of course, as "the Shack." And to this day, all of New York's police commissioners sit at the wooden desk first used by Theodore Roosevelt.

EIGHT

The Play's the Thing

Not quite A-list.

That was Olga Nethersole's place in the Broadway order. She was not in the same firmament as Sarah Bernhardt or Mrs. Patrick Campbell, but the Englishwoman was definitely a star. Her specialty was acting (or overacting, according to George Bernard Shaw[1]) roles that featured bold, independent, and decidedly immodest women. That made her controversial. Fallen women were acceptable in the late Victorian theater as long as they stayed down; many of Nethersole's characters, however, picked themselves up and triumphed. So, for that matter, did Nethersole. When her father died, she worked for two dreary years as a teenage governess before quitting to go on the stage. She quickly became a star of the second order, and she loved it. Nethersole dressed extravagantly, had a string of gentleman callers and produced her own shows. When she came to the United States, she brought barrels of English rainwater for her complexion. A self-made diva who acted as if she were to the manor born,[2] she was regarded by moralists with suspicion. They considered her insulting when she appeared barefoot and vulgar and blew her nose onstage.[3] And then there was the "Nethersole kiss."

The actress had unveiled this stunning innovation in a theatrical version of *Carmen* in 1896. Kneeling at her lover's knees,[4] Nethersole would lean back, close her eyes, and initiate a lip-to-lip pucker[5] of apparent passion and definite duration. (Stagehands bet on how long the notorious kiss would last.[6]) The smooch hinted at such charged sexuality that, the *National Police Gazette* was happy to report, the "scenery shriveled up like scorched paper and the metal buttons on Carmen's dress grew hot."[7] Perhaps it exaggerated.

One contemporary critic called *Carmen* "a filthy play in which lust and animal passion were shown with disgusting frankness" and her performance a "study in lasciviousness."[8] Another did not pronounce on the play's morality, but he knew what he was seeing: "nitroglycerine, pure and simple."[9] The recipient of the kiss had this to say: "In fifteen years experience on the stage, I've never known a leading lady to kiss the way Miss Nethersole does," said Ernest Leicester. "She nearly took me off my feet the first night, don't you know. . . . They're real reckless kisses." Leicester was a trouper, though, soldiering on night after night, an uncomplaining Don José.

Naturally, *Carmen* became a huge hit. Ticket sales rocketed, with young women the most conspicuous, and attentive, spectators. Nethersole modestly disclaimed any credit: "These kisses are not my kisses, but Carmen's. Mine are quite different."[10]

So when Nethersole came back to the United States in 1900 to try out her new production of *Sapho*, the purity police were watching. By then, the public knew pretty much what to expect when she took the stage—a lavish production, with her in the middle of it, milking every bit of emotion and then some.

In *Sapho*, she had a role that fit her persona perfectly. Based on the 1884 French novel by Alphonse Daudet, the play told the story of a courtesan, Fanny Le Grande, who meets a young diplomat, Jean Gaussin, at a ball; she impresses him with her glamour as she climbs a pedestal in her flowing gown to recite poetry. Later that night, she seduces him. But when Jean finds out about her considerable past (among other things, Fanny had posed for a notorious sculpture of Sappho), he is furious. She begs him to stay, offering to shine his boots or be his dog. He leaves anyway.

Fanny is bereft. An earlier lover, the father of her son, returns to her after getting out of jail and offers her marriage. Then Jean returns, pledging his troth, too. In a scene that had audiences in tears all over the country, Fanny leaves a farewell letter on Jean's sleeping breast. She bids good-bye to the love of her life in order to do the right thing by her son, returning to Paris to a marriage that she does not desire. The curtain falls.

Nethersole financed the production herself. After opening in Milwaukee, it played to reasonable reviews and happy audiences in Chicago, Atlanta, Nashville, Louisville, New Orleans, Cincinnati, and Detroit.[11] It struck something of a nerve in Pittsburgh, where a few ministers went public with their fears about the rotten example Fanny Le Grande set for the innocents of the smoky city. Not so at least one drama critic, who had loved Nethersole's *Carmen* and was bowled over by her *Sapho*. Never was the actress "so absolutely unique, more original in conception, more finished or brilliant or various in execution than as Fanny Le Grande,"[12] wrote Willa Cather.

Perhaps unwisely, Nethersole's manager, Marcus Mayer, quietly played up the ministers' fears; hints of indecency were a proven way to swell box office receipts. And sure enough, when the production moved to New York, the rumors that *Sapho* was risqué helped sell out the first four weeks in a day.[13]

But the indecency card can be trumped, particularly in a town with eight daily newspapers, all of them looking for a way to stand out from the pack. When *Sapho* opened at Wallack's Theatre on February 5, 1900, the reviews were mixed. The consensus was that the play was not obscene, just not very good. The exception to this view was the *Tribune's* William Winter, who got out his thesaurus to damn the "dark, dirty, and stupid" play as a "reeking compost of filth and folly." But Winter fell short of calling on the authorities to shut it down; he assumed it would not last long owing to its many flaws. The *Herald* liked the play, although it suggested a little "toning down," while the reviewer for the *World*, a tabloid that was big on morality—particularly ugly, headline-worthy breaches thereof—saw it as vulgar and disappointing, but short of shocking.

It was left to the *Journal* to point out just how dangerous *Sapho* was to Gotham's morals. In a bylined column, "The *Sapho* Indecency," the paper's owner, William Randolph Hearst, laid out the paper's views. "We expect the police to forbid on the stage what they forbid on the sidewalk and in low resorts," he wrote with a forceful illogic that would have kept the murderous Macbeth or the slave-abusing Simon Legree from New York's whitewashed stages. "Since the law treats mercilessly the poor hunted woman of the streets driven into the gutters by want," he vented, "that same law can certainly protect decent women against contagion on the public stage."

The police didn't see it that way. Warned of the possible indecency, a number of them, including Chief Bill Devery, attended opening night, and came away impressed. Inspector Walter Thompson attended almost every day; his eagle eyes never saw what Hearst's did. It was certainly not a play for children, Thompson thought, but there were worse things onstage, and he, for one, liked it.

Though the *Journal* struck the first editorial blow at *Sapho*, it was the *World* that took up the battle in earnest. The *World* had owned the city's lower-middle- and working-class readers ever since Joseph Pulitzer bought the paper in 1883. He had introduced himself to his staff this way: "Heretofore, you have all been living in the parlour and taking baths every day. Now I wish you to understand that, in future, you are all walking down the Bowery."[14] It was as much business statement as editorial vision. Pulitzer went downmarket, serving up a stew of sex and violence. But he also treated his readers with respect, running profiles on local heroes and investigations of things that mattered to them, like dangerous tenements and dirty milk. *World* readers were strivers, and he supported their aspirations. In doing so, he prospered mightily, hiring Stanford White (see Chapter 10) to build him a mansion.

Then came the *Journal*. Since buying the then-moribund paper in 1896, Hearst had turned it into a serious rival, poaching dozens of the *World*'s best reporters and cutting into its circulation.[15] If the *Journal* was going to make a fuss about *Sapho*, the *World* would make a crusade.

For weeks, the paper drummed up hostility to the play. At first, the play's management was delighted. The theater continued to be packed, with ticket scalpers doing a roaring business, and copies of the original novel selling briskly on street corners. Young women proved *Sapho*'s most devoted fans, a sign of the degradation of the weaker sex that the *World* found particularly troubling. Day after day, the newspaper continued its campaign, rounding up pastors, aldermen, clubwomen, teachers, and other worthies, including, curiously, the commissioner of bridges, to denounce the play. Few had actually seen it, but they knew it was bad for the youth of New York. Still, the show went on, and on. It was a hit.

Finally, with the police clearly unwilling to act, the *World* did. It sent one of its reporters, Robert Mackay, to *Sapho*. He found what he was asked to find, and filed a complaint that the producers of *Sapho* had perpetuated a public nuisance by putting on a play that violated public decency. In his affidavit, Mackay explained the reason for his disgust:

> The theme of the play is the portrayal of the life of a lewd and dissolute woman in a way to offend the public decency; that Olga Nethersole, in the recitation of her lines, boasts that she is the mistress of a man, and that the said Olga Nethersole permits, publicly, an actor, one Hamilton Revelle, to carry her up a staircase in a vile and indecent manner.[16]

With an actual complaint in hand, and at least some of the press breathing down his neck, the district attorney, Asa Bird Gardner felt he had no choice. Reluctantly, he called out the troops to arrest Nethersole, Revelle, Mayer, and theater owner Theodore Moss on the misdemeanor. They called Howe & Hummel.

Of course they called Howe & Hummel. By 1900, the firm had the largest and most sophisticated theatrical practice in the country. That was the work of Little Abe, who was so ardent a first-nighter that when he missed one, actors took it as an ill omen.[17] On Broadway, it became something of a badge of honor to be represented by Hummel. His client list ranged from Lillie Langtry and Sir Henry Irving to Jo-Jo, the dog-faced boy.[18] Signed pictures of these and other luminaries pockmarked the walls of his office.[19] When an attempt to blackmail John Barrymore failed—he had no reputation to preserve, he told Hummel—he became a client, too. So did Mark Twain, who hired him to defend him against a lawsuit from a playwright who said he had reneged on a deal regarding a stage version of *The Prince and the Pauper*.[20]

Hummel was counsel for the Actors' Fund and represented theater managers in their successful effort to refuse to honor tickets bought from scalpers.[21] He was also the legal representative of the French Society of Dramatists. On their behalf, he won a landmark decision that granted copyright protection to foreign works. Prior to this, the rule had been that any work published abroad was automatically in the public domain in the United States. Gilbert and Sullivan got so tired of having their work ripped off the second it went onstage that when they brought *The Pirates of Penzance* to the United States in 1880, they did not publish a libretto or score. Unable to plagiarize, U.S producers turned to satire; a spoof called *The Pie Rats of Penn Yan* was on the stage in months. Hummel later won a decision declaring illegal plagiarizing by memorization.[22] He even wrote his own one-act play, *A Case Out of Court*, which apparently never saw the footlights.[23]

Copyrights and contracts were not the stuff of the dramatic courtroom confrontations in which Howe reveled, but Hummel managed to bring a bit of pizzazz to his specialty. In a dispute over the rights to produce *Zaza,* a play almost as notorious as *Sapho*, Hummel bought a box seat for a process server. In the middle of the first act, the young man jumped onto the stage, thrust the papers at Mrs. Leslie Carter and exited stage right.[24] Poor Mrs. Carter had the vapors and had to retire for a few minutes at the end of the first act, but she came back strong.

The theatrical element provided useful economic synergies across the legal practice. At the same time that Howe was readying Carlyle Harris's appeal, for example, he was also defending Colonel William Hayes on a charge of perjury brought by a spurned lover, who said she had lent him $2,000. The case undoubtedly came through Hummel's connections—Hayes had once been accused of bigamy by Loie Fuller, the famed serpentine dancer.[25]

Many a chorus girl greased the blackmail machine that was a lucrative, albeit low-profile, part of the business. As Hummel's fictional alter ego, Quibble, put it: "A family skeleton is the criminal lawyer's stron-gest ally. Once you can locate him and drag him forth, you have but to rattle his bones ever so little and the paternal bank account is at your mercy."[26]

Howe & Hummel actively sought out blackmail prospects, sending younger members of the firm to chat up struggling actresses, singers, and other likely prospects. It was this division of the business that scared people. "Really, old chap," one roué told his lawyer, "if I saw Howe & Hummel on a letter addressed to me, I would die of fright."[27] Hundreds of men knew exactly that feeling. But in their way, Howe and Hummel were honorable. In a Tammany town, staying bought was the height of ethics, and in this they were true. A brazier in Hummel's office took care of the evidence and the lawyers never allowed a girl to hit up the same mark twice for the same offense.

Another benefit of their connection with the theater was that they had no trouble finding people to play sympathetic "family members" in Howe's criminal cases, ranging from bereft grandmothers to sniveling little brothers. For hard-up actors between gigs, it beat waiting tables. Finally, showbiz types had as much difficulty staying married then as they do now, so there were a healthy number of divorce cases. These, in turn, could bring other work.

Consider, for example, one Katherine Viola Clemons. She caught the eye of Buffalo Bill Cody in London in 1887; he was so impressed that he financed two theatrical tours for her, one in England and one in the United States. Alas, her talents were as limited as her charms, but at least to the lion of the Wild West, they were limitless. He lost $70,000 on the ventures.[28] But she and Cody stayed in touch for the next decade.

In 1898, Clemons won the obscure-actress lottery, marrying Howard Gould, the third son of Jay Gould, the railroad baron who had died one of America's richest men. Shortly before their marriage, the *World* published a melodrama in five parts, strongly suggesting that the rela-tionship between Buffalo Bill and the chorus girl might not have been strictly platonic. The Goulds hired Howe & Hummel to sue for libel. At this point, everyone knew who Howe and Hummel were, but Howard Gould knew them for the most painful of reasons: personal experience in being on the wrong side of the men of Centre Street. He had come away from the experience unsettled, poorer—and impressed.

In 1893, Zella Nicolaus—blond, blue-eyed, and with a startling resemblance to Lillian Russell—sued the very married George Gould, Howard's brother, claiming that he had tricked her into giving back a check for $40,000 (for services unstated). The poor young thing was the soul of honesty, both Howe and Hummel declared. "I never had a client," Howe said, "with whose truthfulness I was more impressed."[29] Considering his clientele, that may have been an artful dodge. But the partners would, they hinted, be willing to consider a compromise.

Only 18 at the time, Zella was old beyond her years. It turned out that she had deserted a husband in Joliet, had been known as Rose Lytle in Indianapolis, and had somehow prospered mightily in Chicago, winning the temporary patronage of the mayor as well as that of Buffalo Bill. Chief of Police Thomas Byrnes swore he knew enough about her to regard her as "an adventuress, a blackmailer, and a criminal."[30] To which Howe replied: "We are unrippled and unruffled."

Even if Zella's past had been active, Howe pointed out, that did not prove she was necessarily lying about the $40,000, and George Gould had been seen to visit her several times at her New York boardinghouse. These visits might well have been innocent. It was probably brother Howard who had given the check to Zella. George stopped payment when she tried to cash it and might have been trying to negotiate a settlement. A successful blackmailer—and there is no doubt that this was the fair Zella's profession—needs something to work with. As for Byrnes's opinion, Hummel's response was simple: "Let him bring charges, and we will try the indictment before we bring our present suit to court." In other words, publish and be damned. She's going for the money.

The Goulds blinked first. Accompanied by a Howe & Hummel underling, Zella went on a shopping spree of epic dimensions, including the purchase of a sealskin jacket trimmed with sable.[31] Then she and her "guardians," under the names A. Harris and Miss Graham, boarded the steamer *Lahn*.[32] Hummel saw them off. They were next heard from in London, where the couple booked into a suite at the Savoy as Mr. and Mrs. Rahman.[33] Their eagerness to get to Monte Carlo suggested that their financial future would be anything but stable. But at least she had started off with a nice payoff, courtesy of the Goulds—Howard, George, or both.[34]

Zella, however, broke the code. She and Rahman were back in New York by the end of January and were arguing about the rent with boardinghouse keepers by March. When she reinstituted her suit against the Gould brothers, Howe & Hummel washed its hands of the violet-eyed vixen.[35] She won another settlement, this time for $3,000,[36] then disappeared.

It wasn't long after breaking off with Zella that Howard Gould took up with Clemons, yet another unsuitable blonde. When they married in 1898, no Goulds came to the wedding. Because the family disapproved, half of Howard's $10 million fortune was revoked. But Howard had his bride, and he was tender of her reputation—thus the libel suit. In the Buffalo Bill affair, the parties settled out of court. Cody made his own opinion of the business clear when he later remarked, in reference to Clemons, "I would rather manage a million Indians than one *soubrette*."[37]

The new Mrs. Gould did not take to her station with ease. She kept being sued for things like not paying her dressmaker or reneging on a contract with a portrait painter. Howe & Hummel defended her each time. The firm also helped Mr. Gould when a disgruntled valet sued. And finally, when the marriage predictably withered, Hummel helped Mrs. Gould prepare for the divorce, brought by Howard Gould on grounds of her infidelity—with Buffalo Bill, among others. One of nature's gentlemen, Cody turned down $50,000, at a time when he was close to broke, to testify against his former lover.[38] In short, a good client, Howe & Hummel knew, was a gift that could keep on giving. Showbiz brought lots of good clients.

Lillian Russell, for example, one of the great stars of the era, was a regular consumer of Howe & Hummel's expertise. At first, she didn't like it one bit. Hummel came after her in 1883 for leaving a production in the middle of a run to go to London to appear in a comic opera written by Edward Solomon (he would become her second husband). The experience of tangling with Hummel was memorable enough that Russell never used anyone else.

Hummel also took care of her marriages, which were inevitably followed by her divorces. Her first husband, Harry Braham, proved no problem. Russell had married him when she was 16 and they hadn't lived together for years. She didn't even need to pay the costs of the divorce, although she was the one who had strayed. Asking her to pay for the separation, Hummel argued, was "ungallant." Besides, "the only valuable notes she could utter were vocal, not of hand."[39] Her second husband, Solomon, was in no position to bargain: He was exposed as a bigamist. Hummel had that one annulled.[40]

But husband number three, Giovanni Perugini (real name: Jack Chatterton) threatened to be a nuisance. The couple met in 1894, when they were the leads in *Princess Nicotine*. This ridiculous comic opera was written by Charles Byrne, whose active love life at one point made him a respondent in three divorce cases simultaneously; Hummel was at the other end of all of them.[41] Russell, who was by no means a fool except when it came to men, found herself drawn to the tenor with the dark eyes to whom she made metaphorical love onstage. Two months after opening night, they married.

Somehow Russell had failed to notice what everyone around her had—that the gay signor was just that. Metaphorical lovemaking was the only kind he would offer her; he wanted to be her co-star, not her husband.[42] Besides, he was a nasty, petulant, vain piece of work who tried to embarrass her onstage. She eventually wrote an article for the *Herald*, explaining why she kicked him out. Perugini had threatened and abused her, she wrote. He tried to dictate her friends, fired her servants, and admitted he had married her for his career. Perugini, she said delicately, "showed that he had no right to marry any woman."

The erstwhile Mr. Russell whimpered, in a startlingly misguided rejoinder published in June 1894, a month after they separated. "Why sir, when we had to share apartments, she took all the pillows; she used my rouge; she misplaced my manicure set; she used my special handkerchief perfume for her bath; she always wanted the best mirror when we were making our toilets . . ." The litany of horrors went on.[43] He wanted alimony. He got something, but in the end, he went quietly, too.

Hummel also cleaned up after Russell in her various financial disputes. The queen of comic opera had become notorious for skipping out on contracts. With Hummel at her side, she got distinctly smarter about it. Thus, the affair of the tights. She no longer wanted to wear them on-stage, and she wouldn't perform for producer James Duff, who insisted on it. This was largely a ruse to get out of her contract—she had worn tights for years.

Still, there might have been some sincerity to it. Nature, Russell told the judge hearing the case in 1892, had been "exceedingly generous" to her—a lovely way of referring to her expanding figure. Besides, she might catch a cold and damage her voice if required to wear tights instead of trousers or skirts. The judge saw it her way, ruling that Lillian Russell's "figure was a national asset and had to be protected from all hazards."[44] She got out of the detestable contract, too.

And Hummel became the designated legal expert on tights. When the New York Senate, which apparently had no more serious matters to consider, took up a bill to ban the wearing of tights on the stage in 1897, it was Hummel who represented P. T. Barnum and the theatrical managers against this dastardly infringement on artistic license. He won.[45]

On one memorable occasion, Howe & Hummel got a case that touched on four of its specialties—theater, cops, divorce, and high society. That was the infamous Seeley dinner. This bachelor party on December 19, 1896, was no worse than many a stag night. But it got in the news and stayed there for weeks—a scandal, a joke, and an embarrassment that was so ludicrous in its inception, and got so far out of hand, that Howe & Hummel just had to be there. And so it was.

Where does the story start? It's not easy to say. Perhaps it began when an apparently distraught father called on the police. Perhaps it started when that cop invaded the celebration. Perhaps it started when the high-society partygoers complained loudly (but, they thought, privately) about the raid.

Or perhaps it had started three years before, at the "Streets of Cairo" pavilion at the World's Fair in Chicago. Complete with crooked byways, camels, and a scale model of the Temple of Luxor, this was one of the

fair's most elaborate exhibitions. But the main attraction was not architectural; it was the dancers who did the coochee coochee. A more formal
name for the performance was the *danse du ventre*; a more descriptive
one was the "shimmy and shake." Whatever it was called, nothing like
it had ever been seen in Chicago before. (Or in Cairo for that matter.)
But it looked vaguely Oriental and the things the four could do with
their midsections! A few outraged matrons, supported long-distance by
Anthony Comstock, tried to shut down the dancers for indecency,[46] but
they were laughed off. The publicity did wonders for attendance.[47]

When the World's Fair closed, the shakers and shimmiers headed
east. Gotham, in the guise of Inspector Alexander "Clubber" Williams,
was not ready for them. The tenderness of Williams's feelings was something of a surprise, given his reputation for brutality and his support
for boxing. But in December 1893, he was in a spot of bother. This was
the time when the Rev. Charles Parkhurst was going after the police for
corruption and indifference to duty. Williams, who was one of the city's
best-known and most controversial cops, was in trouble.

So it is likely that Clubber was looking for a high-profile bust to
display his dedication to morality. Four foreigners made a good target.
When he went to the Grand Central Palace to see the *danse du ventre*,
he was duly outraged. The first dancers, three Algerians named Zelika,
Zora, and Fatima (known as "the plump"), passed muster. But then
Egypt-born Ferida started to crouch and writhe and wriggle, to general acclaim. "Wow!" called one enthusiast. "Where is Comstock now?"
shouted another. Comstock was hard at work elsewhere that afternoon,
but Clubber Williams, dry cigar clenched between his teeth, was up to
the job. "Stop that!" shouted the blushing copper. "There can be no more
of this thing here tonight or any other night." He and his sidekick, Captain Berghold, the commander of the precinct, hustled the women offstage. Williams later explained his reasoning: "It is indecent, and offends
the morals of our citizens."

The latter assertion was dubious. People were filling the Palace several times a day to be offended. But New York's Finest were not to be
deterred. When the performers went back to work the next day, Captain
Berghold and two beat cops were ready. As soon as the writhing became

too interesting, they arrested the dancers for violating public decency. Enter Howe & Hummel. "On with the dance," Hummel roared. "We do not care to accept Inspector Williams as a censor of morals."[48]

Hummel got in the first shot at the police court, where he asked for bail and an immediate trial, pending which the dancers would continue their contributions to cultural diversity and the dissemination of global understanding. Zora, age 17, certainly took the experience in that light. "We want to take in everything," she said in fluent French. "You have such funny customs." Nor was 18-year-old Zelika intimidated. As the dancers waited before the judge, she began to sing a ditty from the World's Fair. Ordered to cease and desist, she responded with magnificent disdain: "No sing! No dance! No do noth'n! Mon Dieu! Maybe bimeby [bye and bye] no eat, no drink, no sleep. Z'en I die. Ah!"

Hummel liked Zelika. On first seeing him huddling with her manager, Adolph Delacroix, she had asked, "Who eez zees leetle man?" Hummel drew himself up to his full five feet (in his specially built platform shoes) and chirped, "Why, I'm the great lawyer who is going to defend you." Zelika looked down at him. "Great lawyaire? You never be great lawyaire. No high enough." Then she paused: "All same, you got nice face." Hummel loved it. This was going to be fun; and he went to work.

Look, he argued, Delacroix had invited arrest to settle the matter. (Ferida the plump, knowing this was the case, had declined to perform; her temper was of such a volcanic nature that she was excused.) The dance, he solemnly asserted, "had been given before the crowned heads of Europe." The judge was receptive and scheduled the case to be heard in a couple of days. In the meantime, the dance could resume. "Oh, it won't hurt anyone for a few days," he said. "Out in Chicago, I saw it myself. Bail will be $300 each." The dancers (except for Ferida, still in a snit) were back at work a few hours later. So was Captain Berghold, grimly sketching their movements in a little notebook. They made it easy for the artist, tripping down the stage to shimmy in front of him.

December 6, 1893, might well have been the most enjoyable day Hummel ever spent in court. There was standing room only in the courtroom; hundreds more had been turned away. Except among the killjoys at the prosecution table, an atmosphere of amused anticipation prevailed.

Surveying his legal arsenal, Hummel chose two weapons: the defense of high art and the deployment of high comedy. The *danse du ventre*, he declared, originated with the Phoenicians and the Greeks and represented a state of religious bliss. It was a favorite of the khedive of Egypt, and had passed muster with the best Chicago women, clergymen, and even lawyers. It symbolized the religion and poetry of the mysterious East, a classical dance of profound religious significance that imitated the movements of the planets and had been sanctified by history.

As for the dancer's attire, Hummel decided a picture would tell the story. At his signal, Zora flung off her coat and stepped onto a chair to reveal her costume. The pantaloons and jacket, Hummel intoned, were considerably more modest than the accoutrements of the average ballerina. Several young men fell off their chairs in their effort to discern the lawyer's point. They appeared to agree that there was nothing at all wrong with Zora's figure and scrambled back to their seats at Judge McMahon's scowl. This was no laughing matter, he pleaded. A roomful of muffled giggles argued otherwise.

The nature of the alleged misdemeanor was that the *danse du ventre* was so immodest as to be indecent. That question could only be evaluated by reference to its implementation. But Judge McMahon, who was determined to enforce decorum, turned down the women's kind offer to dance. Without a demonstration, though, how could he decide?

Hummel had the answer to this legal conundrum, which he rolled out during his questioning of the police. Captain Berghold testified that the objectionable aspects of the dance had to do with movements in the stomach area. "Do you know which part of the anatomy the stomach is?" queried Hummel. "No, I'm not a doctor," retorted Berghold. If the good captain could not explain the indecency, Hummel murmured, perhaps he could show it. With determined dignity, the captain rose from his seat, assumed the position, and solemnly wriggled his midsection. Snorts exploded from all corners of the room.

Next up was Policeman Dennis McMahon, all 300 pounds of him.

The very image of the burly Irish beat cop, his interpretation of the *danse du ventre* was given with more abandon, as he adjusted his coat, lifted his feet, and twisted. Ferida sneered. McMahon realized that he had not done justice to the classical dance, but he insisted that the way the performers "extorted" their stomachs was indecent. More pops of suppressed laughter. Sergeant Daniel Archbold did his manful best as well.

Back came Berghold: I know where the stomach is now, he told Hummel in triumph, and indicated the spot on his own anatomy. And the final fillip on the whole affair came in the guise of Anthony Comstock, who stood up and demanded to testify: "I am defending womanhood in this city!"

"So am I," replied Hummel.

And so was the court, noted the justice; sit down, Comstock. Then he gave his decision: guilty as charged. The dancers were fined $50 each and told to go and sin no more. Grumbling, Delacroix paid up, and sent the dancers back out that evening, minus the *danse du ventre*.

So it was a loss, but one that Hummel would not have missed for the world. And like many a celebrated loss, it led to more work.

As New York's leading legal experts on the *danse du ventre*, Howe & Hummel were naturally drawn into the Seeley affair.

All Herbert Barnum Seeley wanted to do was to give a memorable bachelor party for his brother, Clinton Barnum Seeley (their maternal grandfather was circus magnate P. T. Barnum). Herbert threw himself into the project, visiting numerous theatrical agents to get just the right entertainment. He was not specific, but he did make it clear that it was a bachelor party, not a Sunday school class.[49]

It was late in the evening of December 19, 1896, when one William Moore approached police Captain George "Whiskers" Chapman. In great agitation, Moore told the officer that his 18-year-old stepdaughter, Annabelle, a dancer of local renown who had performed her "Butterfly Dance" for one of Thomas Edison's moving picture prototypes,[50] had been approached by James Phipps, a theatrical agent. The proposition—the usual, but could she also dance nude from the waist down? No, she replied. How about just dropping her tights at the end of the dance? "By that time," Phipps explained, "the men would be so drunk that it would make no difference."[51]

Annabelle continued to refuse, but Moore believed that Phipps might have found women of more flexible ethics. (Moore somehow failed to mention that he, too, was an agent, and a rival of Phipps. Nor did Annabelle make it clear that if her modesty had been considered worth $20, rather than the $15 Phipps offered, well, tights be damned.[52]) Moore was sure that there was probably something immoral going on right this minute at Sherry's, one of the city's most famous restaurants. Oh, the horror! Chapman rounded up several of his men. At 1:30 a.m., they went in.

The doors were locked and bolted; Chapman leaned on the bell until someone opened it a crack. Then he and his men muscled their way through. The upstairs door was also locked. They broke it open. Chapman headed to the first door he saw and blundered into the room. Sure enough, he found damsels in *dishabille*—it was their dressing room. But there were also four men in there, laughing and acting thoroughly at home. Chapman chided the men: "You who have sisters and mothers and wives should be ashamed." At this point, young Horatio Harper (of the Harper publishing family) tried to defenestrate the captain. His friends restrained him, and the captain left. An equal-opportunity preacher, Chapman bestowed a fatherly lecture directed at a young woman who had fled behind a curtain: "You ought to be ashamed of yourself, degrading your sex this way."

Then he went in search of the ballroom that was the favored party site for young society. Propelled by frustration and anger, he burst in and saw—nothing. Or, rather, a bunch of men sitting at a round table smoking and drinking. Abashed, Chapman explained that he had come to investigate the charges of an "immoral entertainment." Chapman certainly knew what such entertainment looked like; he was known to collect protection money at Paresis Hall, a boy brothel on the Bowery.[53] At Sherry's, though, there was nothing going on; he would now leave, thanks very much. The men were hardly pleased to see him, but they took it well enough and invited him to have some champagne. Chapman further disgraced himself by revealing that he neither smoked nor drank. Then he went back to his post in the Tenderloin, which was at the height of its glory as the most vice-ridden square mile in the country.

The usual story is that the tenderloin, which had been known as Satan's Circus, got its new moniker from Clubber Williams when he transferred to it from a quiet district in 1876: "I've been living on chuck steak for a long time," he celebrated, "and now I'm going to get a little of the tenderloin."[54] Another story, though, is that the *bon mot* was Hummel's. On meeting Williams at Delmonico's after the transfer, Hummel joked to him, "That's a pretty juicy tenderloin they just handed you."[55]

There is a school of thought that it's not a party worthy of the name unless the cops come. The Seeley dinner fit that profile, and the kerfuffle looked likely to disappear on a froth of gossip. It didn't. Late-night theatergoers had noticed the conspicuous police presence around Sherry's and spread the word of the raid. Manhattan's bush telegraph quivered in excitement. "Policemen in Sherry's!" was the bemused reaction of one contemporary. "The world had not known such a horror since the Commune."[56] By the time the papers published the first stories on December 21, the guests who had been at the Seeley dinner were no longer sheepishly amused. They were furious. Louis Sherry called Chapman's action "an outrage"; the bridegroom's father hinted at legal action.

They would have done better to maintain a discreet indifference. The initial stories of the raid were bland. Even the *World*, which lived to ridicule the elite, could only manage "Funny Raid on Sherry's" as a headline for a half-column story. But the threats of legal action stirred not only the press, but also Chapman and his superiors. These included the chief of police and the Board of Police Commissioners, headed by a Republican reformer who didn't mind the occasional headline: Theodore Roosevelt. TR had made a point of roasting bad cops publicly. If Chapman had erred, he said, let's hear it. And if he hadn't, let's get the story out so he can be cleared.

The latter, of course, was precisely what the men at the dinner realized they did not want. But it was too late. The party was the talk of the city. (The future bridegroom, at work on the floor of the Consolidated Exchange, had to endure the attentions of his fellow brokers, who sang and danced the coochee-coochee around him.) Still, by December 23, all talk of legal action had faded into mutters of let bygones be bygones. Perhaps it would go away.

But Herbert Seeley, a young man whose defining characteristic was poor judgment, gave the affair new life by offering a statement to Police Commissioner Andrew Parker (one of TR's colleagues). In this, Seeley conceded that, yes, there had been men in the women's dressing room; yes, he had contacted agents to arrange a robust entertainment; yes, he had been offered dancers willing to shuck their clothes; but no, he had refused anything so "out and out vulgar." His lapse into honesty gave legs to what should have been a two-day wonder. The *World* got the statement, of course—it had more police friends than Roosevelt ever did—and happily published it, pointing out that young Seeley and Chapman were now telling pretty much the same story. Leaked affidavits from the insulted Annabelle Moore, as well as another theatrical agent who had refused to supply naked dancers, also backed up the idea that the goings-on at Sherry's might not have been strictly decent. Maybe the whole matter really should be aired out. Chapman, for one, welcomed the idea of legal action. Tired of being ridiculed, he was positively eager for his day in court.

On December 30, Clinton Seeley got married, and Chapman got his wish. Though no one involved with the dinner was willing to press charges, Chief of Police Peter Conlin decided that he couldn't let the matter drop. He charged Chapman with conduct unbecoming an officer. Members of the board would hear the case at police headquarters and that would be that, predicted Commissioner Parker. It would take "less than an hour."

Parker was a lawyer, and a smart one, but he could not have been more wrong. Although he was right that none of the guests would want to testify, that still left the talent—and remember, this was showbiz. The performers didn't mind seeing their names on the front pages one tiny bit. Indeed, even before the decision was made to have a hearing, one of them, Ashea Waba, had signed a sworn statement to the effect that she had been recruited and paid $100 to perform two dances—one in stockings, bloomers, and a fetching little bolero jacket; and the other in just her stockings. She had been waiting in a private room, primed with champagne, when Chapman arrived, then was hustled off to hide. She did do her first dance and was more than willing to drop her gauzy bloomers, but because of the concern that the police might return, she was forced to keep her clothes on.

A week later, at the request of Captain Chapman, she came to police headquarters to tell her story. She adored Commissioner Parker ("a prince"), but her first impression of TR was not as positive: "He show me his tooth like this"—and here she bared her own. "He looks so mad. I don't like him." But she did as she was asked. "I make my statement," she said. "I swear. I sign. I go away." And left wreckage in her tripping wake. "I do not know why everybody makes fuss," she mused.

Who was Ashea Waba? Well, her professional name was Little Egypt. Her specialty was the *danse du ventre*. And her lawyers were Howe and Hummel.[57] In an excellent mood at the prospect of such a case, Howe described himself as the "minister for Little Egypt."[58]

The hearing opened on January 7, 1897. But the Seeleys et al were goners before the case began, when their lawyer, Colonel E. C. James, lost a motion that testimony from the witnesses "of the character of Little Egypt" not be allowed. The motion was ridiculous; it was also the only chance for the 22 society men to avoid public humiliation. From the moment the gavel first came down, it was obvious to all that this was not about the legality of Chapman's entry into Sherry's. It was about the hijinks in the ballroom. Not that anyone cared if dancers agreed to flash skin to men who paid to see some. But there was curiosity: How did high society act when no one was looking?

Commissioner Fred Grant (son of Ulysses), the nominal head of the proceedings, was as interested as everyone else in the famous party. He let the matter wander off into fascinating, if irrelevant, byways. By the time the first witness, dancer Cora Routt, finished bussing the Bible and then narrating her theatrical history, everyone understood that tedious notions of rules of evidence would be disregarded. Commissioner Grant, and the hundreds of spectators—this was the hottest ticket in town, in every sense—appeared to be serious about finding out, for the sake of justice, every winsome little detail of the event.

Howe was in rare form, attired in a polka-dot tie and diamonds of awesome dimensions. One lawyer—and there were almost a dozen on hand—argued to be allowed to elicit testimony on what kind of place Sherry's was. "We ought to know if those who patronize the place are Chinamen, or negroes or—"

"Or little Egyptians," offered Howe. The barks of laughter drowned out Grant's ineffectual effort to restore order. At another time, Phipps, the theatrical agent, introduced himself by saying he had been in business for 17 years, furnishing players to clubs, private parties, and churches. Howe instantly interpolated in a stage whisper that carried to Brooklyn, "I wonder if he ever furnished 'Little Egypt' to a church."

All in all, though, the proceedings on the first day were boring enough that Roosevelt was caught yawning; he would not return. What mattered was that the point of the case had already been lost, and would never be recovered. The prosecution was supposed to prove that Chapman had exceeded his authority by entering Sherry's on a flimsy pretext. Looked at this way, it shouldn't have mattered what the entertainers did; the only issue was whether Chapman knew enough to invade the premises, hand out lectures, and the rest of it. But that narrow legalism didn't survive five minutes.

Howe can take a good deal of credit for ensuring that the court did not confine itself to the issue at hand. When the Seeleys' lawyer, E. C. James, tried again to keep out evidence of the dinner on the accurate but irrelevant grounds that it was not germane to the charge against Chapman, Howe delivered a 10-minute stemwinder. There were bits in there about public morality, other bits about the licensing law, and a few thoughts on the role of the courts in democratic society. Lawyer James replied by reciting the charge again—what does any of this matter? It's just a fishing excursion. Let 'em fish, Grant decided.

On day two, it was Herbert Seeley on the hook, providing "details worse than disgusting," in the words of the *World*, which refused to print them. Seeley insisted that he had told Phipps that "I did not want an exposure of the person," just a few "hot" (but not lewd) songs and some acts that had "ginger" (but were not suggestive). The court was beginning to explore these interesting distinctions when the entertainers, kept apart in a separate room, asked if they could go out for lunch. Sure, said the amiable Grant. Escorted by two detectives, the eight women were led to a humble restaurant near the court. But they were looking for a meal of the liquid variety; they quickly found a saloon that suited their purposes. It was a telling moment. Throughout the proceedings, the women managed to have a good time. They adored giving their testimony, relished the chance to even scores, and proved adept at repartee.

One dancer, Cora Routt, had nothing but disdain for Chapman, who had said mean things to her in the dressing room. Asked what she did as he left, she replied, "I said 'Good-bye,' and waved my hand to him like this." She pantomimed an elaborate gesture and blew a kiss toward Howe. He lapped it up. So did everyone else. When Routt descended from the stand, she bowed to Chapman, then swept out. The room had never seen a better exit.

Lottie Mortimer blushed when she told of the toast she had offered ("pure filth," according to the *Sun*; "obscene in the extreme," agreed the *World*). Still, she showed pride in her originality and a cheerful lack of trauma when she was, in her words, "mauled and pulled about" as men tried to cut the straps on her dress. Her bodice would stay up even without the straps, she chortled: "That's where they got fooled." Minnie Renwood calmly repeated the verses that the newspapers deemed unfit to print. And Annabelle Moore enjoyed detailing the subtleties of the butterfly, the borealis, and the sun dance.

But the men—they did not have a good time at all. When they weren't lying, which was most of the time, they were being embarrassed. William Moore, for example, had to admit that he had been living off his 18-year-old stepdaughter's earnings for several years, and had once booked her into the Grotto, a Chicago hall of ill repute. Louis Sherry was irritated and concerned for the reputation of his establishment. James Armstrong appeared blasé when he was accusing Phipps of asking him to provide dancers comfortable in their skin, but markedly less so when grilled about how many clients he had lost to his rival. Phipps squirmed as he told lie after lie. Even Whiskers Chapman, who wanted to be there and was freshly barbered and laundered for the occasion, was made to wriggle when he had to admit he had exchanged pictures with Annabelle. "I told her I was proud to know a woman who would protect her honor," he said nobly, "and said I would protect a woman's honor with my life." He twirled his mustache and endeavored to look magnificent.

But none of this compared to the experience of Herbert Seeley. He arrived with a swagger and left, hours later, in a heap. The statement he had given to Parker kept coming back to bite him, particularly his musings about how he had nothing against nudity per se, but he preferred the mystery of partial covering. Then there was the pesky matter that, well, someone had talked. Although Phipps had lied like a gentleman about the kind of entertainment he had been asked to provide, Chapman's lawyer, W. S. Hart, knew a lot more than anyone anticipated. Hart had the annoying habit of asking questions about things Seeley thought had stayed in that ballroom. There was, for example, the matter of the small gifts the entertainers had been asked to present. That sounded innocent enough—except that one of the gifts was a syringe, an implement that had exactly the same connotation then as now; other items were considered too filthy to mention.

And then, on the afternoon of January 12, the fifth day of testimony, Little Egypt took the stand. William Howe, whose baby-blue tie that day featured a diamond stickpin in the shape of a fork-tailed demon, opened the performance. Addressing Commissioner Grant, the maestro of the courtroom asked, "As Byron says, 'On with the dance.' Shall I bring in my little client, Little Egypt?"

She bounded in happily, then seated herself with a loll and a leer that boggled the room. Howe warned that if the dancer were to tell all she knew about the infamous dinner, she would probably end in prison or at the very least, never be able to work again. "You know that I must protect public morality as far as I have the power, and really—well, it's too dreadful, all of this is." So he would be very careful in his questioning. Then he let her rip.

The story she told, which was consistent with her affidavit, was a simple one. Phipps had hired her to appear before a party of artists (a group known to appreciate the female body). "I say I do what is proper for a-r-r-t," she trilled. Specifically, she agreed to "just a little pose in the altogether, a little Egyptian slave girl, *comprenez vous*? The pose in the altogether was for the encore." The first course was to be the *danse du ventre*.

In the event, Little Egypt was disappointed. As she was getting ready for her entrance, Captain Chapman arrived, and she was abruptly picked up and carried from a nice little blue waiting room, furnished with champagne, to a yellow one, which was similarly stocked. When the good policeman left, she did the *danse du ventre*, keeping her filmy black lace bloomers on the entire time. As she shimmied among the guests, they hugged and touched and squeezed and pinched the lithesome little brunette, who enjoyed it all. But Phipps called off the encore in case the police returned. Little Egypt was sad.

"Fine?" Ms. Waba asked as she concluded her account, delivered in a delightfully fractured mix of French, English, and something all her own. "That's all," agreed Howe. "That's all," repeated Colonel James. The *Herald*'s review: "amusing, outside of the filth."

And that was all. Even Grant realized that things had gone far enough. His motto throughout had been, "The truth will harm no one." He even seemed to believe it, which showed just how little he knew about courts, or New York, or life. (TR's opinion of his fellow commissioner: "a mere dolt." [59]) Herbert Seeley, for one, could have given Grant a tutorial about the hurtfulness of truth. There may also have been an element of class solidarity in Grant's decision. The more serious papers had downplayed the whole thing, burying a few anodyne paragraphs inside. The middlebrow ones like the *Sun* tried for dignity. But the yellow papers wallowed in the affair, and stuff was leaking out all over, among them rumors that "the women were not the only persons in the apartments who were careless about their attire." Unclad dancers were one thing; what could be expected of women of that sort? Dishabille among upper-class men was another.

None of Seeley's guests would be asked to testify; no more humiliation was necessary. Moreover, some of the lawyers had received letters, anonymous but in female writing, asking that they put specific questions to certain men. This looked like divorce in the making. Enough was enough, the commissioners decided; they could make a decision based on the evidence before them.

Looked at logically, Chapman could not win. It was unlikely that he had the right to enter private premises without a warrant, based on the uncorroborated accusation of a stranger. But if Chapman's entry was to be excused on the basis that the dinner was indecent, his apologetic departure from it then becomes problematic. By his own account, Chapman had seen nothing wrong.

But logic had been barred from the hearing right from the start. In effect, the entire four-and-a-half-day spectacle was an exercise in after-the-fact justification. If the dinner was bad, then Chapman must be good. And it worked. The charges against him were dismissed.

Not that matters ended there. Seeley and Phipps were arrested a few weeks later for conspiring to induce Little Egypt and Minnie Renwood to commit the crime of indecent exposure. Howe represented the entertainers, naturally, but the grand jury refused to indict—not because of their presumed innocence, but because "to put the case on trial would be against the interests of public morality."[60] Society had, belatedly, closed ranks.

The dancers, appropriately, profited from the affair. Little Egypt doubled her rate, and a number of the others cashed in on their notoriety by appearing in a burlesque, "Silly's Dinner," that did well for the elder Oscar Hammerstein—until he got indicted.[61] This, too, was dismissed. Annabelle Moore, who didn't perform at the Seeley dinner, probably got more publicity than any of those who did. She became famous enough that even the death of her guinea pig made the papers.[62]

Ashea Waba was not the last Little Egypt. Perhaps a dozen dancers adopted the title—a brand, and a promise, that outlived its creator. The original Little Egypt died in 1908, leaving an estate estimated at $100,000. When her sisters contested some of the terms, they turned to Abraham Hummel—even though he was in jail at the time. When it came to showbiz, Howe & Hummel was a tough habit to break.[63]

There is no reason that Olga Nethersole would have known all of this. She didn't need to. For anyone who was anyone on the stage, Howe & Hummel was as necessary an accessory as a dresser. Whether it was the *danse du ventre*, a husband who needed to be disposed of economically, or as in the *Sapho* case, the imputation of obscenity, Howe & Hummel got the call.

By 1900, Howe was largely tending to his roses. It was Hummel's practice now, and he moved the firm from the criminal work his partner had delighted in toward the civil cases and quiet extortion he preferred. It was lucrative work: One contemporary estimated that the firm was bringing in $300,000 a year.[64]

Of the many mysteries of Howe & Hummel, the economics of the practice is one of the most mysterious. The legend is that it was a cash-only operation that kept no books. At the end of every day, they would repair to the back room of Pontin's restaurant, where there were two tables—one for the partners, one for the judges of the felony court. There Howe and Hummel would empty their pockets and split the takings.[65] With Howe in semi-retirement at this point, it appears that Hummel got slightly more systematic, with a set of books, no doubt highly edited, that were destroyed each year.

There's something a little too pat about the Pontin's picture; it reeks of the kind of thing that would be said of the two. But the idea that record keeping was whimsical rings true. There were no income-tax laws to evade, and a practice with so many secrets did well to cultivate the idea that there was no paperwork to worry about.

Sapho was a natural—a high-profile case with rich theatrical defendants. Dauntless, Hummel stood ready to defend Nethersole against the witless philistines. Reaching for his rhetorical cannon, he called the charge "villainous, perjurious, [and] un-American."

"Un-American-like," echoed Nethersole.

Granted, the play was overwrought. Daudet's novel was an acerbic, antiheroic tale of an older woman without a conscience seducing a younger man without a clue. This had been Americanized into a mawkish tale of hopeless love, complete with a tacked-on moral of the redemptive value of maternal devotion. But so what? Nethersole liked mawkish; she did it well. She had made a career out of it. And now, her carefully contrived (and expensive) star vehicle had turned into a cause célèbre for the yellow press. Now, *that* was obscene.

Released on bail, she went back to work. When she appeared onstage the night of her arrest to the biggest crowd yet—people were crammed into the aisles—she got nine standing ovations. "Are you with me?" she cried. "Yes, yes," came the roar. "With you at my back," she continued, "I can defy the universe." Hummel was less dramatic, but equally confident: "I have absolutely no doubt the case will be thrown out of court after a short hearing."

It wasn't to be that easy. Magistrate John Mott appeared sympathetic to the defense, noting that the police were untroubled by the play and that people likely to be offended did not have to see it. But at the insistence of the district attorney, he grudgingly decided that the legal show, having been started, must go on.

Act one opened on February 23, 1900, in the Centre Street Police Court, steps from Howe & Hummel's offices. It was a ridiculous affair. Fifteen cops, plus police Chief Bill Devery, were on hand, presumably to beat off a rampaging crowd. Crowd there was; rampage, no.

The prosecution offered two witnesses. The first was Robert Mackay, the reporter for the *World* who had brought the charge. He got off to a bad start by being honest. Had he not been asked to by his employer, he testified, he never would have sworn out a complaint. Even so, he objected to the scene at the end of the first act in which the young Jean Gaussin, having escorted Fanny home, takes her in his arms and walks up a spiral staircase. The curtain opens several times to track the couple's progress. This, said the easily shocked reporter from a paper that reveled in reporting grisly crimes, was indecent.

HUMMEL: Tell us the manner in which he carried her.
MACKAY: He picked her up in his arms.
HUMMEL: What did he say before he picked her up?
MACKAY: I don't remember but his words were suggestive.
HUMMEL: Can't you recall any of the words?
HUMMEL: No. I believe, though, Miss Nethersole told him he was awfully good to her.

Hummel asked Nethersole to repeat the dialogue on the staircase, which she did.

FANNY: It was so good of you to bring me home. Thank you and
   good night.
JEAN: You are very tired?
FANNY: Yes.
JEAN: Which is your floor?
FANNY: The third.
JEAN: May not I carry you up?
FANNY: No.
JEAN: I won't let you walk, a great country fellow like I am.
FANNY: Not all the way; only half.

Well, Mackay had to concede, there was nothing filthy there. But
that was not the point, he protested. Fanny and Jean were clearly headed
to her bedroom, and they were not married. How do you know where
they were going? asked Hummel. Was there a room visible? No, replied
Mackay, but he had read the book. "So your deductions are drawn from
the book, and not from the play?" Something like that. ("Awful," Howe
harrumphed in a stage whisper from his seat at the defense table. "Is this
law? Is this justice?")

Hummel went on: "And it is a fact then when the curtain goes down the
two are left standing at the top of the stairs in plain sight of the audience?"

"Yes," said the ragged Mackay, who all too clearly wanted to be anywhere else. Hummel put him out of his misery, turning to the second
witness, the Rev. Phebe Hanaford, Quaker and head of the Women's
Christian Temperance Union. She was no more convincing. The *World*
had given her a ticket to the show, even after she told them that she was
no judge of plays and that she was already prejudiced against *Sapho* on
the basis of what she had heard. Go anyway, pleaded the *World*. So she
did, and found her preconceptions confirmed. "I don't like the theater,"
she said flatly, and the staircase scene was no good. Nethersole should
choose better material.

The defense countered with the tale of the humble omelet, which
Fanny makes for Jean one day in their love nest. Nethersole, Hummel
pointed out, used real eggs in this scene, and real dishware. No strum-
pet, he implied, could be expected to make an omelet with such dex-

terity. The prosecution objected stridently, but futilely, to this stunning evidence of Nethersole's domestic inclinations. At the end of the day, Nethersole got the last word, reciting, with dramatic effect, passages from the last act, when Fanny decides to marry the father of her child— a triumph of morality.

Between the omelet and the declamation, it had been a very good day for the defense. Hummel's accusation that the whole thing had been cooked up by the newspapers might have been speculative, and insulting to the DA's office, but the magistrate allowed it. The vox populi saw it this way, too, and expressed itself in verse.

> *Sapho must stop—it must shut up its shop;*
> *It is vulgar and low and infernal.*
> *That's what those say who have not seen the play*
> *That shocked both the* World *and the* Journal.
>
> *The extraordinary capers of these moral newspapers*
> *Is not at all strange or surprising.*
> *They are yellow, you see, and between you and me,*
> *They sadly need self-advertising.*

Act two opened the following day, with more testimony from *World*-induced theatergoers, such as the president of the Society of Life and the leader of the New York Mothers' Club. They were reluctant witnesses, having been dragooned into seeing a show they would never have bothered with, and then, to their dismay, subpoenaed. But they agreed that *Sapho* was shocking and ought never to be allowed. Even her dress was indecent, a gown so thin as to be diaphanous.

"Like this complaint," Hummel chipped in.

On the third day, the defense took center stage, starting with a now-familiar decimation of another *World* writer/witness, W. O. Inglis. He, too, objected to the staircase scene, but on fresh grounds. Fanny, he agreed, did try to refuse Jean's offer to carry her up the stairs, but her drawn-out "no" was insincere and therefore indecent. Besides, there was also the scantily clad girl in the first act. Hummel was ready, showing a picture of the female. Is this her? Yes. And you say she is indecently dressed? Yes. In the picture, though, her neckline was high and her dress almost to the ankles.

> HUMMEL: Any you said she was a young girl?
> INGLIS: I did.
> HUMMEL: Would it surprise you to know that woman is Carolyn
>   Heustis-Graves, and that she is married?
> INGLIS: I hope she's happy.

Like shooting fish in a barrel.

But Hummel was only warming up. Inspector Walter Thompson had made the arrests. Now he was the star witness for the defense. He testified that he didn't consider the play immoral. He had watched it 20 times, and would have no problem taking a 16-year-old girl to see it. The play was not only not indecent, but morally worthwhile, showing as it did the efforts of a scarlet woman to reform herself. And the skirts were modest; he had measured them himself.

The prosecution did its best to help the defense. Turning to the objectionable letters from former lovers that Fanny read and then burned in front of Jean, an obviously callow assistant district attorney named Richard O'Connor got himself in a fearsome mess. A previous witness had described the letters as "very indecent . . . [they contained] expressions of love, but it was not pure love." Feeling his oats, O'Connor asked Thompson to repeat the contents of the letters. Thompson demurred; his memory was not good enough. Hummel noted that he would be giving a copy of the play, including the letters, to Magistrate Mott.

"No!" shouted O'Connor. "We want the original letters submitted to the court. We want the actual letters read on the stage." Mott could not hide a smile; Nethersole and company were incredulous. They were not only being persecuted by the yellow papers; they were being prosecuted by an idiot. Nor was O'Connor's recovery impressive. Once it was explained to him that there were no actual letters, just pages in the script, he remarked: "Well, I've never seen the play, and don't know anything about it either." Then he went about trying to make the case that the play he had never seen and knew nothing about should be shut down.

At the end of the four-and-a-half days of trial, faced by five lawyers from the DA's office, Hummel must have felt as confident as he appeared to be. All the witnesses for the prosecution were either employed by the *World* or had attended the play at its behest. The alleged bits of indecency—the staircase scene, the letters, the costumes—had proved as flimsy as Sapho's gown. And this was New York, for heaven's sake, where any evening's stroll in the Tenderloin would be an education for the likes of Jean Gaussin, or even Fanny Le Grande.

But Magistrate Mott proved himself a political animal. Unwilling to be painted as the man who allowed indecency to fester, he kicked the case upstairs. Let a higher court decide the matter, he ruled. With similar caution, the police closed *Sapho* until it did.

Not that either the play or Nethersole went away. The latter reopened the theater the next day with *The Second Mrs. Tanqueray*, to riotous applause. And *Sapho* got new life as a spoof, *Sapolio*. In this version, when the couple returns from the ball, the spiral staircase is blocked—so Jean gets in a dumbwaiter and Fanny hauls him up. The program for the show was careful to note that this was a "clean satire."

Verifying the truism that a well-instructed grand jury would indict a ham sandwich, on March 22, this one indicted the *Sapho* crew, in language that even the *World* might have considered excessive. "The said Olga Nethersole, Hamilton Revelle, Theodore Moss and Marcus R. Mayer, being persons of wicked and depraved mind and disposition," it began, put on an entertainment,

> commonly called *Sapho*, in a lewd, indecent, obscene, filthy, scandalous, lascivious, and disgusting manner, make divers lewd, indecent, obscene, filthy, scandalous, lascivious, and disgusting motions, and assume lewd, indecent, obscene, filthy, scandalous, lascivious postures and attitudes . . .

Hummel presented a brave face, swearing that an indictment was what he had wanted all along. "Now," he said, "we shall have a speedy vindication before a jury of twelve good citizens. We have no fear as to the result." Nethersole swooned and took to her bed in nervous prostration, even canceling a performance of *The Profligate*, in which, for a change, she acted the part of a wronged innocent.[66] Art can certainly be made to imitate life.

A week later, the trial opened. Hummel wanted to re-create the famous staircase scene, and the inventor of a collapsible spiral staircase offered to supply one for the purpose. For its part, the prosecution wanted a special jury panel, because the case, it said, was so "complex and intricate." Judge Edgar Fursman denied both requests, and a jury was selected in less than a day. The fate of *Sapho* would be decided by a clerk, a bookkeeper, a broker, a painter, four manufacturers (of pianos, ostrich feathers, flowers, and handkerchiefs), an insurance adjuster, a driver, a clerk, and a secretary.

Both sides were primed. The prosecution had four lawyers on the case (the hapless O'Connor was not among them). Hummel had submitted a list of 50 witnesses. Among them: the entire cast, including Annabelle Moore of Seeley dinner fame,[67] and drama critics from around the country. And William Howe had come along, either for moral support or the sheer fun of it. Sporting a rose in his lapel and a hearty bonhomie, Howe gallantly told the besieged actress, "Nothing but this case would have dragged me" from his garden.

Realizing that neither Mackay nor Hanaford had proved particularly persuasive, the prosecution brought in a new witness, Henry Brevoort Kane. This self-described gentleman of leisure opined, as Nethersole glared at him, that the play was not up to the highest moral standards, citing *Sapho*'s "loose and flowing" gown and the "feline grace" with which she danced. The audience—the appropriate term for the standing-room crowd that had come for a show—snorted. Hummel did not bother to cross-examine the idler, who scuttled from Nethersole's angry glower, never to return.

W. O. Inglis did, however, come back. He objected to the rollicking opening scene of a ball, in which Fanny wore a "flowing, clinging" Grecian gown. But he saved his own dramatic flair for his interpretation of the "woman's no." Prosecutor No. 2 asked the witness to imitate the infamous negative. The reporter leaned back in his chair, threw out his arms, opened his mouth wide, and with both force and a hint of yearning, bellowed a baritone "no-o-o-o!" Hilarity in the courtroom; more curt words from the judge. Hummel had had much of his work done for him in these four syllables, but he decided to have a little fun with Inglis anyway. On cross-examination, he took up the issue of the clinging costume. Gesturing to the painted figure of a woman in the panel of the Fates that decorated the wall behind the judge's bench, he asked:

HUMMEL: Did Miss Nethersole show as much of her leg as you see in that figure?

INGLIS: No. That is a naked leg; she wore tights.

HUMMEL: Well, could you see that much of her tights?

INGLIS: When she got down from the pedestal, I could see more than that.

HUMMEL: Well, as much as you see of the leg in that small figure [on another mural]?

INGLIS: Not as much as that.

Turning to the always interesting topic of breasts, Hummel directed the witness's attention to the figures of "Liberty" and "Science" featured on other walls of the courtroom. Did Miss Nethersole show as much skin as either of these? No.

And that, it turned out, ended both the prosecution and the defense. When a third district attorney called yet another *World* reporter to the stand, Fursman bristled. No need to hear the same things for a third, fourth, or fifth time, he declared. Show me something new or stop. The prosecution stopped. And so, surprisingly, did the defense.

Olga Nethersole had spent her adult life in front of audiences, and now she felt she had a read on the crucial audience of 12 in the jury box. Hummel was in the middle of arguing that he should be allowed to show that the play had been peaceably performed in numerous other cities, when she gestured to him. After a few moments of consultation, he changed tack. The defendants, he said, were willing to go to the jury on the basis of that day's evidence alone.

"I never heard of such a fizzle in my life before," sneered Nethersole as she left the court. It was a harsh review of the proceedings, but not a unique one. Rev. Phebe Hanaford shared it. "The whole case has degenerated into a farce, hasn't it?" she asked leading man Hamilton Revelle during the lunch break. "I'm so glad for Miss Nethersole's sake." The redoubtable Quaker had not enjoyed being rolled by the *World*.

The following morning, each side gave short closing statements. The prosecution had nothing new to say, but Hummel was ready for his close-up. He took to the moment with a gusto more typical of his partner. And Howe was there to listen, in a grass-green vest, red tie, and ruby-and-diamond pin. Hummel did him proud.

First, he sneered:

In the third act, an omelet is made in the full sight of the audience. Mixed and stirred in the presence of innocent women and pure young men, in all its nakedness it is presented to the eyes of the helpless audience. Words cannot tell the criminality of such an invasion of the privacies and the decencies of life. I glory in the journalism that sought out that omelet and brought it into court to be suppressed!

Then, he pleaded:

As the hart panteth after a fountain, as the wearied traveler in the desert longs for the cool waters, so has my defendant longed for this oasis—this moment when she should wash away the stain of this nauseous indictment, which is the outcome of venom, spleen, and rancor.

My defendant is like Caesar's wife—she is above suspicion; and she comes here today strong in the consciousness of innocence. She has been dragged into court by as foul a conspiracy as was ever conceived by a crusade instituted in order to revive the waning circulation of a newspaper.

Ah, gentlemen [his voice cracking]. Has there ever been a smirch on her pure womanhood? After fame and fortune are hers, now comes a charge that she is trying to subvert public morality, and forsooth she is dragged into a criminal court. Poor, defenseless woman!

Greatly moved, Nethersole touched her head to the table and wept. She played the scene beautifully.

But it was the judge's charge that was the hit of the day. Judge Fursman had already hinted broadly at his views, noting how singular it was that of all the thousands of people who had seen the play, it was only a single reporter who had objected to it. Why should that person fix the moral temperature of an entire city?

Now, in his closing remarks, he went considerably further. The members of the jury should not see themselves as "custodians of public morality," Fursman said—a direct hit at the prosecution (and the *World*), which had argued that they should. Their job was to decide a point of law. The play was suggestive, but that was not enough to prove an offense against decency. When they considered that point, they should remember that they could see more female flesh at any ballet, and find more blatant themes in any number of great books and pictures. Moreover, *Sapho* was suggestive of good as well of evil. "The law," said Fursman, "was not made for young boys or girls. It was made for the community as a whole." The jury caught his drift.

At 3:00 p.m., the 12 men filed out.

At 3:12, they filed in: "Not guilty."

This time, Nethersole's tears might have been genuine.

The following night, *Sapho* was back—with four jurors in attendance, and a number of people from the DA's office. Inspector Thompson, *Sapho*'s best friend, was back, too; he brought his wife. And, of course, there were Howe and Hummel. When Nethersole appeared in the clinging, diaphanous, Grecian gown that had occupied three tribunals over six weeks, she stopped the show for ten minutes.

The play sold out the rest of its run, and several companies, including two in Yiddish and one in Japanese, also made a good living for years from the melodrama. Nethersole played the role on and off for the rest of her career.

The defense of *Sapho* was the theatrical highlight of Hummel's career, and the last big case Howe and Hummel would try together. But it could have been bigger. They missed a chance to make a splash on free speech grounds, as they had tried to do with Johann Most. Hummel knew he could win with ridicule. So he did.

Sapho neatly inverted many social norms—the woman was the sexual initiator (no matter how many syllables in her "no"), and the man her sex object. The defense of it, though, was to appeal to the conventional morality it flouted for three-quarters of the play. "What can be more noble in life than a woman who is trying to be good?" Nethersole pleaded. What could be more boring?

Nethersole and Hummel deliberately left matters of principle to someone else—in this case, Fursman. His was the most compelling voice of the trial, sprinkling sense over a soufflé of idiocy. Hummel brought attitude and humor to a winning cause, and he had a good time doing it. But he settled for a limited victory on the grounds of decency, rather than a sweeping one in the defense of freedom.

NINE

The Ice Man Cometh

A few days before Olga Nethersole won the trial of her life, Charles W. Morse became the most hated man in New York. Morse would not connect with Howe & Hummel for another few years. The man was a serial business killer; he would also inadvertently cause the destruction of Howe & Hummel. But in April 1900, he was at the height of his powers. And he used them, deliberately, to make people miserable.

Imagine a hot and sweltering day in New York. The heat literally rises from the sidewalks, accentuating the smells of the city. To move is to resist a palpable weight of humidity. Clothes chafe against sticky bodies; breathing the thick air takes effort. Tempers rise with the temperature. Violence lurks a degree or two beneath the surface.

Now imagine such a day without electricity. This was the natural state of affairs for almost everyone in New York in 1900. But at least they had ice.

Then Morse doubled the price. Literally overnight, ice became a luxury for the poor. This was not just a matter of comfort. Without refrigeration, the ubiquitous wood boxes filled with ice and insulated with rags or newspaper were the only way most New Yorkers could keep their milk drinkable and their food unspoiled. Ice was a matter of public health; doctors warned that infant mortality would rise if ice became prohibitively expensive. It takes a cold heart to double the price of a life-saving commodity for the hell of it; Morse was the man for the job.

It was a tale of capitalist rapacity that Johann Most might have hesitated to make up because it was so outrageous. But it happened, and an unknown number of people—chiefly the weak, the old, and the very young—suffered greatly in Morse's pursuit of monopoly profits. And what did the city's highest public servants do about it? They made sure they got their cut.

Charles W. Morse was born in Maine in 1856 and got into the ice business as a teenager. In 1885, he moved to New York, where he oversaw his various interests. In an immensely profitable circle, he shipped lumber north to Maine's shipyards and Maine's ice south to hot city dwellers. Five years later, he made his first big score. Anticipating that a warm winter would mean a shortfall in the ice harvest, Morse got control of the supply in all of Maine and Canada. Other New York ice companies were not as well positioned, and Morse took over a number of them.

By 1899, he felt strong enough to combine his various interests into the American Ice Company. For one thing, he had cultivated his political connections with care and generosity. Among the stockholders: Tammany boss Richard Croker; his deputy, John Carroll; Mayor Robert Van Wyck, and his brother, who bought their stock for half price, with a low-interest loan from Morse;[1] Hugh McLaughlin, the Democratic boss of Brooklyn; Frank Platt, son of the Republican boss; Corporation Counsel John Whalen; the president of the City Council; the police chief's wife; ten judges; two former mayors; and two commissioners who managed the docks.[2] The latter were particularly useful because the city controlled access to most of the piers through which ice was shipped. (Artificial ice making was in its infancy; almost 90 percent still came from natural sources.[3]) Independent ice dealers, a lawyer for them told the *Times*, "were told to get out by the Dock Department on the plea that what they occupied was wanted for something else. They got out and saw American Ice go into the berths that were vacated."[4] The company controlled 80 percent of the New York market.[5]

That pesky 20 percent became the object of special attention. One independent dealer's stock of ice was accidentally crushed by a trust-owned steamer. Twice.[6] Others could not even bribe their way to get docking privileges. One dealer, driven out of business, decided to make ice instead. He sank his life savings into machinery, but Morse's friends in the Building Department harassed his factory. The ice trust undersold independents, then bought them out. All told, hundreds of small entrepreneurs had to find another way to make a living, while purchasers of American Ice's product were forbidden to resell any surplus, on pain of being cut off.

With an almost complete monopoly in place, in April 1900, American Ice doubled the price of household ice, from 30 to 60 cents per hundred pounds, the amount an average family used in a week.[7] Of even more consequence for the city's poor households (about a million New Yorkers lived in tenements in 1900),[8] the five-cent chunks they could afford would no longer be available. "No trust ever hit the working masses of this city with a tenth part of the force of the recent doubling of rates by the Ice Trust," the *Tribune* editorialized. "The detestation heard on all sides is too varied and violent in its character to admit of proper description."[9]

The company claimed that the ice harvest was way down, accounting for the increased price. That just wasn't so; there were stockpiles of ice all over the east, and the Maine harvest had been huge. On Staten Island, a short ferry ride from Manhattan, ice was selling for 30 cents per hundred, and in New Orleans, much farther from the source, for 25 cents. The real reason for the price rise was simple: The managers of the trust thought they could get away with it. And the trust needed the money. Not only was its ice made of water, so was its stock. Capitalized at $60 million, the company needed inflated profits to stay afloat.[10]

"Resentment for the trust exists under every roof," complained the *Times*, "but there seems to be no way of evading its oppression."[11] Morse probably thought it looked that way, too. The mayor, for one, was not seeing or hearing any evil. A month after the price increase, with the city in a fury, Mayor Van Wyck could only say of the uproar, "I think I have heard a little about it."[12] Of course, he might have been out of the loop, since he had just come back from vacation—to Maine, with Morse, where they inspected ice houses, but of course did not discuss prices.[13]

It looked as if the icemen had perfected a monopoly that could run forever. That, at least, was the opinion of those in the middle of it. "They cannot get ice cheaper, so what are they going to do about it?" one company executive explained. "We don't anticipate any serious difficulty selling ice at our own prices. There will be no outside competition and the chances for making money are good."

Pride goeth before a price fall, though. Morse et al had not considered how factors outside their control could undermine their scheme. And these began to come into play almost immediately. First was nature itself. A heat wave in mid-May that pushed temperatures to 90 degrees made it obvious just how costly a shortage of ice would be in human terms—and how few allies the trust had. Even papers like the *Tribune*, which generally defended trusts as an economic necessity, found this one indefensible. The business classes either stayed silent or roasted the ice merchants. Nathan Straus, who owned Macy's and Abraham & Straus, and had endeared himself to New York by providing pasteurized milk and low-cost food to the poor, called the trust "one of the greatest calamities of the age. It is simply wholesale murder."

People were furious, and they let their ward leaders know it; that message eventually got passed up the political ladder. On May 14, the trust agreed to send wagons to the tenement districts to sell five-cent ice, a display of self-described philanthropy that did its meager reputation no good. Tenement dwellers bought the ice but gave the icemen a scornful, hostile, hissing reception.

Second, the newspapers were all over the controversy, which they saw not just as a good story, but as a genuine outrage. Tammany had long defended itself as the champion of the people; there may have been "honest graft," but the poor got jobs and Christmas turkeys and funeral expenses. It was the rich who got soaked. Boss Croker defended Tammany this way: It "is of the people, created for the people, controlled by the people—the purest and strongest outcome of the working of democratic government under modern conditions."[14]

Things were never that straightforward, but Tammany did enough for enough people that its faux economic populism kept it in power. Not this time: The people whom it professed to represent were the ones hurting most. At 60 cents per hundred, a ditchdigger would have to work half a day just to pay the ice bill. Food costs would also rise as grocers and butchers passed on the expense of monopoly ice. Morse didn't care. "The American Ice Company does not pose as a philanthropic organization," he said. "This company is in business to make money for its stockholders, and this it cannot do if the price of ice to families is made any lower than 60 cents a hundred."[15]

Rubbish, declared the *Journal* and the *World*. These two papers had given the world the term "yellow journalism," derived from their battle over the first comic strip, Richard Outcault's "Yellow Kid." To the quality press, the phrase was an insult, implying a certain gutter sensibility. The papers themselves wore it as a yellow badge of honor. The *World* and the *Journal* were staunchly Democratic and generally amenable to Tammany. But their readers were the poor and near-poor who were, as the *Journal* put it, "suffering from the soul-less greed and grip of one of the meanest forms of monopoly."[16]

The two papers were fierce rivals, and 1900 was near the peak of their antipathy. But together they became an anti ice trust tag team. The *Journal* brought an indictment for conspiracy to create a monopoly in a product that was a "necessary of life."[17] The *World* compelled Mayor Van Wyck and others to answer questions before a judge. The *Journal* forced publication of the stockholders' names; the *World* picked apart the trust's finances. The *Journal* tried to have Van Wyck impeached; the *World* petitioned Governor Theodore Roosevelt to boot the mayor from office. Both aimed heavy editorial and artistic fire at the trust and the politicians it had bought.[18] On May 9, for example, the *World* ran a cartoon of a bloated Tammany pol, his tiger tail showing, holding a small block of ice with a sign "ICE TRUST: 60 cents per hundred. PAY PAY PAY." Behind the Tammany tiger is a grieving mother tending to a sick and scrawny infant.[19] There were also legal battles on several fronts, with city officials being threatened with prosecution for owning the stock and the state attorney general sniffing around, too.

All this was nightmare enough; but then market forces began to mobilize. Sixty-cent ice was easy to undercut, and new competitors saw an opportunity. Denied access to the docks, entrepreneurs brought in ice from New Jersey via the ferries, or shipped it in from Pennsylvania in railroad cars.[20] Others built (and protected) their own pier in Brooklyn; artificial ice makers, including a consortium of saloons,[21] invested in machinery and boosted production. The Waldorf-Astoria hotel, which made its own ice, began selling its surplus. By early June, the trust was secretly matching the prices of the independents. Though American Ice swore that it was not cutting prices, a week later, households were able to buy ice for 40 cents—and the price would go lower still. Before the worst of the summer heat, the trust was busted—or, perhaps, melted. By autumn, there was an ice glut.[22]

None of the various court cases, both civil and criminal, amounted to much, but the consequences of the rise and fall of the ice trust were still momentous. For one thing, the ice trust's well-known Tammany connections helped undermine the presidential campaign of Democrat William Jennings Bryan. He might have lost anyway, but it didn't help that the Democrats' antitrust stance became a national mockery. The ice debacle ended Van Wyck's political career and cost Tammany the 1901 mayoral election. Its monopoly power degraded, American Ice's finances began to fall apart. Less than a year after it tried to cheat poor infants out of their milk, it recapitalized at just $40 million. Between 1900 and 1903, its stock price dropped by 90 percent; by 1902 it was losing money.

Fortune magazine would later write of Morse, "had he been Augustus, [he] might also have found Rome of brick and left it of marble. But there would have been funded debt on the Tiber and an overcapitalized Colosseum."[23] That was being kind: There would also have been sweat-soaked peasants and reeling investors.

Morse would end up wreaking havoc in three different industries— ice, shipping, and banking. He should be remembered as one of the worst businessmen in U.S. history. In comparison, his tawdry attempt to exit a marriage was perhaps the least of his sins. But it was this that made Morse's name a daily feature in the newspapers for the better part of three years. And it was this, incredibly, that destroyed Howe & Hummel.[24]

• • •

Life is not always fair. Morse benefited hugely from the ice trust. He cashed in his chips in May 1901, an estimated $12 million richer.[25] A month later, he made another life-altering decision. He married his housekeeper, a divorced woman named Clemence Cowles Dodge; Mayor Van Wyck was best man. By 1903, Morse wanted out of the marriage so that he could marry Catherine Gelshensen, the widow of one of his partners in the ice trust. But Mrs. Gelshensen was Catholic and would not marry a divorced man. (Apparently, having an affair with one was okay.) Taking no for an answer was not one of Morse's strengths, so he called on Abraham Hummel, New York's legal agony aunt for gentry in matrimonial distress.

Not in person, though. Morse got his uncle, a retired sea captain named Jim Morse, to open the negotiations. Uncle Jim had disapproved of the marriage to Clemence Dodge; he was happy to help break it up. In later court proceedings, he would say he initiated the contact to attempt to have the marriage annulled. But of course that was nonsense: Even if he had succeeded, that could not have killed a happy marriage. The couple would simply have married again. Good old Uncle Jim was a blind, an intermediary. The ice king was the instigator.

Howe had died in his sleep in 1902, so Hummel was on his own. Not that he needed Big Bill for the Morse matter. This kind of thing had been Hummel's specialty for decades. To a lesser mind, how to exit a marriage without divorce, short of murder—and here Howe & Hummel drew the line—might have looked like an insuperable problem. Not to Hummel. All we have to do, he advised the middle-aged lover (via his uncle), is to prove that his wife's divorce was no good. Then she never would have been legally married the second time. Of course, that would require the cooperation of her first husband, Charles Dodge, but maybe something could be worked out. For a retainer of $15,000, I'll see what I can do. Greatly pleased with this elegant solution, Morse told Hummel to go ahead.

The ease with which Hummel came up with the answer suggests that this was not the first time he had encountered the problem. But it would be the last. What ensued was a four-year saga that became known as the "Dodge-Morse tangle." By the time it ended, the matter would embroil half a dozen law firms and almost start a battle between the Texas Rangers and a posse. There would be a chase across the Texas desert; a raid on a boat in the Gulf of Mexico; a bill for false teeth; and enough booze consumed to flood Houston, a tiny place at the time that found itself in the middle of things, much to its amusement. And at the end of it, Hummel would troop across the Bridge of Sighs.

Why did such a trivial affair become such a big deal? Because District Attorney William Travers Jerome insisted on it. Not unlike his cousin, Winston Churchill, Jerome had his limitations but recognized none of them. Jerome wanted to be powerful and saw himself as a future president. He was sure he would be a great one. But his ambition for politics was matched by an impolitic character. He spoke when he should have said nothing, and he sprayed gratuitous insults like buckshot. At a dinner of Mayflower descendants, he once rubbished the Puritans as hypocrites.[26] And he did not endear himself to Tammany, with whom he was loosely allied, by belaboring his conspicuous honesty—not a highly prized commodity in those circles. However favorably Jerome regarded his own abilities, this was not a man with a political future.

He was also a sore loser. Jerome had tangled with Howe & Hummel in the criminal courts and had not enjoyed the experience. Six feet under, Howe was beyond his reach. But Hummel was still out there: Jerome wanted to take him down. Even better, the case gave him a shot at Morse, too. It's hard to say which man Jerome wanted more. But the opportunity to nail both of them was irresistible. Finally, there was simple momentum. Once the case started rolling, it was impossible to jump off, at least not without embarrassment. Jerome had his eye on becoming governor of New York; he could not afford to lose.

And it was all over an uncontested divorce between two nonentities.

Clemence Cowles married Charles Dodge in 1877 in San Francisco. They drifted apart about a decade later as Mr. Dodge's unpleasant habits began to reveal themselves; an enthusiastic libertine, he also had trouble keeping a job. In 1897, Mrs. Dodge, then keeper of a boardinghouse in Brooklyn, decided to make the thing official. She hired William Sweetzer as her lawyer and sued for divorce. Charles Dodge couldn't have cared less, and when his erstwhile wife offered to pay all costs and see the thing through, he said fine, just don't ask for alimony. Sweetzer served Dodge the divorce papers, and brought in Mortimer Ruger to act for him. The divorce was granted in June 1898.

It could not have been more routine, or more legal. But perhaps Hummel could do something about that. The first job was to determine if Charles Dodge could be made to see reason. Hummel dispatched a private detective, Edward Bracken, who found Dodge in Atlanta, about to open a restaurant. There's $500 waiting in New York for you, Bracken suggested.[27] The budding restaurateur agreed that now was an excellent time for a quick trip to the big city.

Dodge arrived in September 1903, and had a parley with Little Abie. Initially, this was a disappointment. Dodge distinctly remembered being served the divorce papers in the Everett House on 17th Street; his wife had gotten him a lawyer named Ruger, with whom he had corresponded several times. Under the gentle coaxing of Hummel, though, Dodge decided he had misremembered. Hummel helped him along, dictating an affidavit stating that Dodge had never been divorced.[28] And if he wasn't, neither was his wife. At the close of business, Hummel gave Dodge $5,000 to salve his wounded feelings over his wife's fecklessness. For that kind of money, the man who had failed at everything would have signed an affidavit that he had assassinated McKinley. A few weeks later, Dodge had to come back to refine his memory further, and was paid again. He was enjoying this. The affidavit was plain:

> I was never served with a summons or complaint in the divorce action and knew nothing about what was going on in reference to it, and the affidavit of proof of service, that I was, on the 31st day of March, served with a summons in this action by William A. Sweetzer, is absolutely false. I do not know said William A. Sweetzer. I have never met or seen him, I never knew of the pendency of the action, nor that this suit was to be brought to trial, nor have I at anytime ever com-

municated with said Mortimer A. Ruger, nor have I ever written him,
or him me.

Hummel, for his part, wrote a letter to Charles Morse, on September
10, 1903, in which he informed the magnate that—surprise!—his current marriage was invalid, since his wife's previous one had never been
legally dissolved. "It is my duty to advise you," Hummel wrote, "that this
decree is collusive and irregular, and it may be doubted whether your
subsequent marriage is a lawful one."

Mrs. Morse must have been somewhat taken aback by this news, but
she accepted it. The only one who didn't was Sweetzer. He remembered
as well as Dodge did that he had served the papers on the rogue husband at Everett House; the implication that he hadn't was an insult that
could cost him his career.

Sweetzer decided to contest the annulment, which went to court in
October 1903. Here he made a major mistake. He thought he was in
a legal dispute. In fact, he was fighting Howe & Hummel, which was
a very different thing. Legalities were necessary but insufficient tools
until the day when Hummel was in the courtroom, as he proved in what
Arthur Train would later call "one of the cleverest traps to discredit a
witness ever devised by human ingenuity."

Here's the situation: If Sweetzer's testimony that he did indeed
serve Dodge could be undermined, there would no longer be grounds
to contest the annulment. So Hummel prepared an ambush. Sweetzer
and Dodge had met only once, six years before. Betting that Sweetzer's
visual memory would be imperfect, Hummel found a sewing machine
salesman named Charles Herpich on the street, and gave him $25 to
come to court. Herpich, who was about the same height, weight, and
coloring as Dodge, was ordered "to sit absolutely still and look wise."[29]

When Sweetzer came into court and saw a colorless little man sitting
next to Hummel, he greeted him as the man he expected to see: "How do
you do, Mr. Dodge?" Game over. Sweetzer's credibility was shot by his
identification of the wrong man. The court decided that Dodge never
had been served. And now Sweetzer was looking at real trouble. The Bar
Association was investigating whether he had behaved unprofessionally.

This was serious; Sweetzer had been arrested in 1897 for blackmail.[30] The charge hadn't stuck, but more trouble could mean disbarment.

Belatedly, Sweetzer came around to Howe & Hummel's view that the best defense was a good offense. He attacked. His determination took him to the offices once occupied by the now-deceased Ruger. There were still a few boxes around; digging through them, Sweetzer struck gold in the form of two letters from Charles Dodge asking Ruger to represent him and confirming that he had gotten the divorce papers from Sweetzer. The letters proved that Dodge had lied through his teeth. The divorce was restored, and with it, the second marriage. Charles W. Morse was right back where he had started—minus the $15,000 retainer.

All very unsatisfactory, but damn, it had almost worked. These things happen. What happened now, though, had never happened before. William Travers Jerome scented his chance. He knew Charles Dodge had lied (everyone knew that), and he suspected that Hummel had been acting for Morse. It didn't take a genius to connect the dots. Jerome surmised that Hummel had paid Dodge to lie. If Jerome could get Dodge to New York, he might be able to get him to tattle on Hummel.

That, as it turned out, was a monumental "if." In fact, it would be almost a year before Jerome was to set eyes on the elusive ex-husband. And Dodge was to have a year to remember. His every whim, however disgusting, was paid for, during an odyssey that stretched from New York to Atlanta to New Orleans to Houston to Galveston to the Texas-Mexico border—but not, crucially, ever across it.

The ubiquitous Bracken got to Dodge first and quietly took him to New Orleans. The police there were known to be cooperative with generous defense lawyers, and the city was renowned for the kind of recreational facilities favored by Dodge. But New York authorities had their own private detective—Jesse Blocher, a small, bland man with a soft voice and the tenacity of a terrier.

Once Dodge was indicted for perjury, the DA's office hired Blocher to find him and told the private detective that there was reason to believe that his quarry was in New Orleans. The cops, both the ones sent by New York and the ones in New Orleans, had been unable to track Dodge down for weeks. It took Blocher an afternoon. He got some bright-red envelopes, addressed them to Dodge, then went from hotel to hotel. He would put an envelope on a hotel counter, then watch the clerk. At the St. Charles, the trick worked. The clerk turned around, spotted the envelope, and put it into a mailbox. Easy as that, Blocher had Dodge's room number—420. Then he got a room on the same floor and watched Bracken and Dodge receive their visitors, among them a number of New Orleans cops, a circumstance that went a long way toward explaining why detectives from two cities had been unable to find the fugitives.

The next day, Dodge and Bracken—perhaps tipped off by people back in New York—boarded a train. Blocher wired his bosses in New York: "Bird flying. Sunset Limited. Destination not known. I am with them."[31]

He got on the same train and chatted with Dodge as they chugged west. Getting a peek at his new friend's ticket, Bracken found that the ultimate destination was Mexico City. This upped the ante quite a bit: Mexico would not extradite a man charged with perjury. Bracken kept sending telegrams back to New York. No answer in Lafayette. No answer in Beaumont. In Houston, finally, he got reinforcements, in the form of a couple of local cops—and the order to arrest Dodge. "Hold the train!" Blocher called. The conductor complied, Blocher boarded— and Dodge got a nasty wake-up call. He spent the rest of January 27 in a Houston jail.

He was out the next morning; Hummel had hired local legal counsel who got him released on a writ of habeas corpus. But Blocher got another warrant and his own set of local lawyers; the Hummel lawyers responded with another writ. Just in case there were not enough people on the case, the DA sent down a New York detective, Sergeant Herlihy. On the same train was lawyer Abraham Kaffenburgh, Hummel's nephew.

Herlihy brought with him a writ for extradition, which he handed to Blocher, who handed it to the governor. Kaffenburgh and two local lawyers (including a former Congressman) argued that the governor should not honor it on the grounds that Dodge was too sick to travel. Besides, the governor of New York hadn't honored Texas requests to extradite some wanted Standard Oil executives. Why should the Lone Star State be more generous? However tempting that argument, on February 3,

Texas Governor S. W. T. Lanham ordered Dodge out of his state. So the Hummel camp found a tame judge and got an injunction keeping Dodge in Texas pending a habeas corpus hearing. A sterner judge looked at the case and ruled that Dodge had to go back. Kaffenburgh appealed and, pending yet another look at the matter, Dodge was released on $20,000 bail. The man who could not hold a job paid up immediately.

The DA's office went ballistic and argued the bond should not be accepted: Dodge wasn't so much a flight risk as a flight certainty. But Kaffenburgh pointed out that there was no precedent for not granting bail in such a case and announced that "any effort to take the prisoner would be resisted by force," the *Houston Post* reported on February 11. Kaffenburgh went so far as to run into the street and offer $5 to anyone who would help him get Dodge out. Kaffenburgh had other duties as well, among them to keep Dodge from talking to anyone else. He did not want Dodge to hear what Jerome was offering—immunity in exchange for information against Hummel.

By now, Blocher knew what he was dealing with; he went to Austin to get a new extradition warrant. If Dodge moved out of the jurisdiction, he could be picked up and returned forthwith. Unfortunately, that left the hapless Herlihy in charge in Houston. All of a sudden, he had tons of new friends, all of whom wanted to buy him a drink. What was a fellow to do? In this case, wake up in a strange hotel room. "In Houston?" he asked hopefully. "In San Antonio," he was told.[32] Herlihy was not alone as a victim of Texas hospitality. A separate set of detectives dispatched from New York to serve a second set of extradition papers made it as far as Austin, before they, too, were waylaid by friendly locals. When they eventually came to, their papers were gone. And no, they couldn't remember the name of the last saloon they had been to.[33]

And where was Dodge? On his way to Mexico, with Bracken and Kaffenburgh to get him there. They had considered taking Dodge to the state fair in San Antonio and shipping him over the border with a circus troupe, disguised as a tattooed woman or a lion tamer.[34] But they discarded the notion. At this point, Dodge was living on a diet of whiskey; any impersonation was going to be beyond the modest talents with which he was endowed. They chose a simpler option.

Leaving Houston on February 10, the trio boarded a ship in the Galveston harbor. Then they transferred to a seagoing tug, leased for $3,000. Next stop, Mexico. Except that Blocher—by far the most competent man representing the forces of law and order—had figured out where they were. He was able to convince the Southern Pacific Railroad, which owned the tug, to order the captain to put in at Brownsville, at the tip of the Texas toe. The captain got into the spirit of the thing, showing the landlubbers the barometer and swearing they could not brave the Gulf of Mexico until the brewing storm had passed. So they sat, for two fine days. And then, in the middle of the Gulf, the captain said, sorry, we can't go to Mexico; the ship doesn't have the right papers.

Meanwhile, Blocher was making his way—by train, cart, and burro—south from Austin to meet his quarry. He stopped in Alice, about 130 miles north of Brownsville, to brief a detachment of the legendary Texas Rangers. The Rangers also got into the spirit of the thing. One went to Point Isabella, a port near Brownsville at the mouth of the Rio Grande, in case the group tried to ease Dodge across that way. And there the tug put in and the two sides encountered each other, although only the Rangers were aware of it.

The Hummelites needed another plan. This one was to go back into the interior, to the railroad junction at Alice, and catch a train for Mexico. They took a stage there and, weary from a dusty, bumpy, 37-hour-long ride—so much for Dodge not being well enough to travel—checked into the City Hotel under assumed names. (Messrs. Dougherty, Koontz, and Barker, of Oklahoma).[35] Blocher had it much worse. He had ridden from Alice to Brownsville, changing horses at prearranged places; now he had to double back to Alice.

The desk clerk was an affable sort. Dodge told his new friend that he was on his way to Mexico for his health. Could the clerk get tickets for him and his companions? Certainly, replied the Texas Ranger in disguise. The next morning, February 15, Dodge, Kaffenburgh, and Bracken settled into their train compartment, and lit up some well-deserved smokes. Mexico, here we come.

And then, just as they were getting comfortable, they looked up to see the stern but satisfied face of Captain Hughes of the Texas Rangers.

You are not going anywhere, he told his quarry. "He will undoubtedly be whisked back to New York," stated the *Houston Post*. "The defense has exhausted their every resource."

Whisking was still months away. The action moved from the plains of Texas to its courthouses, as a dandy jurisdictional squabble, much abetted by the Howe & Hummel offices in New York, broke out. Proud of their work, the Rangers wanted to keep Dodge for themselves. But the state had an order for his extradition; two county courts had issued habeas corpus writs; and the feds now got into the act, ordering Captain Hughes to hand Dodge over to U.S. marshals. With any luck, this fine mess could keep going for months.

But the Texans proved willing to compromise. Eventually, Hughes agreed that a marshal could accompany him as he delivered his quarry to Houston. Dodge arrived in May, and was released on $50,000 bail, again promptly paid. Kaffenburgh was shipped back to New York, a step ahead of a contempt citation.[36] He had made his bones in his uncle's office by trawling the back rooms of Broadway for blackmail material,[37] and he was sorely out of place in Texas, at one point getting arrested and fined for obscene language when the long-distance phone did not work as intended. Hummel replaced him with the more urbane David May. Bracken stayed on as Dodge's minder, procurer, and all-around enabler.

At this point, there were two federal appeals pending, one in a circuit court in Fort Worth, and one in the U.S. Supreme Court in Washington. An escape would hurt his chances in court, so from now on, Dodge stayed put. Actually, that puts it badly. Dodge never stayed still; he traveled much in Houston. Or, as a correspondent would later put it, his acquaintances ensured "that he was never permitted to suffer from ennui." According to one awed Texas Ranger, Dodge once managed to consume 46 whiskeys in 14 hours.

Back in New York, there were two issues to be sorted out. One was the marital status of the woman known, for simplicity's sake, as Mrs. Dodge-Morse. At this point, no one cared to keep the Dodge marriage together; even Charles W. Morse seemed willing to go back to the way things were. Eventually, the first divorce was reinstated, and the annulment of her second marriage was annulled. So the second marriage was back in force; Clemence Cowles Dodge was Mrs. Morse again. How anyone felt about the matter was not reported. Mrs. Morse stayed offstage. News of her presumed bigamy had not appeared to faze her; nor had the annulment, nor the annulment of the annulment. She put her foot down once, requesting a brand new divorce, but gave up quickly, going to Europe in February and staying there until the whole mess was over. She was the catalyst—inert, but essential, and also curiously opaque.

That left the second issue—figuring out what had happened and who, if anyone, should be held accountable. Morse, for one, was determined not to be part of that club. He twice refused to answer questions from the grand jury "on the ground that I am protecting a woman."[38] He got away with it when the judge said the DA was on a fishing expedition.

Hummel also hung tough, continuing to maintain that the divorce was bad, and referring back to Dodge's affidavit: "All I did was what any loyal, faithful lawyer would have done for his clients." And perhaps a bit more, as Benjamin Steinhardt indicated. Steinhardt, a lawyer at Howe & Hummel, had troubled his superiors before, working at cross-purposes with the firm in a long-running defense of racetrack bookies. This time, he told four reporters the exact, unsayable truth—that Howe & Hummel was paying Dodge's bills, with Morse reimbursing the firm.

Hummel immediately denied the statement, but in a Hummelish fashion: "Clearly, unequivocally and absolutely, Charles Morse never retained the firm of Howe & Hummel in any way." (True: It was Uncle Jim who made the contact.) His dear friend Steinhardt was a sick man, Hummel said, his voice cracking. Sometimes he didn't know what he was saying. Steinhardt, who was indeed sick, with locomotor ataxia, grasped the lifeline and promptly remembered that he, too, had misremembered. The papers greeted this change of heart with the skepticism it deserved. Clearly, the issue of who-did-what-to-whom and who was paying, could not be settled in the courtrooms of lower Manhattan—until, that is, Dodge entered one of them.

Texas took back center stage.

• • •

From the start, Dodge had been liberally supplied with whatever he wanted, and he was determined to indulge his various vices to the fullest. On his return to Houston in May 1904 after the Brownsville-Gulf-Alice escapade, he settled into a suite at the Rice Hotel. He had no job and nothing to do except show up in court every once in a while. Given such a chance, he went at the work of dissipation with a single-minded intensity he had never shown for his previous careers. Howe & Hummel would not kill in defense of its clients, but if Dodge wanted to debauch himself to death, the firm would be happy to pay the bills. Bracken carried stacks of cash to help. "It is very hard to keep up with him," Bloch reported to Jerome. "His feet never touch ground."[39] The schedule went something like this:

10 am—breakfast—whiskey
noon—lunch—booze
afternoon—gambling, racetracks, whorehouses, opium
dinner—maybe food, definitely booze
evening—gambling, Louisiana Street brothel[40]
sleep—6:00 a.m. to 10:00 a.m.

Dodge seemed to be enjoying himself so much that it took everyone by surprise when he slipped out of the hotel in July and went to Galveston, ostensibly to rent a fishing boat. The indefatigable Blocher hauled him back. With that, the Dodge entourage settled in and waited for developments. Dodge didn't mind one bit. In fact, he seemed to enjoy the attention. It was a curious situation, with rival detectives and lawyers all circling around—sometimes literally, in the lobby of the Rice Hotel—a man who seemed oblivious to it all.

Blocher, who by this time knew Dodge as well as anyone, could see what his minders were doing to him and had some sympathy for the pathetic little man: "Hard drinkers were thrown into his company, and as he is a man who seldom or never declines an invitation to drink, his stomach was kept full of liquor all the time. He was taken to all sorts of dives, and induced to carouse until he could no longer remain on his feet."[41]

There were more innocent recreations as well. When New York's Department of Finance began to get the bills from their men in Houston, a number of items raised questions—"treats and incidentals" to police officers; several ball games; admission to the circus. By the end of May, New York had spent almost $8,000; the Board of Estimate then allocated another $15,000. Jerome vowed to spend $2 to get Dodge to New York for every dollar the fugitive was spending to stay out.

For the next few months, Dodge kept up his wearying round. By December 1904, his teeth had fallen out and he looked at least a decade older than his 58 years. That month, the U.S. Supreme Court declined to address the extradition question, sending it back to Texas. The decision came back swiftly. The extradition order was good; Dodge would have to go. To make sure that he did not feel like fishing in Galveston again, several New York City detectives stayed within a few feet of him at all times, leading to yet another legal action, this one for harassment. The detectives were ordered to give the man a bit of space.

Dodge took this as permission for a new spree. He sped out of the hotel, accompanied by Bracken and a new Howe & Hummel lawyer, Nathaniel Cohen. They went straight to some kind of den of iniquity—the newspapers are vague—shutting out the detectives, who banged on the door. They failed to get in, Texas madams being a tougher breed than hoteliers or judges. But there was very little privacy left. Or time.

Hummel fired two last shots. One was particularly clever. He argued that since it could not be known that Dodge had committed the offense or had even been in New York when it was committed, he had become the victim of a conspiracy of those who had procured the divorce and were now "prosecuting him to cover their own tracks." What's nice about this is that, in effect, it blamed an unknown "combination" for doing what Hummel had been doing for the past year. By now, though, Texas was weary of these troublesome New Yorkers. The suit was dismissed.

One last, desperate shot: Cohen found yet another tame judge, this one in Wharton County, about 50 miles west of Houston, to give another writ of habeas corpus. Then Bracken and Cohen organized a posse, most of them ne'er-do-wells from rival gangs called the Wood-peckers and the Jay Birds, and paid them $150 each, to get Dodge out of Houston. Blocher suspected that Cohen was looking for a gun battle in which Dodge might catch a bullet. But this plot, too, came to nothing. When a judge caught a rumor of the posse, he ordered Dodge to Galveston. There was one last, slapdash bid to escape, when Dodge, Cohen, and Bracken got a cab and started running. But the lurking detectives got on their horses and overtook them before they were out of the city limits.[42]

On December 16, the last appeal went the wrong way and the judge ordered Dodge to New York, with no more delays. He also strongly suggested that Dodge's legal counsel leave the state, on pain of disbarment. "I'm glad to go," said Cohen, "I would not come back for $1 million." All told, it had cost almost $90,000 to keep Dodge on the loose, and it was not enough.

The following day, December 17, after 11 memorable months, and guarded by five U.S. marshals—all of them fine, strapping, cowboy-hatted specimens of Texas manhood—Dodge left Texas. The entourage went by ship, lest his lawyers try to find a judge in every state to issue more writs. Naturally, the trip was not without incident. Dodge had been living on a diet of booze for months; Cohen said he looked like a cadaver. Anxiety and the travails of the last year had taken a toll, and Dodge tried to throw himself overboard. But there was always a marshal at his side, even sharing his stateroom, and he never got wet. U.S. Marshal Hanson, who had been part of the pursuit for six months, took Dodge aside during the journey and advised him to make a clean breast of things. It was the first time since Dodge had sat in Hummel's office that he was in the company of someone who had no stake in him. (The interests of Texas would end in New York.) He gave the idea some thought.

At 5:00 p.m. on December 23, Dodge landed in New York—along with Herlihy, Blocher, Cohen, and the retinue of marshals. The Texans formed a cordon and rushed him to a waiting carriage. "Drive like hell," Hanson ordered. Entering police headquarters at 300 Mulberry Street from the rear, Dodge was escorted up a private stairway to the commissioner's office. Kaffenburgh, who had met the ship at the pier, Cohen, and another Howe & Hummel lawyer, Bartow Weeks, camped in an anteroom outside. (Weeks was a former prosecutor who had tilted against the firm on occasion. Hummel was not averse to poaching talent, whatever the source—and the offices of Howe & Hummel were not considered so degraded that smart lawyers wouldn't switch sides. And it certainly paid more.)

Inside, Dodge was being stubborn. He knew there was money for the taking if he stayed silent. "Have you really got the goods on me?" he asked his captors again and again. He was convinced they did when they brought in a man he knew from Atlanta who had sworn to Dodge's handwriting. If things had gone this far, Dodge realized, he was sunk. So he began to talk. And talk. And talk.

This, of course, was just what everyone was afraid of. Notified of Dodge's arrival, Hummel left a party he was hosting and hustled to 300 Mulberry Street to look after his client. Ex-client, that is. The four Howe & Hummel lawyers storming around the anteroom blustered and fumed. "I demand to see him or I will make it hot for somebody," Weeks threatened. He was informed that Dodge was a federal prisoner; no New York warrant had been issued (it was in Herlihy's pocket), and Dodge was therefore not in the DA's custody. Since there was no official proceeding going on, there was no need for a lawyer to be present.

Hearing Dodge talking away, the lawyers grew frantic. "I have never seen a proceeding like this in the United States," Weeks shouted. "It might go down in barbarous Russia, but not here. It is a shame and an outrage." And still, the door stayed shut. Hummel pounded on it. Out came a flunky, ordering that all requests be put in writing. Hummel scratched out a note. The answer came back: "Your request duly filed." Desperate, Cohen left the building and climbed a nearby roof. He could see into the office. Dodge, he reported, was talking to an assistant district attorney. Marshal Hanson was also in the room, along with Herlihy and a few others. When Cohen bellowed his rage, Hanson looked up and calmly pulled down the window shades.

Back in the anteroom, Hummel had been reduced to listening in at the keyhole. Around midnight, Jerome had the great satisfaction of telling his old adversary that, in effect, he was fired. Dodge, Jerome said, "tells me he has retained other counsel and that he does not know Mr. Hummel. Good night." The new lawyer was James Osborne, a former assistant district attorney who was on the best of terms with Jerome.

Hummel finally admitted defeat: "It's home for us," he told a reporter who had witnessed the night's proceedings. At 1:40 in the morning, Dodge stopped talking and was taken to the Broadway Central Hotel to rest.

None of what Dodge said in those seven hours in the commissioner's office was official, but he said enough that on Christmas Eve, when the marshals handed him over to New York authorities, he was a free man, released without bail. Not without discretion, though: Dodge would have several detectives for company at all times. The Texas marshals, their duty done, went on a spree of their own.

Back at the Broadway Central, Dodge was getting used to solid food again, including a Christmas dinner with his minders. He was not healthy, but he was no longer going downhill. In fact, he was being well tended. The man who had been the willing stooge of Hummel and Morse was now happy to do Jerome's bidding. There was one huge difference, though: Jerome wanted him alive. "He is recovering from a spree that lasted eleven months," Jerome explained. "Naturally, one cannot shut off all his allowance of drink, but he gets only so much whiskey as the physician orders as necessary to keep him alive."

As 1905 beckoned, Dodge was very nearly ready to untangle the mess. Not that he knew all of it, since he was not a confidant of the Morses. But one question was answered, obliquely, early in the year, when Catherine Gelshensen took off for Cairo, without children or trunks, a few days before a grand jury could call her. The widow, a Catholic, had recently occupied Morse's opera box. No reader could miss the implication.

But there were other witnesses unable or unwilling to flee to Cairo on a moment's notice, and the grand jury was showing an unfortunately expansive curiosity. Hummel, Cohen, Kaffenburgh, and even the office stenographer were all called to testify. So were Morse's accountants; William Sweetzer; Mrs. Morse's lawyer (Judge Fursman of *Sapho* fame); Mr. Morse's counsel (Samuel Untermyer); Dodge; and many others.[43]

There could be only one outcome of such a full ventilation of the affair: On January 27, 1905, Hummel, Steinhardt, Fursman, Dodge, and Bracken were indicted for conspiracy to deceive the courts in connection with the divorce. Hummel and Steinhardt were also charged with two felony counts of suborning perjury. In the event, only Hummel went to trial. Bracken had left the country with a handsome check for his services and was resting in Paris; Steinhardt was sick;[44] the charges against Fursman and Dodge were dropped, the former for lack of information, the latter for his cooperation.

Morse was in Europe, too, and any hope of prosecuting him fell through when Captain Jim came down from Maine in July to take the blame. It was he who contacted and paid Hummel, the bluff seaman swore, but he never knew anything about anything illegal. He thought Hummel was on the level. The story was ridiculous, of course. But nothing could shake the captain, who seemed to radiate Down East honesty. Jerome had to give up the idea of getting the ice king. But at least he could get Hummel.

If he could get to Hummel, that is. Deploying every trick in the book (and inventing some new ones), Hummel's lawyer—DeLancey Nicoll, a former DA who had defended the ice trust and opposed Howe & Hummel on many a memorable occasion—delayed the trial. In a final throw of the dice, in late September 1905, he argued for a change of venue. Hummel, he noted, "is known in almost every part of New York City and to almost everybody, at least by reputation and name." Jerome had been bad-mouthing this famous man for months; a fair trial in Manhattan was impossible. The DA's office argued that the case was so complicated no one could have made up his mind on the basis of the newspapers. The case deserved to stay in New York. It did.

The trial opened on December 13, 1905; Nicoll asked for a special jury panel, which would have meant more delay. But after almost a year of this, the judge was unsympathetic, telling Nicoll that if he was not ready to go ahead, "I will assign counsel" who was. With that, the trial began; ironically, one of the jurors selected was an ice dealer.

How much did Jerome want Hummel? So much that he had the jury sequestered—something that had never been done before in a misdemeanor case. The extraordinary measure was necessary, Jerome said, because "The personal character of the defendant and of his firm is such that it would be injudicious to allow these jurors to separate. It will be impossible to watch them all." In other words, Hummel would try to bribe some of them. The jury was booked into the Broadway Central, Dodge's old home.

When testimony began on December 15, Hummel looked pale and nervous, though his theatrical nature must have been pleased at the sight of crowds storming the doors to get in. The first witness called was Abe Kaffenburgh; perhaps in homage to the late Bill Howe, he was dressed in flash and diamonds. And like both his mentors, he stayed true to the firm's "don't tell" policy. "Were you ever in Texas?" "Who paid Dodge's expenses?" "What were Hummel's orders?" Nicoll objected to every question. The court overruled every time. And then Kaffenburgh took the Fifth. The rhythm finally broke when the prosecutor asked, "Do you know where the Waldorf-Astoria hotel is?" Kaffenburgh did answer that one.

In the afternoon, Nathaniel Cohen proved similarly attached to his constitutional right against self-incrimination. Although Kaffenburgh and Cohen had stayed true to the Howe & Hummel code, their unwillingness to incriminate themselves naturally tended to incriminate their boss. Their lack of cooperation became corroboration.

Morse, who had returned to New York when the legal heat cooled, spent the next day blaming his uncle for most things and Hummel for the rest; there was little for the Hummel defense team to work with. Implicating Morse for his role in the conspiracy would only confirm its existence. Another of Hummel's lawyers, John Stanchfield, was pleased to get in a few shots along the line that the Morses really did worry that something was wrong with the divorce. That was irrelevant to the charge at hand; still, a little smoke never hurt.

The world finally got to hear from Dodge on December 19. After a year of relatively clean living, he looked positively dapper and sounded articulate through his $40 false teeth. Ludicrously, the city auditor had balked at paying this dental bill, which wasn't even a rounding error in terms of the money spent to bring him in. But he got the teeth, and they paid enormous dividends, as Dodge told his story in a clear and confident manner. "He impressed those who looked and listened to him as a person who does not know how to feel ill at ease," the *World* reported. That made him impossible to fluster.

Nicoll tried to dent the little man's composure by eliciting all his various fibs. But Dodge was not discomfited at all; yep, he admitted, he had lied and lied and lied. When he took the money, he said engagingly, he felt he was honor bound to keep lying to earn it. Then, after Captain Jim told his story, the prosecution rested.[45] So did the defense.

There really was nothing to say. Hummel was certainly never going to testify. As Artemis Quibble noted in the fictional retelling of the tale, doing so would "open the door to a cross-examination" of his entire career. "I well knew that there was not a single shady transaction in which we had participated, not one attempt at blackmail, not a crooked defense that would be out of bounds."[46] Like Quibble, Hummel knew his options on the stand would be perjury or taking the Fifth. Neither was likely to be helpful.

His team would do what they could during the closing argument the following morning. And they tried, how they tried: Bill Howe would have approved. The defense started by going after Dodge. How could the jury believe a serial perjurer? "His testimony would not convict a dog!" Nicoll shouted. It was Dodge who led Hummel, not the other way around. The hotelkeeper knew his ex-wife had married a millionaire and saw an opportunity. So he showed up at the office with a story of a dud divorce. Hummel believed it; there was no reason not to. The famous lawyer "was not such an idiot as to draw up a false affidavit."

And what about Mrs. Morse? If she was such an "unhappy victim," why didn't she appear in court? Because the prosecution knew she was tainted. So instead, she hid—first, in Europe and now in New Jersey, out of reach of the New York law. Turning to the useful field of class warfare, Nicoll argued that the whole thing was unfair. "Why should the two millionaires"—that is, Charles W. Morse and his Uncle Jim—and the "hungry, avaricious wolf of Georgia" get off scot-free while "poor little Hummel" went to jail?

As Nicoll spoke, Hummel's eyes welled with tears, which fell at the rousing close: "It is high time for the men who own gas plants, insurance companies, railroads, and steamships, and walk by our courts contemptuously to be brought to justice. They laugh at the efforts of the court to convict them of wrongdoing. Something must be done! It isn't right to oppress the weak and leave the rich and powerful to go and do as they please."

It was a good effort, but the Hummel the jurors had read about for decades did not resemble the weak lamb that the defense was conjuring. And the Dodge the jury saw had not displayed the subtle criminal mind that Nicoll's words painted. Dodge was a liar, but an eminently credible liar.

As the prosecution noted, the idea that there was no case because Dodge was a perjurer made no sense. "Why, that is the whole case— that Dodge is a perjurer and this defendant hired him to commit perjury." Indeed, Jerome went on, the Howe & Hummel offices might be described as the "headquarters of the amalgamated association of supporters of perjury."

The following day, after the judge gave his instructions, the jury filed out. At the first ballot, the vote was 11–1 for conviction. It took two more hours to make it unanimous. A little after 3:00 p.m., the 12 men filed back in. None looked at Hummel, who was chewing gum nervously. He stood up. Silence descended in the court, the street noises of the city filtering in with eerie clarity. And then the jury foreman spoke: "We find the defendant guilty of conspiracy as charged in the indictment." Jerome immediately asked for the maximum sentence—a year in jail and a $500 fine—because Hummel "has been a menace to the community for twenty years." The judge agreed.

Shortly afterward, Abraham Hummel crossed the Bridge of Sighs and entered the Tombs for the first time as an unfree man. There he chatted with his old friends, the reporters—and had a dinner of cold lamb and bread and butter, far from his usual Delmonico's fare. He was released on bail in a few hours.

Hummel would not reenter a jail cell again for another 17 months, but other forms of justice proved swifter and more certain: He was suspended from the practice of law in July 1906 and then disbarred, this time for good. When Kaffenburgh was struck off four months later, Howe & Hummel was finished. The famous sign came down on November 15, 1906.[47]

There was still the matter of the remaining felony indictments for suborning perjury. But in this case, Hummel caught a little luck. Disgraced and unable to practice law, he was no longer a burr in Jerome's side. The DA was disposed to be generous. He also needed Hummel's help.[48]

TEN

Three Shots and an Affidavit

On June 25, 1906, Hummel's appeals were percolating and he was still a practicing lawyer. The Dodge-Morse tangle had gone to the celebrity graveyard, already half forgotten. The Morses were living quietly in New Jersey. Dodge had vanished. Jerome was on vacation.

That evening, at the opening night of a musical, *Mamzelle Champagne*, at the rooftop theater at Madison Square Garden, came three shots heard 'round the country. They were fired from a revolver held by Harry Thaw, playboy heir to a Pittsburgh industrial fortune, and they blew apart the face of Stanford White, the most famous architect in the United States. Thaw then disarmed his weapon, handed it to a guard and said, "He deserved it. He ruined my wife."[1]

Behind those three murderous shots was a story of a beautiful girl, two terrible mothers, a gifted roué, and a strange young man. The beautiful girl was Evelyn Nesbit, who had come to New York in 1900; then 15, she was already gorgeous. She was also poor. Her widowed mother saw in her daughter's beauty the basis of the family fortune. She shopped the teenager around, and young Evelyn graduated from posing for calendars to artist's model to the chorus line. She also fell in love with John

Barrymore, the wastrel son of the famous theatrical family; he was then failing as a journalist, and at 19 was already a well-known libertine.

There was another man in her life, not one she could marry—he was encumbered with wife, son, and reputation—but one who could certainly help her. That was Stanford White. Mrs. Nesbit set about selling her daughter to the middle-aged architect. White was in the market. But, then, White was always in the market for beauty, both professionally and otherwise. He built mansions for the Astors, the Vanderbilts, and Joseph Pulitzer; churches for various Protestants, including a new Madison Square Presbyterian for Charles Parkhurst; the Washington Square arch; and clubs for the moneyed. He helped create the Mall and the Lincoln Memorial in Washington. He designed the ballroom at Sherry's[2] that was the site of the infamous Seeley dinner. He even built Madison Square Garden; atop its tower was a statue of Diana the hunter by Augustus Saint-Gaudens. Anthony Comstock objected: Diana was nude as she aimed her bow. The 13-foot statue, a graceful representation of girlhood that is one of the sculptor's masterpieces, was hardly an affront to the innocent, since it was more than 300 feet above the ground. Diana stayed. Madison Square Garden was massive; its main hall could seat 8,000 and quickly became one of the city's favorite places, holding everything from horse races to aquatic demonstrations. It was on the Garden's rooftop theater garden that Stanford White died.[3]

While many of White's achievements were written in stone, his greatest one was more subtle: He was the man who taught New York beauty, the definer of taste and sophistication for new money that wanted such a gloss and older money seeking to affirm that they counted for more than their bank accounts. When White wasn't working, he was playing, most often around Broadway, where he became known for his not entirely paternalistic interest in young female talent. That he and Evelyn would come together was inevitable.

On August 1, 1901, he invited two dancers from the hit musical *Florodora*, a Broadway phenomenon that sent several of its talents into marriages with millionaires,[4] to lunch at his home on West 24th Street. One of these was 16-year-old Evelyn Nesbit. White was 47. After lunch, he took the girls up to his studio on the top floor, whose main feature was a red velvet swing. He pushed Evelyn higher and higher until her dainty foot pierced a paper parasol. And then she left, with a reference to a dentist to fix a slightly flawed front tooth.

The friendship flourished, particularly when he started bestowing expensive gifts on the Nesbit family, including a suite at the Wellington Hotel, a huge step up from their modest boardinghouse.[5] White paid for Evelyn's brother's schooling, introduced her to Dickens and Shakespeare, and provided her with a piano and a teacher. Her mother was charmed, particularly when he started paying the family a $25 a week stipend. She regarded White as "heaven sent."[6] When a friend warned Evelyn that White's intentions might not be entirely honorable, she dropped the friend. Mrs. Nesbit apparently trusted White completely. In September 1901, she left New York for a few days and asked the architect to look after her Evelyn. When White's partner, Charles McKim, heard this, his reply was, "My God!"

White did attend to Evelyn. At a late-night supper for two, he poured her champagne, then brought her to a mirrored room that delighted her. She had more champagne. And then he showed her a secret room, deep purple with a four-poster bed. There were mirrors and special lighting, and a silk cord to open the coverings around the massive bed. There was a glass of champagne for her there, too, though this one was "bitter and funny tasting,"[7] she would later recall. Evelyn passed out, and when she woke up, she was lying in bed, in very few clothes, next to Stanford White, who wore none at all. She screamed and wept. White was attentive, "Don't cry, kitten," he murmured. "It's all over."[8]

He took her home; distraught, she shivered in a chair for hours. Later that day White visited her, to reassure, to comfort—and to inform her of some other facts of life. "It was a terrible thing to talk. A girl must never talk," he told her, or her own reputation would suffer. "Don't talk, Evelyn—tell nobody, and nobody will know." The advice was cynical and self-serving, of course. Whether the champagne was drugged or simply liberally bestowed, Stanford White was behaving vilely. But he was also right. He was unlikely to suffer much from one more revelation of one more evening with one more chorus girl. If Evelyn spoke out, though, she would find herself friendless and unemployed.

Evelyn did not tell, not then, anyway; nor did she shun Stanford White. The man had become part of her life. She did not so much forgive what she would later call her "unvirgining" as transform it into power. White was enthralled as never before; and Evelyn, whose father had died young, couldn't resist being part of the world White could show her—sumptuous dinners at Rector's, lunches with Augustus Saint-Gaudens. After her unconscious debut, she became White's willing mistress. Mrs. Nesbit did not interfere. She had brought the family to New York in the hope of making money off her daughter; and Evelyn had delivered. From February 1902 to May 1903, White gave the Nesbits about $3,500.[9]

As generous a benefactor as White was to the Nesbit clan, he was married. A more permanent arrangement would be preferable. So when 31-year-old Harry Thaw came courting in 1902, Mrs. Nesbit was happy to encourage him. Thaw had studied poker at Harvard and was invited to leave. His besotted and unwise mother then gave him a generous allowance to do whatever he wanted, which he did. He was known as "Mad Harry" to his contemporaries and the "Pittsburgh queer" to Manhattan madams.[10] (He would pay extra to use his whips on their girls.) Thaw was the kind of playboy who gave playboys a bad name, mixing snobbery with sadism and buying his way out of trouble. But he was single, his family was worth $40 million, and he was not Jack Barrymore. That was good enough for Mama Nesbit.

Evelyn was getting restless, too. White was undoubtedly infatuated, and the apartment at the top of the 300-foot tower of Madison Square was a garden of delights. But she became aware that she was not the only young, lovely, fatherless actress to experience them. With Jack Barrymore gone, she was ready for someone new. Although she didn't like Thaw at first, she was won over by his persistence and generosity. In 1902, when Evelyn was operated on for appendicitis, he offered to arrange a trip to Europe for her and her mother to recuperate. They accepted.

It was in London that Evelyn saw the scary side of Thaw, when he whipped a boy; the act, Evelyn recalled, "in some way seemed to gratify him."[11] But Evelyn was enjoying herself, and her mother seemed to have no problem with Thaw either. It was her daughter she couldn't stand.

Sick of bickering with her willful offspring, Mrs. Nesbit went home, leaving her daughter in Thaw's tender care. One evening in Paris, Thaw asked Evelyn to marry him, not for the first time. Whimpering, Evelyn told the story of White's seduction, and turned Thaw down because of it. "I said it would affect him and his family, and it would not be a good thing for him."[12] Thaw had always been suspicious of White; now the architect began to loom ever larger in his twisted mind. "Poor child, poor child," he sobbed.

The two continued their unchaperoned tour of Europe. Thaw remained attentive, but also given to sarcastic remarks about Evelyn and White. Even a statue of Joan of Arc brought his nemesis to mind: "She would not have been a virgin if Stanford White had been around," he wrote in a guest book. Then he snapped. They were living in the Schloss-Katzenstein castle high up a mountain in the Austrian Tyrol. One night, Harry broke into Evelyn's room, and tore off her gown. Naked, he began whipping her[13] until "all of a sudden, the demon in Thaw died out," she recalled. "The sadistic orgy exhausted him."[14] He did it again the following morning.[15] It was weeks before her bruises healed and she could get off the mountain. He beat her in Switzerland. He beat her in Paris. Evelyn escaped back to New York in October 1903.

Reader, she married him. Not until 1905, and not with the approval of his family (or of White). But when he wasn't a raging maniac, Thaw could be sort of appealing. And his money was always charming.

But that is certainly not what Evelyn had in mind when she first got back to New York. She just wanted to work, and to put the memory of the Schloss behind her. She was used to turning to Stanford White for advice, and she did so this time. White warned her against Thaw, telling her stories about his morphine use and other unsavory habits. Then he did one more thing: He took her to see Abe Hummel.

White had been a Howe & Hummel client for about a decade, paying an annual retainer[16] to the firm to take care of his romantic entanglements. And while White might not have known this, Hummel was familiar with the Thaw family. In 1901, Howe & Hummel had brought suit on behalf of the Earl of Yarmouth—known on stage as Eric Hope.[17] The nobleman was aghast that the *Daily Telegraph* had written that not only was he a bad actor, but that he was courting Sylvia Green, daughter of the stockbroker and famous miser Hetty Green, for her money.[18] The newspaper claimed truth as a defense. Somehow it lost, but the jury decided the nobleman's reputation had only suffered $2,757 in damages. That must have stung.[19] Hetty Green saw off the impecunious aristocrat; the matriarch of the Thaws was not as sharp. The Earl courted various Thaw females before settling on Alice, Harry's sister.[20] They married in 1903; it was not a happy union.

An expert in self-preservation, White sensed that Hummel was what Evelyn needed. Although she was undoubtedly a victim, she was also a poor showgirl, while Thaw was the son of a powerful family. Her protection would be White's, too. Both he and Thaw had taken advantage of a young girl; getting her to accuse Thaw of sexual sadism, in writing, would be an excellent preemptive blow.

Evelyn, not yet 18, had not heard of the famous lawyer. Her first impression was an unflattering one. She saw a "gnomelike, undersized [man], with a top-heavy bald head, prominent warts on his face and watery eyes." Hummel tried to put her at ease by showing her the autographed pictures of famous actresses that dotted the walls of his office. There were some good divorces there, he remembered fondly. At White's urging, she told Hummel her story; then Hummel called in a stenographer, and started dictating his version of the trip to Europe and all that happened there. Much of this account, Evelyn later said, was embellished, but she did not demur at the time, and signed the document.

Never shy about shilling for business, Hummel later suggested that she sue for breach of promise. Evelyn thought that was absurd—Thaw was the one who wanted to get married, not her. "Oh, that doesn't matter," was Hummel's airy reply. "Lots of rich men were sued for breach of promise by actresses."[21] When she refused, he was angry. And when she tried to get the affidavit back, he turned her down; White was his client, and it was his property, not hers. When she insisted, White brought her back to the office, where Hummel made a production of burning a paper with her signature on it. She was under the impression that the affidavit had gone up in smoke. It hadn't; Hummel had photographed it first. As usual, the older men in her life were deceiving her.

The legal consultation did not settle the troubled contours of Evelyn's life. Her story was no longer in her own hands, and the rivalry between the two men in her life continued to simmer. Thaw had detectives following White, and even tried to sic Comstock on him. The architect kept coming to Evelyn with stories of Thaw's depredations. Thaw was sure that White had hired Monk Eastman's gang to attack him.[22] White blackballed Thaw from a number of clubs.[23]

As much from exhaustion as anything else, Evelyn married Thaw in April 1905, then spent a paralyzingly dull year in Pittsburgh in a wing of the family mansion, under the disapproving eye of Harry's mother. After partying with the likes of Jack Barrymore, sipping tea with the church ladies of Pittsburgh was agony. At first, marriage seemed to suit Thaw; he was calm and reasonable and almost a pleasure to have around. But after a few months, he returned to his obsession. At home with his bride, he would wake her in the middle of the night to demand more details of the unvirgining. He insisted that Evelyn refer to White, if she must refer to him at all, as "the Beast."[24]

Evelyn was only 21, but she must have felt that her life was wrecked. At least there was a trip to Europe to look forward to. They would sail for London on June 26 and spend a week in New York to get ready for it. The shots on the rooftop meant they never sailed.

There was no doubt that Thaw shot White. Literally hundreds of people had witnessed the event. He himself was proud to acknowledge it. Ensconced in the Tombs, where he dined on champagne and squab delivered hot from Delmonico's,[25] Thaw relished telling visitors how he, Harry the Avenger, had struck a blow on behalf of the virgins of New York.

But the numerous defense lawyers—one of them John Stanchfield, who had helped to defend Abe Hummel in the Dodge-Morse affair—went for a not-guilty plea anyway. They developed two lines of argument. One was that Thaw was obeying the "unwritten law" in defense of his wife, killing the man who had ruined her. (The Thaws cooperated in this by underwriting a movie with that title.[26]) If the man-protecting-hearth-and-home approach didn't seem to be working, the defense lawyers were also ready to argue extremely temporary insanity—that Thaw, on seeing his wife's victimizer, was overcome by a brainstorm that lasted a few frantic moments. Before and after, Thaw was as sane as any member of the jury. Under the rules of the time, the defense could, and did, pursue both arguments. This would give the jury a useful out. If they wanted to free Thaw on the "higher law" idea, they could justify it by nodding to the brainstorm folly.

The prosecution, in turn, had two lines of attack. One was that Thaw was a murderer who had coolly planned the death of a man he had long hated. The other was that he was insane. Jerome was not averse to an insanity plea in principle; he was totally opposed to letting Thaw walk on the basis of a two-minute "brainstorm."

And that was where Hummel's affidavit came in. It contradicted both defenses. In it, Evelyn said that she refused to sign a statement Thaw had written charging an unnamed married man with her ruin. The pertinent sentence read: "The said Thaw had begged me time and time again to swear to written documents which he had prepared, involving this married man and charging him with drugging me when I was 16 years of age. This was not so; and I so told him." The implication was that Evelyn had refused to sign the document because the incident had never happened. Thaw was therefore not fulfilling the "unwritten law"; he had simply killed a man he didn't like.[27]

And second, the affidavit, in horrifying detail, related Thaw's beatings, drug use, and erratic behavior. He had, in short, been a sick man for a very long time. So Jerome needed Hummel, the man with the affidavit. And Hummel, facing two felony charges, was ready to help. It was he, after all, who had told Jerome of the existence of the affidavit, less than two weeks after the killing.[28] Hummel knew a bargaining chip when he saw one.

Evelyn, who needed the Thaws for their financial support as much as they needed her for appearances, stood by her husband. In court, she dressed like a particularly prim schoolgirl—a long dress, with a high-necked Peter Pan collar—and under the gentle questioning of the defense, she played the role of injured innocent brilliantly. For two days, she told a spellbound country her story, a melodrama that far outstripped anything that would have been allowed onstage. The highlight was the story of the night in Paris when she told Thaw she could not marry him because . . . she was not a virgin, thanks to Stanford White.[29] "He wanted every detail," she related in a girlish lisp, "and I told him everything. He would sit and sob or walk up and down the room as I told him." The courtroom throbbed with pity.

And it went over just as intended—the loyal wife admitting to her own disgrace to save her husband. The *Chicago Tribune* caught the national mood in an illustration it published on February 10. The pen-and-ink drawing shows Evelyn in a distant profile, body hunched and head bowed, hands in her lap. The caption: "The Sacrifice."[30] In her account, Thaw was an attentive husband who was normal on every subject but one—Stanford White.

Jerome was considerably less tender with the damsel. If White's character was in play, then Evelyn's would be, too. She was forced to admit knowing Barrymore rather well; to being White's mistress, and then Thaw's; and to watching the cakewalk at the Dead Rat café in Paris, which Jerome apparently considered proof of extreme decadence. Never beaten, Evelyn was bowed into something like honest self-awareness when she gave her final thoughts on White: "I say that outside this one terrible thing about Stanford White, he was a very grand man," she told the court. "He was kind and considerate and exceedingly thoughtful—much more thoughtful than most people. He had a very peculiar personality. People liked him very much. He made a great many friends and always kept them."[31]

To the end of her days, Evelyn would feel grateful to White, and angry with him. It was a complex relationship, a mix of destructiveness and empathy. White was both abuser and lover, Evelyn both naïve and knowing. They used each other and gloried in doing so. There was love there, and fear, delight and darkness.

With the history of her relationship with White public in all its peculiarities, Evelyn could admit to her ambivalence. The affidavit was another matter. It was much too damning. The defense scorned it as a forgery, and Evelyn did not demur. The prosecution would not let her off so easily. So she lied. Reading from a copy, Jerome asked about its contents in detail; Evelyn denied everything. That wasn't her handwriting in the affidavit; nor was it White's notes in the margins. She never told Hummel that Thaw beat her with a whip; or that she had seen a hypodermic needle among his things; or that he had threatened to kill her; or that he had tried to make her sign a statement to the effect that a married man had wronged her. She never signed any affidavit. "I never did, sir," was her refrain. No, no, no; never happened, none of it, as she lisped and trembled and cast yearning glances toward her husband. She really was an actress of much greater talent than she had ever been able to display on the stage.

Hummel was in the best position to attack Evelyn's denials. He would have to testify. The irony of this was lost on no one. Jerome was asking Hummel, whom he had recently convicted for faking an affidavit, to swear to the authenticity of this one. After a series of numbing legal wrangles,[32] Hummel took the stand in one of his last appearances in a courtroom. His task was to prove that Evelyn Nesbit Thaw had lied. He did his best, telling how he had interviewed her; written the affidavit; had it typed, including a carbon copy; and then photographed it before burning the original. The office stenographer confirmed the account, adding that he had specifically asked Evelyn if she had read it before signing. She said she had.

The defense attacked Hummel's veracity with, one juror later judged, rather too much enthusiasm. "The scathing denunciation of the little lawyer was undoubtedly calculated to tear a reputation to pieces," commented juror Harry Brearly after the trial, "but it was first necessary to assume that the reputation previously existed. [Defense attorney] Delmas was from California, however, and had not been long in New York."[33] Hummel had to admit that he had once been disbarred and was now suspended.

But the testimony was in, and a few days later, so was the affidavit itself: On March 18, the jury had the entire thing read to them. If the prosecution expected this to be a bombshell, it was wrong. There was nothing in it that everyone had not already heard. Worse, Hummel was caught in a lie, or at least a mistake: In court, he testified that White was his client; in the affidavit, he is described as Evelyn's attorney. Even if it was an honest error, the contradiction impeached his already supremely impeachable character.[34]

Besides, regardless of whether Evelyn signed the a statement or not, Thaw clearly knew something of the events at White's love nest. The account of the rawhide whippings was awful, but it could be untrue. Remember, Evelyn said Hummel had put in things that had never occurred. It came down to her word against Hummel's, and his could hardly be taken on faith. There was no smoking gun here, just a small-caliber shot in the dark—damaging but not deadly.

All that was left for the jury to do was to assimilate the testimony of the various medical "experts." Jerome did not make this easy for them. He sculpted a 13,000-word hypothetical, touching on every detail of the case. Printed, it was 39 pages long; spoken, it took 78 minutes to recite. Blessedly, the defense agreed to use the same hypothetical; and unsurprisingly, the defense and prosecution doctors drew opposite conclusions. The defense doctors argued that Thaw was temporarily insane, the prosecution that he was sane enough.

In his closing argument, the lead defense attorney, Delphin Delmas, displayed why he was considered the Big Bill Howe of the West. He praised Evelyn for her virtue, then rubbished Hummel as a perjurer and White as a satyr. If Thaw wasn't insane (and he might have been, for just a few moments), he was a Sir Galahad who, in the defense of the Angel Child, did the world a service by getting rid of a lecher.

The heart of Delmas's six-hour argument is encapsulated by a few lines in the middle of it: Thaw "knew not, he reasoned not, but struck as does the tigress to protect her home—struck for the purity of American homes—struck for the purity of American wives. He struck, and who shall say he was not right?"[35] In a much-quoted expansion on this theme, Delmas went on,

> And if Thaw is insane, it is with a species of insanity known from the Canadian border to the Gulf. If you expert gentlemen ask me to give it a name, I suggest that you label it *Dementia Americana*. It is that species of insanity that inspires every American to believe his home

is sacred. It is that species of insanity that persuades an American that whoever violates the sanctity of his home or the purity of his wife or daughter has forfeited the protection of the laws of this state or any other state.[36]

Jerome was more direct in his closing. This was no act of chivalry, he argued, just another "vulgar, sordid, common murder of the Tenderloin." If Thaw was insane, then he should go to an asylum; if he was not, he was guilty of first-degree murder and should pay for it with his own life. Hummel "was not an upright man," Jerome admitted, but there was corroboration from the stenographer to the creation of the affidavit. It was Evelyn, not Hummel, whose word was unsupported. A study in perjury, she had lied time and again, about things big and small, for days on end. The "Angel Child" was a serial liar who had played two besotted men against each other.

What it came down to, Jerome asked, was this: "Will you acquit a cold-blooded, deliberate, cowardly murderer, because his lying wife has a pretty girl's face?" And then, grasping the revolver that killed White, he pulled the trigger three times. The clicks echoed in the chamber, shocking the crowd into silence. Those sounds, at least temporarily, were sharp reminders that this was serious business. One man was dead, and another at risk of death. In his last words, Jerome rejected the unwritten law to remind jurors of a written one: "Thou shalt not kill."

After a dispassionate charge from Judge Thomas Fitzgerald, who hinted that an insanity finding would not be such a terrible thing, at 5:12 p.m. on April 10, 1907, it was time for the gentlemen of the jury. Forty-seven hours later, they gave up, deadlocked: seven in favor of conviction, five in favor of insanity.

The second trial, in January 1908, was a more subdued and sensible affair, taking three weeks instead of almost three months. Thaw's new counsel, mindful that in the previous trial seven jurors had wanted to convict his client, went straight for an insanity plea—not *Dementia Americana*, not a two-minute brainstorm. Thaw, he said, had long been insane, and the family history was rich in mental illness; a cousin, for example, doted on pet rats.[37] The jury agreed, as did Jerome. Hummel did not appear. Thaw was packed off to an asylum in upstate New York.[38]

The story did not end there and it did not end well. Thaw escaped from the asylum and went to Canada; the authorities there shipped him back. Mama Thaw kept lobbying for his release and got it in 1915. He divorced Evelyn and was rearrested for whipping a teenage boy nearly to death in 1917. He spent another seven years in another asylum. Released in 1924, he was the subject of various rumors and lawsuits, but he stayed out of institutions until his death in 1947.

The Thaws were not generous to Evelyn, even after she gave birth to a son, Russell, who looked strikingly like Harry (he denied paternity). When Harry was sent to the asylum, they cut her off. Evelyn went back on the stage, but she never recaptured the glory of her youth—she was a has-been before she was 25. She also began to drink and take drugs; her despair translated into headlines of fights, evictions, arrests, and suicide attempts. In the late 1930s, she was appearing in a second-rate Chicago nightclub when she saw John Barrymore, by then a ruin of a man, in the audience. They looked at each other and wept.[39]

ELEVEN

The Legend Ends

Delay, delay, delay: Hummel and his team did their best. But the clock eventually ran out. Jerome dropped the felony indictments for suborning perjury, citing the help Hummel had given the Thaw prosecution.[1] Still, he refused to budge on the conspiracy conviction. Hummel would have to serve his time.

On May 16, 1907, he gave a banquet at his townhouse, where some of his showbiz friends performed in the drawing room under a portrait of Stanford White. Two days later, Hummel sneaked out to the 70th Street dock, where he picked up a boat that dropped him off at the north end of Blackwell's Island. From there, he walked to the jail, thus avoiding the dozens of reporters who had camped out to record his shame. Arthur Train had to admit that the lawyer went out in style: "Now that the game was going against him, he met fate with a smiling face and accepted ruin like the gambler he was."[2]

Always a careful man, Hummel had his head and mustache shaved by a barber of his choice, rather than trusting to the prison staff. But he had to submit to a search, shower, and new wardrobe—a striped uniform of coarse flannel. Indignity was added to insult; there was no uniform small enough for him, and he had to turn up the trousers a good five inches. The prison shoes were huge, too, and the shirt draped him like a dress. The ridiculous outfit, under the circumstances, was a small thing, but it loomed large to Hummel, who prided himself on his appearance. "I guess that most of what they say about me is true," he told another lawyer during the Dodge-Morse tangle. "I'm a crook and I'm a black-mailer. But there's one thing about me. I'm a neat son of a bitch."[3]

Holding up his clothes, Hummel shambled to his four-by-eight cell, furnished with a cot and a wooden slop bucket. For the next year, he could anticipate the following routine: 6:00 a.m. breakfast of coffee and bread; work in the commissary from 8:00–4:00; dinner; back to the cell; lights out at 9:30. He could have one bath a week, and three visitors on Sunday. It took only a day for him to crack. A cold night weakened him, and he ended up in the prison hospital.

Hummel would spend almost all of his incarceration in the hospital wing. In July, he was said to be near death; in September, he was depressed and indifferent. In November, he refused to celebrate Thanksgiving and was reportedly suffering from kidney disease. In a December interview with a reporter who had posed as a criminology researcher, he was fretful and finicky, complaining about his weak eyes, the fetid air, and not getting his medicine in capsule form.[4] With nothing else to do, he brooded about the "harrowing contrast of myself here and with myself of the recent past," calling such thoughts a "veritable hell." He never wanted to drink milk again.

But he survived the ordeal and was even allowed to grow a mustache a few months before his release, so that he looked pretty much like his old self when he left Blackwell's Island on March 19, 1908. Down to 121 pounds, he could still throw his weight around, finagling a special boat to take him back to Manhattan to avoid reporters.

A couple of days after his release, Hummel sailed to London on the *Lusitania*. His last words were a mix of bitterness and pride—bitter that he was convicted on what he called "perjured testimony" and that the newspapers had, in his mind, turned against him. And proud that he hadn't squealed. Hummel could have taken down dozens of people. But, paid generously for his silence, he kept it. "Had I been willing to tell some secrets that had been entrusted to me, I could not have been convicted," he said. "I resolved, however, to show that I did not belong to those who turn on their friends. . . . So I took my punishment and I believe that I am now entitled to live my own life in my way."

That is exactly what he did, living in luxury on Grosvenor Square in London with his sister. He also spent a good deal of time in Paris, where he became a friend of the theatrical community and bought a movie theater. It was a quiet life, and one that tolled no echoes.

Except once. On an around-the-world trip in 1911, Hummel ran into his past in the form of a man in a Yokohama rickshaw. In the early 1870s, the partnership had worked behind-the-scenes in the famous trial of Ned Stokes for the murder of Jim Fisk. Hummel's job: to spirit away the only eyewitness to the shooting, with a fat retainer and orders never to return. It was this man he ran into on the streets of Yokohama.[5] What a remembrance of things past that brief encounter must have provoked.

In general, though, Hummel did not spend much time looking into the past; once he left New York, he never came back. The memories were too much, his anger too deep—until his death in 1926, when he returned for good.

At their peak, Howe & Hummel were so famous that they were the subject of well-understood jokes on vaudeville, and reporters would trek up to the Saratoga racetrack just to check on them. Even after the partnership ended with the death of Howe and the humiliation of Hummel, their celebrity lingered.

For one thing, lawyers love to gossip, and Howe & Hummel's fame continued to flicker in the form of "Did you hear the one about . . ." stories, to be told with gusto in the convivial precincts of Pontin's or other lawyerly hangouts. As late as the mid-1940s, when *New Yorker* writer Richard Rovere went looking for Howe & Hummel lore, it was easy to find: The partners were "still spoken of by cops and lawyers, police reporters and court attendants along Centre Street with the same respect for dead giants that other people show for Sarah Bernhardt [and] Christy Mathewson."[6]

For another, some of their most famous cases continued to resonate. The saga of Carlyle Harris, with its dandy combination of class, sex, and overweening mother love, cropped up whenever there was a murder in the upper crust. Ditto for the unfortunate Guldensuppe. Any time a body was stuffed in a trunk, or chopped up, or both, the grisly demise of Bathhouse Willie would be retold.[7] And finally, Artemis Quibble and Ambrose Hinkle, the eponymous stars of humorous novels unmistakably drawn from the Howe & Hummel body of work, introduced the duo, however backhandedly, to a new generation.

But lawyers die; new atrocities displace old ones; and not many comic novels outlast their time. Even great defense lawyers falter against the forces of time and death. Gradually, the legend began to fade. Nor did either man have more conventional forms of remembrance. Howe had a daughter; when she married, the name passed out of circulation. Hummel had an illegitimate son, the product of a long liaison with an opera singer.[8] Once Henry Hummel got a cut of his father's estate, he returned to his bakery wagon in Maine, and to obscurity.[9]

The partners probably would not have minded that their fame had a limited shelf life. William Howe and Abraham Hummel were men of their times, and of the moment. They loved their lives—the charms of Pontin's, the courts, the races, and even the Tombs, endured to the end. They never seemed to give a thought to the future, either in the form of the consequences of their actions, or in the larger sense of posterity. If they were given to reflections about mortality, they never shared them openly. They seemed to be of the opinion that once this mortal coil was shuffled off, well, to hell with it.

With all the secrets he knew, Hummel could have written a racy bestseller, in several volumes, that would have kept his name alive—and would have been prime source material for future historians. True to his own code of honor, he never did. Ditto for Howe. He did write *In Danger*, but that was advertising, not the juicy autobiography he had in him. The partners didn't buy art or endow scholarships or do any of the things the Gilded Age elite did to ensure posthumous fame. The men for whom the Saratoga racetrack was a second home never even named a horse after themselves.

This reticence extended to their deaths. Howe asked to be buried in Brooklyn's Green-Wood Cemetery, a verdant and lovely place that was made for him. Here he would lie among friends, such as his former associate Joseph Moss; kindred spirits, like Boss Tweed; critics, like Horace Greeley; and notables who had featured in some of his famous cases, such as Lola Montez and Henry Ward Beecher. Given Howe's ability to milk the drama out of anything from a murder trial to a tiepin, it would have been in character for him to want to make a statement in death, perhaps a statue of the Goddess of Justice, with a wink instead of a blindfold. Such a memorial would have fit right in among the mausoleums and obelisks and other self-referential totems to earthly importance that Green-Wood is stuffed with.

In fact, there is nothing of the sort. Map in hand, it is possible to stand on William Howe's burial place; but there is no tangible remembrance of the man, not even a simple tombstone. In death, he eschewed the attention that he had sought all his life. Hummel, too, was discreet. He was buried in a private plot in a private cemetery outside Manhattan that is accessible only to family members.

But even if it was inadvertent, Howe and Hummel did leave a legacy, in two ways. First, because they were willing to take up lost causes, they were often ahead of their times. Howe's defense in 1887 of Johann Most, the anarchist, on free speech grounds, for example, feels pretty sound even today. Hummel's plea on behalf of the allegedly obscene *Sapho* in 1900 set down the useful principle that it was no crime to produce provocative plays not authored by Shakespeare. And their very outrageousness helped force the bar to raise its standards.

Their other legacy is a subtle one. Howe and Hummel went into practice just as the media was becoming available to the masses. Before their time, the idea of a famous criminal lawyer would have been ludicrous: What went on in the courts was not something the average dockworker or housewife knew or cared about, and there was no culture of celebrity to speak of. It was on the partners' watch that crime became a news staple and lawyers could be stars.

As the highest-profile lawyers in the first generation of high-profile counsel, Howe & Hummel designed the template for a certain kind of lawyering. Those who wanted to follow in their footsteps adopted their style; so did the next generation, and the one after that, so that to this day there is a faint tracing of the original. Bill Howe, with his flashy dress, big voice, love of publicity, and willingness to say the unthinkable looks and feels an awful lot like any number of high-profile defense attorneys seen today. And Hummel was a role model for the power-behind-the-throne kind of lawyer, subtle and unprincipled.

In their own times, Howe and Hummel were probably more famous than they deserved to be; but their subsequent obscurity also seems inappropriate. In their life and work, they connected the threads, both golden and dark, that made up the Gilded Age. New York has never seen their like again—and that's probably not a bad thing.

NOTE ON NEW YORK CITY'S 19TH-CENTURY JUSTICE SYSTEM

THE COURTS

Here is how the court system operated in New York City during the era of Howe & Hummel, 1869–1907.

From the bottom up:

Police Courts

The police courts had original jurisdiction over minor offenses like boozing and pickpocketing. The justices—15 of them, operating in six courts scattered around the city—could decide the case or send it to another court for trial. The defendant could also ask for the case to be transferred. Justices were appointed by the mayor to ten-year terms and often had no legal background. In the mid-1870s, they disposed of almost 85,000 arrests a year.

Court of Special Sessions

Created in 1858, these courts operated out of the Tombs and adjudicated misdemeanors—about 6,000–7,000 cases a year. They were presided over by a rotation of three police justices. They could decide the case, or transfer it; a defendant could also ask for a jury trial.

Court of General Sessions

Operating out of a building in City Hall Park, slightly south of the Tombs, these courts presided over jury trials in felony cases. There were four judges: the Recorder, the City Judge, and two Judges of the Court, elected to 14-year terms. All had the same pay and responsibilities, but the Recorder was considered first among equals. (For the sake of simplicity, I refer to everyone as Judge.) Death penalty cases usually started here; they could be appealed directly to the state Court of Appeals, which did not hear testimony but would consider new arguments.

Court of Oyer and Terminer (from the French for "hear and determine")

This was presided over by a judge of the Supreme Court of the State of New York who tried cases—typically those of a more serious or complex nature—at the request of either defense or prosecution, four or five times a year. It was abolished in 1896.

JAILS AND PRISONS

Ludlow Street

For federal prisoners and those arrested by the sheriff of New York County. Many of its inhabitants were imprisoned for debt.

Blackwell's Island

For those sentenced for minor crimes such as prostitution, pickpocketing, or conspiracy to subvert justice.

The Tombs

The famous jail had a number of different purposes. It had something like a drunk tank, called Bummer's Hall; it also housed people who were awaiting trial and witnesses whom the authorities feared would flee unless they were caged. Finally, until New York adopted the electric chair and centralized executions in Sing Sing, those doomed to death by the City of New York awaited, and suffered, their fate here.

Sing Sing

This was, and is, a state prison for repeat offenders and those convicted of serious crimes.

THE NEW YORK POLICE DEPARTMENT

The police force in the Howe & Hummel era had the following shape:

The NYPD was supervised by a civilian board of political appointees; the panel adjudicated police transgressions, oversaw the pension fund and, until 1895, decided promotions and appointments. The top uniformed cop was known as the superintendent of police and later as chief of police. For simplicity's sake, I use the term "chief" throughout.

Under the chief, there were four inspectors; then there was a captain for each precinct—36 of these in Manhattan and the Bronx, prior to the creation in 1898 of Greater New York, which combined Manhattan, Brooklyn, Queens, the Bronx, and Staten Island. About 160 sergeants ran day-to-day operations at each station house; several hundred "roundsmen" supervised the patrolmen on the beat.

In 1895, there were about 3,200 beat cops, plus a scattering of surgeons, doormen, and matrons. And yes, the stereotype is true: The force was overwhelmingly Irish. In the 1890s, a third had been born in Ireland, and most of the rest had at least one Irish-born parent. About 7 percent were of German descent.

NOTE ON SOURCES

I first came across Howe & Hummel in a few pages of Luc Sante's wonderful *Low Life*, about life on the periphery of New York from roughly 1840 to 1919. The bibliography led me to *Howe & Hummel: Their Scandalous History* by Richard Rovere, a reprint of a 1947 book, *The Magnificent Shysters*, which was based on four articles Rovere wrote for the *New Yorker*.

Rovere's book was an important starting point, leading me to some of the famous cases and convincing me that there was a story here worth telling. Rovere also had the great advantage of talking to people who remembered both Howe and Hummel. By the time I came to the story, of course, all their contemporaries were long dead. That said, I did not rely on Rovere when I could check things for myself. While I found Rovere generally reliable, he was not infallible. For example, he wrote that the defense of Olga Nethersole (Chapter 8) was for the famous kiss and on the basis of art. That is not quite right. He also repeats the incorrect death date of George Leonidas Leslie (Chapter 6), a mistake that keeps cropping up in other sources; and that Ella Nelson shot six times (it was four; Chapter 5). This is not to criticize Rovere. As far as I can tell—which is pretty darn far, at this point—he made very few significant errors. Therefore, on things of consequence that were otherwise unverifiable, I have felt confident repeating his assertions, especially if I could find some kind of confirmation from another source.

For example, Howe & Hummel's blackmailing practice was, by its nature, a hidden one. But Rovere spoke with people who knew firsthand about that aspect of things, and I was able to find contemporaneous comments that reinforced these assertions. On that basis, I was willing to go ahead and say, yes, this was part of their practice. By the same token, if Rovere asserted something that I could find no evidence of elsewhere, I usually decided not to use it. So, for example, he said that the great counterfeiter Charles Brockway was a Howe & Hummel client. Brockway, who was a wonder at this job, was surely the partners' kind of man, but I could find no inkling anywhere else that they represented him.

Rovere's book was an invaluable start, but only a start. Most of the research for this book came from going through the newspapers of the era. At the New York Public Library, I trawled through the following newspapers: the *New York Herald*, the *New York Journal*, the *New York Sun*, the *New York Times*, the *New York Tribune*, and the *New York World*. There were other newspapers circulating in this era, but these covered the range of low, middle, and high brow. Each chapter notes which newspapers I used. In addition, the Municipal Archives of the City of New York has a collection of scrapbooks from the district attorney's office from 1884 to 1902. These contained clippings about notable cases, giving me access to many other newspapers for this period.

I have not footnoted each newspaper reference, simply because it would be tedious. But the reader should know that every quotation in the book, if it is not footnoted, comes from a contemporaneous newspaper. So how did I go about picking and choosing what quotations and references to use? With discretion.

In an era before tape recorders and in which court transcriptions were not routine (typically, the defense paid for a stenographer, and many of these transcripts, sadly, were thrown out), the modern author has to rely on what the reporters wrote. It is humbling, as a journalist, to note that it was not often that the reporters wrote the same remarks exactly the same way. They were, however, generally very close. So what I have done is to choose the pithiest quotation of the various entries. What I have not done, which did happen occasionally, is to choose the one that is different. If four newspapers have reported testimony the same way, with slightly different words, I disregarded the fifth that was at odds with the rest.

Because I am relying so heavily on the journalism of the era, it is fair to ask: How good was it? Sometimes astonishingly good. I was awed reading a comprehensive account of the murder of Jane Hull in Boston a day after the fact. (Howe & Hummel represented her killer, Chastine Cox, who hanged for it.) Everything was there, and there was little "row back" (correcting mistakes in subsequent articles without acknowledging the errors). And sometimes it was astonishingly bad; see the Nethersole imbroglio, in which the *New York World* created a controversy where there was none. And sometimes it was both. The *Journal* did admirable investigative work in the Guldensuppe murder; it also printed spurious "confessions" and statements from the authorities. So I trod warily. If there was a major break or accusation or development in a case that was reported in one newspaper and not subsequently picked up by the rest, I went on the assumption that the story had been too good to be true and decided not to include it. This may not be an infallible approach, but I think it gives the best odds of recounting something resembling reality.

Other important resources were the Municipal Archives of the City of New York and court transcripts at the John Jay College of Criminal Justice. The city's archives have indictment files going back to the 1600s. This is a remarkable achievement of storage. More important, it is a testament to the ideal of the rule of law. Even after spending years in the company of Howe and Hummel, who regarded this notion lightly, I consider this an ideal well worth our effort. The indictment files were intermittently useful. Most often, the affidavits were boilerplate. But they could at least confirm when Howe & Hummel were the attorneys of record and sometimes presented other nuggets to mine, such as the no doubt perjured testimony of those who said that Danny Driscoll's chief accuser (see Chapter 4) was a lying slut.

The court transcripts were more of an experience in treasures lost; in the 1970s, tons of historic court records were thrown out before an alert professor saved the rest. Only 18 cases featuring Howe & Hummel have been preserved, few of them interesting. Though the transcripts proved not to be all that useful in the preparation of this book, they presented the undeniable thrill of being as close as possible to the moment.

Naturally, secondary sources were important in learning about things like prison life, the death penalty, and attitudes about abortion. All references and insights from these are footnoted.

NOTES

PREFACE

1. *New York World*, December 9, 1890.

2. *Chicago Tribune*, December 21, 1905.

3. This was the second building known as the Tombs; the first was replaced in 1902.

4. *New York Times*, December 21, 1905.

5. Richard Rovere, *Howe and Hummel: Their True and Scandalous History* (New York: Farrar, Straus and Giroux, 1985), p. 8. First published as *The Magnificent Shysters* in 1947.

6. The term was used in the *New York Herald*, September 3, 1902; *New York Times*, September 3, 1902; *New York Tribune*, September 7, 1902.

7. Francis Wellman, *Gentlemen of the Jury* (New York: Macmillan, 1924), p. 99.

8. Rovere, *Howe and Hummel*, p. 126.

9. Ibid., p. 15.

10. *New York Herald*, September 3, 1902.

11. Theron Strong, *Landmarks of a Lawyer's Lifetime* (New York: Dodd, Mead, 1914), p. 294.

12. Arthur Train, *True Stories of Crime* (New York: Charles Scribner's Sons, 1908), p. 317.

13. Rovere, *Howe and Hummel*, p. 5.

14. Wellman, *Gentlemen of the Jury*, p. 101.

15. *Cosmopolitan*, May 1908, p. 596.

16. *New York Tribune,* November 23, 1901.

17. *New York Herald,* February 25, 1890.

18. *New York Morning Journal,* January 17, 1893.

19. Strong, *Landmarks,* p. 301; *New York Tribune,* September 3, 1902.

20. Tom Buk-Swienty, *The Other Half* (New York: W. W. Norton, 2008), p. 162.

21. Ibid., p. 165.

22. Rovere, *Howe and Hummel,* p. 126.

23. *The Bar: Journal of the West Virginia Bar Association,* November 1907, p. 27.

24. Ibid., p. 25.

25. Randolph Churchill, *Winston S. Churchill: Youth, 1876–1900* (Boston: Houghton Mifflin, 1966), p. 258.

26. Ben Macintyre, *The Napoleon of Crime,: The Life and Times of Adam Worth, Master Thief* (New York: Farrar, Straus & Giroux, 1997), p. 32.

27. Arthur Train, *My Day in Court* (New York: Charles Scribner's Sons, 1939), pp. 29–30.

28. *New York Times,* November 18, 1870.

29. The subhead is: *Being the ingenuous and unvarnished history of Artemis Quibble, Esquire, one-time practitioner in the New York Criminal Courts, together with an account of the divers wiles, tricks, sophistries, technicalities and sundry artifices of himself and others of the fraternity, commonly called "shysters" or "shyster lawyers"* (New York: Charles Scribner's Sons, 1911).

30. Arthur Train, *The Confessions of Artemis Quibble* (New York: Charles Scribner's Sons, 1911), p. 88.

31. Ibid., p. 71.

32. Wellman, *Gentlemen of the Jury,* 254.

33. Francis Wellman, *Success in Court* (New York, Macmillan, 1941), p. 60.

34. *New York Mail and Express,* April 28, 1893.

35. George Lankevich, *New York City: A Short History* (New York: New York University Press), p. 103.

36. "The Heirs of Howe & Hummel," *Victorian Bar News* 2004, p. 39.

37. George Martin, *Causes and Conflicts: The Centennial History of the Association of the Bar of the City of New York, 1870–1970* (Boston: Houghton Mifflin, 1970), p. 135.

38. Edwin Burrows and Mike Wallace, *Gotham: A History of New York City to 1898* (New York: Oxford University Press, 1999), p. 968.

39. *New York Times,* December 21, 1905.

40. Wellman, *Gentlemen of the Jury,* p. 116.

ONE · THE LEGEND BEGINS

1. *New York Tribune*, October 7, 1888.

2. *New York Herald*, March 1, 1891.

3. Rovere and others estimate the sign at 40 feet, but in the only picture I have seen, it is the width of a low-rise building, which was typically built on a 25-foot-wide lot.

4. *Chicago Tribune*, January 24, 1906.

5. Strong, *Landmarks*, p. 296.

6. Rovere, *Howe and Hummel*, pp. 59–60.

7. In 1893, he referred to incidents in his "early legal training" in England (*New York Times*, March 17, 1893).

8. Charges of the Bar Association of the State of New York, vol. 1, p. 377.

9. *New York Times*, December 5, 1874.

10. *Chicago Tribune*, December 25, 1892.

11. *New York Times*, August 28, 1860, and August 14, 1861.

12. *The Bar: Journal of the West Virginia Bar Association*, November 1907, p. 28.

13. Thomas Byrnes, *Professional Criminals of America*. Introduction by Arthur Schlesinger (New York: Chelsea House, 1969), p. xv.

14. James McCabe, *Lights and Shadows of New York Life* (New York, Farrar, Straus and Giroux, 1970), p. 522. Facsimile of 1872 original.

15. Charges of the Bar Association of the State of New York, vol. 1, p. 377.

16. *New York Times*, December 11, 1871. The newspaper never names Howe and/or Hummel, but internal evidence, such as the cases cited, makes it clear that they are the subjects.

17. *New York Times*, December 11, 1871, and April 9, 1873.

18. Train, *True Stories*, pp. 72, 73.

19. Hummel admitted this during his testimony at the murder trial of Harry Thaw in March 1907.

20. *New York Times*, October 9, 1875.

21. *New York Times*, February 2, 1870.

22. *New York Times*, February 22, 1870.

23. "Trial and Conviction of Jack Reynolds for the Horrible Murder of William Townsend," pamphlet compiled by A. H. Hummel, pp. 11–17, 37.

24. Ibid., p. 23.

25. Ibid., p. 37.

26. Ibid., p. 48.

27. *New York Times*, March 20, 1870.

28. *New York Times*, February 18, 1870.

29. *New York Tribune*, April 21, 1870.

30. Gustave Lening, *The Dark Side of New York Life and Its Criminal Classes from Fifth Avenue Down to the Five Points* (New York: Fred Gerhard, 1973), p. 718.

31. *Brooklyn Daily Eagle*, April 20, 1870.

32. *New York Herald*, February 22, 1870.

33. *New York Herald*, February 22, 1870.

34. *New York World*, June 12, 1892.

35. *New York World*, February 24, 1870.

36. *New York Times*, March 30, 1870.

37. *New York Times*, February 22, 1871.

38. Lawrence Friedman, *American Law in the 20th Century* (New Haven: Yale University Press, 2002), p. 35.

39. *New York Herald*, April 10, 1872.

40. *New York Times*, February 19, 1872.

41. George Martin, *Causes and Conflicts: The Centennial History of the Association of the Bar of the City of New York, 1870–1970* (Boston: Houghton Mifflin, 1970), p. 75.

42. James Lardner and Thomas Repetto, *NYPD: A City and Its Police* (New York, Henry Holt, 2000), p. 96.

43. www.harpweek.com; essay accompanying a cartoon by Frank Bellew that appeared May 25, 1872.

44. Andrew Kaufman, *Cardozo* (Cambridge, MA: Harvard University Press, 1998), p. 7.

45. Quoted in Martin, *Causes and Conflicts*, p. 77.

46. Charges of the Bar Association of the State of New York, vol. 1, p. 379.

47. Kaufman, *Cardozo*, p. 8.

48. Transcript of report of the Bar Association, *New York World*, April 10, 1872; also Bar Association, p. 401. Howe said in his testimony to the Judiciary Committee that this was all easily explained. He got the writs in cases where only one judge had presided, pending further judgment. But the story does not stand up: Why only Cardozo?

49. *New York Times*, February 25, 1872.

50. Bar Association, vol. 1, pp. 429–430.

51. Transcript of report of the Bar Association, *New York World*, April 10, 1872.

52. Charges of the Bar Association of New York, vol. 1, p. xiii.

53. Kaufman, *Cardozo*, p. 11.

54. *New York World*, April 15, 1872.

55. Martin, *Causes and Conflicts*, p. 76n.

TWO · THE GHASTLY TRUNK

1. James Mohr, *Abortion in America* (New York: Oxford University Press, 1979), p. 51.

2. Ibid., p. 53.

3. *Medical and Surgical Reporter*, October 14, 1871.

4. Mohr estimates that by the 1860s, there may have been as many as one abortion for every five births, p. 50.

5. James Lardner and Thomas Repetto, *NYPD: A City and Its Police* (New York, Henry Holt, 2000), p. 10.

6. $10 in 1872 is equivalent to about $180 today; $300 is equivalent to $5,400.

7. Edwin Burrows and Mike Wallace, *Gotham: A History of New York City to 1898* (New York: Oxford University Press, 1999, p. 808.

8. At the northeast corner of 52nd Street.

9. Luc Sante, *Low Life: Lures and Snares of Old New York* (New York: Vintage, 1992), p. 187.

10. James McCabe, *Secrets of the Great City* (New York: Jones Brothers, 1868), p. 207.

11. Stewart did his reputation no good by carelessly allowing his body to be robbed after his death; the thieves held it for ransom. That kind of thing did not happen in the best families.

12. Eric Homberger, *Mrs. Astor's New York: Money and Social Power in a Gilded Age* (New Haven: Yale University Press, 2004), p. 123.

13. McCabe, *Secrets of the Great City*, p. 159.

14. Clifford Browder, *The Wickedest Woman in New York* (New York: Archon, 1988), p. 9.

15. "Wonderful Trial of Caroline Lohman, alias Madam Restall," pamphlet, p. 6.

16. Speech to the May 1990 "Celebration of Our Work" conference, which was sponsored by the Rutgers University Institute for Research on Women. http://www.kenschaft.com/restell.htm.

17. Sante, *Low Life*, p. 187.

18. Edward van Every, *Sins of New York* (New York: Ayer, 1970), p. 91.

19. Browder, *Wickedest Woman*, p. 124.

20. *New York Times*, August 23, 1871.

21. Unless otherwise specified, this story is drawn from accounts in the contemporaneous newspapers, specifically the *New York Herald*, *New York Sun*, *New*

York Times, *New York Tribune*, and *New York World*. All covered the events in detail. (Interestingly, the *Times* was among the first with the story, and the early accounts in the *Tribune* show clear traces of plagiarism from that source.)

22. The *New York Tribune* on August 30 even noted a "small blue tub full of clothes that were soaking in readiness for the washerwoman." For two days, it apparently did not occur to anyone to look in the tub.

23. Browder, *Wickedest Woman*, p. 136.

24. Ibid.

25. *Woodhull & Claflin's Weekly*, September 16, 1871.

26. *New York Sun*, January 31, 1872.

27. Arthur Train, *The Confessions of Artemis Quibble* (New York: Charles Scribner's Sons, 1911), p. 77.

28. Burrows and Wallace, *Gotham*, p. 1017.

29. *New York Herald*, April 10, 1872.

30. *New York Times*, November 28, 1872, and June 27, 1875.

31. *New York Times*, November 28, 1872.

32. Rovere, *Howe and Hummel*, p. 160.

33. The first would be the killing of Jim Fisk; Howe & Hummel played a behind-the-scenes role in that one, apparently getting a key witness out of town (see Rovere, *Howe and Hummel*, pp. 50–52).

34. Edmund Lester Pearson, *Studies in Murder* (New York: Macmillan, 1924), p. 134.

35. *New York Times*, September 13, 1872.

36. *New York Herald*, September 19, 1872.

37. *New York Times*, September 19, 1872.

38. *New York Herald*, September 23, 1872.

39. *New York Herald*, November 10, 1889.

THREE · SISTERS IN LAW

1. Gerald Johnson, "Dynamic Victoria Woodhull," *American Heritage*, June 1956, pp. 45, 49.

2. Francine du Plessix Gray, *The New Yorker*, April 20, 1998, p. 95.

3. Luc Sante, *Low Life: Lures and Snares of Old New York* (New York: Vintage, 1992), p. 326.

4. Ibid., p. 327.

5. "Our Fundamental Propositions," *Woodhull & Claflin's Weekly*, p. 1.

6. Madeleine Stern, *The Victoria Woodhull Reader* (Weston, MA: M&S Press, 1974), p. 5.

7. Ibid.

8. *Woodhull & Claflin's Weekly*, November 2, 1872.

9. *New York Times*, August 28, 1872.

10. Debby Applegate, *The Most Famous Man in America* (New York: Doubleday, 2006), p. 420.

11. Applegate, *Most Famous Man*, p. 415; Tilton would later say that Woodhull forced him to write the biography, threatening to tell about Beecher if he refused.

12. Leon Oliver, *The Great Sensation* (Chicago: Beverly, 1873), p. 167.

13. Ibid., p. 120.

14. *Woodhull & Claflin's Weekly*, January 23, 1873.

15. Mary Gabriel, *Notorious Victoria* (Chapel Hill, NC: Algonquin Books, 1988), p. 188.

16. Helen Campbell, Thomas Knox, and Thomas Byrnes, *Darkness and Daylight: Lights and Shadows of New York Life* (Hartford: Hartford Publishing, 1895), p. 345.

17. M. M. Marberry, *Vicky: A Biography of Victoria C. Woodhull* (New York: Funk & Wagnalls, 1967), p. 113.

18. *New York Herald*, November 3, 1872.

19. *New York Times*, February 11, 1878.

20. George Walling, *Recollections of a New York City Chief of Police* (New York: Caxton Book Concern, 1887), p. 392.

21. Walling, *Recollections*, p. 390.

22. Barbara Goldsmith, *Other Powers: The Age of Suffrage, Spiritualism and the Scandalous Victoria Woodhull* (New York: Alfred A. Knopf, 1998), p. 365.

23. *New York World*, November 5, 1872.

24. *New York Herald*, November 9, 1872.

25. Diary entry, quoted in Heywood Broun and Margaret Leech, *Anthony Comstock, Roundsman of the Lord* (New York: Albert & Charles, 1927), p. 117.

26. Stern, *Woodhull Reader*, Chapter 3.

27. Goldsmith, *Other Powers*, p. 365.

28. *Chicago Tribune*, April 23, 1873.

29. *New York Tribune*, April 23, 1873.

30. Broun and Leech, *Anthony Comstock*, p. 125.

31. Donna Dennis, *Licentious Gotham: Erotic Publishing and its Prosecution in Nineteenth-Century New York* (Cambridge, MA: Harvard University Press, 2009), p. 241.

32. Marberry, *Vicky*, p. 139.

33. Broun and Leech, *Anthony Comstock*, p. 119.

34. *New York Sun*, June 28, 1873.

35. Tennie and Victoria suffered some very lean years after all their trials. But in 1877, they got lucky: their mentor, Commodore Vanderbilt, died. The chief beneficiary of his $100 million fortune, his son William, paid the sisters to leave the country so that his siblings could not use the stories about spiritualism and séances to contest the commodore's mental soundness. They took the money—rumor put the figure at $100,000—and ran to London, leaving Colonel Blood behind. He drifted through a series of increasingly menial jobs and died in 1885.

    In London, both sisters married well, Tennie into the nobility, and Victoria into happiness, to banker John Biddulph Martin. Enough people knew about their past that London society did not immediately take to the sisters. Over time, though, their natural charms prevailed, and when the Prince of Wales visited the Martins, they were in. But the sisters paid a price for their acceptance. Victoria flatly denied she had ever been a free lover and began writing exceptionally conventional things about the virtues of monogamy. To the end, though, she retained some of her fire. Well into her 80s, she was known to dismiss chauffeurs who would not drive as fast as she wanted. And she outlived her bête noire, Anthony Comstock, by 12 years, dying in 1927.

36. Burrows and Wallace, *Gotham*, p. 1015.

37. Ralph Andrist, "Paladin of Purity," *American Heritage,* October 1973.

38. Burrows and Wallace, *Gotham*, p. 1016.

39. Eric Homberger, *Scenes from the Life of a City* (New Haven, Yale University Press, 1994), p. 134; Browder, *Wickedest Woman*, p. 159.

40. Ibid., p. 139.

41. Over time, Comstock lost his constituency. He seriously overreached in 1906, when he attempted to prosecute the Art Students' League, a renowned school for artists, for publishing a magazine that included two pages of student depictions of nudes. The only person on the scene when he swooped down was the bookkeeper, who took the fall. "It was just one of our ordinary raids and arrests," Comstock defended himself. But it was a raid too far. Comstockery, a term created by George Bernard Shaw, became ridiculous. H. L. Mencken summed up the crusader with precision: "A good woman, to him, was simply one who was efficiently policed." Comstock died in 1915.

42. Robert Shaplen, *The New Yorker*, June 12, 1954, p. 65.

43. Marberry, *Vicky*, p. 121. Train was obviously no violent threat; the authorities apparently sent him to Murderers' Row hoping to scare him into giving up.

44. *Woodhull & Claflin's Weekly*, January 23, 1873.

45. *National Police Gazette*, April 2, 1881.

46. Byrnes, *Professional Criminals of America*, p. 313.

47. *New York Herald*, November 20, 1873.

48. *New York Times*, August 6, 1873.

49. *National Police Gazette*, December 11, 1880.

50. *New York Times*, March 20, 1881.

51. Charles Sutton, *The New York Tombs* (Montclair, New Jersey: Patterson Smith, 1874), pp. 30–31.

52. http://www.archaeology.org/online/features/wtcartifacts/index.html

53. http://r2.gsa.gov/fivept/fphome.htm

54. Walling, *Recollections*, p. 398.

55. Herbert Asbury, *All Around the Town* (New York: Alfred Knopf, 1934), p. 184.

56. *New York Times*, November 20, 1873.

57. Rona Holub, "Fredericka 'Marm' Mandelbaum, 'Queen of Fences': The Rise and Fall of a Female Immigrant Criminal Entrepreneur in 19th Century New York City," PhD dissertation, Columbia University, 2007, p. 52.

58. *New York Herald*, November 20, 1873.

59. Rovere, *Howe and Hummel*, p. 26.

60. *New York Times*, November 20, 1873.

61. *New York Times*, November 21, 1873.

62. *New York Times*, February 7, 1875.

63. Timothy Gilfoyle, *A Pickpocket's Tale* (New York: W. W. Norton and Company, 2006), p. 131.

64. Ibid., p. 133.

65. *New York Times*, December 22, 1872.

66. *New York Times*, March 28, 1873.

67. George Train, *My Life in Many States* (New York: Appleton & Company, 1902), p. 326.

68. *Boston Globe*, March 31, 1873.

69. *New York Sun*, May 3, 1873.

70. *New York Tribune*, May 21, 1873.

71. George Train, *My Life in Many States and Foreign Lands* (London: William Heinemann, 1902), p. 219.

72. Ibid, p. 327.

FOUR · GANGSTERS OF NEW YORK

1. Charles Dickens, *American Notes* (London: Chapman & Hall, 1842), p. 215.

2. For most of the 19th century, these streets were known as Anthony, Orange, and Cross; the names were changed in the late 1870s to remove the stigma from people who lived there (see *New York Herald*, December 27, 1891).

3. Tyler Anbinder, *Five Points* (New York: Free Press, 2001), p. 344.

4. For a fascinating account of the economic fortunes of a specific group of Irish emigrants, whose passage to New York was paid by their landlord, see "From Famine to Five Points: Lord Lansdowne's Irish Tenants Encounter North America's Most Notorious Slum," by Tyler Anbinder, *American Historical Review*, April 2002.

5. T. J. English, *Paddy Whacked: The Untold Story of the Irish American Gangster* (New York: Regan Books), p. 19.

6. According to Anbinder's original research, in 1880, 31 percent of the adult population in the area had been born in Ireland; 23 percent in Italy; 22 percent in the United States, 11 percent in Poland, and 7 percent in Germany. The momentum of demographic change continued; by 1890, almost half of the residents had been born in Italy; 18 percent were Jewish, probably born in eastern Europe; and only 10 percent Irish and 1 percent German (*Five Points*, pp. 344–345).

7. *New York Herald*, December 27, 1891.

8. Herbert Asbury, *Gangs of New York* (New York: Alfred A. Knopf, 1928), p. 226.

9. English, *Paddy Whacked*, p. 34.

10. Asbury, *Gangs*, p. 229.

11. *New York Herald*, December 27, 1891.

12. Asbury, *Gangs*, p. 226.

13. *New York Herald*, December 27, 1891.

14. This account is derived from the *New York Times*, the *New York Herald*, and the *New York World*.

15. *New York World*, January 17, 1885.

16. *New York World*, January 17, 1885.

17. "The New York Police Department," *Harper's Magazine*, 1886 [from W. H. Smith, ed., *New York: A Collection from* Harper's Magazine (New York: Gallery Books, 1991), p. 430].

18. Timothy Gilfoyle, *A Pickpocket's Tale* (New York: W. W. Norton, 2006), p. 61.

19. Helen Campbell, Thomas Knox, and Thomas Byrnes, *Darkness and Daylight: Lights and Shadows of New York Life* (Hartford: Hartford Publishing, 1895), p. 704.

20. Thomas Byrnes, *Professional Criminals of America,* p. xvii.

21. James Richardson, *The New York Police* (New York: Oxford University Press, 170), p. 211.

22. Ibid., p. xviii.

23. Larry Hartsfield, *The American Response to Professional Crime, 1870–1917* (Westport, CT: Greenwood 1985), p. 44.

24. Byrnes, *Professional Criminals*, pp. 147, 167, 169, 270.

25. Smith, *New York*, p. 430.

26. *New York Sun*, January 26, 1885.

27. *New York World*, January 17, 1885.

28. A. E. Costello, *Our Police Protectors* (New York: self-published, 1885), p. 405.

29. Ibid., p. 407. But he also claimed to have recovered nearly $600,000 in stolen property. The contradiction is beyond the author's capacity to resolve.

30. James Lardner and Thomas Repetto, *NYPD: A City and Its Police* (New York, Henry Holt, 2000), p. 83.

31. *New York Times*, February 27, 1893.

32. Byrnes, *Professional Criminals*, p. xvii.

33. Lardner and Repetto, *NYPD*, p. 85.

34. This was actually a double execution; the other was of Pasquale Majone, an itinerant musician who shot his wife, suspecting her of infidelity, and his mother-in-law; he then tried to kill himself.

35. *New York Herald*, December 27, 1891.

36. *New York Herald*, December 27, 1861.

37. *New York Times*, August 14, 1912.

38. Anbinder, *Five Points*, p. 270.

39. *National Police Gazette*, February 4, 1888.

40. *New York Herald*, December 27, 1891.

41. It was this kind of reckless courage that kept McCullagh rising through the ranks; he would be the first chief of police after the consolidation of the five boroughs into greater New York in 1898.

42. *New York Herald*, December 27, 1891.

43. The story of the murder and the trial is drawn from the *New York Herald*, the *New York Sun*, the *New York Times*, the *New York Tribune*, and the *New York World*.

44. *New York Herald*, December 27, 1891.

45. *New York World*, February 5, 1891.

46. English, *Paddy Whacked*, p. 36.

47. *New York Herald*, December 3, 1887.

48. Not that Atkinson always acted professionally. In late 1888, returning drunk from a job on Long Island, "he pulled the black cap and noose from his pocket, drew the cap over his head and showed how he had hanged Hawkins" (*New York Tribune*, December 13, 1888).

49. Bruen's career as gang leader was a short one; a few months later, he was arrested and convicted of assault, and sent to Sing Sing for nine years.

50. *New York Herald*, December 27, 1891.

51. *New York Times*, October 31, 1888; another newspaper said he was a member of the Morgue gang. But the two were not mutually exclusive.

52. *New York Herald*, December 13, 1888.

53. *New York Herald*, February 22, 1891.

54. *New York Times*, August 2, 1884.

55. *New York Herald*, December 2, 1879.

56. Mark Essig, *Edison and the Electric Chair* (New York: Walker and Company, 2003), pp. 95–96.

57. Stuart Banner, *The Death Penalty: An American History* (Cambridge: Harvard University Press, 2002), p. 169.

58. Essig, *Edison*, pp. 99, 116–117.

59. Banner, *Death Penalty*, p. 182.

60. Essig, *Edison*, p. 159.

61. *New York Times*, August 7, 1890. There was one man who was pleased with the day's proceedings. A Buffalo physician who had lobbied for the electric chair was a witness to the event. Dr. Southwick called the event "the grandest success of the age" and called himself "one of the happiest men in the State of New York."

62. Craig Brandon, *The Electric Chair: An Unnatural American History* (Jefferson, NC: McFarland, 1999), p. 187.

63. Charles E. Still, *Styles in Crime* (Philadelphia: J. B. Lippincott, 1938), p. 291.

64. *New York Times*, August 9, 1891.

65. *New York Times*, July 8, 1891.

66. *New York Herald*, March 10, 1891.

FIVE · MURDER, INC.

1. Richard Morris, *Fair Trial: 14 Who Stood Accused* (New York: Alfred A. Knopf, 1952), p. 335.

2. Edmund Pearson, *Masterpieces of Murder* (Boston: Little, Brown, 1961), p. 188.

3. *New York Times*, April 29, 1893.

4. Charles E. Still, *Styles in Crime* (Philadelphia: J. B. Lippincott, 1938), p. 166.

5. *New York Times*, March 22, 1891, and May 8, 1893.

6. The Trial of Carlyle Harris, official stenographer's minutes, p. 214.

7. Ibid, p. 215.

8. *New York Sun*, January 30, 1892.

9. *New York Mail and Express*, April 28, 1893; the paper reprinted a facsimile of the letter, which was on Howe & Hummel stationery, on the front page.

10. *New York Mail and Express*, April 28, 1892.

11. Statement of grounds of appeal in Carlyle Harris file, Municipal Archives of the City of New York; report of argument, *New York Times*, December 7, 1893.

12. Carlyle Harris, *Articles, Speeches and Poems. Ed. by "Carl's Mother"* (New York: J. S. Ogilvie, 1893).

13. *New York Times*, March 17, 1893.

14. Harris, *Articles*, p. 136.

15. Ibid.

16. *Boston Globe*, May 9, 1893.

17. *Washington Post*, May 9, 1893.

18. Richard Rovere, *Howe and Hummel: Their True and Scandalous History* (New York: Farrar, Straus and Giroux, 1985), pp. 66–67.

19. Howe, William F., "Some Notable Murder Cases," *Cosmopolitan*, August 1900, p. 381.

20. Matthew Pinkerton, *Murder in All the Ages* (Chicago. A. E. Pinkerton, 1898), p. 487.

21. Pearson, *Masterpieces*, p. 229; Still, *Styles*, p. 163.

22. *New York Journal*, September 3, 1897.

23. *New York Sun*, July 8, 1897; Charles Edwarde, *The Guldensuppe Mystery* (New York: True Story Publishing, 1897), p. 105.

24. *New York World*, July 10, 1897.

25. *New York Sun*, July 10, 1897.

26. *New York World*, November 9, 1897.

27. *New York Journal*, November 8, 1897.

28. *New York Journal*, November 9, 1897.

29. *New York Times*, November 7, 1897.

30. *New York Journal*, November 9, 1897; one feathered messenger, known as the Flying Dutchman, completed the journey in eight minutes.

31. *New York Times*, August 10, 1897.

32. *New York World*, November 11, 1897.

33. *New York Journal*, November 12, 1897.

34. *New York Sun*, November 10, 1897.

35. *New York Times*, November 13, 1897.

36. *New York World*, November 11, 1897.

37. *New York World*, November 29, 1897.

38. *New York World*, November 25, 1897.

39. *New York Journal*, November 29, 1897.

40. *New York World*, December 4, 1897.

41. *New York Times*, December 6, 1897.

42. Rovere, *Howe and Hummel*, p. 132.

43. *New York World*, December 5, 1897.

44. *New York Times*, January 11, 1898.

45. *The People v George Evans*, Box 199, Folder 1996, DA Indictment Files, Court of General Sessions, Municipal Archives of the City of New York.

46. *New York World*, April 8, 1896.

47. Theron Strong, *Landmarks of a Lawyer's Lifetime* (New York: Dodd, Mead, 1914), p. 305.

48. *New York World*, January 29, 1885.

49. *New York Herald*, January 30, 1885.

50. The account of this case comes from the DA scrapbook files in the Municipal Archives—chiefly from the *New York Herald*, *Morning Advertiser*, *New York Sun*, *New York Times*, *New York Tribune*, and *New York World*.

51. And a few years later, Granville would come clean; Goodwin, she said, had fallen over the cuspidor. (DA scrapbook files, Municipal Archives, September 4, 1897).

52. Francis Wellman, *Gentlemen of the Jury*, p. 116.

53. He served seven-and-a-half. His sentence was commuted to ten on appeal and, with time off for good behavior, he was released in April 1899. He lived mostly on the charity of his friends and died in 1916. Evelyn Granville had the squalid future predicted by everyone who ever met her. Her notoriety guaranteed her an audience when she went back on the stage, but her skill could not keep her in work. She took to drink, and was arrested several times for alcohol-related incidents, such as threatening with a fork the woman with whom she shared a room. She resided on Blackwell's Island on several occasions and did a stint in the Workhouse. When she died in 1938, Granville was working on a WPA-sponsored sewing project. She was so not worth the death of one man and the ruin of another.

54. *New York Tribune*, October 17, 1887.

55. Rovere, *Howe and Hummel*, p. 44.

56. A. E. Costello, *Our Police Protectors* (New York: self-published, 1885), p. 254.

57. *New York Star*, October 15, 1887.

58. *New York Sun*, October 15, 1887.

59. *New York Herald*, October 15, 1887.

60. *New York Times*, January 31, 1887.

61. *New York Times*, May 8, 1910.

62. *New York Sun*, February 18, 1887.

63. *New York Herald*, February 16, 1887.

64. *New York World*, June 12, 1892.

65. *New York World*, June 12, 1892.

66. Michaels's account is taken from the transcript of the trial, pages 23–26; Trial #15, John Jay College Library. The general account is from the *New York Herald*, *New York Sun*, *New York Times*, *New York Tribune*, and *New York World*, in addition to the DA Scrapbook of clippings.

67. Box 428, Folder 3949, DA Indictment Files, Court of General Sessions, Municipal Archives of the City of New York.

68. *Sunday Advertiser*, April 9, 1893.

69. Costello, *Police Protectors*, p. 227.

70. Arthur Train, *The Prisoner at the Bar* (New York: Charles Scribner's Sons, 1906), p. 251.

71. *New York Herald*, June 19, 1891.

72. Trial transcript, p. 150.

73. *New York Herald*, June 20, 1891.

74. Trial transcript, p. 151.

75. Strong, *Landmarks*, p. 303.

76. Wellman, *Gentlemen of the Jury*, p. 105. Wellman was incorrect in his recollection, though, when he said the moment came around 10:00 at night; it was actually around 5:30. He also made the charge of pinching (which Howe denied, with a smile) contemporaneously; see the *New York Herald*, April 23, 1892, when he makes a reference to it without naming the case, and the *New York World*, June 12, 1892, when he makes the charge explicitly.

77. *New York Herald*, June 21, 1891.

78. Wellman would get payback of a kind the following year when he prosecuted Annie Walden, the Man-Killing Racetrack Girl. Walden had walked up to her husband of a few months—the two of them had met at the track and their marriage was a tempestuous one, marked by neither maturity nor fidelity—and shot him in the face. He died; she called Howe & Hummel. With the Nelson imbroglio at the front of his mind, Wellman took care to inoculate the jury against his rival's techniques. "Mr. Howe," he told the jury, "is a great actor, and

these trials, with all their pathos and pitiful appeals, are merely his plays. Suppose you had heard him, as I have, say to a jury, 'Convict this woman and then go home and look your wife in the eye if you can' and then suppose you had seen him, as I have, go behind the woman prisoner and pinch her and make her scream pitifully. Do not be deceived. Every furious outburst of his, every pitiful fainting spell of his clients—all, all are carefully studied line upon line and rehearsed perhaps a hundred times" (*New York Herald*, April 23, 1892). Even though Howe abused the dead man with energy and did his best to transform Walden from good-time girl around town to tragic little wife, the jury didn't buy it. Walden was convicted of second-degree murder; she escaped the death penalty only because of her sex. She was pardoned in 1900 by Governor Theodore Roosevelt after rescuing a baby during a prison fire.

79. The partners were so closely associated with the place that for years after Howe's death, a portrait of him hung on the wall of the stairway leading to the upper floor (see Arthur Bartlett Maurice, *New York of the Novelists* [New York: Dodd, Mead, 1917], p. 73).

80. *New York Times*, October 19, 1898.

SIX · THE MANDELBAUM SALON

1. Frank Moss, *The American Metropolis* (New York: Peter Fenelon Collier, 1897), p. 209.

2. Nell Kimball, *Nell Kimball: Her Life as an American Madam by Herself*, edited by Stephen Longstreet (New York: Macmillan, 1970), p. 143.

3. George Walling, *Recollections of a New York Chief of Police* (New York: Caxton Book Concern, 1887), p. 236.

4. Cleveland Moffett, "The Great Northampton Bank Robbery," *McClure's*, 1895, p. 257.

5. Scott died in prison in 1882; as he lay ill, he asked his wife to try to get Dunlap, whom he regarded as a protégé, pardoned. Mary Scott Rowland went to work, and Dunlap was pardoned in 1892, five years short of his sentence.

6. *New York Times*, August 13, 1877, and February 1, 1878; *New York Herald*, May 8, 1879. Some accounts say that Leary came out wearing his coat, and then reached in his pockets and brought out two cocked guns. I think this version is probably wrong; it came out after the first accounts. Moreover, Leary's criminal record was light on violence, and the cops seemed to like the guy, even after his escape. That would not have been the case had he threatened to shoot. The less dramatic account, all in all, seems likely to be the one closer to the truth.

7. Burrows and Wallace, *Gotham,* Edward van Every, *Sins of New York* (New York: Ayer, 1970), p. 236.

8. Kimball, whose husband was a safecracker who learned some of his trade from Leslie, put the figure at 70 percent and $10 million, but conceded that this was a guess.

9. Helen Campbell, Thomas Knox, and Thomas Byrnes, *Darkness and Daylight: Lights and Shadows of New York Life* (Hartford: Hartford Publishing, 1895), p. 659.

10. Walling, *Recollections*, p. 270.

11. Every, *Sins*, pp. 236–237.

12. Walling, *Recollections*, p. 278; Every, *Sins*, p. 242.

13. James Ford, *Forty Odd Years in the Literary Shop* (New York: Dutton, 1921), p. 50.

14. Rona Holub, "Fredericka 'Marm' Mandelbaum, 'Queen of Fences': The Rise and Fall of a Female Immigrant Criminal Entrepreneur in 19th Century New York City," PhD dissertation, Columbia University, 2007, p. 234.

15. *National Police Gazette*, May 15, 1880.

16. And they couldn't even sell them back; the bank got Congress to pass special legislation to provide new bonds to replace the stolen ones.

17. Affidavit in the Nugent file; Municipal Archives of the City of New York.

18. *New York Times*, September 7, 1902.

19. Moss, *American Metropolis*, p. 211.

20. *National Police Gazette*, January 9, 1897.

21. *National Police Gazette*, February 9, 1895.

22. *New York Times*, February 1, 1880.

23. *New York Times*, June 27, 1875.

24. Jay Robert Nash, *Look for the Woman: A Narrative Encyclopedia of Female Poisoners, Kidnappers, Thieves, Extortionists, Terrorists, Swindlers, and Spies* (New York: Evans Publishing, 1981), p. 355.

25. Eddie Guerin, *Crime: The Autobiography of a Crook* (London: John Murray, 1928), p. 90.

26. Moses King, *King's Handbook of New York* (Boston: self-published, 1892), p. 456.

27. Kathleen De Grave, *Swindler, Spy, Rebel: The Confidence Woman in Nineteenth-Century America* (Columbia: University of Missouri Press, 1995), p. 62.

28. Ibid., p. 257.

29. Guerin claimed that one of the reasons Sophie went to Europe was that domestic criminals had begun to suspect her of working with the Pinkertons. He regarded her as a "low down snitch" and a "female Judas" and charged that she tried to blackmail him out of a share in an 1888 French bank robbery. The latter sounds very much in character; as to whether Sophie was a snitch, it's impossible to know. The charge is not a common one against Lyons, but it does serve to show the degree of suspicion that existed even at the highest levels of crookdom.

30. Guerin, *Crime*, p. 105.

31. *National Police Gazette*, November 1, 1902.

32. *National Police Gazette*, February 9, 1895.

33. *National Police Gazette*, January 5, 1895.

34. Nash, *Look for the Woman*, p. 259.

35. *New York Times*, February 2, 1916.

36. Asbury, *Gangs*, p. 190.

37. *New York Times*, June 14, 1879.

38. *New York Times*, June 15, 1879.

39. Wellman, *Gentlemen of the Jury*, p. 245.

40. *People ex rel Nugent v. Board of Police Commissioners*; Court of Appeals of New York, May 3, 1889.

41. *New York Times*, July 29 and 31, 1883.

42. The lawyer was Peter Mitchell, an associate with the firm.

43. *McClure's*, p. 267.

44. Account of the escape taken from the *New York Times* and *New York Herald*, May 8, 1879.

45. In fact, Ludlow Street was so porous that the *National Police Gazette* referred to it as "Hotel Ludlow" and the *Times* as the "Ludlow Street Sieve." To wit: In October 1875, a counterfeiter named James McGrath shaved off his whiskers and got a change of clothing, then simply walked out with the group when it was time for the dozen or so visitors who had come for Sunday services to leave the jail. In November 1879, five counterfeiters got out by breaking the bars on the window and climbing the 30-foot wall, which had been helpfully provided with cross bars that made a dandy ladder. The Ludlow keepers waited more than three hours to notify the police of their absence. And in 1881, John Jourdan, alleged bank robber, feigned sickness at Ludlow and was taken to Bellevue Hospital, accompanied by his sister Maggie, the woman who had helped William Sharkey escape from the Tombs (see Chapter 3). Jourdan left no more than 90 minutes later. Maggie, ever helpful, had his overcoat.

46. *National Police Gazette*, November 15, 1879; *New York Times*, February 11, 1879.

47. *New York Herald*, May 9, 1879.

48. *National Police Gazette*, May 24, 1879.

49. *National Police Gazette*, February 19, 1881.

50. *New York Times*, February 5, 1881.

51. That would not change for some years. In the *Herald* on March 2, 1891, a reporter recounted how he got himself arrested and sent to Ludlow Street; Howe & Hummel had sworn out the warrant on behalf of a client. There he managed

several lovely furloughs with the keeper, including dinner and the theater and post-performance drinks. Gambling took place in the chaplain's library, and the most privileged boarders were served breakfast in bed.

52. Moss, *American Metropolis*, p. 211.

53. Kimball, *Nell Kimball*, p. 175.

54. Ibid., p. 176.

55. Gilfoyle, *Pickpocket's Tale*, p. 150.

56. Guerin, *Crime*, p. 58.

57. Asbury, *Gangs*, p. 216; Luc Sante, *Low Life: Lures and Snares of Old New York* (New York: Vintage, 1992), p. 211.

58. Asbury, p. 326.

59. There is no proof of this, but the reference pops up in several sources. Considering Howe & Hummel's connection with Mandelbaum, which would have required them to build substantial contacts with the police, they would be a plausible choice to hold the valuables. On the other hand, that also implies direct criminal involvement of the kind Howe & Hummel avoided (outside of discreet blackmail). But then, the practice of selling back securities to banks was routine, so perhaps it didn't feel illegal to men of undoubtedly elastic ethics. In short, it cannot be proved either way; the larger point is that among Howe & Hummel's contemporaries, the idea that a wanted bank burglar dropped his swag at their offices before fleeing the country was not at all implausible. By the 1880s, Howe & Hummel were doing just fine without taking such risks. Macintyre, *Napoleon of Crime*, p. 40; Court TV: The World in His Pocket (trutv.com/library/crime/gangsters_outlaws/cops_others/worth/8.html).

60. Asbury, *Gangs*, p. 216. The $5,000 a year retainer from Mandelbaum is one of those barnacles that cling to the Howe & Hummel story, repeated every time their name comes up. But is it true? Asbury is not wholly reliable on many details, but he knew people who knew both Mandelbaum and Howe & Hummel. Moreover, lawyer Frank Moss, who knew a lot about the criminal underworld, wrote in his 1897 book that Mandelbaum "employed famous criminal lawyers on yearly fees." Another contemporary, Chief of Police George Walling, also wrote that Howe & Hummel were on a $5,000 retainer. So all in all, I think it is likely that Howe & Hummel did have some kind of retainer arrangement. Given their reputation, and Marm's assets, $5,000 seems a reasonable, if unprovable, figure.

61. Holub, "Fredericka 'Marm' Mandelbaum," p. 1.

62. Ibid., p. 234.

63. Moss, *American Metropolis*, p. 210.

64. Macintyre, *Napoleon of Crime*, p. 29; Walling, *Recollections*, p. 283.

65. Kimball, *Nell Kimball*, p. 175.

66. Holub, "Fredericka 'Marm' Mandelbaum," p. 240.

67. *Boston Globe*, November 11, 1883.

68. Every, *Sins*, p. 242; *New York Star*, July 27, 1884.

69. Every, *Sins*, p. 30; $10 million in 1885 dollars is equivalent to about $238 million in 2009 dollars.

70. Holub, "Fredericka 'Marm' Mandelbaum," p. 1; $500,000 would be about $12 million in 2009 dollars.

71. *New York Times*, July 24, 1884.

72. Walling, *Recollections*, p. 281.

73. Gilfoyle, *Pickpocket*, p. 151; *New York Sun*, July 23, 1884; *New York Times*, July 24, 1884.

74. Gilfoyle, *Pickpocket*, p. 148.

75. Yes, consumers suffered, too, in the form of higher prices—but not in a way that would make them complainants in a criminal action.

76. *New York Times*, January 24, 1884.

77. *New York World*, July 24, 1884; Gilfoyle, *Pickpocket*, p. 152.

78. *New York Times*, July 24, 1884, editorial.

79. *New York Times*, December 16, 1883.

80. *New York Times*, December 12, 1883.

81. Arthur Train, *The Confessions of Artemis Quibble* (New York: Charles Scribner's Sons, 1911), p. 116.

82. Gilfoyle, *Pickpocket,* p. 388; Lexow Committee transcript, pp. 5671–72).

83. *New York Times*, July 24, 1884.

84. *New York Times*, January 6, 1885.

85. Timothy J. Gilfoyle, "America's Greatest Criminal Barracks: The Tombs and the Experience of Criminal Justice in New York City, 1838–1897," *Journal of Urban History*, July 2003, pp. 538–540.

86. *Harper's Magazine* counted 100 to 125 cases a day disposed of, in six hours.

87. The police schedule was a nightmare: In 1882, it went something like this: A patrolman worked a 24-hour shift—13 hours on patrol, 3 for eating, 8 "on reserve"; the latter required him to be at the station, in uniform, where he could sleep on a cot in an on-site dormitory. Then he had most of the following day off—unless he had to bring prisoners to court—returning to patrol from 6:00 p.m. to midnight; then sleep, and return to the 24-hour shift at 6:00 a.m. (See *Harpers*, April 29, 1882.) There was one day and one night off in every eight-day rotation. It was not until January 1, 1902—a date that former Chief Cornelius Willemse described as "the policeman's 4th of July" that the department established a more humane three-shift schedule, in which an officer was on eight hours, on reserve eight, and off eight.

88. The homage to Rumpole of the Bailey is deliberate. Howe is definitely Rumpoleish in both size and sensibility.

89. Holub, "Fredericka 'Marm' Mandelbaum," p. 234.

90. Thomas McMorrow, *The Sinister History of Ambrose Hinkle* (New York: J. H. Sears, 1929), p. 4.

91. *National Police Gazette*, September 4, 1886.

92. Mandelbaum died in Canada in February 1894. One of New York's German-language newspapers, the *Staats Zeitung*, said of her: "Mutter Mandelbaum is dead. With her stiffening body, a piece of New York the way we know it will be taken to the grave."

SEVEN · THE ACCIDENTAL REFORMERS

1. Yes, really. This was the work of the Flower Mission; see Campbell, Knox, and Byrnes, *Darkness and Daylight: Lights and Shadows of New York Life*, p. 308.

2. Riis, who was rarely popular with those in power, was not invited to the opening; his account of the new park can be found in the *American Review of Reviews*, August 1895.

3. Clay McShane, *Down the Asphalt Path* (New York: Columbia University Press), p. 53.

4. Elliott Gorn, *The Manly Art: Bare-Knuckle Prize Fighting in America* (Ithaca, NY: Cornell University Press, 1986), p. 196.

5. *New York Times*, June 9, 1877.

6. Gorn, *Manly Art*, p. 216.

7. Alexander Johnston, *Ten—and Out!* (London: Chapman and Hall, 1928), p. 61.

8. van Every, *Sins*, p. 261.

9. Michael Isenberg, *John L. Sullivan and His America* (Chicago: University of Illinois Press, 1988), p. 94.

10. Every, *Sins*, p. 151.

11. The account of the match and subsequent legal proceedings is taken from the *New York Herald, New York Sun, New York Times, New York Tribune*, and *New York World*, with a few other clippings from the DA scrapbooks.

12. *New York Sun*, November 18, 1884.

13. Isenberg, *John L. Sullivan*, p. 178.

14. Johnston, *Ten*, p. 64.

15. *Boston Globe*, November 20, 1884.

16. *New York World*, February 12, 1887.

17. Rovere, *Howe and Hummel*, p. 28.

18. *National Police Gazette*, December 6, 1884.

19. New Orleans legalized prizefighting with gloves in 1890, and gradually so did many other cities and states. New York went back and forth. In 1896, Albany passed the Horton Law, which allowed glove fights to take place in members-only clubs. This proved impossible to enforce and the state went back to abolition in 1900. This, too, proved impossible to enforce, so in 1911, New York passed the Frawley Law, which limited bouts to ten rounds but otherwise liberalized the laws of boxing. This provision died in 1917 and three years later was replaced by the Walker Law, which finally legalized and regulated prize-fighting.

20. Patrick Myler, *Gentleman Jim Corbett: The Truth behind a Boxing Legend* (New York: Rolson Books, 1998), p. 101.

21. The roommate was Helene Minkin; it was a common-law marriage, of course, and an unhappy one. Emma Goldman, *Living My Life* (Dover Books, 1930), p. 44; Frederic Trautmann, *The Voice of Terror: A Biography of Johann Most* (Westport, CT: Greenwood Press, 1980), p. 251.

22. Tom Goyens, *Beer and Revolution* (Chicago: University of Illinois Press, 2007), p. 43.

23. The account of the Schwab affair is drawn chiefly from the *New York Herald, New York Sun, New York Times,* and *New York Tribune.*

24. Schwab died in 1900; his funeral was a day of rare unity for the cause. Goldman and Most both attended, as did about 2,000 others (*New York Times,* December 21, 1900).

25. Richard Drinnon, *Rebel in Paradise* (Chicago: University of Chicago Press, 1961), p. 34.

26. *New York Times,* June 3, 1886.

27. Three others were sentenced to prison. In June 1893, Governor John Peter Altgeld, in a monumental act of political courage, reversed the verdict and gave the three an absolute pardon, citing numerous flaws in the trial.

28. *New York Times,* December 1, 1887.

29. *New York Tribune,* September 13, 1887.

30. The People Against John Most, Motion for new trial, Municipal Archives of the City of New York, December 8, 1887.

31. Drinnon, *Rebel in Paradise,* p. 53.

32. Goldman, *Living My Life,* p. 105.

33. Trautmann, *Voice of Terror,* p. 225.

34. Ibid., p. 252; *New York Times,* April 2, 1906.

35. Paul Avrich, *Anarchist Voices* (Princeton: Princeton University Press, 1995), pp. 18–19.

36. *American Heritage,* December 1967.

37. *New York Herald,* September 22, 1868. The varmints were often provided by a

local businessman known as Dick the Rat. He was paid to clean out local hostelries, and would then sell the critters he caught for two cents a pair to the rat pits. Ragged Dick made a good if unorthodox living and was generally left alone to his work. One day, though, a policeman saw him coming out of a basement with what looked like a bag of swag. Escorted to the police station, he was ordered to dump the contents of his bag. Dick demurred. "Empty out that bag," the captain insisted. So he did (*National Police Gazette*, June 12, 1880).

38. Martin and Herbert Kaufman, "Henry Bergh, Kit Burns and the Sportsmen of New York," *New York Folklore Quarterly*, March 1972, p. 23.

39. Ibid., p. 25.

40. Saved from the dogs, the rats were nonetheless doomed. The cops dumped the cage into the East River.

41. *New York World*, December 31, 1893.

42. *New York Herald*, September 14, 1893.

43. *New York Times*, October 6, 1893.

44. M. H. Dunlap, *The Gilded City: Scandal and Sensation in Turn-of-the-Century New York* (New York: HarperCollins, 2001), p. 247.

45. *Boston Globe*, November 12, 1893.

46. *New York Sun*, November 16, 1893.

47. Newspapers consulted: chiefly the *New York Herald, New York Sun, New York Times, New York World*; also the DA clipping files.

48. *Munsey's*, December 1911, p. 337.

49. More precisely: conspiring to cheat and defraud by criminal means, and conspiring to obtain money or property by false pretenses.

50. John Mulholland, *Beware Familiar Spirits* (New York: Arno Press, 1938), p. 256.

51. The proceedings, however, were actually held in the Court of Special Sessions at the Tombs, which had more room than the Police Court there.

52. After her stint in jail, Debar went back to work, persuading Harriet Beach, wife of the editor of *Scientific American,* to support her. Mrs. Beach was later committed to an insane asylum, in part because of her connection to Diss Debar; Howe acted for Beach's husband in the matter.

Diss Debar—who ditched the general but kept his name—then bounced from boardinghouse to boardinghouse in Brooklyn, and appeared onstage, briefly, as Cupid. She filed a lawsuit against having to wear tights; with no Abe Hummel, the world's leading expert in tights, to appear for her, she lost. Indicted for a couple of minor fiddles in Illinois, she served two years in prison there and was last heard of in 1901 when she was convicted of aiding and abetting a rape at the Theocratic Unity temple.

As for Luther Marsh, he gave up on the Diss Debars but not on spiritualism. Not long after the trial, he moved upstate to dedicate the remainder of his life to the memory of his wife. Unfortunately, that meant more spiritu-alism. He found a new and better medium, Clarissa Huyler, whose messages from the biblical authorities he took down and published in a book, *Voices of the Patriarchs*. In turn, Huyler took Marsh for various pieces of real estate and also induced him to transfer several life insurance policies; her husband later estimated she took him for at least $35,000. When Huyler died in 1901, she was kind enough to provide in her will that Marsh's own funeral expenses be provided for from these policies. She also willed Marsh various spirit pictures; the curious thing is that he already owned them. But perhaps property rights are unsettled in the spirit world. Marsh died in 1906 at age 90.

53. *New York Times*, March 15, 1884.

54. *New York Times*, March 25, 1901.

55. Burrows and Wallace, *Gotham*, p. 1167.

56. Chad Heap, *Slumming: Sexual and Racial Encounters in American Nightlife, 1885–1940* (Chicago: University of Chicago Press, 2009), p. 17.

57. Dunlop, *Gilded City*, p. 135.

58. Ibid., pp. 135–137.

59. Burrows and Wallace, *Gotham*, p. 1168.

60. Edward Robb Ellis, *The Epic of New York City* (New York: Carroll and Graf Publishers, 1966), p. 426.

61. Luc Sante, *Low Life: Lures and Snares of Old New York* (New York: Vintage Books, 1992), p. 285.

62. Ellis, *Epic of New York City*, p. 428.

63. *New York Times*, March 14, 1892.

64. Sante, *Low Life*, p. 286.

65. Wallace and Burrows, *Gotham*, p. 1169.

66. Ellis, *Epic of New York City*, p. 428. The *New York Times*, which was much the most sympathetic to Parkhurst, ran the whole sermon on March 14, 1892.

67. Rovere, *Howe and Hummel*, pp. 82–83.

68. *New York World*, May 6, 1892.

69. *New York World*, May 6, 1892.

70. *New York World*, May 6, 1892.

71. *New York Herald*, May 7, 1892.

72. Sante, *Low Life*, p. 287.

73. *Harper's Magazine*, June 30, 1894.

74. Richard O'Connor, *Courtroom Warrior: The Combative Career of William Travers Jerome* (Boston: Little, Brown, 1963), p. 48.

75. Ibid.

76. *New York Times*, October 3, 1894.

77. *New York Times*, May 5, 1892.

78. O'Connor, *Courtroom Warrior*, p. 49; Lexow Committee transcript, p. 4186.

79. Nell Kimball, *Nell Kimball: Her Life as an American Madam by Herself*, edited by Stephen Longstreet (New York: Macmillan, 1970), p. 178.

80. Lexow Committee transcript, p. 3598.

81. Ibid., p. 4654.

82. Works Progress Administration, *New York City Guide* (New York: Octagon Books, 1970), p. 104.

83. Timothy Gilfoyle, *A Pickpocket's Tale* (New York: W. W. Norton, 2006), pp. 147, 288.

84. *New York Times*, June 20, 1894.

85. Gilfoyle, *Pickpocket*, p. 214. The proceedings of the 1894 Lexow Committee (Chapter 7) left no doubt of the connections between cops and the green goods men; see, for example, George Appo's testimony, *New York Times*, June 15, 1894.

86. *New York Times*, June 17, 1896.

87. *New York Times*, September 11, 1894.

88. *New York Times*, June 17, 1896.

89. Lexow Committee transcript, testimony of George Appo, pp. 1647.

90. Ibid., p. 44.

91. *National Police Gazette*, May 12, 1894; *New York Times*, November 28, 1886.

92. *New York Times*, September 14, 1884.

93. Every, *Sins*, p. 199.

94. Walling, *Recollections*, p. 484.

95. *National Police Gazette*, May 5, 1894.

96. Lexow Committee transcript, pp. 2961+.

97. *Boston Globe*, December 23, 1894.

98. *Harper's Magazine*, January 5, 1895.

99. Lexow Committee transcript, p. 5363.

100. Lexow Committee transcript, pp. 5343, 5349.

101. Lexow Committee transcript, p. 5382.

101. Lexow Committee transcript, p. 5383.

101. James Lardner and Thomas Repetto *NYPD: A City and Its Police* (New York, Henry Holt, 2000), p. 111.

104. Justin Kaplan, *Lincoln Steffens: A Biography* (New York: Simon and Schuster, 1974), p. 89.

105. *The Outlook*, September 5, 1917, p. 406.

106. Ibid., p. 25; *Chicago Tribune*, November 3, 1894; *New York Times*, November 3, 1894.

107. *New York Times*, May 25, 1907.

108. *New York Times*, October 29, 1895.

109. *National Police Gazette*, June 22, 1878.

110. James Richardson, *The New York Police: Colonial Times to 1901* (New York: Oxford University Press, 1970), p. 205.

111. *New York Evening Post*, March 1891.

112. Lexow Committee transcript, p. 5466.

113. Lexow Committee transcript, p. 5457.

114. *New York Times*, December 30, 1894.

115. This was a deeply satisfying win for Goff, who had been charged with contempt of court for protesting Smyth's vigorous pro-prosecution rulings during the trial of Parkhurst detective Charles Gardner on trumped-up charges of extortion. Ironically, Goff would get a reputation of being even tougher than Smyth.

116. Hermann Hagedorn, *The Theodore Roosevelt Treasury: A Self-Portrait from His Writings* (New York: G. P. Putnam's Sons, 1957), p. 96.

117. Theodore Roosevelt, *American Ideals* (New York: AMS Press, 1898), p. 182.

118. Lincoln Steffens, *The Autobiography of Lincoln Steffens* (Berkeley, CA: Heyday Books, 2005), p. 261.

119. Edmund Morris, *The Rise of Theodore Roosevelt* (New York: Modern Library, 2001), pp. 562–563.

120. Rovere, *Howe and Hummel,* p. 104.

121. Lloyd Morris, *Incredible New York: High Life and Life from 1850 to 1890* (Syracuse: Syracuse University Press, 1951), p. 233.

122. When Schmittberger went back on the take, his bagman in the Tenderloin was Charles Becker, until the two fell out in the early 1900s. Becker, who was a protégé of Clubber Williams, later became the first New York City cop executed for murder.

123. Hagedorn, *Theodore Roosevelt Treasury*, p. 99.

EIGHT · THE PLAY'S THE THING

1. Judith Fisher and Stephen Watt, eds., *When They Weren't Doing Shakespeare: Essays on Nineteenth-Century British and American Theatre* (Athens and London: University of Georgia Press, 1989), p. 108.

2. Mildred Davis Harding, *Air-Bird in the Water: The Life and Works of John Craigie (John Oliver Hobbes)* (Madison, NJ: Fairleigh Dickinson University Press, 1996), p. 364.

3. "Sex Dramas To-Day and Yesterday," *The Green Book*, 1913, p. 32; Olga Nethersol file, New York Public Library for the Performing Arts.

4. *New York Journal*, December 20, 1896.

5. Abe Laufe, *The Wicked Stage: A History of Theater Censorship and Harassment in the United States* (New York: Frederick Ungar, 1978), p. 24. Apparently lip-kissing was the innovation.

6. Katie N. Johnson, *Sisters in Sin: Brothel Drama in America, 1900–1920* (New York: Cambridge University Press, 2009), p. 45.

7. *National Police Gazette*, January 25, 1896.

8. Lewis Strang, American Actresses; http://home.comcast.net/~m.chitty/nethersole.htm

9. *New York Journal*, December 20, 1896.

10. *New York Journal*, December 20, 1896.

11. Fisher and Watt, *When They Weren't Doing Shakespeare*, p. 111.

12. Willa Cather, *The World and the Parish: Willa Cather's Articles and Reviews, 1893–1902*, selected and edited by William M. Curtin (Lincoln: University of Nebraska Press, 1970), p. 688.

13. Charles Burnham, "State Indecency, Then and Now," *Theater*, September 1925, p. 16.

14. Edwin Burrows and Mike Wallace, *Gotham: A History of New York City to 1898* (New York: Oxford University Press, 1999), p. 1152.

15. David Nasaw, *The Chief: The Life of William Randolph Hearst* (Boston: Houghton Mifflin, 2000), pp. 100–111.

16. *New York Sun*, February 22, 1900. The rest of this account will be drawn from New York newspapers, unless otherwise specified. The papers consulted are the *New York Herald*, *New York Journal*, *New York Sun*, *New York Tribune*, *New York Times*, and *New York World*.

17. *New York Herald*, October 27, 1889.

18. *New York Times*, December 28, 1887.

19. *Law Notes*, September 1907.

20. Twain lost; for details, see coverage January–March 1890.

21. James Trager, *New York Chronology: The Ultimate Compendium of Events, People, and Anecdotes from the Dutch to the Present* (New York: HarperResource, 2004), p. 29. The lawyer for the scalpers was Max Steuer, who would later come to prominence as the lawyer who defended the factory owners in the Triangle Shirtwaist Factory fire.

22. Mitchell C. Harrison, *Prominent and Progressive Americans*, vol. 2 (New York: Tribune Publishing, 1904), p. 124.

23. *New York Herald*, July 6, 1901.

24. William Winter, *The Life of David Belasco*, vol. 2 (New York: Jefferson Winter, 1925), p. 91.

25. *New York Herald,* January 18, 1893.

26. Train, p. 86.

27. *The Bar*, West Virginia Bar Association, November 1907, p. 27.

28. *New York World*, October 2, 1898.

29. *New York World*, December 7, 1893.

30. *New York World*, December 9, 1893.

31. *New York Herald*, December 13, 1893.

32. The incident wrought a characteristic Hummelism. He told the papers: "I declare most solemnly that I was not on the steamship *Normannia* on Tuesday . . . and that neither Mrs. Nicolaus nor Mr. Rahman sailed on that steamship." He left the distinct impression that they were still holed up somewhere in Manhattan. Asked about this when they surfaced in London, he replied, "I said that Mrs. Nicolaus did not sail on the *Normannia*; neither did she. I said nothing one way or the other about her having sailed on any other steamer."

33. *New York World*, December 21, 1893.

34. *New York Times*, March 10, 1894.

35. *New York Herald*, January 30, 1894.

36. *New York Herald*, December 1, 1895.

37. Robert Carter, *Buffalo Bill Cody* (New York: John Wiley & Sons, 2000), p. 358.

38. Larry McMurtry, *The Colonel and Little Missie* (New York, Simon and Schuster, 2005), p. 205; *New York World*, December 9, 1907.

39. *New York Times*, May 7, 1885.

40. *New York World*, November 17, 1893.

41. *National Police Gazette*, March 24, 1894.

42. John Barker, *Duet in Diamonds* (New York: G. P. Putnam's Sons), 1972, pp. 91–96.

43. Parker Morrell, *Lillian Russell* (New York: Random House, 1940), p. 152.

44. Armand Fields, *Lillian Russell: Biography of America's Beauty* (Jefferson, NC, and London: McFarland, 1999), p. 56.

45. *New York Herald*, April 8–9, 1897; *New York Times*, March 13, 1897.

46. *Chicago Tribune*, August 4, 1893.

47. Toni Bentley, *Sisters of Salome* (New Haven: Yale University Press, 2002), p. 37.

48. *Chicago Tribune*, December 5, 1893.

49. *Chicago Tribune*, December 31, 1896.

50. Terry Ramsaye, *A Million and One Nights: A History of the Motion Picture*, vol. 1 (New York: Simon and Schuster, 1926), p. 117.

51. *St. Louis Post-Dispatch*, January 10, 1897.

52. M. H. Dunlap, *The Gilded City: Scandal and Sensation in Turn-of-the-Century New York* (New York: HarperCollins, 2001), p. 171.

53. Lloyd Morris, *Incredible New York: High Life and Life from 1850 to 1890* (Syracuse: Syracuse University Press, 1951), p. 219.

54. Luc Sante, *Low Life*, p. 17.

55. Trager, *New York Chronology*, p. 181.

56. Ibid., p. 337.

57. Many sources say that Little Egypt did the *danse* at the World's Fair, but there is no evidence of this in the Chicago papers of the period.

58. Chapman thoroughly enjoyed his moment in the spotlight and began to see himself as a stalwart defender of womanhood. In 1897, he became a figure of ridicule for what became a habit of arresting women who were out after dark by themselves; in a couple of cases he entered homes without a warrant to arrest women he assumed were disorderly. (See *New York Sun*, July 1, 1897: "Chapman is at it again.") It went so far that one newspaper noted in June, "Before long, when Chapman orders an arrest, it will be regarded . . . as prima facie evidence that the accused is innocent" (DA scrapbook, unidentified clipping, June 1897).

59. Paul Grondahl, *I Rose Like a Rocket* (New York: Free Press, 2004), p. 231.

60. Dunlap, *Gilded City*, p. 181.

61. Unless specified otherwise, what follows is taken from the newspaper accounts from the *New York Herald, New York Journal, New York Sun, New York Times, New York Tribune*, and *New York World*.

62. Ramsaye, *Million and One Nights*, p. 339.

63. Herbert Seeley proved no more judicious in later life. In 1900, he won control of his portion of the Barnum estate, shedding the oversight by his aunt and brother that his careful grandfather had stipulated. Five years later, he had blown through it all and was working as a ticket-taker at the Hippodrome. Divorced in 1903, he died in obscurity in 1914. Clinton Seeley's marriage got off to a rough start, but it lasted until his wife's death in 1957. He became a banker and local notable in Bridgeport, Connecticut.

64. *Law Notes*, September 1907; a decade before, the guess was $100,000 (see *The Law*, September 1890). There is no reason to believe that these are anything but semieducated guesses. The point, though, is that Howe & Hummel's contemporaries in the legal profession were sure they were making a fortune.

65. *Cosmpolitan*, May 1908, p. 595; Rovere, *Howe and Hummel*, p. 27.

66. Johnson, *Sisters in Sin*, p. 62.

67. Ramsaye, *Million and One Nights*, p. 339.

NINE · THE ICE MAN COMETH

1. *The Outlook*, June 16, 1900, p. 376.

2. HarpWeek.com; explanation of cartoon of October 6, 1900; *New York Tribune*, June 5, 1900; also *New York Journal*, May 24, 1900.

3. David Hemenway, *Prices and Choices* (New York: Ballinger, 1988), p. 190.

4. *New York Times*, May 6, 1900.

5. John Moody, *The Truth about the Trusts* (New York: Moody Publishing Company, 1904), p. 228.

6. *New York Times*, May 9, 1900; *New York Journal*, May 9, 1900.

7. *The Outlook*, May 19, 1900, p. 144.

8. *New York World*, May 17, 1900.

9. *New York Tribune*, May 9, 1900.

10. *New York Tribune*, May 9, 1900.

11. *New York Times*, May 6, 1900.

12. *New York Times*, June 10, 1900.

13. *New York Times*, May 9, 1900.

14. H. W. Brands, *T.R.: The Last Romantic* (New York: Basic Books, 1997), p. 275.

15. *New York Journal*, May 8, 1900.

16. *New York Journal*, May 8, 1900.

17. *New York Journal*, May 8, 1900.

18. The *Journal* and the *World* were co-belligerents, rather than allies, a position the *Journal* made clear on May 23, when it referred to the *World* as a "persistent but stupid imitator."

19. *New York World*, May 9, 1900.

20. *New York Herald*, June 6, 1900.

21. *New York Times*, June 13, 1900.

22. Hemenway, *Prices and Choices*, p. 196.

23. "Water Still Freezes," *Fortune*, May 1933, p. 74.

24. Unless otherwise indicated, the following account is from the New York newspapers—most commonly the *New York Times*, *New York Tribune*, and *New York World*—as well as the *Houston Post*.

25. *New York Times*, November 8, 1908; Henry Pringle, *The Life and Times of William Howard Taft: A Biography* (New York: Farrar and Rinehart, 1939), p. 629.

26. Richard O'Connor, *Courtroom Warrior: The Combative Career of William Travers Jerome* (New York: Little, Brown, 1963), p. 114.

27. Ibid., p. 127.

28. Train, *True Stories of Crime* (New York: Charles Scribner's Sons, 1908), p. 325.

29. *New York Times*, December 17, 1905.

30. *New York World*, September 29, 1897.

31. Train, *True Stories*, p. 349.

32. O'Connor, *Courtroom Warrior*, p. 135.

33. Rovere, *Howe and Hummel*, p. 152.

34. Ibid.

35. Train, *True Stories*, p. 358.

36. O'Connor, *Courtroom Warrior*, p. 138.

37. Rovere, *Howe and Hummel*, p. 94.

38. *New York World*, February 24, 1904.

39. Rovere, *Howe and Hummel*, p. 156.

40. O'Connor, *Courtoom Warrior*, pp. 139–140.

41. *Washington Post*, January 8, 1905.

42. *New York Times*, December 8, 1904.

43. The *New York Times* (January 27, 1905) puts the figure at "almost 100," but that seems high.

44. Steinhardt's lawyer was John Dos Passos, father of the novelist. Steinhardt died in June 1907.

45. In 1908, the rumor surfaced that Hummel had sold letters from Morse to a group of lawyers; these letters would have given the lie to Captain Jim, and much else, and saved Morse from being charged in the divorce tangle. Hummel had nothing to lose by selling the letters; his own case would be unaffected either way, and Morse, through the lawyers, provided him with a handsome sum for his retirement. Nothing can be proved, but the late entrance of Captain Jim into the case was always curious, and this rumor is one explanation. And Hummel did enjoy a comfortable retirement.

46. Train, *Confessions*, p. 222.

47. *New York Tribune*, November 16, 1906.

48. Though Morse won the most notoriety for his botched divorce, he really should be remembered as one of the worst businessmen in American history. As part of the group that tried, and failed, to corner United Copper, he helped to touch off the Panic of 1907. The following year he was sentenced

to 15 years for misappropriating funds and falsifying the books of one of his banks. (One of his neighbors in the Atlanta pen was Charles Ponzi, a small-time scamster compared to Morse.) His devoted wife launched a pardon campaign that went nowhere until Morse, apparently wasting away and propped up on pillows, convinced a panel of army doctors that he had only a few months to live. It turned out that he had swallowed a chemical cocktail. "This shakes one's faith in expert examinations," President Taft would later reflect.

Leaving prison in February 1912, Morse stiffed his lawyers, traveled to Italy and Germany for a few months, and on his return, went back into the shipping business. In 1915, he was sued for unfair competition. During World War I, he thrived, but he was later prosecuted for war profiteering and mail fraud; he paid the government $11 million in a civil settlement. Morse died in Maine in 1933. Ironically, the marriage he tried so hard to exit turned out to be an enduring and happy one. When Clemence Dodge Morse died in July 1926, *Time* magazine praised her as an "extraordinarily loyal wife" who had sold her furs and jewels in the effort to get her husband released from prison. At the time of her death, her husband was facing yet another criminal charge, this one for mail fraud.

TEN · THREE SHOTS AND AN AFFIDAVIT

1. Richard O'Connor, *Courtroom Warrior: The Combative Career of William Travers Jerome* (Boston: Little, Brown and Company, 1963), pp. 174–177.

2. Paul Baker, *Stanny: The Gilded Life of Stanford White* (New York: The Free Press, 1989), p. 345.

3. Michael MacDonald Mooney, *Evelyn Nesbit and Stanford White: Love and Death in the Gilded Age* (New York: William Morrow, 1976), pp. 35–36.

4. John Kobler, *Damned in Paradise: The Life of John Barrymore* (New York: Atheneum, 1977), p. 71.

5. Paula Uruburu, *American Eve: Evelyn Nesbit, Stanford White and the Birth of the "It" Girl* (New York, Riverhead Books, 2008), p. 116.

6. Ibid., p. 122.

7. Evelyn Nesbit, *Tragic Beauty, The Lost 1914 Memoirs of Evelyn Nesbit*, edited by Deborah Doran Paul (London: John Long, 2006), p. 46.

8. Uruburu, *American Eve*, p. 137.

9. *New York Herald*; Delmas's closing statement, April 9, 1907. The *New York Times* (February 27, 1907) puts the figure closer to $3,000.

10. O'Connor, *Courtroom Warrior*, p. 195.

11. Nesbit, *Tragic Beauty*, p. 53.

12. *New York Tribune*, February 9, 1907.

13. Uruburu, *American Eve*, p. 223.

14. Evelyn Nesbit, *Prodigal Days: The Untold Story of Evelyn Nesbit* (New York: Julian Messner, 1934), p. 109.

15. F. A. Mackenzie, ed., *The Trial of Harry Thaw* (London: Geoffrey Bles, 1928), p. 139.

16. Ibid., p. 149.

17. *New York Herald*, May 8, 1901.

18. *New York Times*, May 8, 1901.

19. *New York Times*, May 15, 1901.

20. *New York Herald*, February 27, 1903. Yes, they did marry; and no, they were not happy.

21. Mackenzie, *Trial of Harry Thaw*, pp. 87–88.

22. Reported in the newspapers during the trial; Thaw repeats the charge in his 1926 book, *The Traitor*, his disjointed account of the trial. The theme is that it was all a put-up job by "The Traitor," who is unnamed but probably his first lawyer, Lewis Delafield.

23. *New York Times*, April 10, 1907.

24. *New York Times*, April 10, 1907, p. 262.

25. *New York Times*, January 21, 1907.

26. Uruburu, *American Eve*, p. 302.

27. A copy of the affidavit can be found at http://www.law.umkc.edu/faculty/ projects/ftrials/thaw/evelynstory1.html. Without delving too deeply into the technicalities, it's interesting that Evelyn would not sign the statement because it "was not so." For the rest of her life, she would say it was. One possibility that would have allowed her to sign the affidavit without actually lying: It refers to her as being 15 at the time of the alleged incident. In fact, she was 16; in that sense, then, the accusation "was not so." It does feel like the Hummel touch.

28. See Hummel's testimony during the Thaw trial, i.e., the transcript in the *New York Herald*, March 16, 1907.

29. The joke around New York was that Thaw shot the wrong man. John Barrymore had probably taken care of Evelyn's virginity before White ever touched her.

30. Reprinted in the *New York Times*, February 10, 1907.

31. O'Connor, *Courtroom Warrior*, p. 225.

32. These had to do with the admissibility of a carbon copy of the affidavit, plus a photograph of the last page, and whether Hummel's testimony would violate the lawyer-client privilege.

33. *New York Times*, April 14, 1907.

34. A later written account by one of the jurors, Harry Brearly, confirms the affidavit's fizzle. Brearly said the jury did not put much stock in it "because of the circumstances surrounding its origin" (*New York Times*, April 14, 1907).

35. Alvin Sellers, *Classics of the Bar*, vol. 1 (Baxley, GA: Classic Publishing Company, 1917), p. 143.

36. *New York Times*, April 10, 1907.

37. *New York Times*, July 10, 1906.

38. In her later years, Evelyn found a measure of contentment, living in California near her son and teaching ceramics. She came back into prominence in 1955 with the release of the movie *The Girl in the Red Velvet Swing*; Joan Collins played the young Evelyn after Marilyn Monroe turned down the part. Evelyn Nesbit died in 1967.

39. Kobler, *Damned in Paradise*, p. 339.

ELEVEN · THE LEGEND ENDS

1. *Washington Post*, June 19, 1907.

2. *Cosmopolitan*, May 1908, p. 602.

3. Richard Rovere, *Howe and Hummel: Their True and Scandalous History* (New York: Farrar, Straus and Giroux, 1985), p. 20.

4. *New York World*, December 8, 1907.

5. Rovere, *Howe and Hummel*, p. 52.

6. Ibid., p. 11.

7. See, for example, *New York Times*, March 15, 1921, and August 27, 1927.

8. *New York Times*, November 23, 1926; her name was Leila Farrell; she died in 1896.

9. Rovere, pp. 169–170.

INDEX